WRITER AND OCCASION
IN TWELFTH-CENTURY BYZANTIUM

In twelfth-century Constantinople, writers worked on commission for the imperial family or aristocratic patrons. Texts were occasioned by specific events, representing a link both between writer and patron and between literary imagination and empirical reality. This is a study of how one such writer, Constantine Manasses, achieved that aim. Manasses depicted and praised the present by drawing from the rich sources of the Graeco-Roman and Biblical tradition, thus earning commissions from wealthy 'friends' during a career that spanned more than three decades. While the occasional literature of writers like Manasses has sometimes been seen as 'empty rhetoric', devoid of literary ambition, this study assumes that writing on command privileges originality and encourages the challenging of conventions. A society like twelfth-century Byzantium, in which occasional writing was central, called for a strong and individual authorial presence, since voice was the primary instrument for a successful career.

INGELA NILSSON is Professor of Greek and Byzantine Studies at Uppsala University and currently Director of the Swedish Research Institute in Istanbul. Her most recent publications include *Raconter Byzance: la littérature au XIIe siècle* (2014) and, edited with Adam J. Goldwyn, *Reading the Late Byzantine Romance: A Handbook* (Cambridge, 2019). Nilsson is a member of the Royal Swedish Academy of Letters, History and Antiquities.

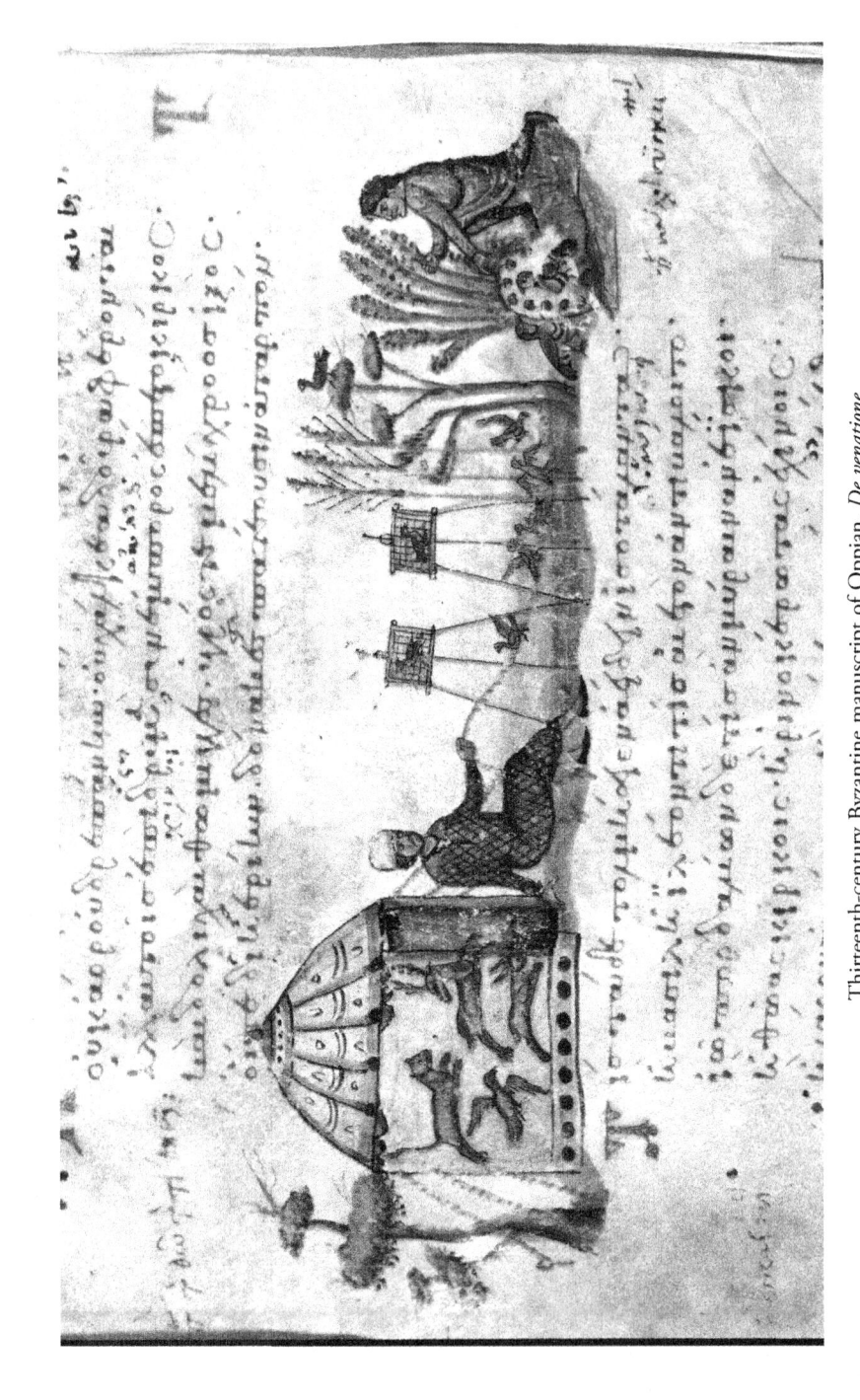

Thirteenth-century Byzantine manuscript of Oppian, *De venatione*

WRITER AND OCCASION IN TWELFTH-CENTURY BYZANTIUM

The Authorial Voice of Constantine Manasses

INGELA NILSSON

Uppsala University, Sweden

CAMBRIDGE
UNIVERSITY PRESS

University Printing House, Cambridge CB2 8BS, United Kingdom

One Liberty Plaza, 20th Floor, New York, NY 10006, USA

477 Williamstown Road, Port Melbourne, VIC 3207, Australia

314–321, 3rd Floor, Plot 3, Splendor Forum, Jasola District Centre, New Delhi – 110025, India

79 Anson Road, #06–04/06, Singapore 079906

Cambridge University Press is part of the University of Cambridge.

It furthers the University's mission by disseminating knowledge in the pursuit of education, learning, and research at the highest international levels of excellence.

www.cambridge.org
Information on this title: www.cambridge.org/9781108843355
DOI: 10.1017/9781108910217

© Ingela Nilsson 2021

This publication is in copyright. Subject to statutory exception and to the provisions of relevant collective licensing agreements, no reproduction of any part may take place without the written permission of Cambridge University Press.

First published 2021

A catalogue record for this publication is available from the British Library.

Library of Congress Cataloging-in-Publication Data
NAMES: Nilsson, Ingela, author.
TITLE: Writer and occasion in twelfth-century Byzantium : the authorial voice of Constantine Manasses / Ingela Nilsson, Uppsala University, Sweden.
DESCRIPTION: Cambridge, UK ; New York : Cambridge University Press, 2020. | Includes bibliographical references and indexes.
IDENTIFIERS: LCCN 2020023801 (print) | LCCN 2020023802 (ebook) | ISBN 9781108843355 (hardback) | ISBN 9781108824262 (paperback) | ISBN 9781108910217 (epub)
SUBJECTS: LCSH: Manasses, Constantine, -1187–Criticism and interpretation. | Byzantine Empire–In literature.
CLASSIFICATION: LCC PA5319.M3 N55 2020 (print) | LCC PA5319.M3 (ebook) | DDC 880.9–dc23
LC record available at https://lccn.loc.gov/2020023801
LC ebook record available at https://lccn.loc.gov/2020023802

ISBN 978-1-108-84335-5 Hardback

Cambridge University Press has no responsibility for the persistence or accuracy of URLs for external or third-party internet websites referred to in this publication and does not guarantee that any content on such websites is, or will remain, accurate or appropriate.

Contents

Acknowledgements		*page* vii
A Note on Texts and Translations		ix
List of Abbreviations		x
1	The Authorial Voice of Occasional Literature	1
	Writer, Text and Occasion	4
	Constantine Manasses and His Texts	13
	Narrative Strategies and Extraliterary Ends	20
2	Praising the Emperor, Visualizing His City	25
	In Praise of the Emperor	28
	Imperial Praise in Ekphrastic Guise	35
	A Constantinopolitan in Temporary Exile	46
	To Be on the Outside or the Inside	54
3	The Occasion of Death: Patronage and the Writer on Command	58
	Your Sorrow is My Concern	64
	Yours, As Ever	71
	My Goldfinch is Dead!	76
	The Good Teacher and the Generous Donor	82
4	In Times of Trouble: Networks and Friendships	86
	Rhetorical Skill at Work	91
	The Need to Address the Logothete	99
	With a Little Help from My Friends	106
5	On an Educational Note: The Writer as *Grammatikos*	113
	Gazing at the Stars	117
	An Ancient Life in Verse	124
	Enigmatic Exercises	130
	The Model Author and the Teacher	138

6 Life, Love and the Past: Self-Quotation and Recycling   142
   A Pleasant Reading of the Past   145
   Excerpted Love and Envy   153
   A Moral Poem à la Manasses   160
   Whose Emotions, Whose Life?   166

7 Occasional Writing as a Creative Craft   170
   Recycling the Past, Recycling the Present (1)   171
   Recycling the Past, Recycling the Present (2)   176
   Occasional Literature Between History and Fiction   181
   The Voice, Story and Career of Constantine Manasses   185

Bibliography   191
Index locorum   215
General Index   217

Acknowledgements

I have spent many years in the company of Constantine Manasses; too many years, perhaps, but I seem to have needed them in order to decide how to deal with the persistent voice that was calling for my attention. The time has come to 'relax the oar and let the ship rest', as he may have put it, and I feel more than ready to say farewell.

My interest in Manasses was first prompted by D. Roderich Reinsch, who suggested that I should look more carefully at the *Verse chronicle*. Under his direction, my postdoctoral years in Berlin helped to shape not only the first part of the project, but also me as a scholar. I am most grateful for the guidance and support that Roderich still offers, and I wish to thank the Alexander von Humboldt Stiftung and Wenner-Gren Foundation for their financial support during my Berlin years. Various research environments have followed in Uppsala, Paris, Oslo, Vienna and Istanbul; I feel privileged to have worked in such favourable milieus, willing to give me both the peace and the stimulation that I needed for this and for various other projects. A fellowship at the Swedish Collegium for Advanced Study gave me the opportunity to develop a first expanded version of the project that eventually turned into this monograph; Riksbankens Jubileumsfond for the Advancement of the Humanities and Social Sciences sponsored a sabbatical that made it possible to actually write it.

Many colleagues have offered their encouragement and support over a long period of time and in very different ways, ranging from discussions of problems to the reading of drafts: Panagiotis Agapitos, Beata Agrell, Lars Berglund, Carolina Cupane, Adam Goldwyn, Olof Heilo, Martin Hinterberger, Krystina Kubina, Karin Kukkonen, Marc Lauxtermann, Margaret Mullett, Paolo Odorico, Stratis Papaioannou, Andreas Rhoby, Roger Scott, Fredrik Sixtensson, Myrto Veikou and Nikos Zagklas. Panagiotis and Stratis were kind enough to read all translations and offer their advice at the very end of the journey, Nikos checked numerous last-minute references for me in the Vienna library and Adam took the time to read the entire manuscript and revise my English, regardless of how tired he must have been of Manasses by then. I am most grateful for their generous help. I would also like to thank the anonymous reviewers for useful remarks. Needless to say, any mistakes remain my responsibility.

There is one person in particular who has been instrumental in bringing this project to an end: Charis Messis, without whose relentless support this book would never have come into being. When I was ready to give up, he was the one who convinced me that the book was already in my head – *il faut juste sortir*. I truly cannot thank Charis enough for being such a knowledgeable, kind and critical colleague and friend.

Last but not least, many thanks to Michael Sharp for good advice and for graciously guiding me through the process of publishing with Cambridge University Press. I am also grateful to my content manager Bethany Johnson, who has been most patient and helpful in the final production phase of the book, and to my copy-editor Malcolm Todd, who has saved me from numerous inconsistencies and mistakes.

A Note on Texts and Translations

Many of the texts by Constantine Manasses cited in this book have not previously been translated into English. Many of them were also edited more than a century ago and accordingly appear in old and sometimes unreliable editions. It was my decision to go ahead nevertheless with what I had at my disposal and not do any manuscript studies for this monograph, which means that I cite the available editions even when I find them problematic (in which case I comment on that in the notes). My translation is an attempt to follow the Greek without producing unreadable English and although each translation is an interpretation and thus always open for discussion, I hope the reader will find them useful.

I also decided to use English titles for all works cited here instead of the traditional mixture of Greek and Latin. Accordingly, I speak of, for example, the *Verse chronicle* and the *Origins of Oppian* rather than of the *Synopsis Chronike* and the *Vita Oppiani*. I hope this will not be confusing for the reader. A complete list of works, indicating editions and translations (in the case they occur), is to be found at the beginning of the bibliographical section.

My hope is that the material presented here will encourage other scholars to engage in new editions, translations and studies of Manasses' literary output.

List of Abbreviations

BMGS	*Byzantine and Modern Greek Studies*
BSl	*Byzantinoslavica*
Byz	*Byzantion*
ByzF	*Byzantinische Forschungen*
BZ	*Byzantinische Zeitschrift*
CFHB	*Corpus Fontium Historiae Byzantinae*
CSHB	*Corpus Scriptorum Historiae Byzantinae*
DBBE	Database of Byzantine Book Epigrams (www.dbbe.ugent.be)
DNP	*Der Neue Pauly = Brill's New Pauly online*, ed. H. Cancik and H. Schneider
DOP	*Dumbarton Oaks Papers*
GRBS	*Greek, Roman, and Byzantine Studies*
JÖB	*Jahrbuch der Österreichischen Byzantinistik*
LBG	*Lexikon zur byzantinischen Gräzität besonders des 9.–12. Jahrhunderts*, ed. E. Trapp et al. (Vienna 1994–2017)
MEG	*Medioevo greco*
ODB	*The Oxford Dictionary of Byzantium*, 3 vols., ed. A. P. Kazdan (Oxford and New York 1991)
PG	*Patrologia Graeca*, ed. J.-P. Migne (Paris 1857–66)
REB	*Revue des études byzantines*
RSBN	*Rivista di studi bizantini e neoellenici*
VizVrem	*Vizantiiskii Vremennik*
WSt	*Wiener Studien*

CHAPTER I

The Authorial Voice of Occasional Literature

In the wake of reader-response criticism and reception studies, the reader's role and significance for the interpretive process has become part of an intellectual awareness that marks philological, linguistic and literary scholars alike. Ancient and medieval literature has been reconsidered from this perspective and scholars have, over the last decades, underlined the widely differing perspectives of historical authors and audiences in comparison to those of modern readers. Such fundamental differences concern, among many others, concepts like originality, spontaneity and individuality. While these were central for the romantic understanding of literature that was established in the late eighteenth and early nineteenth centuries, they are generally agreed to have been understood very differently in pre-modern contexts. Originality should be considered rather as a skilful use of conventions, creating a tension between and careful balancing of tradition and innovation. And while linguistic and rhetorical devices could be used in order to create stylistic effects that gave the impression of an original, spontaneous and individual voice – ranging from the lyric expressions of Sappho to the vernacular works of Chrétien de Troyes – that effect should not be confused with the romantic notion of spontaneity.

Previous generations of readers had a different approach. When Nicolae Iorga (1871–1940) – the Romanian polymath and writer, to Byzantinists known above all for his *Byzance après Byzance* (1935) – took on the task of writing a cultural history of Byzantium, he did it with a passion and open subjectivity that now would seem unusual. In the third volume of his *Histoire de la vie byzantine* (1934), Iorga devoted several pages to the twelfth-century writer Constantine Manasses, who was elaborately praised as a Byzantine Turgenev:

> Ceux qui parlent du manque de sens pour la beauté de la part des Byzantins n'ont que lire le joli morceau de Manasses, dans son récit de chasse qui présente les charmes de ce rivage de la Propontide où « la mer solitaire se

I

joue avec les berges et sourit doucement au rivage », « une fête pour les yeux, une joie pour les sens ». Le spectacle dans la nuit embaumée rappelle les plus belles pages de Tourguénieff sur la beauté des orées russes dans l'obscurité.[1]

The text that Iorga refers to and cites here is an ekphrasis, the *Description of the catching of siskins and chaffinches*, which had been edited and published some 30 years earlier.[2] In addition to this text by Manasses, Iorga also discussed the *Description of a crane hunt* and the *Encomium of Emperor Manuel Komnenos*,[3] the so-called *Itinerary* (*Hodoiporikon*)[4] and the *Verse chronicle* (*Synopsis Chronike*).[5] The *Itinerary* was described in terms of 'spontaneity' and 'imagination', while the *Verse chronicle* – by Iorga referred to as a *poème historique* – was compared to the work of John Milton: 'C'est sans doute de la meilleure poésie, qui n'est pas inférieure à celle d'un Milton.'[6]

What is interesting about the enthusiastic attention that Iorga thus paid to the literary production of Manasses is not his unreserved praise of its 'beauty' or 'charm', but the way in which he brought together a number of works and noticed certain similarities that characterize them. He observed that both the hunting ekphrasis and the oration to Manuel are useful for their historical detail,[7] while the *Verse chronicle* was compared to the epic. Iorga did not make any distinction between works written in prose or verse, nor did he note any clear difference between fiction and reality in these works – it seems to have been rather, in all cases, a question of literary beauty and imagination. This distinguishes Iorga from some earlier admirers of Manasses, who had focused only on the *Verse chronicle*, such as the sixteenth-century German philologist Martin Crusius (1526–1607) or the Greek enlightenment poet Kaisarios Dapontes (1713/14–84).[8] An important reason for Iorga's wider perspective was the availability of edited texts, many of which had appeared at the beginning of the twentieth century. His tendency to describe the literary qualities that he saw in Manasses by means of comparison to authors as different as John Milton (1608–74) and Ivan Turgenev (1818–83) may be seen as a wish to make

---

[1] Iorga 1934: 63.
[2] Sternbach 1902 and Horna 1905. See also Iorga 1934: 62, on the same ekphrasis. For the lines cited in translation by Iorga, see below, n. 13.
[3] Both edited by Kurtz in 1906.
[4] First edited by Horna in 1904, but now see Chryssogelos 2017.
[5] Iorga most probably relied on Bekker's edition of 1837, but now see Lampsides 1996.
[6] Iorga 1934: 64.   [7] Iorga 1934: 62.
[8] On Crusius and Manasses, see Rhoby 2014: 392; Paul and Rhoby 2019: 1–3 and 57. On Dapontes and Manasses, see Lampsides 1969.

1 The Authorial Voice of Occasional Literature

the Byzantine author comprehensible and relevant to modern readers, without offering classicizing references. The comparison to Milton's *Paradise Lost* thus seems to sustain Iorga's characterization of the chronicle as epic (with special attention to the opening Creation ekphrasis), while Turgenev here may mirror the idea of simple or rustic realism.

Some might argue that Iorga was neither a literary scholar nor a Byzantinist,[9] and that his ideas on the quality of Manasses' works are of no interest to today's readers. His admiring and strongly evaluative comments seem outdated to a contemporary student of Byzantine literature. However, they offer a suitable point of departure for a study of Manasses' literary production, simply because they express the first known discussion of more than one of his works: they seek to identify what is 'Manasses' in a series of different kinds of texts. In that sense there are certain similarities between Iorga's almost 90-year-old discussion and the present investigation, although my focus is not on literary quality as such but on that impression of an original, spontaneous and individual voice which was mentioned above and which Iorga attempted to identify and describe. In the case of Manasses, it is the voice of a teacher and a writer on commission, a producer of occasional literature, and as such it has often been described as having the aim of mere entertainment or self-display.[10] Occasional literature has thus been seen as inferior to romantic poetry, in which the spontaneous poet expresses his original feelings on the spur of the moment. William Wordsworth's famous definition of poetry as the 'spontaneous overflow of powerful feelings', taking 'its origin from emotion recollected in tranquillity' (1798), has come to dominate modern thinking about poetics, in spite of its ideological and clearly romantic character.[11] As a result, the form of occasional texts has often been seen as 'empty', as a display of beauty with no function beyond the moment at which it is performed. According to that approach, the writer on command

---

[9] For an interesting and personal reflection on this question, belonging as early as in the 1940s, see Laurent 1946.

[10] See e.g. Magdalino 1997: 162, stating that Manasses 'writes only to entertain or to instruct on a very basic level', and E. Jeffreys 2012: 276: 'Most of Manasses' literary output known today consists of short pieces, in both prose and verse, written either for sponsors or for self-display.' See also below, n. 71.

[11] The source of this quotation is the preface to the second edition of *Lyrical Ballads* (1800: 26). The first edition, a joint venture with Samuel Taylor Coleridge, had been published in 1798 but not received much attention; see Butler 2003. As early as 1919, T. S. Eliot rejected Wordsworth's definition of poetry in his *Tradition and the Individual Talent*, arguing that a writer should be impersonal and his writings devoid of personal emotion and feelings; see Eliot 1950 and cf. Ferguson 2003: esp. 101.

does not have an individual voice, but one that fits each separate occasion. The writer on command thus remains a writer, not an author.

This study takes as a point of departure the idea that writing on command privileges originality and encourages the challenging of conventions. A society in which occasional poetry and rhetoric have central positions calls for a strong and individual voice of the author, since the voice is the primary instrument for a successful career. By 'voice' I do not mean point of view or focalization in the narratological sense, but a writer's combined linguistic, stylistic and rhetorical means to express oneself publicly – all that usually goes under the term 'style'. An authorial voice should not be expected to be stylistically static, but to be flexible so that it can be used for various occasions but still be recognizable across generic boundaries and in different social contexts. Constantine Manasses is a good example of an author who projected such a voice in a society that demanded such social performances. The texts that have been preserved allow us to study his particular characteristics across different genres, in both prose and verse, in texts written for various patrons and situations. Such a study reveals not only the literary and rhetorical preferences as such, but also the compositional techniques that helped convey the individual voice: on the one hand, the insistent and elaborate use of the same or similar words, verses and phrases in different texts, on the other a series of recurring motifs and narrative techniques such as characterization or the handling of time and space. My aim is to show how Manasses used this stylistic and narrative 'author brand' as a way to promote his literary production, but also to create a winning self-representation – his own 'personal' *qua* authorial story, as it were.

Writer, Text and Occasion

In the *Description of the catching of siskins and chaffinches* ("Ἔκφρασις ἁλώσεως σπίνων καὶ ἀκανθίδων τοῦ σοφωτάτου κυροῦ Μανασσῆ), praised and cited by Iorga in the passage discussed above, Manasses offers a description of a pleasure trip to the other shore of the Marmara Sea.[12] The narrator begins by explaining the reasons for leaving Constantinople and travelling across the water:

---

[12] The text has survived in two mss: Vat. Urb. Gr. 134 and Escorialensis Y.II.10, of the fifteenth and thirteenth century respectively. Both mss contain more than one text by Manasses.

There was once in Constantinople a lack of hot baths and the upper side of the Propontis was crowded with people who came there to bathe. The location is pleasurable and well worth idle stays: there are gardens everywhere, thickly wooded and wide-spreading, and an abundance of clear streams; the sea plays gently with the shore and smiles with light waves at the mainland, and this becomes a feast for the eyes, a joy for the senses. I too went there, for the itching of my flesh demanded so; it was the time right after the vintage.

Ἐσπάνισέ ποτε καὶ ἡ Κωνσταντινούπολις λουτηρίων θερμῶν καὶ τὸ ἀναπλεόμενον μέρος τῆς Προποντίδος ἐστενοχωρεῖτο τοῖς περαιουμένοις ἐπὶ λουτρά· χαρίεις δὲ ὁ χῶρος καὶ διατριβῶν ἀνεσίμων κατάξιος, παράδεισοί τε πανταχοῦ κατάδενδροι καὶ ἀμφιλαφεῖς καὶ ναμάτων διειδῶν ἀφθονία· θάλασσα ταῖς ἠϊόσιν ἠρέμα προσπαίζει καὶ ταῖς ἠπείροις ἡμέρῳ κύματι προσγελᾷ, καὶ γίνεται ταῦτα πανήγυρις ὀφθαλμῶν, ἑορτὴ τῶν αἰσθήσεων. Ἀνῄειν κἀγώ· τῆς γὰρ σαρκὸς ὁ κνησμὸς οὕτως ἐκέλευεν· ἦν δὲ καιρὸς ὁ μετὰ τὴν τρύγην εὐθύς.[13]

As soon as he gets off the boat, the narrator is greeted by one of his closest friends. After the much-awaited bath he spends the night in his friend's tent.[14] At dawn they are woken up by a loud noise as a group of boys and young men, accompanied by an older man, set off for a bird hunt. The hunt – a catching of small birds by means of lime and other traps – is then described in great detail. The text closes in a traditionally ekphrastic manner, as the narrator is asked by his friend to bring what he has seen onto paper. He does so 'as a favour offered to my host and for myself a way of preserving the memory of the spectacle' (τῷ ξεναγῷ χαριζόμενος καὶ ἐμαυτῷ περισώζων τὴν τῶν θεαμάτων ἀνάμνησιν).[15]

Even this short introduction raises a number of questions concerning the form, content and function of the text. Is the narrator to be identified with Manasses himself? Does the ekphrasis describe an event experienced by Manasses or is it merely a fiction, a literary pleasure mirrored in the rural pleasure of the image painted in words? For what occasion and audience was it composed – does the very good friend of the narrator exist or is he merely a pretext for the description, an ekphrastic trope? Such

---

[13] Manasses, *Description of the catching of siskins and chaffinches* 1–8 (Horna).
[14] On the significance of tents in Byzantine literature, see Mullett 2013a, 2013b, 2017 and 2018. As for literary and iconographic representations reminiscent of the one in Manasses' ekphrasis, note esp. the 'tent poem' by Manganeios Prodromos (Anderson and Jeffreys 1994) and the illumination to Pseudo-Oppian's *Cynegetica* in Marc. Gr. 479, f. 2ᵛ, depicting a scene of bird-catching with a tent, in turn decorated with scenes of a hunt (Spatharakis 2004: fig. 4). See the cover and frontispiece of this book.
[15] *Description of the catching of siskins and chaffinches* 206–7 (Horna). I return to this text below, Chapters 2 and 5.

issues are discussed in this study in relation to the respective texts by Manasses, but my primary concern here is with this text as an example of occasional literature. That term has in Byzantine Studies often been limited to cases of epideictic rhetoric or ceremonial poetry, addressed to a specific person at a specific event, but I should like to argue that all preserved texts by Manasses were potentially occasional. So was most, if not all, Byzantine literature of the twelfth century, as were numerous texts produced in Europe up until at least the end of the eighteenth century. As noted by Volkhard Wels, employing the corresponding German term *Gelegenheitsdichtung*:

> Was also bleibt von der Dichtung der Frühen Neuzeit [*c.*1500–1800], wenn man die 'Gelegenheitsdichtung' außer Betracht lässt? – Offensichtlich nichts. Die gesamte Dichtung der frühen Neuzeit ist 'Gelegen-heitsdichtung', insofern diese Dichtung immer in einen konkreten kommunikativen Zusammenhang eingebettet ist.[16]

These concrete communicative contexts are what made texts written by Manasses and his peers occasional, or perhaps rather occasioned: they had a pretext. Importantly, this pretext – the occasion – was not the function of the text, but an opportunity to achieve its extraliterary aim. Within the basically political and social system of patronage in the twelfth century, the aim of literature was not to *be* but to *do* – to achieve something for its author.[17] Most often it was a question of social and professional advancement, achieved through a display of one's learning, but there could also be other reasons for writing, such as socio-political and/or personal rehabilitation.[18]

While the significance of patronage in the Komnenian period has been acknowledged and frequently referred to since Margaret Mullett's pioneering article in the 1980s,[19] the poetics of occasional literature have been largely avoided both within and beyond the field of Byzantine Studies. Mullett's interest in genre, author and performance has often taken her in the direction of the occasional, as in her study of the intersection between

---

[16] Wels 2010: 20–1; cited by Kubina 2020: 167.
[17] Cf. Tompkins 1980 on patronage in the Renaissance, applying the necessary reader-response perspective. I return to this issue below.
[18] As in the case of Anna Komnene, whose *Alexiad* was not occasioned by a specific event or written with the aim of financial support, but still part of a system in which literature had extraliterary functions.
[19] Mullett 1984 was followed by several studies on the topic, considered from various angles, see e.g. Mullett 2007; Theis, Mullett and Grünbart 2014; Drpić 2016. For a discussion on literature and patronage in eleventh-century Byzantium, see Bernard 2014: 291–333. I return to the issue of patronage below, esp. Chapters 3–4.

immediate occasion and inherited form,[20] but the term 'occasional poetry' has most often remained a designation for ceremonial or courtly poetry and rarely taken into consideration orations or other performative pieces in prose.[21] Wolfram Hörandner's definition of an occasional poem underlined the 'special purpose' of literature in Byzantium, but by bringing in the term *Gebrauchstexte* he also conveyed the confusion between use and function inherent in that concept.[22] As noted by Krystina Kubina, both *Gelegenheitsdichtung* and *Gebrauchsdichtung* are fuzzy terms,[23] and an important reason is exactly this unclear status of use vs function. While a text is *used* at a specific event, its *function* most often goes beyond that event.

In a recent and rare discussion of the occasional in the case of prose oratory, Emmanuel Bourbouhakis underlines (as Wels above) the concrete setting of the performance of the text: 'an actual physical and ceremonial context, an *event*'.[24] An occasional text is thus 'a text recited before a particular audience in a specific place'.[25] I agree with the importance of such a definition, but that specific place and audience – the text's performative circumstances – are in many cases lost to us as modern readers. Moreover, I am interested in the specific relation between the text's literary construct and the occasion (the pretext or use), on the one hand, and the occasion and the aim (function) on the other. My own understanding of the occasional is accordingly less categorical and includes both commissioned and uncommissioned works,[26] that is, also self-promotional works produced in the hope of future commissions, performed before an audience (or intended for such performance), written in either poetry or

---

[20] Mullett 1992.
[21] See e.g. Hörandner 1987 and 2003 and cf. 2017: 91–116. As for Hörandner's distinction between court poetry and poetry on commission, cf. Zagklas 2018. See also Lauxtermann 2003: 34–53 on the function of poetry and the relation between poet and patron. Agapitos 2007: 6 uses the term occasional poetry for a book epigram, but without any discussion or definition of the term. For an excellent critical discussion of occasional poetry in the case of Manuel Philes, see Kubina 2020: 163–287.
[22] Hörandner 1987: 236: 'The German term, rather en vogue of late, is "Gebrauchstexte", texts intended for use. Consequently, these poems are characterized in disposition and contents by their function.'
[23] Kubina 2020: 165: 'Der zweite oft verwendete Begriff, "Gebrauchsliteratur", ist noch unschärfer und unmöglich zu definieren, da er alle Texte umfasst, denen eine Zweckhaftigkeit zugrunde liegt.' Kubina here offers a useful survey of the term *Gebrauchsdichtung* and its background in German philology of the 1970s.
[24] Bourbouhakis 2017: 47*.   [25] Bourbouhakis 2017: 59*.
[26] Cf. Kubina 2020: 235–8 on 'Externe und interne Motivation', including uncommissioned poems ('ohne Bestellung').

prose, in a short period or over a long period of time.[27] But how can we move on to define the concept and avoid the 'fuzziness' that seems to haunt the term?

With the exception of some work on ancient, Renaissance and seventeenth- and eighteenth-century circumstances, occasional literature has on the whole attracted little interest from modern scholars, not least in critical discourse.[28] It seems that there are difficulties in defining or situating occasional texts because they somehow lack what is demanded – according to the romantic definitions referred to above – by 'poetry proper': an individual voice. Occasional literature, according to such romantic notions, is most highly valued when it gives up its own status and so to speak merges with the occasion, but in pre-romantic contexts it is exactly the occasion that lends the texts their status. The occasion offers the writer, the artist or the composer a pretext to display their craft and, moreover, an opportunity to reach a more specific goal (a reward, fame, perhaps another commission) – which is ultimately the function of the work. This is one of the reasons why the occasional fell into disrepute in the nineteenth century: political and social conditions changed and literary patronage largely disappeared from the public sphere, or at least in the form that was known before. In practice, patronage is an important agency in the cultural sphere even today.

Writing in a period when the inferior value of occasional literature had already been established, Friedrich Hegel reflected on its status between 'poetry' and 'reality' in his *Lectures on Aesthetics* (1835–8). Hegel's interest in the occasional stemmed from his concern with art's relation to human existence (*Dasein*) and must therefore be seen in the wider perspective of his philosophical understanding of aesthetics, but his brief comment offers considerations that are relevant also for the present discussion. Hegel first notes that occasional pieces (*Gelegenheitsgedichte*) express most amply the 'living connection with the real world' (*die lebendige Beziehung zu dem vorhandenen Dasein*) in the form of 'occurrences in public and private affairs' (*privaten und öffentlichen Angelegenheiten*).[29] While such a description could designate most poetic works, he continues, the more narrow

---

[27] On the synchronic vs diachronic aspects of occasional literature, see further below, Chapter 6.
[28] For a recent exception, see Küpper, Oster and Rivoletti 2018. Note also Tompkins 1980; Keller et al. 2010.
[29] Hegel 1970: 269. The passage in which Hegel comments on the occasional is placed in a section on 'Das freie poetische Kunstwerk', a subsection of 'Das poetische und prosaische Kunstwerk', in turn part of the larger section on 'Das poetische Kunstwerk im Unterschiede des prosaischen'. For Hegel, the difference between the poetic and the prosaic was not primarily a question of form, but one of art's relation to human existence; he saw the world of the ancients as fundamentally poetic (a world in which poetry was not merely written, but lived), while his own age was prosaic (a world prosaically understood in scientific terms). For a detailed discussion, see Shapiro 1975.

sense indicates 'Produktionen ... welche ihren Ursprung in der Gegenwart selbst irgendeinem Ereignisse verdanken, dessen Erhebung, Ausschmückung, Gedächtnisfeier usf. sie nun auch ausdrücklich gewidmet sind.' Then follows a brief but significant explication of the close connection between 'the poetic' and 'the real', which according to Hegel is what has lent occasional literature an inferior position:

> Durch solch lebendige Verflechtung aber scheint die Poesie wiederum in Abhängigkeit zu geraten, und man hat deshalb auch häufig diesem ganzen Kreise nur einen untergeordneten Wert zuschreiben wollen, obschon zum Teil, besonders in der Lyrik, die berühmtesten Werke hierher gehören.[30]

The contradiction that Hegel notes at the end of this passage is significant. The lack of prestige of occasional literature is due to an 'entanglement' (*Verflechtung*) with life, by means of which it falls into a position of 'dependence' (*Abhängigkeit*). And yet, the great lyric poets of the past, such as Pindar, composed their works under exactly such circumstances, without being accused of dependence and empty flattery.[31] Hegel's notion of 'entanglement' with life is central for the way in which occasional poetry has been understood (as something primarily dependent and low) from the nineteenth century onwards, but the question is to what extent that entanglement should be seen as a problem. Or to put it differently: does occasional literature really give up its own status? Do writers on commission relinquish their own voice?

Let us return to the ekphrasis by Manasses and my definition of it as an occasional piece – a piece that has an extraliterary end and by which the author wishes to achieve something. Ekphraseis are often not read in this manner, but as representations of objects or events.[32] It is, however, likely that such descriptions were performed in twelfth-century Constantinople before an audience at a specific occasion, which means that their function could be occasional.[33] Many of Manasses' preserved texts display such

---

[30] Hegel 1970: 269–70.
[31] Cf. the definition in *DNP* (s.v. Occasional poetry): 'A form of poetry created for a specific occasion, not as a result of the poet's autonomous desire. From a perspective that privileges original thinking, occasional poetry (OP) is often regarded as inferior ... but this is unjustified since large parts of ancient poetry from the earliest periods on are OP in a broader sense, as can be seen – in what appears to be self-reflection – in the song of Demodocus in Hom. Od. 8,250ff. Homer himself is attributed with OP in the biographical tradition.' In spite of such scholarly insights, Homer and Pindar are usually not portrayed as occasional or 'dependent' poets in literary history.
[32] For a recent survey of ekphrasis scholarship from the art-historical perspective, see Foskolou 2018: 72–6.
[33] Cf. Macrides and Magdalino 1988: esp. 80–2. For a discussion of such functions of ekphrasis, going beyond the merely representational, see below, Chapter 2.

characteristics, even when they are not explicitly epideictic. For a teacher hoping for social and financial advancement, even grammar exercises could have the aim of self-promotion, especially if they were later recycled and used for other occasions in imperial or aristocratic court settings. Self-promotion could lead to commissions, which in turn led to other assignments.[34] The circumstantial character of such a literary production is often misunderstood for its function, but a commission is not a function – it is merely a characterization of the circumstances under which a certain text was produced. Most such situations vary from case to case so that the function of each individual text is different, even if they all may be said to fall within the wider category of self-promotion aiming at social advancement.

The ekphrasis in question accordingly has a function that reaches beyond that of mere representation of an event; its specific occasion is not known to us, but it still conditions the way in which the text should be understood not as passive or self-referential, but as active and referential – a potentially powerful tool. This brings us back to the implications of Hegel's passage: that occasional pieces somehow fall between 'the poetic' and 'the real', between the imaginary and the referential. Literature's representation of the real has since been subject to numerous discussions and it is beyond the scope of the present study to offer a detailed survey. A basic assumption here is that all literature could be seen as 'entangled' with reality or 'suggested by real life', since all artistic expression is necessarily based on human experience. Moreover, literature is seen as a sphere in which human existence can be imagined and negotiated, offering an important tool for commenting on and relating to 'reality'; in the words of Gregory Jusdanis, 'the role of literature ... is to highlight itself as a separate realm of human practice wherein we can imagine alternative possibilities of human relationships and political institutions'.[35]

To what extent is occasional literature then different from any literary expression? How can it be seen as particularly 'entangled' with life? The answer may lie in its referential character, which offers a more direct connection to a specific event, rather than human experience in general. But here we need to provide Hegel's notion of entanglement with a distinction between two kinds of referentiality: on the one hand, the text's

---

[34] See Zagklas 2014 on the case of Theodore Prodromos and the different settings of court poetry as 'communicating vessels'. Cf. the situation of Renaissance poets who would typically dedicate various versions of their work to a number of potential patrons in the hope of securing recognition and remuneration; see Lytle and Orgel 1981. See also further below, Chapters 5 and 7.
[35] Jusdanis 2010: 5.

connection to the occasion (pretext/performance); on the other, its (literary/potentially fictive) representation of a 'reality' that is relevant to that occasion. This becomes particularly clear in the case of, for instance, poems celebrating a wedding or orations commemorating a military victory, in which case authors can more openly explore the relation between the actual event and the imaginary of the text and use it to their advantage.[36] But also other kinds of occasional texts, such as the ekphrasis discussed above, are referential and once offered a link between an actual occasion and its literary imaginary, even if that moment has been lost to a modern reader such as myself.[37] The *Description of the catching of siskins and chaffinches* could accordingly be described as a textual inscription of an occasion: the text and its pretext cannot be easily distinguished, so even if the occasional origin has been lost it still needs to condition its critical reception. Edward Said has described this connection between text and historical occasion in a manner that seems particularly apt in a discussion of occasional literature:

> My position is that texts are worldly, to some degree they are events, and, even when they appear to deny it, they are nevertheless a part of the social world, human life, and of course the historical moments in which they are located and interpreted.[38]

Seen from that angle, literary pieces occasioned by specific circumstances simply cannot renounce their own status (as 'occasioned literature'), because they would then lose their special power to achieve an extraliterary end and have a function beyond the occasion.

According to the more traditional way of looking at occasional literature, it is produced in the service of the patron, whether that patron is an individual, a nation or an empire. From such a perspective, the successful occasional author 'must, for the moment, fuse himself so completely with the nation that he is in essence the nation. He must speak so clearly that all men must recognize his voice as the voice of the nation.'[39] Such an obliteration of the self is what has led occasional texts to be seen as subservient and less valuable or creative than other kinds of literature. However, if one accepts the ideas outlined above – the occasional text as

---

[36] We will see several examples of this below, most notably in Chapters 2 and 3.
[37] Cf. Foskolou 2018: 92–5 on the 'topicality' of Manasses' *Description of the Earth*, i.e. the relation between the represented object and its possible model.
[38] Said 1983: 4. Interestingly, Said's position here is expressed partly as a reaction to Hayden White's claim that there is no way to get past text in order to apprehend 'real' history, a claim which Said 'in the main' accepts.
[39] Lord 1935: 154.

explicitly referential in relation to both occasion and representation – the service it lends is not so much to the patron as to the writer himself and whatever aims they wish to achieve. This has several consequences for our understanding of the writer on command. Most importantly, commissioned writers do not necessarily relinquish their own voice; on the contrary, for writers who need to establish themselves so as to get more commissions and climb the social ladder, a clearly recognizable voice is crucial. Such a voice can be achieved in various ways, linguistically, rhetorically and narratologically. In the case of Manasses it includes various strategies of recycling and repetition with variation on both linguistic and narrative levels. The recognizable authorial voice is a means of communicating with both patron and audience, carrying a message that is relevant to them but yet keeping the writer's trademark.[40]

The authorial voice is accordingly as indistinguishable from the text as is the pretext (the occasion), and it is often marked by the same position between 'the real' and 'the imaginary' as is occasional literature itself. This is by no means limited to the Byzantine twelfth century, but characteristic of the entire Graeco-Roman tradition: the author taking on an unreliable literary *persona* that suits the occasion (often lost to us) and the literary imaginary that goes with it, but which does not necessarily mirror the historical person who composed it. Such a voice can still be distinct and characteristic, even if it takes on different positions as regards politics, social strata or gender.[41] The reasons behind such flexibility lie exactly in the occasioned nature of much pre-modern literature, demanding adaptability and availability to the caprice of circumstances. What is particularly prominent in the twelfth century and the case of Manasses is that the authorial voice tends to explicitly comment on or implicitly allude to its own occasioned status. In the case of the *Description of the catching of siskins and chaffinches*, the narrator (Manasses/his authorial *persona*) was asked by his friend (the addressee/the potential audience) to compose a written representation of the event, which turns out to be the product that the reader/listener has just received.[42] Even if such a device is part of the ekphrastic topos, it also draws attention to the role of the commissioned writer – this is his trade and the characteristic voice, as we will see, is his trademark.

---

[40] Cf. Zagklas 2018: esp. 69.
[41] In the case of ancient literature, Sappho is a case in point; see the important studies by Lardinois 1989, 2010 and 2014. On voice and *persona* in Byzantine literature, see Papaioannou 2013 and 2014; now also Kubina 2020: 187–99. See further below, Chapter 4.
[42] Manasses, *Description of the catching of siskins and chaffinches* 200–7 (Horna).

Since the text here is understood not as passive, but as active and referential, a reader-response perspective becomes necessary and conditioned by the patronage system which offered occasions for literary performances.[43] Jane Tompkins has described occasional poetry in the Renaissance as a kind of 'public relations': 'a source of financial support, a form of social protection, a means of securing a comfortable job, an instrument of socialization, a move in a complicated social game, or even a direct vehicle of courtship'.[44] As we will see, such a description is apt also for the circumstances in which Manasses worked, with a literary work being 'not so much an object, therefore, as a unit of force whose power is exerted on the world in a particular direction'.[45] This triangulation of text, pretext and authorial voice, entailed by the position of occasional literature between 'the imaginary' and 'the real', serves as the theoretical basis of my investigation.

Constantine Manasses and His Texts

As is the case with numerous Byzantine authors, Constantine Manasses (c.1115–after 1175) is known primarily through his own texts.[46] The few biographical details that are known are almost exclusively based on his own inclusion of them in various literary contexts. The approach outlined above necessarily problematizes the reading of such details as biographical or 'true' in the modern sense of the word. Nevertheless, several studies over the past few decades have been devoted to mapping and understanding the socio-cultural and literary characteristics of the Komnenian period (1081–1185), which makes it easier to place the life and work of Manasses in a relevant context and critically interpret his many authorial comments. The image of the twelfth century that has gradually emerged, starting with the seminal study of Manuel I Komnenos by Paul Magdalino,[47] is one of an aristocratic and courtly sponsored society in which patronage played an important role. Such a society allowed or even demanded occasional literature to thrive; it called for writers on

---

[43] Performance in Byzantium has been subject to numerous studies over the past few years, not the least as regards the twelfth century; see e.g. Mullett 2003 and 2010, Marciniak 2007 and 2014, Bourbouhakis 2011. See further below, Chapter 3.
[44] Tompkins 1980: 208.   [45] Tompkins 1980: 204.
[46] On the dating of Manasses' birth to c.1115, see Lampsides 1988: 104–10 and 1996: xiii–xvii, followed by Paul and Rhoby 2019: 4 and Rhoby (forthcoming). Cf. Horna 1904: 320, suggesting c.1130, followed by Karpozilos 2009: 536. The latter date does not seem reasonable in light of the preserved production and the likely dating of the *Verse chronicle* to the 1140s; see further below.
[47] Magdalino 1993.

commission who could draw attention to and praise the central characters and the system itself, both publicly and in more limited literary circles. The system allowed for social climbing based on education and the performance of rhetorical skills, which lent pedagogical positions – ranging from a simple *grammatikos* to a coveted chair as *maistōr tōn rhētorōn* – a particular prestige.

Manasses was only one of several writers who 'lived by the pen', offering their services as teachers and rhetoricians in exchange for money, protection and social advancement in the form of pedagogical, administrative or ecclesiastical positions. The self-conscious authorial voice that is often pointed out as characteristic of Komnenian writers was at least partly caused by the patronage system and the necessary self-promotion that came with it.[48] The literary products, occasioned by the various needs of the patrons, were accordingly important vehicles for public relations, since the navigation of sponsorships and friendships was central for a successful career. The works by Manasses that have come down to us represent a wide range of literary forms that were useful in such a system: orations of different kinds and other rhetorical pieces in prose such as ekphraseis; narrative and didactic poems, ranging from a large verse chronicle to a poetic account of an embassy; a romantic novel in verse (preserved only in excerpts); letters in prose; and grammar exercises (*schede*) elaborating with both prose and verse. All in all, there are almost 30 texts (some of which fragmentarily preserved) attributed with some certainty to Manasses.[49]

As already mentioned, most of these texts quite frequently contain comments on the system in which they were composed and performed. For instance, the most well-known work by Manasses, the *Verse chronicle*, was written for Sebastokratorissa Eirene (1110/12–1152/3), probably in the 1140s, and opens with an address to her, referring to the roles of both patron and writer.[50] Another kind of 'autobiographical' remark is included in the *Funerary oration on the death of Nikephoros Komnenos* (died c.1173),

---

[48] On authorial identities and self-consciousness in the twelfth century, see below, Chapter 4, esp. n. 13.

[49] For a complete list of works, with editions and translation, see the Bibliography section. For further information on manuscripts and transmission, see the first citation and discussion of the respective work. For previous inventories of Manasses' works, see Nesseres 2014: 340–4; Chryssogelos 2017: 13–20; Paul and Rhoby 2019: 5–7 (a discussion rather than an inventory); Rhoby (forthcoming).

[50] Manasses, *Verse chronicle* 1–26 (Lampsides). The Sebastokratorissa is praised also in nine hexameter verses preserved after the chronicle in some manuscripts, but printed before the text in Lampsides' edition and therefore also in the translations; see Rhoby 2009: 324; Paul and Rhoby 2019: 15. On the dating of the chronicle, see below, Chapter 6. On the Sebastokratorissa as a literary patron, see Lampsides 1984, Rhoby 2009 and E. Jeffreys 2014.

composed some 30 years later in Manasses' career. Here the author recalls a grammar contest in the imperial palace at which Nikephoros put children to trial and very successfully presented the most difficult kind of schedography.[51] Based on this passage, along with another mentioning of grammar contests in the *Encomium of Michael Hagiotheodorites* and five preserved *schede*, Manasses has been identified as a teacher, possibly in the so-called Patriarchal School.[52] In addition to such information drawn from Manasses' texts, there have also been attempts to identify the author Manasses with a certain metropolitan of Naupaktos (*c*.1180), which has been firmly refuted.[53] His possible identification with the metropolitan of Panion (today's Banıdoz), whose name has been preserved on a lead seal dated to *c*.1170, has also been found unlikely.[54] Representations of Manasses dressed as a bishop in two manuscripts – Cod. Vind. Phil. Gr. 149, depicting how the author hands over his *Verse chronicle* to the Sebastokratorissa Eirene, and Cod. Vind. Hist. Gr. 91, depicting the author seated on a bishop's throne with the chronicle in his hands – indicate that a late Byzantine tradition saw him as a bishop, which does not necessarily represent the historical situation in the twelfth century.[55] It is not unlikely that someone like Manasses would have ended his career as metropolitan bishop, given his relative success in imperial and aristocratic circles, but there is no irrefutable evidence to support this.

The entire corpus of preserved texts by Manasses has not previously been analysed together, even though the stylistic characteristics of Manasses were noted by early editors.[56] The Manassean style distinguishes

---

[51] Manasses, *Funerary oration on the death of Nikephoros Komnenos* 453–66 (Kurtz). The oration is discussed below, Chapter 3.

[52] Polemis 1996: 280–1. On the location and function of the so-called Patriarchal School, both of which remain questioned, see Browning 1962. On Manasses as teacher, perhaps at the Orphanotropheion, see below, Chapter 5.

[53] First suggested by Bees 1930; refuted by Lampsides 1988 and 1996: xvi; more recently by Paul and Rhoby 2019: 4–5 and Rhoby (forthcoming). See also Wassiliou-Seibt 2016: 297. Cf. Treadgold 2013: 399–401, who rejects Lampsides and argues that Manasses was a younger relative of Athanasios Manasses, Greek patriarch of Antioch in 1157.

[54] See Rhoby and Zagklas 2011. For the seal, see Wassiliou-Seibt 2016, no. 1988.

[55] Cf. the manuscripts of the *Verse chronicle* in which Manasses is called 'the later metropolitan of Naupaktos'; see Bees 1930 and Lampsides 1988. On the Vienna codices, see Paul and Rhoby 2019: 7 with n. 37; for Cod. Vind. Phil. Gr. 149 (fourteenth century), f. 10ʳ, see Rhoby 2018: 367–9; for a reproduction of Cod. Vind. Hist. Gr. 91 (fourteenth/fifteenth century), f. 1ʳ, see Yuretich 2018: 19. For a discussion of Manasses as a teacher and a potential man of the Church, see further below, Chapter 6.

[56] Most notably by Horna and Kurtz, who both edited several texts by Manasses; see e.g. Horna 1902: 16–17 and Kurtz 1906: 77. More recent discussions of style (based only on the *Verse chronicle*) include Augerinou-Tzioga 2003; Taxidis 2017; Yuretich 2018: 9–10; Paul and Rhoby 2019: 47–51.

itself across genres in its rich vocabulary and varied syntax, the frequent use of neologisms – often long compound adjectives that appear in several of his works but not in other authors – and its many gnomic expressions. There is a tendency to mix high and low, so that the high style and Homeric references are placed next to vernacular expressions or words, especially in the *Verse chronicle*.[57] An overall predilection for repetition with variation, both within and across works, and for recycling his own words, sentences and verses, made Manasses an interesting case for philologists of the early twentieth century using stylistics as a means to identify authors of anonymous or falsely attributed texts.[58] More recently, Manasses' style has been analysed and described as an efficient means of creating literary portraits and dramatic effects in the *Verse chronicle*.[59] In spite of this new focus on style as a means to achieve a literary and narrative effect, the Manassean style is still described as 'baroque',[60] 'overblown' or marked by 'inflated language'.[61]

For my own concerns in this study, the consistent use of a characteristic style that goes beyond the boundaries of genre and occasion, as well as those of prose and verse, is interesting not primarily as a philological paternity test, but as a crucial aspect of Manasses' 'author brand' and self-representation. It is my assumption that a word such as βελεμνοτοξοφόρος (carrying-bow-and-arrows)[62] is created not only to be 'inflated' or to fit the second half of a fifteen-syllable verse, but also to function as an authorial signal to the audience, while the use of a word like καλλίστομος creates connections between texts, perhaps also between occasions, and accordingly has a function that goes beyond that of linguistic ingenuity.[63] Taking all of the preserved texts attributed to Manasses into consideration in one study accordingly allows a contextualization of the more well-known texts (such as the *Verse chronicle* and the *Itinerary*) and an important focus on the less known, but no less significant texts. Above all, such a study enables an observation and analysis of how the works interact with each other on linguistic and authorial levels.

---

[57] Trapp 1993: 119. Paul and Rhoby 2019: 48–9. Lampsides saw the (in his view) 'simple' and 'popular' language of Manasses as one of three novelties that marked a break with the previous chronographical tradition (Lampsides 1996: xliv–xlv).

[58] This tendency can be observed in almost all early editions of Manassean works, but most notably in those that offer editions of anonymously transmitted texts, e.g. Miller 1875, Sternbach 1902 and Horna 1906.

[59] Taxidis 2017; Paul and Rhoby 2019: 51.   [60] Yuretich 2018: 9.   [61] Foskolou 2018: 96.

[62] Manasses, *Verse chronicle* 565 (Lampsides).

[63] Manasses, *Encomium of Michael Hagiotheodorites* 259 (Horna); *Monody on the death of his goldfinch* 3.10 (Horna).

In light of my understanding of Manasses' production as occasioned and performative, I see the writer on command as a craftsman rather than an author in the romantic sense – a Greek *poiētēs* ('maker')[64] more than a Latin *auctor*. However, I do not refrain from using the terms 'author', 'authorship' and 'authorial' throughout this study; they are indispensable in critical practice and I see no need to try to replace them by coining new terms. To call someone a craftsman instead of an *auctor* does not indicate a lower quality – on the contrary, it takes great skill and above all adaptability to work on commission and use one's technical skill (*technē*) for various occasions and different circumstances. My approach to the author-writer thus mirrors the instrumental–performative understanding of authorship characteristic of the pre-modern period, before the shift to the modern personalization of the author characterized by creative originality.[65] Contrary to the traditional expression of these two understandings of authorship, I see no contradiction between the instrumental–performative and the individual–creative. As outlined above, I argue instead that a literary production with extraliterary ends demands a strong individual voice from an author who wishes to distinguish himself and achieve his own and his patron's aims. Such an approach draws on cultural history and the concept of authorship as a 'cultural performance' within a 'cultural topography', always in connection with social contexts as well as political and cultural developments.[66]

In a similar vein, genres are here understood from a social perspective, as typified rhetorical ways of acting in recurring situations – in that sense, as means of communication between writer, patron and audience.[67] Such a genre perspective avoids the definition of genres as neat boxes in which texts can be placed and emphasizes the communicative role played by rhetorical and literary conventions. If combined with the understanding of authorship described above, one could say – in the words of Anis Bawarshi – that 'writers invent within genres and are themselves invented

---

[64] I use this word here in its most basic sense and not indicating a poet; cf. Bernard 2014: 47–8.
[65] On this development, see Wetzel 2000.
[66] See e.g. Berensmeyer et al. 2012. Cf. Spiegel 1990: 85, arguing that texts should be located within 'specific social sites that themselves disclose the political, economic, and social pressures that condition a culture's discourse at any given moment. ... Only after the text has been returned to its social and political context can we begin to appreciate the ways in which both language and social reality shape discursive and material fields of activity and thus come to an understanding of a text's "social logic" as situated language use.'
[67] I draw here on Miller 1984, defining genre as 'social action', and its later reception in genre studies. For an early discussion of genre from a social perspective in relation to Byzantine literature, see Mullett 1992 and 1997: 20–3.

by genres'.⁶⁸ This is not exclusively a Byzantine feature, but a prominent process in antiquity onwards, encompassing all literary cultures in which textual forms are organized in a generic system. In fact, such generic conventions and uses thereof characterize not only literature but also most other artistic expressions, such as music, art and architecture. To work within and against conventions is the task of any artist, and often of particular significance for those who work on command. The fact that such challenges were part of Byzantine twelfth-century writers' concerns is clearly voiced in a poem by Manganeios Prodromos, paraphrased by Michael Jeffreys in the following manner:

> He describes a world of exhausted rhetoricians, overwhelmed by the majesty of Manuel Komnenos, who is constantly providing even greater subjects for their encomiastic talents, challenging them to find new ways within the strict rules of reaching higher and higher levels of encomium.⁶⁹

We may assume that this situation was representative for all writers in similar situations, even if less tightly connected to the Komnenian court than Manganeios might have been. Such procedures are most often and quite rightly understood from a rhetorical perspective as 'mixing of genres',⁷⁰ but they may also be seen as a flexible use of available rhetorical and literary forms, the manipulation of which is unavoidable in contextualized practice.

Manasses has often been described as an author particularly concerned with an easily available literary form, to the extent that his work has become associated with 'classics made easy'⁷¹ or pleasurable (implicitly empty) display produced by a typical 'Byzantine courtier'.⁷² Of course, Manasses had the same tools at his disposal as had his peers: a solid education in grammar and rhetoric, allowing him to express himself for various occasions in either verse or prose. He is not more or less literary than other authors of his time, although his *Verse chronicle* may come across as surprisingly entertaining for being a Byzantine chronicle.⁷³ Needless to say, in a Byzantine context – as in any pre-modern setting – 'literary' and 'literature' mean something different from the modern notion

---

⁶⁸ Bawarshi 2003: 7.
⁶⁹ M. Jeffreys 2003: 94, referring to Manganeios Prodromos, *Poem* 10.309–25 (Bernardinello).
⁷⁰ See M. Jeffreys 2003: 94; also Agapitos 1998 and Zagklas 2018.
⁷¹ Kaldellis 2009b: 23. Cf. E. Jeffreys 2014: 180 on the *Verse chronicle* as 'coffee-table book'.
⁷² See above, n. 10.
⁷³ For the scholarly discussion of Manasses' *Verse chronicle* as 'literary', 'novelistic' or 'poetic', see Lampsides 1996: xl–xlv; Reinsch 2002, Nilsson 2006 and Rhoby 2014. Cf. Signes Codoñer 2005: 38 and Lauxtermann 2009: 46, on which Hörandner 2017: 132 and now also Nilsson 2019: 530–3.

of writing as associated with written text, leisure and entertainment.[74] As we have already seen, a Byzantine author of the twelfth century produced texts in the service of the empire or the aristocracy, often on commission, mostly for public declamation and primarily within the frame of rhetorical training and display. What modern scholars call literature – texts ranging from historiography and hagiography to romantic novels and satire – was accordingly understood in terms of rhetoric and discursive practices (ῥητορική and λόγοι). The first referred to the style or register of language that could be used for all kinds of discourse; the latter included any text informed by rhetoric, but also intellectual learnedness per se.[75] The strong influence of rhetoric and the primarily practical function of texts (for administrative, educational or ideological purposes) has led to a general idea of Byzantine literature as devoid of artistic ambition, aesthetical concerns and, indeed, 'literariness'. A basic assumption here is instead that rhetoric largely converges with what we understand as literature,[76] and that literary and narratological concerns were of major importance for authors of the twelfth century.[77]

For such an approach, it is vital to accept the connection between literature/rhetoric and social standing: in the twelfth century, rhetorical skills carried social meaning, because with such skills one could acquire cultural competence that was available to and controlled by a professional elite (not always to be equated with an economic elite).[78] This cultural competence rendered to the author a special place in the social structure of the empire, a position that created an extreme self-consciousness that imbued most texts produced.[79] Just as the commissioned texts needed to express a metanarrative of the empire and/or individual receiver, in a similar manner the author was continuously constructing the story of

---

[74] For a tentative, partly problematic definition of Byzantine literature, see Kazhdan and Constable 1982: 98–9, arguing that literature 'begins when a text contains not only exact information but also unformulated elements that are only indirectly connected with information. This superinformation may appear as a general context ... or it may be an artificial or rhetorical embellishment of the narrative, such as metaphor, simile, rhyme, rhythm, or word play.' Cf. Ljubarskij 2003.

[75] For useful discussions, see Bernard 2014: 41–7; Barber and Papaioannou 2017: 18–19. See also Papaioannou 2013: 17–18.

[76] Barber and Papaioannou 2017: 18.

[77] For the particularly narratological perspective, see Nilsson 2014.

[78] Cf. Bernard 2014 and his 'utilitarian' approach inspired by Bourdieu; see esp. the introductory chapter and pp. 7–9 on poems as socially meaningful acts, helping persons to cultural positions and material advantages in the eleventh century.

[79] See Magdalino 1993: 429, noting that Komnenian rhetoricians 'praised the emperor with a strong sense that their learning and eloquence placed them at even footing with their lords'. See further below, Chapter 3.

himself as a skilful rhetorician.[80] The intense focus on artistic concerns such as style, form and pleasure in the works of Manasses is to be seen from this perspective of authorial self-construction. Manasses indeed shares these features with many of his fellow literati of the period, which is why a study of his production could be seen as a case study of a twelfth-century writer.[81] At the same time, this monograph is intended as a study of an individual writer with his own preferences and ideas.[82] This is not a biography of Manasses as seen through his texts, but a study of his texts as a partial reflection of a twelfth-century writer.

Narrative Strategies and Extraliterary Ends

In light of these theoretical considerations, let us return to the aim and method of this study. As already stated, I wish to investigate the entire preserved production of Manasses in order to understand and define his individual voice on both stylistic and narrative levels. This method entails a certain circumvention of separate works and the division into genre, so that my focus may remain on characteristics that transcend generic boundaries. These characteristics are 'authorial' in the sense that they stem from the writer, but they are here for the most part seen as an expression of an authorial *persona* or a 'model author' rather than the 'empirical author'.[83] It is common to ascribe emotions or political positions stated by Byzantine authors in their texts as reflecting their own personal views, as if literature necessarily mirrors the identity of the author.[84] In the case of Manasses, it has, for instance, more than once been suggested that he had been badly treated because of envy – a motif that is prevalent in the *Verse chronicle* and in some other texts. The question is whether the descriptions of falling out of favour and being subject to envy are autobiographical or a prevalent theme in the courtly environment of the Komnenian period.[85] The one

---

[80] Cf. Chryssogelos 2016: 155–60 on the 'social skills' of Manasses, making his long career possible; but we know little or nothing about Manasses' social skills and more about his projected voice and *persona*.
[81] Cf. Tsolakis 1967: 22, on the particular case of Manasses and the need for cross-generic analysis. Cf. Bees 1930: 124.
[82] Cf. the desideratum expressed in Trapp 1993: 128, to focus on the synchronic aspects of texts and 'to stress more the whole personality of an author within his milieu', which I take to mean the linguistic and literary personality of any given author (rather than his psychological character).
[83] For this terminology, drawn from Umberto Eco, see a more detailed discussion below, Chapter 4.
[84] The case is very similar for ancient literature and Sappho is, again, a case in point; see above, n. 41.
[85] See e.g. Magdalino 1997: 163 (on envy as a 'courtly' theme) and Reinsch 2007: 267 (on the story of Palamedes in Manasses' Trojan war narrative as a reflection of court envy). On envy in the *Verse chronicle*, see now Paul and Rhoby 2019: 37–41 with a useful summary of previous research.

does not necessarily exclude the other; the relation between literature and the 'real' is, as already noted, complex and there is no clear boundary between the two – especially not, as I see it, in occasional literature. The letters by Manasses seem to confirm the picture gained from the chronicle, but even in the case of letters with their allegedly personal voice we cannot be entirely sure that the content reflects the historical personality of the author, that the narrator is the 'real' Manasses rather than a literary *persona*.[86] That said, I am not excluding the possibility that they do, at times, coincide.

Such issues of interpretation of the literary text and its relation to the author are central to this investigation and are here considered from a primarily narratological perspective.[87] What kind of authorial story (or self-representation) does the writer present the reader with and how does it relate to the 'reality' in which he worked? To what extent can it be seen as an expression of his authorial intentions? Is the ascription of meaning with reference to aspects of the empirical author theoretically legitimate and fruitful? Or is, on the contrary, the distinction between empirical author and the authorial *persona* problematic? These questions are considered in more detail further on in this study, but the relation between writer and text is central for the way in which I have structured my analysis and therefore needs to be underlined here. Of course, the position of the reader also conditions the analysis of any given text, and therefore my own theoretical stance as a twenty-first-century reader of Byzantine literature has shaped the present study in its choice of focus and structure.

Methodologically, a narratological perspective is accordingly applied not only to the analysis of Manasses' texts, but also on the levels of authorial self-referentiality (how the author wishes to display himself and his skills), individual works (narrative techniques across genre boundaries) and the literary production as a whole (how individual works fit into the overall story of a literary production). My analytical focus is on primarily four aspects of Manasses' narrative technique: his use of Graeco-Roman and Biblical material; his recycling of parts of his own texts; his authorial comments on his own situation as a writer; and his handling of patrons and peers in imperial and aristocratic circles. All aspects may be considered in relation to the occasional character of Manasses' literary production,

---

[86] On the letters by Manasses, see further below, Chapter 4. On envy as a motif in Manasses' texts and modern interpretations, see below, Chapter 6.
[87] Cf. Jannidis 2000.

contributing to the achievement of extraliterary ends for both writer and patron.

Of particular interest in this respect is the use of ancient literature and fictional devices as a means of both sustaining and manipulating the status of occasioned pieces as referential in relation to the literary tradition *and* to the represented occasion. While the use of ancient literature in Byzantium was once seen as imitative practices of a more or less perfunctory kind, a jargon sometimes void of meaning, it is now generally accepted that the process of appropriation that went on throughout the Byzantine millennium, and became particularly prominent in the twelfth century, was highly complex and significant.[88] Practices of imitation and appropriation can thus offer important keys for our interpretation of Byzantine texts, and occasional pieces offer a particularly interesting case. If we accept the notion of occasional literature as having an in-between status (between the 'imaginary' and the 'real'), the use of fictional markers in the form of citations of or allusions to ancient literature become part of an interplay involving author, text and audience. Such interplay tends to confuse modern readers because it does not allow us to offer one single interpretation, as demanded by philological practices but evaded by the ambiguous Byzantine text.[89]

Such an ambiguous message seems to be conveyed in another of Manasses' ekphraseis, the *Description of a little man*, depicting a dwarf who has travelled to and now performs at the imperial court at Constantinople.[90] In light of what we know about the Komnenian courtly entertainment from other sources, it seems probable that such a man existed and was observed by Manasses, who then described the sight (*theama*) as a performance (*drama*) in words for an audience who had seen the same thing and could remember one or more such events. At the same time, Manasses' use of ancient literature and especially his references to Homer and the ancient Greek novel by Achilles Tatius point in a fictional direction, underlining the 'unrealistic' experience of watching the 'monstrous little man' with his deformed limbs. Above all, they blur the boundaries between what is true and not, so that nature turns out to

---

[88] See e.g. Nilsson 2010 and Marciniak 2013. The use of ancient literature ties in with the overall question of originality and innovation, a topic that was brought to the fore in Kazhdan and Epstein 1985, then in Littlewood 1995. For more recent discussions from various perspectives, see Ödekan, Akyürek and Necipoğlu 2010; Nilsson 2014: 25–31; Spanos 2014.
[89] Cf. Mango's idea of Byzantine literature as a 'distorting mirror'; Mango 1975, cf. Ljubarskij 2003: 117–18.
[90] Messis and Nilsson 2015 and 2021.

reflect and confirm literature, which is the way in which occasional literature, according to my understanding, functions. The meaning of the ekphrasis must thus be sought beyond its representational character, in what is implied by the combination of 'real' (Constantinopolitan courtly space) and imaginary or 'fictional' (a sight that is known from Homer and reminds the observer of Tatius). In accordance with such reasoning, the little man has been interpreted as both a realistic representation and a literary metaphor, the latter as an alter ego of the author on command – an entertainer of the court, secretly despising the aristocrats in whose hands his success lies.[91]

By considering the use of ancient literature from such an occasional and narratological perspective, I do not wish to shift the scholarly focus away from other kinds of imitation or appropriation, but to sharpen our eyes to the meaning of such procedures and in particular its significance for the triangulation of writer, occasion and patron.[92] We must assume that uses of ancient literature of the kind described above meant something not only for the writer, but also for his audience (both patron and peers) and that it therefore was part of his overall strategy to achieve, by his texts, an extraliterary end. In the *Description of a little man*, the metaphorical message seems to be directed at fellow writers on command, but having no available information about the text's occasion we can only make probable assumptions based on the text as it has come down to us. A reasonable assumption in this case is that Manasses took advantage of the partly referential, partly fictional status of the occasional piece that he composed in order to shape his own authorial *persona*. He offers a self-representation that may be seen as playful or ironic, but which suits well the storyworld in which twelfth-century writers tend to place themselves.[93] In that storyworld they are weary poets, struggling under the constraints of their patrons, as in the poem by Manganeios Prodromos discussed above, or poor beggars doing anything to catch the emperor's attention in order to put food on the table. The begging poet is now by many scholars seen as a literary *persona* and not a part of Byzantine reality,[94]

---

[91] Messis and Nilsson 2015 and 2021.
[92] On this particular relationship, see below, esp. Chapters 3 and 4.
[93] For a contrasting idea, see Foskolou 2018: 79–80: 'Though he himself probably did not come from nor did he ultimately belong to this class, he composed a tale of aristocratic glamour and at the same time the myth of his own social group', with reference to Magdalino 1984. On storyworlds, a narratological concept developed by Herman 2002, in the context of Byzantine literature, see several contributions in Messis, Mullett and Nilsson 2018. I return to these contrasting storyworlds below, Chapter 7.
[94] Hörandner 2017: 100. Cf. Kulhánková 2008 and 2010; now also Kubina 2018.

which means that the hardship of writers in Komnenian Constantinople straddles the real and the fictional in a way that is similar to the status of occasional writing itself.

With a point of departure in these considerations, my analysis of Manasses' texts has been arranged not according to dating or genre, but according to contextual, functional and thematic concerns. Such a structure may help us to distinguish how a writer on command worked across genre boundaries, choosing content and form depending on the occasion rather than on the genre as such. The idea has been to map and thus better understand the position of Manasses in relation to his patrons and peers: which topics would suit which occasions, which level of style would be appropriate for each individual addressee, and to what degree the writer could express himself within the confines of the respective occasion. Comparisons with contemporary authors have been kept to a minimum in order to keep the analytical focus on Manasses' production, but occasional glances at his peers have in some cases been deemed relevant. I have deliberately avoided repeating my previously published analyses, which means that the *Verse chronicle* and some of the ekphraseis receive limited space in this study.[95] My intention is to make known the variety of texts composed by Manasses, rather than underlining the common view of him as an historian and an 'expert in ekphrasis'.[96]

Reconsidering Manasses' literary production from this angle reaches beyond superficial descriptions of his literary production as merely entertaining, didactic or novelistic, and instead acknowledges him as a writer concerned with the use of a literary heritage for extraliterary purposes. Even though such Byzantine recycling of literature, composed for students or on commission for wealthy patrons, sometimes has been seen as uncreative and void of literary aspiration, it is clear that Manasses was a successful writer – for some readers even a 'new Orpheus' and an 'embodiment of charm and sweetness'[97] – and that his authorship offers us important information not only on his own career, but on the Komnenian socio-cultural and literary culture more widely.

---

[95] References to relevant publications are included throughout.
[96] Hunger 1978, I: 183: 'ein Spezialist für Ekphraseis', frequently cited.
[97] I cite here an epigram preserved in one of the witnesses to *Aristandros and Kallithea* and partially in one manuscript of the *Verse chronicle*, edited as *Aristandros and Kallithea* frg. 181 (Mazal); tr. with brief notes in E. Jeffreys 2012: 337. For a discussion of this poem, see below, Chapter 6. On other book epigrams on the *Verse chronicle*, see Paul and Rhoby 2019: 59–61 and below, Chapter 7.

CHAPTER 2

Praising the Emperor, Visualizing His City

Constantinople has been experienced and described by inhabitants and visitors countless times over the centuries. At the centre of attention has often been the emperor and his court, but also various spatial components of the city: buildings – such as churches, palaces and libraries, parks and gardens – and, no less important, people of different origin and status. The geographical location of the city, with its mythologized foundation by Constantine the Great, has also triggered the imagination of spectators – a city bestriding the shores of Europe and Asia, embraced and cherished by both. The magical qualities of certain places and monuments were gathered and preserved in the tenth-century *Patria*, while also echoing in much later literary representations of the golden city of the Byzantines, turning it into a site for exotic allurement, astrology and magic. Stories and descriptions of Constantinopolitan space often connect a place or an object to a moment in the capital's glorious past. They seem to present a particular configuration of time and space, indicating their 'intrinsic connectedness' as proposed by Mikhail Bakhtin and subsequently underlined by cognitive narratology,[1] while also embodying a symbolic value that lies exactly in that configuration. The past thus becomes a relevant issue for the present and objects (statues or other works of art, but also monuments and buildings) function as its representatives.

This symbolic or metaphorical value of the various components of the city – including the emperor and the people – was central to any Byzantine writer concerned with Constantinople, but especially for writers aiming at celebrating its historical and imperial value. One could perhaps argue that all texts produced in Constantinople (and quite a few of those composed in other places) were concerned with the emperor and his capital, simply because the focus of many writers seems to have been on advancement

---

[1] The famous chronotope; see Bakhtin 1981: 84. For the relation between time and space in cognitive narratology, see e.g. Ryan 2003 and Herman 2014 (with substantial bibliography).

made possible through imperial channels. However, the everyday experience of the city and the more specific workings of court culture were unique for writers who made a living in that space. Such an experience is relevant for the way in which twelfth-century literature in this study is seen as occasional, or rather as occasioned by specific events: the presence of the writer and the audience both at the occasion and in the environment they describe or refer to enhances the referentiality of occasional pieces and makes them more likely to convey a clear and efficient message.

If we take Manasses' *Verse chronicle* as an example, it is necessarily concerned with the Byzantine Empire, since it narrates history from Creation until the beginning of the Komnenian reign. Several of the events narrated are placed in Constantinople and accordingly function as reminders of spatio-temporal configurations of the kind mentioned above, alluding to the symbolic value of various aspects of the city: the foundation of Constantinople by Constantine the Great (306–37)[2] or the destruction of the library of the Patriarchal School by Leo the Iconoclast (717–41).[3] Since Manasses' historical account ends just when the Komnenian reign begins, there are only few direct references to the present, among which the opening address to Sebastokratorissa Eirene and a brief praise of Manuel I Komnenos.[4] A brief ekphrastic note on Constantinople at the end of the reign of Constantine the Great may, however, function as both a reference to the contemporary (lived) city and an encomium of the prosperous Komnenian reign:

> the greatest city, the city of New Rome, | a Rome without wrinkles, that never grows old, | a Rome forever young, forever renewed, | a Rome from which streams of graces flow, | which the mainland embraces, the sea receives, | the palms of Europe gently embrace | and the mouth of Asia kisses from the other side.
>
> πόλιν τὴν μεγαλόπολιν, πόλιν τὴν νέαν Ῥώμην,
> Ῥώμην τὴν ἀρρυτίδωτον, τὴν μήποτε γηρῶσαν,
> Ῥώμην ἀεὶ νεάζουσαν, ἀεὶ καινιζομένην,
> Ῥώμην ἀφ' ἧς προχέονται χαρίτων αἱ συρμάδες,
> ἣν ἤπειρος προσπτύσσεται, θάλασσα δεξιοῦται,
> ἠπίως ἀγκαλίζονται παλάμαι τῆς Εὐρώπης,
> ἀντιφιλεῖ δ' ἑτέρωθεν τὸ τῆς Ἀσίας στόμα.[5]

---

[2] On which see Nilsson 2005: 137–9. [3] See Nilsson 2021a.
[4] Manasses, *Verse chronicle* 1–26 (Lampsides) (to Eirene), 2507–12 (to Manuel). On the dating of Manasses' chronicle and the inclusion of these addressees, see further below, Chapter 6.
[5] Manasses, *Verse chronicle* 2320–6 (Lampsides). The English translation of the *Verse chronicle*, Yuretich 2018, appeared when I had already made my own translations, which are consistently used in this book.

2 Praising the Emperor, Visualizing His City

The city may here accordingly function in lieu of a more elaborate praise of the Komnenians, at the same time reminding the audience of the symbolic *qua* contemporary value of their imperial space.[6]

In this chapter, I focus primarily on three texts that thematically tie in much closer with Constantinople and the imperial court: the *Encomium of Emperor Manuel Komnenos*, the *Description of a crane hunt* and the *Itinerary*. To this group of texts concerned with the imperial space of Constantinople belong also the four other preserved ekphraseis by Manasses: the *Description of the catching of siskins and chaffinches*, the *Description of the Earth*, the *Description of the Cyclops* and the *Description of a little man*.[7] All seven texts, I argue, express praise of imperial space and can be seen as different forms of panegyric.[8] This is obvious for the oration to the emperor, a *basilikos logos*, which according to Menander's definition is a form of *encomium*.[9] Such praise would traditionally focus on the emperor's origin, his physical appearance, his deeds (usually his success in war) and his imperial virtues as a wise and generous ruler. Presented on specific occasions, it would 'represent and reinforce values' familiar to and supposedly shared by orator, emperor and audience.[10] In that sense it is clearly occasioned, both by the occasion and by the object of praise. That does not mean that epideictic oratory is a mere variation on obvious and known facts, without any ambition to convince or influence the audience. Ruth Webb has shown how epideictic rhetoric can achieve 'a shift in the audience's feelings about or perception of the topic', as does rhetorical argumentation of all types.[11] Part of that process was the use of classical rhetorical figures such as, for instance, *synkrisis*, in order to show that the object of praise was worthy, but also ekphrastic and narrative strategies.[12] Descriptions of physical appearance and imperial settings along with stories of success in war or philanthropic acts were all part of creating the overall narrative of a successful emperor.

---

[6] On this passage as an example of a 'spatial narrative of time', see Veikou 2018: 21. On the representation of Constantinople as a woman, often threatened rather than embraced, in twelfth-century texts, see Magdalino 1993: 425 and Schmidt 2016: 167 and n. 26. For the same imagery in laments on the fall of Constantinople, see Goldwyn 2014.

[7] Since I have dealt with these texts in some detail elsewhere and, to some extent, above in Chapter 1, they are here used only for parallels and comparison. See Nilsson 2005 and 2011, along with Messis and Nilsson 2015 and 2021.

[8] On the ekphraseis of Manasses as 'indirect *encomia*' of Manuel, see Magdalino 1993: 455; see also Magdalino 1997: 164; Nilsson 2014: 153–6, 158–60.

[9] On Menander Rhetor and his influence on Byzantine rhetoricians, see e.g. Magdalino 1993: 415–16 (focusing esp. on the twelfth century) and Webb 2003. See also E. Jeffreys 2010: 171.

[10] Webb 2003: esp. 127 and 133. See also Magdalino 1993: 418. [11] Webb 2003: 127–8.

[12] Cf. E. Jeffreys 2010: 174 (on how 'narrative played a part' in the *basilikos logos*).

Something that connects the texts discussed here is, accordingly, that they all go beyond the purely representational and interact with the experience of imperial space – a characteristic of ekphrasis and ekphrastic discourse that is now receiving increasing scholarly attention. Such an approach takes its point of departure in a basically narratological definition of three ekphrastic functions (narrative, aesthetic and exegetic) which are combined in order to communicate an ideological or political message to the audience.[13] According to that way of defining ekphrasis, it is not merely representational – it also does something, it has agency, for both the writer and the audience – perhaps even for the object.[14] It has recently been argued by Myrto Veikou that descriptions of space take on a particularly potent role, since space cannot simply be 'looked at' or merely 'represented': 'instead, space is physically, bodily and mentally experienced, and it is being lived through iterative embodied spatial practices. In brief, accounts of spaces mean historical accounts of cultures.'[15]

Not all texts analysed in this chapter are descriptions, but they all contain descriptive sequences and they all refer to imperial space in a way that makes them involved in the spatial experience of Constantinople. By means of embedded uses of different text types – or, if one prefers, embedded uses of rhetorical techniques – the writer can thus control and manipulate the effects of his texts, in close and constant relation with the 'reality' of the occasion. The following examination of three texts that belong to different genres but similar occasions allows us to observe the recurring use of words, phrases and imagery employed by Manasses in his representation of imperial space.

In Praise of the Emperor

Six orations by Manasses have been preserved in their entirety: two encomiastic orations, three funerary orations and one consolatory discourse. With one exception, they all address members of the Komnenian elite and indicate the audience for which Manasses was writing his occasional pieces.[16] The *Encomium of Emperor Manuel Komnenos* (Πρὸς τὸν βασιλέα κυρὸν Μανουὴλ τὸν Κομνηνόν) offers an encomium of Manuel's

---

[13] Nilsson 2021b.
[14] Webb 2017, Veikou 2018 and Nilsson 2021b. Cf. also Peers 2017 and Foskolou 2018.
[15] Veikou 2018: 16.
[16] The exception is the *Monody on the death of his goldfinch*. In addition to these six pieces, one funerary oration has been fragmentarily preserved; see Sideras 1994: 190–5. On these texts, see further below, Chapters 3 and 4.

victories against Hungarian tribes in the last years of the 1160s.[17] The dating of the text should be to the end of that period, or at the very latest to the first part of the 1170s,[18] which means that it belongs to the later period of production by Manasses. The text has been preserved next to the *Description of a crane hunt* in a single manuscript, the thirteenth-century Cod. Barocc. 131.[19] Since the oration has not been translated into English, nor been discussed in detail in modern research, it is worth citing the opening passage in full as a point of departure for closer analysis.

> O Emperor, most enduring and most versed in military command of all emperors ever, you have already put to shame orations impossible to humble and raised by free wings, no longer daring to praise the sparkling of your trophies; having defeated both the pride and daring of arrogant barbarians, you have now also shackled the tongues of rhetoricians and bound their right hands to their elbows. They are conspicuously defeated by your strong unconquered right hand; and only now for the first time was it made known to them, that they are not able to measure up to deeds that extraordinary; it is indeed impossible even for a sophist's tongue to fly next to a swift-flying eagle and keep up with the sun; surely even the giant sun, enormous and shining resplendently, knows rising and experiences setting, but you are another and swifter light-bringer, gushing out the rays of myriads upon myriads of brave deeds, an eye that never wants to sleep, a strong hand, an arm of iron, a nature that exceeds the firmness of steel, more steadfast than copper, a nature unyielding, unassailable, impossible to humble. The orations beheld you, Emperor – your profound mind, strong hands, swift feet – and they are head over heels in love with your beauty and long to flutter toward you; but they are defeated by your height, they are conquered by your course and their wings no longer raise them into the air, and while in the past energetic hands and palms were second to sophistic refinery and gracious Muses, now things have taken a turn for the opposite (one might say): deeds are almost divine and truly heavenly, but words are now bending downwards and close their eyes to such absolute radiance of sun-like labours.
>
> Ὦ βασιλεῦ τῶν πώποτε βασιλέων καρτερικώτατε καὶ στρατηγικώτατε, ἤδη καὶ τοὺς ἀταπεινώτους λόγους καὶ πτεροῖς ἐλευθέροις κουφιζομένους

---

[17] On Manuel's campaigns against Hungary (1162–72), see Magdalino 1993: 78–83. On Byzantine–Hungarian relations in the twelfth century, see Makk 1989: 79–106; Stephenson 1996: 33–59; Stephenson 2000: 247–61.

[18] Kurtz 1906: 70–1, arguing that the text cannot be dated earlier than spring 1170.

[19] In the manuscript, the oration follows immediately after the ekphrasis, so that both texts cover ff. 180ᵛ–184ᵛ. This explains why Kurtz chose to publish them together in his edition of 1906. The Barocc. 131 was copied in Nicaea and Constantinople between 1250 and 1280 and contains also other pieces by or attributed to Manasses. On the ms, see Wilson 1978; also Papaioannou 2013: 263.

ἐξήλεγξας μηκέτι θαρροῦντας ἐπεντρανίζειν ταῖς τῶν σῶν τροπαίων μαρμαρυγαῖς· καὶ βαρβάρων ὑπερφρόνων ὀφρὺν καὶ θράσος καταβαλών, ἤδη καὶ ῥητόρων γλώσσας ἐπέδησας καὶ δεξιὰς ἀπηγκώνισας. ἥττονταί σου περιφανῶς τῆς δεξιᾶς τῆς ἀνικήτου τῆς βριαρᾶς· καὶ νῦν πρώτως αὐτοῖς ἐπῆλθε μαθεῖν, ὡς ἔργοις οὕτως ὑπερφύεσιν ἀντιφερίζειν οὐ σθένουσι· ναὶ γάρ τοι καὶ λίαν ἀμήχανον, γλῶσσαν σοφιστικὴν ἀετῷ συνίπτασθαι τῷ ταχυπετεῖ καὶ ἡλίῳ συμπεριφέρεσθαι· καίτοι γε ἥλιος μὲν οὗτος ὁ γίγας ὁ μέγας ὁ φεραυγὴς καὶ φαῦσιν οἶδε καὶ δύσιν ἔγνω, σὺ δὲ φωσφόρος γίνῃ δρομικώτερος ἕτερος, μυρίας ἐπὶ μυρίαις ἀριστευμάτων σελασφορίας ἐκβλύζων, ἀνύστακτος ὀφθαλμός, χεὶρ κραταιά, βραχίων σιδήρεος, φύσις ὑπὲρ τὸν ἀδάμαντα στερεμνία, παγιωτέρα χαλκοῦ, φύσις ἀνένδοτος ἀνάλωτος ἀταπείνωτος. εἶδον οἱ λόγοι σε, βασιλεῦ, τὰς φρένας βαθύν, τὰς χεῖρας πολύν, τοὺς πόδας ὀξύν, καὶ κατάκρας μὲν ἐρωτιῶσι τοῦ κάλλους καὶ προσπτερύξασθαι γλίχονται· ἀλλ' ἥττηνταί σου τοῦ ὕψους, ἀλλὰ νενίκηνταί σου τοῦ δρόμου καὶ τὸ πτερὸν αὐτοῖς οὐκέτι μετάρσιον, καὶ πάλαι μὲν χεῖρες καὶ παλάμαι δραστήριοι κομψείας σοφιστικῆς καὶ μουσῶν χαρίτων εἶχον τὰ δευτέρα, νῦν δ' ἀλλ' εἰς τοὐναντίον (εἴποι τις ἄν) τὸ πρᾶγμα μετέστραπται καὶ τὰ ἔργα θεῖά τινα καὶ ἀληθῶς ὑπερνέφελα, κάτω δὲ οἱ λόγοι κυπτάζουσι καὶ πρὸς οὕτως ἄκρατον αἴγλην ἄθλων ἡλιωδῶν ἐπιμύουσιν.[20]

The oration accordingly opens by asserting the secondary status of oratory in relation to the glorious deeds of the emperor. The orator underlines not his own humble status, as is common in rhetorical discourses of all kinds, but the impossibility of *logoi* – his own primary tools – to represent justly the 'reality' of Manuel's actions.[21] At the same time, the traditional imagery of both the *basilikos logos* and other rhetoricians praising Manuel is woven into this alleged denial of oratory: the wise mind and strong hands of the emperor, his skill in war and his competitiveness – in brightness and speed – with the sun.[22]

---

[20] Manasses, *Encomium of Emperor Manuel Komnenos* 1–22 (Kurtz).

[21] The motif seems to be a variation on the praise of imperial talent in oratory, here transferred to the 'deeds' rather than the 'words'; cf. Theophylact on Alexios I Komnenos, cited and translated by Magdalino 1993: 430: Ὁ δὲ καὶ ἄλλως μὲν ἐν ταῖς πρὸς βαρβάρους ὁμιλίαις πάντας ἀποκρύπτει καὶ φιλοσόφους καὶ ῥήτορας τῶν νοημάτων τῇ στιβαρότητι καὶ τῶν ῥημάτων τῇ καθαρότητι (Gautier 224, 20–3). Eustathios of Thessalonike employs a similar figure in his funerary oration on Manuel, praising the rhetorical skills of the emperor; Eustathios of Thessalonike, *The epitaphios for Manuel I Komnenos* 13 (Bourbouhakis), on which see Nilsson 2014: 163–4. As noted by Magdalino in the case of Theophylact, with such a motif 'the rhetor is creating the emperor in his own image'; Manasses is rather underlining the difference between words and deeds in his oration.

[22] On the representation of Manuel as the sun, see Karla 2008: 673–4; on the ancient pedigree of the solar imagery, see Magdalino 1993: 417–18. It may be noted that Manasses uses the solar imagery rather frequently and thus recycles his epithets in various contexts; cf. e.g. *Encomium of Emperor*

In Praise of the Emperor

The orator continues:

Let others marvel at your qualities, o you of a lofty mind and empyrean hands, and as if having picked golden gifts from an abundant meadow, rich in thick bloom, let them become weavers of wreaths and compose praising hymns or as if from a sweet sea let them lead water and cultivate the garden of their speeches – one may speak of your manliness, another may applaud your sound judgement, by one your deeds in Asia may be sung, by another those of Europe may be spoken, your forbearance may sharpen one's tongue, your bounteousness and generosity may set another's hand in motion. I, however, will not waste my time on the Scythians and Persians and Cilicians and the subjugation of countries and the relocation of entire peoples, nor will I make out of all this a confused blend, but at this great thing that is unattainable for all tongues, as if attainable for discourse, shall I wonder. For what should one do? Where should one fly? Not yet has any rhetorician spoken about the events of Isaurians and Cilicians, and the deep-eddying Istros saw you flooding the rule of Rhomaians with abundant deeds of prowess. Not yet have the mouths of rhetoricians been opened for the events for which even the Nile with her seven mouths praised you, subduing Egypt into the paying of tribute, and already you flew against the Triballoi and the Gepids, rustled with your wings against the land of Pannonians, and carried off for your nestlings a large spoil such as the sun had never seen.

Ἄλλος μὲν οὖν ἄλλο τι τῶν σῶν θαυμαζέτω καλῶν, ὦ καὶ τὰς φρένας αἰθέριε καὶ τὰς χεῖρας ἐμπύριε, καὶ ὡς ἀπὸ λειμῶνος εὐπόρου, βαθεῖαν πλουτοῦντος τὴν ἄνθην, χρυσίζοντα δῶρα δρεψάμενος στεφανηπλόκος γινέσθω καὶ συντιθέτω τὸν ὑμνητήριον ἢ ὡς ἀπὸ γλυκείας θαλάσσης ὀχητηγείτω καὶ κηπευέτω τοῦ λόγου τὸ φυτηκόμημα· ὁ μὲν λεγέτω τὴν εὐανδρίαν, ὁ δὲ κροτείτω τὴν εὐβουλίαν, τῷ μὲν τὰ τῆς Ἀσίας ὑμνείσθω, τῷ δὲ τὰ τῆς Εὐρώπης λαλείσθω, τοῦ μὲν τὴν γλῶτταν θηγέτω τὸ ἀνεξίκακον, τοῦ δὲ κινείτω τὴν χεῖρα τὸ μεγαλόδωρον καὶ φιλόδωρον· ἐγὼ δὲ Σκύθας μὲν καὶ Πέρσας καὶ Κίλικας καὶ χωρῶν ἀνδραποδισμοὺς καὶ ὅλων ἐθνῶν μετοικισμοὺς οὐ περιεργάσομαι οὐδ᾽ οἷον κρατῆρα κεράσομαι πάμφυρτον, ἀλλὰ τὸ μέγα τοῦτο καὶ πάσαις γλώσσαις ἀνέφικτον, ὡς ἐφικτὸν τῷ λόγῳ, θαυμάσομαι. τί γὰρ καὶ δράσει τις; ποῖ καὶ πτερύξεται; οὔπω τὰ τῶν Ἰσαύρων καὶ Κιλίκων ὁ ῥητορεύων ἀπερρητόρευσε, καὶ ὁ βαθυδίνης Ἴστρος σε ἔβλεψε τὴν Ῥωμαίων ἡγεμονίαν ἀφθόνοις καταλοῦντα τοῖς ἀριστεύμασιν. οὔπω τὰ τῶν ῥητόρων ἠνοίγησαν στόματα ἐφ᾽ οἷς καὶ Νεῖλος ἑπτά σε στόμασιν ὕμνησεν, εἰς φόρων ἀπαγωγὴν καταστρεψάμενον Αἴγυπτον, καὶ πάλιν εἰς Τριβαλλοὺς ἐπετάσθης καὶ Γήπαιδας καὶ Παννόνων γῆν ἐπιρροιζήσας

Manuel Komnenos 9–10 (Kurtz): ἥλιος μὲν οὗτος ὁ γίγας ὁ μέγας ὁ φεραυγὴς with *Verse chronicle* 108 (Lampsides): ὁ μέγας γίγας ἥλιος, ὁ ζωοτρόφος λύχνος.

σου τοῖς πτεροῖς, μέγα τι καὶ οἷον οὔποτε ἥλιος ἔβλεψε τοῖς σοῖς νεοσσοῖς ἐκόμισας θήραμα.²³

The orator thus specifies his own task in contrast to that of other rhetoricians: he leaves the flowery praise and events already dealt with to them – he himself will speak about events not yet properly commemorated and eulogized. The tone of this passage is potentially critical or at least imbued with rivalry: other orators are made to sound like they are idly picking flowers for their praise, putting together wreaths or mixed bowls, while this orator will raise his voice for events that have been passed over; his own oration will somehow tie in closer with 'reality'. This close and complex relation between rhetoric and reality that is underlined from the very beginning of the oration is significant, not least because of the role of the writer on command and his relationship with his patrons, to which I return below in a comparative discussion. First, I should like to concentrate primarily on two aspects of the imperial imagery employed in this oration: the emperor as an eagle, soaring through the air against his enemies, and as a representation of imperial models of the past.

As we have seen, the emperor is from the very start described as a swift-flying eagle, whose wings compete with and outrun those of rhetoric (γλῶσσαν σοφιστικὴν ἀετῷ συνίπτασθαι τῷ ταχυπετεῖ). The orations are made to recall small birds fluttering around and towards the eagle, their wings too weak to keep up with his pace (προσπτερύξασθαι γλίχονται· ἀλλ' ἥττηνταί σου τοῦ ὕψους, ἀλλὰ νενίκηνταί σου τοῦ δρόμου καὶ τὸ πτερὸν αὐτοῖς οὐκέτι μετάρσιον). The struggle of orators is in this way directly connected with the bellicose character of Manuel, who flies against his enemies and brings home spoils for his nestlings (ἐπιρροιζήσας σου τοῖς πτεροῖς . . . τοῖς σοῖς νεοσσοῖς ἐκόμισας θήραμα). As the oration moves on to describe the events in more detail, this imagery becomes even more overt and more focused on war, for instance in Manuel's fight against the Teutons (Germanic or Celtic tribes) and Gepids (Hungarians):

> You flew upon, you attacked like an airborne and swift-moving eagle, whipping the air with eager movements upon seeing a snake crawling into

---

²³ Manasses, *Encomium of Emperor Manuel Komnenos* 23–41 (Kurtz). Manuel's expedition to Egypt took place in 1169; see Magdalino 1993: 73–5. According to John Kinnamos, *History* 6.9 (Meineke), the expedition as such failed, but since the Egyptians feared a second expedition they offered much gold in order to be left alone in the future. On these events as described by Manasses, see also Kurtz 1906: 70–1, discussing the expedition and noting the difficulties in deciphering some of the historical events to which the oration refers.

his own nest, or like a roaring and deep-voiced lion that has realized another beast is attacking his cubs.

Ἐπέπτης, ἐπέδραμες ὡσεί τις αἰθεροδρόμος καὶ ταχυκίνητος ἀετὸς συντονωτέραις τὸν ἀέρα μαστίζων κινήσεσι, κατὰ τῆς ἑαυτοῦ καλιᾶς ἰδὼν ἑρπύζοντα δράκοντα, ἢ λέων βρυχηματίας καὶ βαρυηχὴς ἕτερον θῆρα κατανοήσας τοῖς σκύμνοις ἐπιτιθέμενον.[24]

The imagery does not only underline the bravery, swiftness and strength of the emperor, but also the barbaric and beastly qualities of the enemies – snakes and beasts attacking the nestlings of Manuel the eagle: the Rhomaian people. The vivid image that is created is one of present and relevant experiences – until now, as emphasized by the orator at the beginning of the oration, untold and unpraised. This immediate present is contrasted later on in the oration, or rather sustained by a glorious past to which Manuel has a close relation.

Manuel's recent victories are compared with historical battles and his unique leadership is contrasted with the actions of Egyptians, Persians and Romans of the past. But unstained with blood and peaceful, Manuel's victory is novel and unheard of (τὸ ἀναίμακτον ταύτην μάχην καὶ τὸ καινὸν καὶ ἀνήκουστον εἰρηνικὸν), thanks to his identification with the sun: 'The Pannonians saw your fiery radiance and drew back as from shining and flaming fire and bent their necks; for who could stand in the face of fire?' (εἶδον σου τὴν πυριμάρμαρον αἴγλην οἱ Παννόνες καὶ ὡς ἀπὸ πυρὸς φωτίζοντος καὶ φλογίζοντος ὑπεστάλησαν καὶ τοὺς αὐχένας ὑπέκλιναν· ἀπὸ προσώπου γὰρ πυρὸς τίς ὑποστήσεται;).[25] The orator, based on these comparisons, then states that three rulers of the past are particularly apt for Manuel's representation:

> To three past rulers can I, o emperor, capture your likeness: Alexander, son of Philip, David, prophet and ancestor of Christ, and the august nephew of Caesar [Augustus]; against the latter I measure you in accordance with the amazing portents before your reign, anticipating the future, to David in accordance with his ascent to kingship, and to the Macedonian in

---

[24] Manasses, *Encomium of Emperor Manuel Komnenos* 58–62 (Kurtz); cf. also lines 103–14 of the same oration. On the emperor as a lion in the twelfth century, see Schmidt 2016 (not including the present oration); see also further below. Cf. also the imagery used in Manasses, *Verse chronicle* 6487–8 (Lampsides), then for Romanos IV Diogenes: ὁ λέων θήρα γίνεται πανθήρων λυσσητήρων, | ταῖς νυκτερίσιν ἀετὸς κρατεῖται χρυσοπτέρυξ; cited and translated in Schmidt 2016: 168.

[25] Manasses, *Encomium of Emperor Manuel Komnenos* 276–9 (Kurtz). The imperial power is here underlined with a Biblical allusion, as Manasses combines Psalms 67:3 (ὡς τήκεται κηρὸς ἀπὸ προσώπου πυρός) and Sirach 43:3 (καὶ ἐναντίον καύματος αὐτοῦ τίς ὑποστήσεται;).

accordance with those great struggles and noble combats and victories and the suppression of unconquerable peoples.

Πρὸς τρεῖς ἐγὼ τῶν πώποτε κρατησάντων, ὦ αὐτοκράτορ, θηρῶμαι σοι τὴν ἐμφέρειαν, Ἀλέξανδρον τὸν Φιλίππου, Δαυὶδ τὸν προφήτην καὶ θεοπάτορα, καὶ τὸν Σεβαστὸν τὸν Καίσαρος ἀδελφόπαιδα, τῷ μὲν ἀντιπαραβάλλων σε κατὰ τὰ πρὸ τῆς ἡγεμονίας τεράστια τοῦ μέλλοντος προμηνύματα, τῷ Δαυὶδ κατὰ τὴν εἰς βασιλείαν ἀνάβασιν, τῷ δὲ Μακεδόνι κατὰ τοὺς μεγάλους ἐκείνους ἀγῶνας καὶ τὰς γενναίας μάχας καὶ νίκας καὶ τῶν ἀκαταγωνίστων ἐθνῶν τὴν καταπολέμησιν.[26]

This passage is followed by further explanations of this comparison (lines 287–300), pointing out the detailed similarities in nature and deeds. This re-presentation (in the literal sense of 'bringing back into the present') of ancient rulers in the character of Manuel brings together the three key elements of Byzantine culture: Greek, Roman and Biblical history, literature and imagination.[27] That representation is sustained by numerous allusions and citations from these three areas, creating a dense web of linguistic and literary significance as a background for Manuel's glorious deeds. Past and present – historically and literarily – are in this manner intertwined in the person of the emperor, reflecting the history of the Byzantine empire and its capital Constantinople. The orator takes on the *persona* not only of imperial panegyrist, but also exegete of events past and present: he reads the past in order to interpret the present and even lay some claim to understanding the future: 'In this manner I madly yearn for and imagine the future events' (οὕτως ἐγὼ περὶ τῶν μελλόντων δυσερωτιῶ καὶ φαντάζομαι).[28] Thus ending the oration with a traditionally optimistic wish for a successful future yet to come, brimming with sonorous effects and drawing on both the Psalter and Oppian, the orator once more states the unparalleled nature of Manuel, 'incomparable among emperors, unrivalled among rulers' (ὁ ἐν βασιλεῦσιν ἀσύγκριτος, ὁ ἐν αὐτοκράτορσιν ἀπαράμιλλος).[29]

The form and content of this oration is fully in accordance with that of other twelfth-century orations. The use of the past in order to celebrate the

---

[26] Manasses, *Encomium of Emperor Manuel Komnenos* 280–6 (Kurtz).
[27] Cf. Magdalino 1993: 415–16 on the combination of ancient rhetoric and literature with Christian sources and imagery in Byzantine oratory, and 431 on the frequent *synkrisis* to classical heroism in orations to Manuel.
[28] Manasses, *Encomium of Emperor Manuel Komnenos* 329–30 (Kurtz).
[29] Manasses, *Encomium of Emperor Manuel Komnenos* 330 (Kurtz). Cf. Manasses, *Verse chronicle* 2507–12 (Lampsides), wishing Manuel and the Komnenian dynasty a successful reign, probably written some 25–30 years earlier.

present, the frequent use of ancient and Biblical sources and the way in which the imperial character is praised are all part of a typical *basilikos logos*. The vivid and at times ekphrastic representation of the emperor as an eagle – king of all animals as the emperor is king of all people – ties in with a symbolic imagery well established in antiquity, not least in ancient Rome, and present also in Byzantium.[30] Even the orator's emphasis of his own important role – presenting something different and reporting something new – is typical of the authorial self-confidence and rhetorical rivalry of the time.[31] What is particularly interesting is the comparison we can make with other texts by the same author: texts in which Manasses uses the same words, images and techniques, which may help us better understand the form and function of such pieces occasioned by the writer's interests at the Constantinopolitan court. Here it accordingly offers a background against which to read the *Description of a crane hunt*.

Imperial Praise in Ekphrastic Guise

One of Manasses' longest and most detailed ekphraseis is the *Description of a crane hunt* (Τοῦ Μανασσῆ κυροῦ Κωνσταντίνου ἔκφρασις κυνηγεσίου γεράνων), preserved in the same manuscript as the oration to Manuel.[32] The text offers a close-up of Byzantine falconry, with the emperor himself and his falcon taking centre stage.[33] There are no clear indications of the dating of the ekphrasis except for the reference to Manuel's reign (1143–80), but it is possible that it was performed in relative proximity to the oration.[34] Regardless of the dating, the ekphrasis should most probably be placed in the same occasional frame as the oration, in the imperial circles that included the emperor himself, as well as aristocrats and other orators. Here I wish to focus on the aesthetic beauty of hunting, strongly emphasized by the narrator and connected with manly heroism,

---

[30] For Manuel as an eagle (and his son Alexios II as an 'eaglet') in contemporary oratory, see e.g. Eustathios of Thessalonike, *Oration* 11, 190.77–84 (Wirth).

[31] See Magdalino 1993: 128–30.

[32] See above, n. 19. In spite of being rather well known and fairly often mentioned in passing when it comes to falconry, the ekphrasis has not been analysed in detail beyond the discussions in Kurtz 1906 and Nimas 1984. See now the new edition with introduction and translation by Messis and Nilsson 2019.

[33] On falconry in Byzantium, partly in a comparative perspective, see Külzer 2018; Messis and Nilsson 2019: 17–37. On falconry and its political meaning in Byzantium, see Maguire 2011. The twelfth century offers particularly rich evidence: in addition to Manasses' ekphrasis, there is also the description by Constantine Pantechnes; see Miller 1872; Messis and Nilsson 2019: 29–33.

[34] I return to this question below, in this chapter.

personified by Manuel in a laudatory passage. That tone is set from the very start, so let us begin by looking at the opening passage:

> Horse racing and hunting and other such things that men have invented do not contribute only to exercise and the strengthening of the body, they also instil pleasure in the hearts and tickle the senses. For they are good because they make men healthy, rejecting anything causing disease and contributing to what supports life, but they are also good because they accustom [men] for war, teaching them to ride and attack and keep the ranks and not leap ahead of the phalanx, and preparing them for the direct pursuit and the one turning left and right, either by yielding to the horses and encouraging them to run with relaxed reins or by pressing them and holding them back with the bridle that iron softened by fire has made.
>
> All this would be, so to say, an exercise in moderate things, as a reminder of greater things; this is a battle without deaths, an Ares unarmed who does not have his right hand covered by blood, nor a spear drenched in murder. These and other such activities are accordingly good and only for those who do not love beauty are they without grace or unwanted; they are in fact graceful, because they relieve the insufferable burden of the soul and drive away what eats the heart and expel what brings sorrow.
>
> Ἱππηλάσια δὲ ἄρα καὶ κυνηγέσια καὶ ὅσα ἄλλα τοιαῦτα τοῖς ἀνθρώποις ἐπινενόηται, οὐ πρὸς γυμνάσια μόνον καὶ πρὸς ἐπίρρωσιν σωμάτων συμβάλλεται, ἀλλὰ καὶ ταῖς καρδίαις τέρψιν ἐνστάζει καὶ ταῖς αἰσθήσεσι γάργαλον· καλὰ μὲν γὰρ καὶ ὅτι τοὺς ἀνθρώπους ἀνόσους ποιοῦσι, πᾶν τὸ νοσηματικὸν ἀποκρίνοντα καὶ πρὸς τὸ ἔμβιον συναιρόμενα· καλὰ δὲ καὶ ὅτι πρὸς τὰ πολέμια προεθίζουσιν, ἱππεύειν καὶ ἐπελαύνειν διδάσκοντα καὶ τάξιν τηρεῖν καὶ μὴ τῆς φάλαγγος προπηδᾶν καὶ τὴν ἐπευθὺ προπαιδεύοντα δίωξιν καὶ τὴν εἰς τὰ ἐπαρίστερα καὶ ἐνδέξια, πῇ μὲν ἐνδιδόναι τοῖς ἵπποις καὶ ἀνέτοις ῥυτῆρσι σφᾶς ἐπὶ δρόμον προτρέπεσθαι, πῇ δὲ πιέζειν καὶ ἄγχειν περιστομίοις δεσμοῖς, οὓς σίδηρος ἐργάζεται πυριμάλακτος.
>
> Καὶ εἶεν ἂν ταῦτα μετρίων, ὡς ἂν εἴποι τις, ἄσκησις πρὸς τὴν τῶν μειζόνων ὑπόμνησιν· ταῦτα μάχη οὐκ ἀνδρολέτειρα, ταῦτα Ἄρης ἀσίδηρος καὶ μὴ λυθρόφυρτον ἔχων τὴν δεξιὰν μηδὲ τὸ δόρυ φονοσταγές. Καλὰ μὲν οὖν ταῦτα καὶ τὰ τοιαῦτα καὶ μόνοις ἐκείνοις ἀχαρίτωτα καὶ ἀθέλητα, ὁπόσοι ἀνέραστοι τοῦ καλοῦ· χαρίεντα δὲ οὐχ ἧττον, ὅτι καὶ ψυχῆς ἄχθος δυσάγκαλον ἐλαφρύνουσι καὶ τὸ δακέθυμον ἀποκρούονται καὶ τὸ λυποῦν ἀπελαύνουσι.[35]

The narrator then turns to the effect of music as a parallel, making men brave, chasing sorrow away and bringing pleasure, before offering a concluding remark on the pleasure of hunting:

---

[35] Manasses, *Description of a crane hunt* 1–19 (Messis and Nilsson).

Imperial Praise in Ekphrastic Guise   37

> For it recalls carrying of arms and killing of men and thudding of shields and blood-thirsty Ares, and it drives away a cloud of faintheartedness and produces rays of pleasure; and nobody could have such a piercing distress in his heart that it would not be healed upon seeing a doe hare with a coward heart appear, being hunted and fleeing from running dogs.

> Ὁπλοφορίας τὲ γὰρ καὶ ἀνδροκτασίας ὑπομιμνήσκει καὶ ἀσπίδων δούπου καὶ Ἄρεος φιλαιμάτου καὶ νέφος ἀθυμίας ἀπορραπίζει καὶ ἀκτῖνας ἡδονῆς ἐπαφίησι· καὶ οὐχ οὕτω δριμεῖαν ὀδύνην ἔχοι τις ἂν ἐπικάρδιον, ὡς μὴ ταύτην ἀκέσασθαι, λαγίναν ἰδὼν δειλοκάρδιον ἀνισταμένην, διωκομένην, κύνας δρομικοὺς ἀλυσκάζουσαν.[36]

This general description of the emotional and aesthetic characteristics of hunting – imbued with masculinity and potential eroticism[37] – is then confirmed by the authorial I, who steps in to confirm his own eyewitness experience:

> I myself, being present at a crane hunt, being filled with the sight of them and seeing how birds with such small bodies make a rustling sound with their wings and fly lightly into the air and bring down these birds with long legs to the ground, had my soul filled with immense pleasure and praising also for other reasons blessed nature I admired also this part, that she armed those small-bodied animals with much strength and added in vigour what she had removed in size.[38]

> Ἔγωγέ τοι θήρᾳ γεράνων παρατυχὼν καὶ τῆς τούτων θέας ἐμφορηθεὶς καὶ ἰδὼν ὅπως ὄρνιθες οὕτω βραχύσωμοι τὰ πτίλα ἐπιρροιζοῦσι καὶ μέχρις αἰθέρος ἐλαφριζόμενοι τοὺς τετανοσκελεῖς ἐκείνους εἰς γῆν καταφέρουσιν, ἡδονῆς τε ἀπλέτου τὴν ψυχὴν ἐγεμίσθην καὶ τὴν μακαρίαν φύσιν κἂν τοῖς ἄλλοις ἀποθειάζων, καὶ τοῦτο τὸ μέρος ἐθαύμαζα, ὅτι τῶν ζώων τὰ ταπεινόσωμα κραταιοτέρως ἐφώπλισε καὶ τοῦ μεγέθους ἀφελομένη τῇ ἰσχύι προστέθεικεν.[39]

The narrator goes on to describe other kinds of hunts that he has witnessed, ranging from deer hunting to the catching of small birds with lime, concluding that the most pleasurable (ἐπιτερπέστερον) is the crane hunt – involving falcons, not glue on twigs, and being a manly activity, not

---

[36] Manasses, *Description of a crane hunt* 25–9 (Messis and Nilsson).
[37] The 'pleasant' image of a female hare being pursued by the male dogs represents a male gaze, including both the animal prey of the hunt and the fleeing enemies of a battle. As such, it seems to tie in with the representation of Manuel – soon to enter the hunt – as exceedingly manly and *erotikos*; see Magdalino 1992. For a recent analysis of the imagery of hunted females and male hunters, see Goldwyn 2017: 39–84 (with both Western and Byzantine examples).
[38] The 'small-bodied birds' refers to the falcons employed for crane hunting, while the birds with 'long (or straight) legs' are the cranes themselves.
[39] Manasses, *Description of a crane hunt* 30–6 (Messis and Nilsson).

child's play.⁴⁰ He then states that he must describe what he has seen: 'What I have seen must now be confined to writing; for what stops me from delighting in describing this, if even Homer offered an account of the hunt of Ithacian men?' (Δοτέον τοίνυν τὰ ὁραθέντα γραφῇ· τί γὰρ κωλύει κἂν τῇ γραφῇ τῷ πράγματι ἐντρυφῆσαι με, εἴ γε Ἰθακησίων ἀνθρώπων κυνηγεσίου καὶ Ὅμηρος μέμνηται;).⁴¹

Having thus prepared a suitable setting – one of war, manly deeds and potentially erotic pursuit – the emperor enters the stage. He is presented in an encomium that is brief, but still follows the basic guidelines of a traditional *basilikos logos*.

> Once the triumphant emperor went hunting, he whom purple had brought to birth and whose purple robe proclaimed his breed, whom wisdom and bravery and intelligence and the entire catalogue of graces embraced and breastfed and offered the milk of myriads of virtues. His hands are huge hands, his heart is a chamber of prudence, his soul is protected by the hands of God – his mind is elevated and lofty, close to rivalling the minds of angels. His hunting and exercise appear to aim at pleasure and relaxation, but in truth they aspire to victories and trophies and the arrangement of important affairs and the preservation of the rule of Rhomaians. Like a lion's cub who even in sleep kept watch with the eyes of his soul, he watches and protects and follows; he protects against the attempt of attacking enemies and he leaps with ferocious eyes without their anticipating his charge.⁴² Moving like an eagle his wings of profound judgement and rustling his feathered plumage of high counsel, he terrifies entire herds of enemies. Once when he appeared to go hunting wild animals, he returned having pursued foreign satraps and rulers.⁴³

---

⁴⁰ Manasses, *Description of a crane hunt* 58–60 (Messis and Nilsson): Ἀλλά μοι τὸ χρῆμα τῆς τῶν γεράνων ἄγρας τοσοῦτον ἐκείνων ἐπιτερπέστερον, ὅσον ἀκανθυλλίδων καὶ σπίνων αἱ μακραύχενες ὑπερέχουσι γέρανοι καὶ λύγων ἐξοφόρων ἱέρακες δραστικώτεροι καὶ ὅσον γυμνασίων ἀνδρικωτέρων παιδαριώδη ἀθύρματα λείπεται. On this passage and its relation to the *Description of the catching of siskins and chaffinches*, see further below, n. 77, and Chapter 5, 'An Ancient Life in Verse'.

⁴¹ Manasses, *Description of a crane hunt* 63–5 (Messis and Nilsson).

⁴² Cf. Manasses, *Encomium of Emperor Manuel Komnenos* 58–62 (Kurtz), cited above. On Manuel as a cub rather than a lion, see Schmidt 2016: 164–5, citing a poem by Manganeios Prodromos from the 1140s: 'By referring to Manuel as the "lion cub", Prodromos places him in the tradition of John II, the lion-like protector of the empire, and stylizes him as Byzantium's current saviour, possessing the same regal and heroic features as his father.'

⁴³ This is an allusion to an occasion on which Manuel was hunting during a military campaign that led to victory and the captivity of enemies; either the campaign of 1148 against the Cumans, when Manuel, during a hunt, found out about the enemy attack and organized a counterattack which led to the victory of the Byzantines (Kinnamos, *Hist.* 3.3 [Meineke]), or the campaign of 1159 in Antioch, when Manuel, during a hunt, was ambushed by the enemy (Kinnamos, *Hist.* 4.21 [Meineke]).

Ἐξῄει ποτὲ πρὸς θήραν ὁ καλλίνικος βασιλεύς, ὃν πορφύρα μὲν ἐμαιεύσατο, ἁλουργὶς δὲ τεχθέντα προσεῖπε, σοφία δὲ καὶ ἀνδρεία καὶ σύνεσις καὶ ὁ τῶν χαρίτων κατάλογος ἐνηγκαλίσαντο καὶ ἐμαστοτρόφησαν καὶ γάλα μυρίων προτερημάτων ἐπότισαν· οὗ χεῖρες, γίγαντος χεῖρες, οὗ καρδία, φρονήσεως θάλαμος, οὗ ψυχὴ παλάμαις δορυφορεῖται θεοῦ· ᾧ νοῦς ὑψηλὸς καὶ αἰθέριος, μικροῦ καὶ πρὸς τοὺς ἀσωμάτους[44] νόας ἀνθαμιλλώμενος· οὗ κυνηγέσιον καὶ γυμνάσιον τὸ μὲν δοκεῖν εἰς τέρψιν ὁρᾷ καὶ διάχυσιν, τὸ δ' ἀληθές, εἰς νίκας καὶ τρόπαια καὶ μεγάλων διαθέσεις πραγμάτων καὶ τῆς Ῥωμαίων ἡγεμονίας συντήρησιν τελευτᾷ· ὡς γὰρ λέοντος σκύμνος καὶ καθεύδων τοῖς τῆς ψυχῆς ἐγρήγορεν ὀφθαλμοῖς καὶ βλέπει καὶ προφυλάττεται καὶ ἐφάπτεται· φυλάττεται μὲν πεῖραν ἐχθρῶν ἐπιόντων, ἐφάλλεται δὲ βλεφάροις ἀγριοθύμοις μηδὲ προϊδοῦσι τὴν ἔφοδον· καὶ ὡς ἀετὸς τῆς βαθυγνωμοσύνης τὰ πτίλα κινήσας καὶ τὸ πτέρωμα τῆς μεγαλοβουλίας περιρροιζήσας ὅλας ἀγέλας πολεμίων φοβεῖ. καί ποτε πρὸς ἄγραν ζῴων δόξας σταλῆναι, ὁ δὲ ἀλλὰ σατράπας, ἀλλὰ χωράρχας θηράσας ἐπαλινόστησεν.[45]

This combative emperor goes hunting and the narrator, he says, comes along, 'to observe the pleasure of the hunt' (τὸ τῆς θήρας τερπνὸν ἐποψόμενος).[46] What follows is a very careful description of the organization of the hunt, one of the most detailed Byzantine accounts that have come down to us.[47] At the centre of the scene is the emperor and his falcon, an impressive bird from Georgia, 'old and noble' (παλαιόχρονόν τινα καὶ γεννάδα),[48] which receives a detailed description of some 50 lines.[49] It has been trained by the emperor himself and its body and colours are balanced and beautiful, matching the brave emperor on whose left hand it is sitting. It outshines by far the other birds of prey that are

---

[44] ἀσωμάτους scripserunt Messis and Nilsson. The manuscripts have ἐν σώματι, accepted by Kurtz, but it seems to make no sense in the context. Manasses wishes to underline the unworldly, nearly divine nature of Manuel.
[45] Manasses, *Description of a crane hunt* 66–82 (Messis and Nilsson).
[46] Manasses, *Description of a crane hunt* 83–4 (Messis and Nilsson).
[47] For a brief introduction to hunting in Byzantium, see Dennis 2009. For more substantial contributions, see Koukoules 1932, Patlagean 1992 and Delobette 2005. For examples of Byzantine hunting descriptions, see Messis and Nilsson 2019. It may be noted that references to Oppian's treatise – formative for Byzantine accounts of hunting – in both the *Encomium of Emperor Manuel Komnenos* and the *Description of a crane hunt* underline the authority of the texts and, at the same time, present their author as knowledgeable. Manasses not only frequently used Oppian's didactic poems on hunting and bird-catching in his texts, he also wrote the *Origins of Oppian* in verse; see below, Chapter 5.
[48] Manasses, *Description of a crane hunt* 125–6 (Messis and Nilsson).
[49] Manasses, *Description of a crane hunt* 117–64 (Messis and Nilsson). This passage is coupled with a description of the crane first captured in *Description of a crane hunt* 298–314 (Messis and Nilsson).

present, presumably just as the emperor outshines the aristocrats – the falcon is his extended arm, his alter ego.[50]

The hunt itself is described in terms of war, in which the ranks of both hunters (falcons) and game (cranes) are portrayed as soldiers taking part in a battle.[51] The image of troop movements is combined with sounds and cries of war – more specifically, the whirring of wings in this 'aerial battle' (μάχην ἀερίαν): '... with crying and whirring they attacked each other ... a confused and thundering noise filled the air, the rattling of wings resounded in the ears and a rushing Ares fell madly upon both armies' (... κλαγγῇ καὶ ῥοιζήμασιν ἀλλήλοις συνέπεσον ... θροῦς δὲ καὶ βόμβος τὸν ἀέρα ἐγέμιζε καὶ κατεκτύπουν τὰς ἀκοὰς τὰ τῶν πτερῶν παταγήματα καὶ θούριος Ἄρης παρ' ἀμφοῖν τοῖν στρατοῖν ἐπεμαίνετο).[52] The choice of word for depicting the sound of wings (ῥοιζήμασιν) reflects the representation of Manuel as an eagle attacking his enemies both in the *Encomium of Emperor Manuel Komnenos* and in the encomium inserted in the description, underlining the war–hunt analogy.[53] So does the anthropomorphic representation of falcons and cranes,[54] displaying fear, courage and other human emotions in this epically coloured depiction.[55] The epic tone is underscored by several allusions to the *Iliad*, including the use of dual, the explicit reference to Homer cited above (used as a justification of depicting a hunt) and yet another mention of Homer in the depiction of the hunting party.[56] Both references to Homer are placed at the beginning of the account, even before the ekphrasis of the hunt itself, functioning as signals of the forthcoming war.[57]

---

[50] On the falcon of the emperor (not taking part in the battle) vs the goshawks of the hunting party (described in lines 184–210), see Messis and Nilsson 2019: 42–3.

[51] On the intimate and significant relationship between hunting and war in Byzantine imagery, see Messis and Nilsson 2019: 12–17.

[52] Manasses, *Description of a crane hunt* 250–4 (Messis and Nilsson).

[53] Manasses, *Encomium of Emperor Manuel Komnenos* 40 (Kurtz): ἐπιρροιζήσας; *Description of a crane hunt* 80 (Messis and Nilsson): περιρροιζήσας.

[54] Noteworthy are also the anthropomorphic description of the birds' physical characteristics, partly mirroring those of the emperor himself. Cf. the way in which the dwarf in the *Description of a little man* is described in zoomorphic terms, including a comparison to a crane; see Manasses, *Description of a little man* 50 (Messis and Nilsson) and Messis and Nilsson 2015: 173–4.

[55] Note especially the emotions of the spectators as depicted in lines 207–9; cf. the little mouse in the *Description of the Earth* 144–63 (Lampsides), displaying the same kind of hesitation (Nilsson 2005: 125–6).

[56] Manasses, *Description of a crane hunt* 106–8 (Messis and Nilsson): ᾔεσαν δὲ πάντες ἐν κόσμῳ καὶ σιωπῇ καὶ ὡς Μενεσθέα προδιέγραψεν Ὅμηρος ἐν τοῖς πολέμοις τοὺς Ἕλληνας κατατάττοντα· Cf. Hom. *Il.* 2.552–4.

[57] The use of Homer for epic effect is thus combined with the use of Oppian for an expert tone. Cf. the use of Homer for the expression of Komnenian heroism, on which Magdalino 1993: 431 (referring to the hexameter poems by Theodore Prodromos: Hörandner nos 3, 6 and 8).

The text closes by returning to the beauty and pleasure of crane hunting, underlined at the beginning of the piece. In comparison to other hunts, says the narrator, crane hunting is both amusing and effortless (ἐπιτερπὲς ὁμοῦ καὶ οὐκ ἔγκοπον)[58] – since the birds of prey do all the work, men are left to watch the spectacle and wait for the game to fall from the sky. This aspect of crane hunting may have contributed to its high status, being a manly, sophisticated and aristocratic, yet painless pleasure, in which the war of hunting was not only performed but also enjoyed as an 'air show'. This would have allowed the spectators to focus on the aesthetic aspects of the battle, underlined by Manasses and possibly referring also to the aesthetic pleasure of re-experiencing a sight in the form of a carefully structured ekphrasis: just as the hunt is pleasurable and amusing, so is the presumed performance of the description for those who listen. This performative aspect of the text, along with its similarities to the *Encomium of Emperor Manuel Komnenos* in terms of imperial imagery, indicate a Constantinopolitan setting in which both pieces were performed, perhaps in proximity to each other as regards time and space. Such proximity is indicated by the use of similar imagery and sonoric effects, here assumed to have been recognized and appreciated by the audience. It may also be supported by the transmission of the two texts next to each other in the same manuscript, copied within less than a century of the texts' original performance.[59] The imagery of hunting as a parallel to war is to be found in texts like Byzantine military manuals,[60] but it also ties in with imperial concerns of the time, making it relevant and potentially popular for rhetorical display, perhaps also appealing to a wider audience.

This imperial and aristocratic interest in hunting is well documented, not least in the so-called historical poems of Theodore Prodromos. As noted by Wolfram Hörandner, interest and skill in hunting were among the ideal characteristics of Komnenian emperors.[61] Anna Komnene

---

[58] Manasses, *Description of a crane hunt* 315–16 (Messis and Nilsson).
[59] Cf. Magdalino 1993: 455 on the *Description of a crane hunt* as 'undatable'. On the transmission of texts in the same manuscript and the clues such a transmission may offer as regards the original context, see Zagklas 2017. Cf. also the transmission of both orations to John Kontostephanos in the same manuscript, on which see below, Chapter 3.
[60] Cf. Dennis 2009: 132, citing the *Strategikon of Maurice* 7.45–8 (Dennis and Gamillscheg): Κυνηγίῳ δὲ ἔοικε τὰ τῶν πολέμων. Ὥσπερ γὰρ ἐκεῖ διά τε κατασκόπων καὶ δικτύων καὶ ἐγκρυμμάτων καὶ παρασκόπων καὶ κατακυκλώσεων καὶ τοιούτων σοφισμάτων μᾶλλον ἢ δυνάμει ἡ θήρα τούτων περιγίνεται, οὕτως δεῖ καὶ … Such manuals contained detailed descriptions that may have influenced writers of rhetorical texts such as ekphraseis and *encomia*. See further Messis and Nilsson 2019: 13.
[61] Hörandner 1974: 95.

mentions in her *Alexiad* that her father and uncle used to hunt when they were free from state business: 'Both brothers indulged often in hunting, when there was no great pressure of work, but they found military affairs more exhilarating than hunting' (ἄμφω δὲ τἀδελφὼ κυνηγεσίοις μὲν πολλάκις ἀπένευον, ὁπηνίκα οὐ πολλή τίς αὐτοῖς ἐπέρρει πραγμάτων φροντίς, πολεμικοῖς δὲ μᾶλλον ἢ κυνηγετικοῖς ἔχαιρον πράγμασιν).[62] As for the reign of Manuel, John Kinnamos notes that aristocrats were expected to decorate their houses with paintings depicting 'the emperor's achievements in war and in the slaying of wild beasts' (τὰ βασιλέως ... ὅσα ἔν τε πολέμοις καὶ θηροκτονίαις αὐτὸς εἴργαστο).[63] The Komnenian focus on hunting can be traced back to the eleventh century, and literary descriptions of the twelfth century seem to echo a series of letters by Michael Psellos, addressed to John Doukas (died *c.*1088).[64] One of the letters describes a crane hunt and even if the details offered by Psellos are few, the imagery is similar to that of the *Description of a crane hunt* and may be seen as a potential model or source of inspiration for Manasses.[65]

In the case of Emperor Manuel as represented by Manasses, hunting is made part of his character – he does not hunt for pleasure, he is at war even when he hunts. We may compare with another encomium of Manuel by Michael the Rhetorician, where the intimate relation between hunting and war is expressed in similar terms: 'You practise fighting against enemies by fighting wild beasts and you rightly consider hunting to be identical to preparation for war ... thus, hunting is close to war.' (τὰ ἐναγώνια τῶν πολεμίων ἐν θηρσὶν ἀγρίοις καταγεγύμνασαι καὶ παρασκευὴν στρατιωτικὴν κυνηγετικὴν εἶναι δι' αὐτῶν πραγμάτων φιλοσοφεῖς ... οὕτως ἐγγὺς πολέμου τὸ κυνηγέσιον.)[66] Such a merging of the two activities is also underlined by Manasses in the anecdote of him ostensibly going hunting, but in fact going after enemies, cited above.[67] The representation of Manuel as an eagle, experienced and noble just like his falcon, would accordingly have emphasized not only an imperial ideal common to

---

[62] Anna Komnene, *Alexiad* 3.3.5 (Reinsch and Kambylis); tr. Sewter, rev. Frankopan 2009. On the death of Anna's brother John II Komnenos in a hunting accident, see Browning 1961.
[63] John Kinnamos, *Hist.* 6.6 (Meineke); tr. in Mango 1972: 225. Cited by Maguire 2011: 137.
[64] Psellos, *Letters* 54, 67 and 76 (Papaioannou). See also Psellos, *Chronographia* 7.72 (Reinsch), on which see Patlagean 1992: 259; Delobette 2005: 288. Cf. also a reference to the qualities of the same emperor as hunter in Psellos, *Letter* 142.56–64 (Papaioannou).
[65] Psellos, *Letter* 67 (Papaioannou), on which see Messis and Nilsson 2019: 28–9. On the presence of Psellos' letters among intellectuals of the twelfth century, see Papaioannou 2012.
[66] Michael the Rhetorician, *Encomium of Manuel I Komnenos* 180.4–6 and 10–11 (Regel and Novosadskij).
[67] Manasses, *Description of a crane hunt* 80–2 (Messis and Nilsson).

all Komnenian rulers, but also a specific characterization of Manuel in relation to both aristocrats and military troops. Both the oration and the ekphrasis would thus have functioned as *encomia* of his recent victories, and the narrator's alleged presence at the hunt may have been aimed at enhancing Manasses' own status as part of the emperor's close circle.

Three other ekphraseis by Manasses display a similar portrayal of the narrator as a person who moves in aristocratic circles, having access to and observing imperial space. The *Description of the Earth* depicts a mosaic that the writer has seen in the old parts of the imperial palace,[68] while the *Description of the Cyclops* expounds on an object that he has seen at the house of an aristocrat, a red stone with a representation of Odysseus and the Cyclops.[69] The recipient of the latter, addressed by the narrator of the ekphrasis as a benefactor or patron, has been tentatively identified as the *megas hetaireiarches* Georgios Palaiologos.[70] Both descriptions relate to objects of the past, representing the Graeco-Roman heritage in a Constantinopolitan setting, described in words of that same heritage – important symbols of core values of the time.[71] The *Description of a little man* is a rare depiction of a court entertainer: a man suffering from dwarfism who has travelled to the capital to entertain aristocrats.[72] Regardless of the potentially ironic and metaphorical aspects of this description, it closely relates to a court environment that is shared by a number of people moving in imperial circles, including the narrator himself. The fifth preserved ekphrasis by Manasses, *Description of the*

---

[68] The full title of the two mss (Marc. Gr. Z412 and Athen. 2953, both incomplete) is long and descriptive: Τοῦ φιλοσόφου καὶ ῥήτορος κυροῦ Κωνσταντίνου τοῦ Μανασσῆ ἔκφρασις εἰκονισμάτων ἐν μαρμάρῳ κυκλωτερεῖ, κατὰ μέσον μὲν τυπούντων τὴν γῆν ἐν μορφῇ γυναικός, κύκλῳ δὲ παρόντων ὀπωρῶν καὶ τινων ζῴων θαλασσίων καὶ ἄλλων διαφόρων. For the sake of convenience, the short title Ἔκφρασις γῆς (as in Lampsides 1991) is employed here. For analyses, see Bazaiou-Barabas 1994; Nilsson 2005: esp. 124–6 (with partial translation); Foskolou 2018; see also Magdalino 1997: 165.

[69] The full title in the single ms (Vat. Barb. Gr. 240) is Τοῦ Μανασσῆ κυροῦ Κωνσταντίνου ἔκφρασις εἰκονισμάτων ἐν μαρμάρῳ κυκλωτερεῖ κατὰ μέσον ἐχόντων τὸν Κύκλωπα τοὺς Ὀδυσσέως ἑταίρους διασπαράσσοντα καὶ ἐσθίοντα καὶ Ὀδυσσέα οἴνου ἀσκὸν προφέροντα καὶ δεξιούμενον πόσει τὸν Κύκλωπα. For an analysis, see Nilsson 2011 (with partial translation). See also Mango 1963: 68; Maguire 1992: 139–40; Dauterman Maguire and Maguire 2007: 25–6 (with partial translation).

[70] The identification was made by Magdalino 1997: 162. On the addressee as 'a friend of those who are nourished by speeches', i.e. a benevolent patron, see Nilsson 2011: 128. The *megas hetaireiarches* Georgios Palaiologos may be the same Palaiologos who is addressed in one of Manasses' letters as *pansebastos* Georgios; see further below, Chapter 4.

[71] Magdalino 1997: 164: 'these texts evoke the beauty and antiquity of the court environment'. See also Nilsson 2014: 153–6, 158–60.

[72] The title in the single ms (Escorialiensis Y.II.10) is Τοῦ Μανασσῆ κυροῦ Κωνσταντίνου ἔκφρασις ἀνθρώπου μικροῦ. On this ekphrasis, see Messis and Nilsson 2015 and (briefly) above, Chapter 1.

catching of siskins and chaffinches, may be seen as different in the sense that it takes the narrator out of Constantinople, on a 'holiday' outside the city.[73] This does not, however, mean that the event described does not relate to Komnenian concerns; on the contrary, the depiction of the catching of small birds closely mirrors an ekphrasis inserted in the Komnenian novel *Hysmine and Hysminias*, probably dating from the 1140s.[74] Presuming that Manasses wrote his own novel *Aristandros and Kallithea* slightly later, but in emulation of and perhaps competition with those by Eumathios Makrembolites, Theodore Prodromos and Niketas Eugenianos, that description should have been known to him.[75]

That kind of hunt, and possibly even the ekphrasis itself, is referred to also in the *Description of a crane hunt*, as the narrator describes other kinds of hunting in which he has taken part:

> I have also seen chaffinches being caught and siskins and goldfinches[76] and all such birds that have small wings and for which twigs covered in sweet bay prepare a trap, putting forward foreign foliage and stretching forth twigs covered in glue. I was once amused by a black-winged starling and a twittering chaffinch and the chattering siskin and other such small birds, who were trapped by reeds covered in glue; they wished to escape and fluttered their wings, but were hindered by those sticky bonds, with their hearts pounding heavily as if running for their life; they were then grabbed and stabbed with small knives and thrown in a basket, but some of them were preserved alive, namely those which the embellishing nature had provided with the most abundant beauty.
>
> Εἶδον δὲ καὶ ἀκανθυλλίδας ἁλισκομένας καὶ σπίνους καὶ ἀστρογλήνους καὶ ὅσοις ὅλοις μικρὰ τὰ πτερύγια καὶ οἷς δαφνοστοίβαστοι ῥάβδοι τὸν δόλον ἀρτύνουσι, φυλλάδας ἀλλοτρίας προβεβλημέναι καὶ προϊσχόμεναι λύγους ἀληλιμμένους ἰξῷ. Ἔτερψέ με ποτὲ καὶ μελάμπτερος ψὰρ καὶ λάλος ἀκανθυλλὶς καὶ ὁ στωμυλώτατος σπῖνος καὶ ἄλλ' ἄττα στρουθάρια, δόναξιν ἰξῷ κεκαλυμμένοις σχεθέντα καὶ θέλοντα μὲν φυγγάνειν καὶ πτερυγίζοντα, εἰργόμενα δὲ τοῖς ἐνύγροις ἐκείνοις δεσμοῖς καὶ πυκνὰ

---

[73] On this ekphrasis, see above, Chapter 1, and below, Chapter 5.
[74] Eumathios Makrembolites, *Hysmine and Hysminias* 4.4.12 (Conca).
[75] On the dating of the Komnenian novels, see E. Jeffreys 2012: 7–10 (*Rhodanthe and Dosikles*), 161–5 (*Hysmine and Hysminias*), 275–6 (*Aristandros and Kallithea*), 342–3 (*Drosilla and Charikles*); on their internal sequence and an attempt to problematize issues of dating and sequence, see Nilsson 2014: 83–6. Cf. also the use of bird-catching imagery in the *Funerary oration on the death of Nikephoros Komnenos* and the *Encomium of Michael Hagiotheodorites*, discussed below, Chapters 3 and 5.
[76] Bird species are notably difficult to identify and translate; in all passages cited here I have aimed at representing the linguistic variety of Manasses, not ornithological accuracy. On the three species mentioned by Manasses here (and in other texts), see Koukoules 1952: 399–400, esp. n. 7.

πυκνὰ τὰ στέρνα πατάσσοντα, οἷα τρέχοντα τὸν περὶ ψυχῆς, ἁλισκόμενά τε καὶ μαχαιρίδι κεντούμενα καὶ κατὰ βόθρου ἀκοντιζόμενα, ἔνια δὲ ζωγρούμενα καὶ τηρούμενα, ὁπόσοις δηλαδὴ δαψιλεστέρου κάλλους ἡ κομμώτρια φύσις μετέδωκεν.[77]

The 'For once I was delighted by' (Ἔτερψέ με ποτὲ) could be a reference to the *Description of the catching of siskins and chaffinches*, which would allow us to date it earlier than the *Description of a crane hunt*. It could also indicate a knowledge of that text among Manasses' presumed audience, or perhaps a wish for them to know about it – an indication of an authorial strategy to place oneself in a wider context as regards both experiences (different kinds of aristocratic pleasures, whether experienced in real life or imagined) and textual production (a larger corpus of ekphraseis and other texts). As we shall see, the songbirds and sparrows appear in different guise in several texts by Manasses, to the extent that the bird becomes a kind of literary mascot or an animal to associate with his voice. In addition to that imagery, 'the embellishing nature' (ἡ κομμώτρια φύσις) at the end of the cited passage is a Manassean expression that appears in two other texts, including the *Monody on the death of his goldfinch*.[78] Imagery and language accordingly work together here in order to project a recognizable voice as a tool of self-promotion.

Whether they are 'true' or not, the two descriptions of different kinds of bird hunting offer two different sides of what a modern reader may see as one activity: as underlined by Manasses in the sentence immediately following the short description of the catching of small birds cited above, and reflecting the wider tradition of hunting in Byzantium, the trapping of small birds using lime is described as 'childish pastimes' (παιδαριώδη ἀθύρματα) in comparison to the 'more masculine activities' (γυμνασίων ἀνδρικωτέρων) of crane hunting.[79] As a means to express praise of the masculine and 'erotic' character of Emperor Manuel, crane hunting was accordingly highly suitable. The catching of birds, by contrast, is

---

[77] Manasses, *Description of a crane hunt* 45–56 (Messis and Nilsson). The similarities between this passage, the *Description of the catching of siskins and chaffinches*, the descriptions of the grammar competitions in the *Funerary oration on the death of Nikephoros Komnenos* and the *Encomium of Michael Hagiotheodorites*, and the passage in *Hysmine and Hysminias* are remarkable. All were clearly influenced by the prose paraphrase of Oppian's *Ixeutica*; see further below, Chapter 5.

[78] Manasses, *Monody on the death of his goldfinch* 8.14 (Horna) and *Encomium of Michael Hagiotheodorites* 4 (Horna). See below, Chapters 3 and 4.

[79] Manasses, *Description of a crane hunt* 57–60 (Messis and Nilsson): Ἀλλά μοι τὸ χρῆμα τῆς τῶν γεράνων ἄγρας τοσοῦτον ἐκείνων ἐπιτερπέστερον, ὅσον ἀκανθυλλίδων καὶ σπίνων αἱ μακραύχενες ὑπερέχουσι γέρανοι καὶ λύγων ἰξοφόρων ἱέρακες δραστικώτεροι καὶ ὅσον γυμνασίων ἀνδρικωτέρων παιδαριώδη ἀθύρματα λείπεται. On crane hunting in Byzantium, see Messis and Nilsson 2019: 37–41.

represented rather as a bucolic idyll or even a painting – a suitable outing for a tired citizen of Constantinople, possibly undertaken in the narrator's youth rather than in his more mature years.[80]

A Constantinopolitan in Temporary Exile

The third text to examine in this chapter takes us out of Constantinople and much further than just across the Sea of Marmara: the *Itinerary* is a narrative poem, composed in dodecasyllables, in which Manasses describes an embassy to the court of Tripoli with the aim of finding a new wife for Emperor Manuel.[81] The embassy would have taken place in 1160/61, after the death of Manuel's first wife Bertha-Eirene.[82] The *Itinerary* has been interpreted by some scholars as a personal or 'egocentric' eyewitness account,[83] by others as a 'novelistic' rendering of a factual event.[84] Here it is read in relation to the texts discussed above: as part of Manasses' larger production of texts relating to the imperial court of Manuel, the eulogy of his reign and the spatial experience of Constantinople. The 'reality' vs 'fictionality' of the poem is not addressed in any detail here, since it is assumed throughout this study that all literary expression contains elements of both and that Byzantine literature in this respect is no different from other, earlier or later cultures. That is to say, the historical context of the poem (or any other text) is necessary in order to understand on the one hand its narrative and rhetorical form, on the other its occasional character and potential addressees, but there is little use in arguing for or against the

---

[80] While the narrator here does not necessarily coincide with Manasses, one could argue that the *Description of the catching of siskins and chaffinches* is likely to have been composed in the early years of Manasses' career, when such imagery seems to have been in fashion (see above, nn. 74–5). In that case, the use of the same imagery in the *Funerary oration on the death of Nikephoros Komnenos*, dated to c.1173, is related to the 'young days' described in the oration. See further below, Chapters 3 and 6.

[81] The full title in the Vatican ms is Τοῦ Μανασσῆ κυροῦ Κωνσταντίνου εἰς τὴν κατὰ τὰ Ἱεροσόλυμα ἀποδημίαν αὐτοῦ; no title or author is indicated in the other two manuscripts. For more details on the mss, see below, n. 86, and Chryssogelos 2017: 87–95. The title *Odeporicum* was given to the poem by Leo Alatius in the seventeenth century; see Marcovich 1987: 286, n. 27.

[82] The event is recorded in both Western and Byzantine sources (William of Tyre and John Kinnamos respectively). On the historical circumstances, see Horna 1904: 315–17; Marcovich 1987: 277–8; Külzer 1994: 17–20, and 2003.

[83] See Galatariotou 1993 ('personal reality'), Aerts 2003 ('egocentric document'), Marcovich 1987 ('personal soliloquy'); cf. Mullett 2002, who emphasizes the 'textual reality' of the *Itinerary* in response to Galatariotou 1993, and Külzer 2002 and 2003, who reads the *Itinerary* in the context of Byzantine accounts of pilgrimage to the Holy Land but underlines its lack of objectivity.

[84] Marcovich 1987, now also Chryssogelos 2017. Cf. Nilsson 2014, trying to explain what 'novelistic' could signify in a twelfth-century context.

'truth' of the narrative beyond the self-expression of the author.[85] As for the different versions of the poem in the manuscript tradition, I assume here that the long version of the *Itinerary*, consisting of four 'strophes' (*logoi*) and including a long ekphrasis of the intended bride, was composed as a coherent whole, while the shorter version (without the ekphrasis) was a later redaction.[86] My focus is not on the narrated events as such, but rather on the way in which the narrator presents himself – the story in which he takes part.

The poem opens with a prophetic dream, anticipating and leading up to the arrival of a 'fatal message' demanding that the narrator accompanies the *sebastos* (John Kontostephanos) to Jerusalem and Palestine – a journey that turns out to be a very unpleasant experience. The function of dreaming here and in other works by Manasses has been considered in some detail by other scholars;[87] here I wish to underline the function of the verses that precede the dream and present an initial setting for the narrative of the poem.

> Just escaping a loud and roaring storm | and the foaming ocean of affairs, | to which I had been treated by my simple life | which had no knowledge of mankind's vicissitudes, | I had just reached the harbour of tranquillity, | where richly blew a breeze of sweet untroubledness, | and found the abundant pleasures of my books | and I was imitating the industry of bees. | Working hard and toiling in the night, | holding in my hands the work of the man from Naucratis, | sleep attacked and closed my eyes | and carried me off for a ride on frightening dreams.

> Ἄρτι θροούσης ἐκφυγὼν ζάλης ῥόθους
> καὶ τὴν ἐπαφρίζουσαν ἅλμην πραγμάτων,
> ὧν μοι προεξένησεν ἁπλότης τρόπου
> ἀνθρωπίνης τε κακίας ἀπειρία,
> μόλις προσέσχον εὐγαλήνῳ λιμένι
> πλουτοῦντι τερπνὴν αὖραν ἀταραξίας
> καὶ δὴ βίβλων χάριτας εὑρὼν ἀφθόνους

---

[85] Cf. Lauxtermann 2014: 158–9, discussing the reading of Bourbouhakis 2007.
[86] See Nilsson 2012, arguing for the poem as a coherent whole. In short, the *Itinerary* has been preserved in three manuscripts, of which one (Vat. Gr. 1881) contains the long version, but omits vv. 1.124–212. The Marcianus Gr. 524 has only the first *logos* of the poem, vv. 1.1–269, while the Constantinopolitanus Μονῆς Παναγίας Καμαριωτίσσης (Χάλκης) 68 (included for the Chryssogelos edition) transmits the first 43 lines of the third *logos*. Horna suggested that the description of the prospective bride, Melisanda of Tripolis, was removed after that marriage had fallen through and Manuel had instead married Mary of Antioch. Cf. below, Chapter 6.
[87] Chryssogelos 2013a (on the *Itinerary*) and Pizzone 2011 (on the novel fragments). The dream motif ties in with an overall interest of the period, explored in the novels and other texts; see also e.g. MacAlister 1996; Angelidi and Calofonos 2014.

> τοὺς τῶν μελισσῶν ἀπεμιμούμην πόνους.
> νυκτὸς δέ μοι κάμνοντι καὶ πονουμένῳ
> κἂν ταῖν χεροῖν φέροντι τὸν Ναυκρατίτην
> ὕπνος πελάσας καὶ βλέφαρα συγκλίνας
> ἐνυπνίοις με παρέπεμψεν ἀγρίοις.[88]

The description of the narrator's situation in these verses may be read programmatically, offering an ideal situation (reading Athenaeus of Naucratis in the safety of his home) that is presented as desirable but highly unstable (preceded and followed by various 'storms'). It is the beginning of more than one narrative, on both intra- and extradiegetic levels. Within the story, the storm from which the narrator claims to have just escaped mirrors at least two forthcoming storms: the one to be experienced in the dream (1.13–47) and the ones that will be suffered on the ensuing journey – both the literal tempest at sea (1.209–12) and the overall hardships of the trip. The storm of the dream, following the practice of both dream-books and the ancient novel, anticipates the latter storms, real and metaphorical.[89] Such a play between the 'real', the fictional and the metaphorical is well known from both ancient and Komnenian novels, which also offer a narrative model for the kind of sudden abduction that the narrator suffers in his dream: John Kontostephanos appears and drags the narrator aboard a ship against his will.[90] The use of the dream, also frequent in the novels, underlines the confusion between fiction and reality and creates a certain suspense, playing on belief and disbelief, themes explored also later on in the poem.[91] The use of such 'novelistic' motifs does not necessarily make the *Itinerary* a 'novelistic' poem, but points rather to the popularity in the twelfth century of narrative strategies drawn from the novels.[92]

On a different narrative level, relating to the narrator's personal situation outside of the story, the storm from which he has just escaped does not only prefigure the coming journey – it also offers a contrast to the quiet

---

[88] Manasses, *Itinerary* 1.1–12 (Chryssogelos). Here and in the following, I use the translation by Aerts 2003, but since it is in verse and sometimes strays a bit far from the original Greek, I have modified it so as to stay closer to the original at the cost of its metrical form.

[89] On the motif of the storm in the *Itinerary* and the relation to the novel, see Mullett 2002 and Chryssogelos 2013a: 71–3. See also Chryssogelos 2013b on tempest and draught as 'key motifs' of the poem.

[90] Manasses, *Itinerary* 1.17 (Chryssogelos): συνεφελκύοντα κἀμὲ πρὸς βίαν.

[91] See esp. *Itinerary* 4.7–13, expressing the disbelief of the narrator at the sight of and return to Constantinople.

[92] Nilsson 2012 and 2014: 186–96. Note also Mullett 2002, showing how the 'exile discourse' was common to several Byzantine genres, including hagiography and epistolography; see also Mullett 1995.

home with the writer studying one of his model authors, Athenaeus.[93] The narrator is not simply tired after a hard day's work – he is exhausted after some sort of crisis.[94] The reference to previous storms indicates, for an audience familiar with such narratives, that the pleasant reading session will not last.[95] The setting accordingly combines various motifs in order to create a sense of uncertainty as regards both the previous (extradiegetic) situation of the narrator (whose earlier misfortunes are alluded to but not related in any detail) and the coming (intradiegetic) development of events. While various well-known motifs, techniques of citing ancient authors and recycling of formulaic verses connect the *Itinerary* to other works by Manasses, the poem is from the perspective of self-representation – here in the form of an extradiegetic authorial narrative – also closely related to his own narrative of being a writer in twelfth-century Constantinople.

I have previously argued that the *Itinerary* is concerned not so much with the journey as with Constantinople itself and its advantages for a rhetorician.[96] The poem, describing the *apodēmia* or temporary 'exile' of the narrator, becomes a means of praising the qualities of the capital and the emperor. Describing the horrors of the 'outside' becomes a praise of the 'inside'. Such concerns – an open fear of travelling and a deep nostalgia for the capital – are commonly voiced in twelfth-century texts and seem to reflect a shared sense of suspicion toward 'outsiders'.[97] In the *Itinerary* these concerns are more clearly connected to the role of the writer and the tasks of the rhetorician. When the main part of the embassy and the tour

---

[93] Athenaeus is only one of the ancient authors employed by Manasses, but there are at least two rather clear uses of the *Deipnosophistae* in the *Itinerary* (3.76 and 4.8, noted by Horna 1904: 347). See also further below.

[94] Cf. Chryssogelos 2013a: 68. As noted by Chryssogelos 2017: 157, the passage is reminiscent of Manganeios Prodromos 6.1–5 (Bernadinello): Ἤδη πάντως ἀπήλλαγμαι τῶν ἔξωθεν φροντίδων | καὶ τοῦ παρενοχλοῦντός με φόβου πάμπαν ἐλύθην· | οὐκ ἔχει πάλιν ταραχὰς τόσας ὁ λογισμός μου, | ἐφησυχάζων δ' ἀτρεμεῖ τῆς ζάλης στορεθείσης | καὶ βλέπω καθαρώτερον χωρίς τινος νεφέλης. The imagery thus seems to be shared by other twelfth-century writers and signifies something more than just regular weariness. See also further below, Chapter 4.

[95] The instability of fortune is a frequent motif in several of Manasses' texts. For the *Itinerary*, see e.g. 2.45–52 with the inserted gnomic statement on the instability of life: αἴ, αἴ, πολυστένακτον ἀνθρώπων γένος, | κακῶν ἄβυσσε, βυθὲ τῆς δυσποτμίας· | αἴ, αἴ, πολυστρόβητε, κυκητὰ βίε, | ἀλλοπρόσαλλε, τρισκατάρατε, πλάνε, | ἄνισε, παντόφυρτε, βάσιν οὐκ ἔχων· | σκώληξ σὺ πικρός, καρδίας κατεσθίων, | δυσχείμερος θάλασσα μυρίων κακῶν, | ἀνήμερον πέλαγος μυρίων κακῶν. On the so-called 'principle of alternation' in Greek narrative, i.e. the idea that no human life is without vicissitude, see Cairns 2014.

[96] Nilsson 2012. See also Mullett 2002: 261–2, on the 'exile discourse' of the *Itinerary*, and Chryssogelos 2013b: 35, on fear of travel and sadness at leaving the capital as 'thematic axes' (θεματικοί άξονες) of the *Itinerary*.

[97] See e.g. Hörandner 1993; E. Jeffreys and M. Jeffreys 2001; Magdalino 2000; Kislinger 2008.

of the Holy Land is over and the narrator, who has fallen ill because of the bad water and poor food, is recovering in Cyprus, he laments his fate – 'For what is the dull flicker of the modest stars | compared with that all-feeding flame of the sun? | In comparison with the City of Constantine, | what's Cyprus in its totality and particulars?' (2.87–90: τί γὰρ ταπεινῶν ἀστρίων ἀμαυρότης | πρὸς τὴν τὸ πᾶν βόσκουσαν ἡλίου φλόγα; | ἢ τί πρὸς αὐτὴν τὴν Κωνσταντίνου πόλιν | ἡ Κύπρος ἡ σύμπασα καὶ τὰ τῆς Κύπρου;).[98] This image of the capital as the sun outshining the stars is reminiscent of the depiction of Emperor Manuel as the sun, employed in the oration discussed above; it thus imbues the capital with imperial power. The narrator then focalizes his own experience of that power and compares it to his situation in Cyprus:

> Oh toil, oh education, oh these learned men's books | with which from childhood I was senselessly stuffed; | oh torment of my body, oh these lengthy nights | which I spent in the company of books, | awake, not letting my eyes close for sleep, | isolated like a sparrow in my room, | or rather like a night owl in the dark.[99] | I live here in a land where literature is scarce, | I sit here idly, my mouth is bound, | I'm unemployed, immobile like a prisoner, | a rhetorician without a tongue, with no liberty of speech, | a rhetorician without a voice, without his exercise. | Like a garden that remains unwatered | withers away from the want of water, | parches up from the lack of rain | and drops the splendid leaves from its trees, | in the same way have I suffered: I died | and lost the beauty which I used to enjoy. | Idling away my time I feed myself with hope | or wait for the movement of waters | just as in older times the lame did for his health. | Oh Rhomaian land, ornament of all the Earth, | my eyes tear up thinking of you.

> Ὦ μόχθος, ὦ μάθησις, ὦ σοφῶν βίβλοι,
> αἷς συνεσάπην ἀνοήτως ἐκ νέου·
> ὦ σώματος κάκωσις, ὦ νυκτῶν δρόμοι,
> ἃς ἀνάλωσα ταῖς βίβλοις ἐντυγχάνων,
> ἄϋπνος, οὐ βλέφαρα κάμπτων εἰς ὕπνον,
> ὥσπερ μονάζων στρουθὸς ἐν δωματίῳ,
> ἢ μᾶλλον εἰπεῖν, ἐν σκότει νυκτικόραξ.
> Εἰς γῆν παροικῶ τὴν σπανίζουσαν λόγων·
> ἀργὸς κάθημαι, συμπεδήσας τὸ στόμα,
> ἀεργός, ἀκίνητος ὡς φυλακίτης,
> ῥήτωρ ἄγλωσσος οὐκ ἔχων παρρησίαν,

---

[98] Cf. *Itinerary* 2.154–5 (Chryssogelos) on Constantinople as ὀφθαλμὲ τῆς γῆς, κόσμε τῆς οἰκουμένης, | τηλαυγὲς ἄστρον, τοῦ κάτω κόσμου λύχνε. Manasses is not always consistent in his imagery; see further below on the use of unstable images and motifs.

[99] An adaptation of Psalms 101:7–8 (ὡμοιώθην πελεκᾶνι ἐρημικῷ, | ἐγενήθην ὡσεὶ νυκτικόραξ ἐν οἰκοπέδῳ, | ἠγρύπνησα καὶ ἐγενήθην | ὡσεὶ στρουθίον μονάζον ἐπὶ δώματι).

A Constantinopolitan in Temporary Exile

ῥήτωρ ἄφωνος οὐκ ἔχων γυμνασίαν.
ὥσπερ δὲ παράδεισος, οὐκ ἔχων ὕδωρ,
συγκαίεται μὲν ὑπὸ τῆς λειψυδρίας,
συμφρύγεται δὲ παρὰ τῆς ἀνομβρίας
καὶ φυλλοριπτεῖ δενδρῖτις εὐκοσμία,
οὕτω κἀγὼ πέπονθα· καὶ διεφθάρην
καὶ κάλλος ἀπέβαλλον, οὗπερ ηὐπόρουν.
Ἀργὸς διάγω, βόσκομαι ταῖς ἐλπίσιν
ἢ τὴν κίνησιν καρτερῶ τῶν ὑδάτων,
ὡς πρὶν ὁ παράλυτος ὑγείας χάριν.
Ὦ Ῥωμαΐς γῆ, κόσμε τῆς γῆς ἁπάσης,
ἔρρευσε τὰ βλέφαρα προσδοκῶντά σε.[100]

The suffering intellectual is familiar from other Komnenian authors, perhaps most well-known in the version of the third poem by Ptochoprodromos,[101] but Manasses offers a decisive twist of the motif: the toils of learning are contrasted with the province, void of learning and – most importantly – without a function for a Constantinopolitan rhetorician.[102] A few verses below, the narrator describes the fate of such a voiceless orator, likening his situation to that of crickets in the winter:

> What dew-consuming crickets suffer, | who sing their musical tunes in summer | but die as soon as the cold arrives. | For the wretched race of humans, | as long as cherished by the sun rays of happiness, | raises its voice louder than Stentor's | and unfolds the instrument of his rib cage | and creates a well-turned and harmonious sound; | but if it is chilled by the cold of distress, | it wastes away, alas, not enduring the frost.

Ὁ τέττιγες πάσχουσιν οἱ δροσοφάγοι,
θέρους μὲν ὑπᾴδοντες ἔμμουσον μέλος,
νεκρούμενοι δὲ τοῦ κρύους πεφθακότος.
τὸ γὰρ πολυμέριμνον ἀνθρώπων γένος,
θαλφθὲν μὲν ἁβροῖς ἡλίοις ἀλυπίας,
τὴν γλῶσσαν ὑψοῖ Στέντορος τορωτέραν
καὶ τὴν ἐπιστήθιον ἁπλοῖ μαγάδα
καὶ φθόγγον εὐτόρνευτον, ἐμμελῆ πλέκει·
ἂν δ' ἀποπαγῇ τῷ κρύει τῶν θλίψεων,
μαραίνεται, φεῦ, τὸν κρυμὸν μὴ βαστάσαν.[103]

---

[100] Manasses, *Itinerary* 2.91–111 (Chryssogelos).
[101] See Alexiou 1986 and 1999; Beaton 1987; Kulhánková 2008 and 2010.
[102] The dark province, void of learning, is more or less a topos among intellectuals who had to leave the city; see e.g. the case of Theophylact of Ochrid (eleventh century) and his 'exile' in Mullett 1997: 274–6, or Michael Choniates (twelfth century) and his sense of displacement in Livanos 2006 and Kaldellis 2009a: 145–65.
[103] Manasses, *Itinerary* 2.119–28 (Chryssogelos).

Thus withering away like a cricket in winter, the narrator wishes to express his gratitude to his current benefactor in Cyprus, probably the governor Alexios Doukas,[104] 'this Nile of benefactions, flowing floods of gold' (ὁ τῶν χαρίτων Νεῖλος, ὁ χρυσοβρύτης).[105] However, in spite of the rich food and these 'showers of dew' (ὀμβροβλυτεῖ με δρόσον),[106] the narrator is sick at the thought of Constantinople (2.137–40). He offers yet another zoomorphic *persona* to describe his indisposition:

> For even a songbird caught in a cage, | albeit plentifully fed, more than enough, | longs for the freedom of spreading its wings | and hating life together with humans | it is constantly searching for secret escapes. | For nothing is so sweet and desirable | as freedom's light, a careless life.

> Καὶ μουσικὸν γὰρ ἐγκαθειρχθὲν στρουθίον,
> κἂν λιπαρῶς τρέφοιτο, κἂν ὑπὲρ κόρον,
> ἐλευθερίων γλίχεται πετασμάτων
> καὶ δυσχεραῖνον τὸν μετ' ἀνθρώπων βίον,
> ἀεὶ διώκει κρυφίας διεξόδους.
> Οὐδὲν γὰρ οὕτως ἡδὺ καὶ ζητητέον,
> ὡς φῶς ἐλευθέριον, ἄφροντις βίος.[107]

As noted above, this is an image presumably well-known to an audience familiar with Manasses' work.

After a brief prayer to Christ asking for a safe return, the narrator closes the second strophe of the poem with six verses that echo the closing verses of the first and third strophes, together creating a sort of refrain with variation.[108] They all express the longing of the narrator for his home and the sense of security that the imperial capital offers. The end of the first strophe in particular mirrors closely the image of the narrator offered in the second strophe:

> Oh, Byzantine land, oh City built by God, | which made me see the light and fostered me, | if only I were in you to see your beauties. | Yes, I wish I were in your embracing arms; | yes, I wish I were under your wings | while you look after me like a little bird.

---

[104] Alexios Doukas is known to have befriended men of letters and was thus a known patron; see Magdalino 1997: 162. Alexios Doukas was grandson of Anna Komnene, as were John Kontostephanos and also Nikephoros Komnenos, whose death Manasses lamented in one of his funerary orations; see below, Chapter 3.
[105] Manasses, *Itinerary* 2.130 (Chryssogelos). See Nilsson 2016 on this imagery of rivers and fountains for patronage in the twelfth century.
[106] Manasses, *Itinerary* 2.132 (Chryssogelos).   [107] Manasses, *Itinerary* 2.141–7 (Chryssogelos).
[108] Nilsson 2012.

Ὦ γῆ Βυζαντίς, ὦ θεόδμητος πόλις,
ἡ καὶ τὸ φῶς δείξασα καὶ θρέψασά με,
ἐν σοὶ γενοίμην, καλλονὰς βλέψαιμί σου.
Ναὶ ναί, γενοίμην ὑπὸ τὰς σὰς ἀγκάλας·
ναὶ ναί, γενοίμην ὑπὸ τὴν πτέρυγά σου
καὶ διατηροίης με καθὰ στρουθίον.[109]

The imagery used by Manasses in the *Itinerary* accordingly describes the situation of the narrator as follows. The task of the rhetorician (a cricket, a bird) is to sing the praise of the emperor (the sun). The emperor, who also represents Constantinople, outshines the stars (other rulers and aristocrats) and offers protection under his wings. Outside of the city, other patrons may offer 'rivers of gold' or refreshing 'dew',[110] but if such channels are cut off the writer (a garden) withers and dies.[111] These elements all come together in an authorial metanarrative that marks many texts written by Manasses and which is visible also in the choice of words and images in the *Encomium of Emperor Manuel Komnenos*. As already noted, the emperor as the sun is an image shared also by other rhetoricians, but the way in which oratory and orators are represented in terms of fluttering wings and birds in both texts offers a more distinct imagery that contributes to the extradiegetic narrative of Manasses: the 'free wings' of *logoi* may be 'shackled' by the deeds of the emperor, just as the tongues of rhetoricians may be 'shackled' by their absence from the city and their lack of work.[112] The orations are like small birds, desperately fluttering around the emperor, just as the rhetoricians are like small songbirds wishing to be under the protecting wings of the emperor;[113] the products of rhetoricians are like

---

[109] Manasses, *Itinerary* 1.331–6 (Chryssogelos). Cf. *Itinerary* 1.77 on leaving the city, Τῆς γλυκυτάτης ἀπάρας βασιλίδος, and 4.1–35 on the disbelief and happiness at returning home. Cf. also the representation of Constantinople in Manasses, *Verse chronicle* 2319–26 (Lampsides), cited at the beginning of this chapter, and the similar eroticized depiction of imperial space.

[110] Cf. Manasses, *Verse chronicle* 16–17 (Lampsides): καὶ τὸν τοῦ κόπου καύσωνα καὶ τῆς ταλαιπωρίας | αἱ δωρεαὶ δροσίζουσι κενούμεναι συχνάκις.

[111] For the same imagery in other texts by Manasses, see Nilsson 2016 and below, Chapter 4.

[112] Cf. Manasses, *Encomium of Emperor Manuel Komnenos* 5 (Kurtz): ἤδη καὶ ῥητόρων γλώσσας ἐπέδησας καὶ δεξιὰς ἀπηγκώνισας, with Manasses, *Itinerary* 2.99 (Chryssogelos): ἀργὸς κάθημαι, συμπεδήσας τὸ στόμα, | ἀεργός, ἀκίνητος ὡς φυλακίτης.

[113] Cf. Manasses, *Encomium of Emperor Manuel Komnenos* 8–9 (Kurtz): λίαν ἀμήχανον, γλῶσσαν σοφιστικὴν ἀετῷ συνίπτασθαι τῷ ταχυπετεῖ καὶ ἡλίῳ συμπεριφέρεσθαι, and 15–17 (Kurtz): καὶ κατάκρας μὲν ἐρωτιῶσι τοῦ κάλλους καὶ προσπτερύξασθαι γλίχονται· ἀλλ' ἥττηνταί σου τοῦ ὕψους, ἀλλὰ νενίκηνταί σου τοῦ δρόμου καὶ τὸ πτερὸν αὐτοῖς οὐκέτι μετάρσιον, with Manasses, *Itinerary* 1.335–6 (Chryssogelos): ναὶ ναί, γενοίμην ὑπὸ τὴν πτέρυγά σου | καὶ διατηροίης με καθὰ στρουθίον and 2.141–3 (Chryssogelos): καὶ μουσικὸν γὰρ ἐγκαθειρχθὲν στρουθίον, | … ἐλευθερίων γλίχεται πετασμάτων.

gardens filled with flowers, carefully watered and cultivated, just like the rhetoricians themselves need to be tended and watered by their patrons.[114]

The imagery is far from consistent and may sometimes seem contradictory, such as the ambiguous image of the emperor as at the same time a fierce eagle and a protecting 'mother sparrow' (στρουθιομήτωρ) – a word not used in the *Itinerary*, but certainly recalled by the image in 1.335–6 (ναὶ ναί, γενοίμην ὑπὸ τὴν πτέρυγά σου | καὶ διατηροίης με καθὰ στρουθίον).[115] But the contrast depends on the choice of focalization: to his enemies, Manuel is a dangerous predator, protecting his people; to his people (his nestlings), he offers a protective wing.[116] The task of the rhetorician is to explore such contrasting perspectives and use them to his and his addressee's advantage, depending on the needs of the specific occasion. Manasses does the same with the role of the orator: taking on a condescending *persona* at the beginning of the *Encomium of Emperor Manuel Komnenos* – describing other orators as picking flowers, drawing on ancient literature and repeating what others have said – but doing more or less the same in practice, both in this and other texts.

To Be on the Outside or the Inside

In all the texts discussed in this chapter, imperial and Constantinopolitan space (including persons, objects and activities) is represented as experienced from various perspectives, but always with an encomiastic end. The ekphraseis should be seen not as descriptions of superficial beauty, but as 'thick descriptions' with important social functions of their key characteristics.[117] Ancient objects and buildings, represented in ancient language, mediate on both narrative and aesthetic levels a social meaning that may be interpreted by the rhetorician and put in relation to the contemporary experience of the city.[118] In this way, the text becomes a way of 're-presenting' the past while at the same time expressing in words the

---

[114] Cf. Manasses, *Encomium of Emperor Manuel Komnenos* 26–7 (Kurtz): ὡς ἀπὸ γλυκείας θαλάσσης ὀχητηγεῖτο καὶ κηπεύετο τοῦ λόγου τὸ φυτηκόμημα, with Manasses, *Itinerary* 2.103: ὥσπερ δὲ παράδεισος, οὐκ ἔχων ὕδωρ.
[115] For the 'mother sparrow' as emperor, see Manasses, *Aristandros and Kallithea* frg. 60.1 (Mazal): Λέγεται γάρ τοι βασιλεὺς στρουθιομήτωρ ὄρνις.
[116] See also Schmidt 2016: 173 on Manuel as both predator and protector.
[117] The term was developed by the anthropologist Clifford Geertz (1973) and indicates descriptions that not only describe but also explain, so that the object or action described becomes comprehensible also for an outsider. For the concept of 'thick description' applied to Byzantine culture, see Veikou 2018.
[118] See Veikou 2018 and Nilsson 2021b.

aesthetic pleasure of the object. A very similar function may be observed in the case of more open imperial praise, representing the emperor as a reflection or even embodiment of great rulers of the past. The ekphraseis accordingly benefit from being analysed in relation to other texts by Manasses, since that comparative study may help us to place them in their historical and occasional context.[119]

Comparison is also relevant for the interpretation of the *Itinerary*, since it opens up a better understanding of its 'autobiographical' characteristics as part of a larger authorial metanarrative created by Manasses throughout several of his texts. Most often, such details are not part of the intradiegetic narrative but rather referred to in passing or made part of an extradiegetic story, as in the *Itinerary*.[120] If we return for a moment to that opening passage, picturing the narrator at home with his book, it may offer yet another piece of the puzzle of self-representation. The intradiegetic reading of Athenaeus, author of the *Deipnosophistae*, is probably not a random choice.[121] Athenaeus' account of the discussions of 'dinner sophists' at a symposium held at the house of Publius Livius Larensis, a wealthy book-collector and patron of the arts, seems to fit Manasses' authorial narrative rather well. Athenaeus, the narrator of the story, is a Roman concerned with Greek learning and entertaining takes on ancient history, not very different from a twelfth-century *grammatikos*, while the mighty Larensis has similarities with contemporary patrons such as John Kontostephanos or Alexios Doukas. Moreover, the reference in *Itinerary* 1.8, directly preceding the two lines on the nightly reading of Athenaeus, describes the narrator as 'imitating the industry of bees' (τοὺς τῶν μελισσῶν ἀπεμιμούμην πόνους), that is, gathering honey from ancient authors.[122] The many borrowings from various ancient sources throughout the *Itinerary*, including Athenaeus himself,[123] indicate that the opening setting of the poem is more than just a convenient place to start.

The situation narrated in the *Itinerary* could perhaps be described as taking an 'insider' and placing him on the 'outside'. That situation stands

---

[119] Such an approach to ekphraseis was prompted as early as Macrides and Magdalino 1988: esp. 81–2.

[120] There are exceptions though, as in the letters and the oration discussed below, Chapter 4.

[121] Horna 1904: 347 first identified the *Naukratites* in this passage as Athenaeus, author of the *Deipnosophistae*. Cf. Chryssogelos 2017: 157–8, on the use of the word *Naukratites* as a pun, tying in with the motif of the passage.

[122] Cf. Manasses, *Verse chronicle* 4856–8 (Lampsides) on Emperor Theophilos as a busy bee, studying his books: ὁ κράτωρ γὰρ Θεόφιλος βίβλοις ἀεὶ σχολάζων | καὶ σίμβλα τὰ τῆς γνώσεως κηροπλαστῶν ἐντεῦθεν, | ὡς μέλισσα φιλόπονος ἀνθῶν ἐκ λειμωνίων.

[123] See above, n. 93.

in stark contrast to the *Encomium of Emperor Manuel Komnenos* and the *Description of a crane hunt*, where the narrator explicitly presents himself as being on the 'inside', having access to detailed information of the emperor's deeds and, in the case of the hunt, even being an eyewitness. At the same time, the three texts represent merely different perspectives of the same phenomenon: the struggle to be on the inside – in Constantinople and in imperial circles. By focalizing the outsider's experiences in the *Itinerary*, Manasses turns the spotlight on the insider's privileges. He employs a similar technique of 'refocalization' in the *Description of a little man*, where the narrator assumes a seemingly neutral position in his description of the curious outsider, with the result that the aristocrats who are mocking the dwarf – by definition insiders – are portrayed in a slightly derisive manner. The narrator seems to take the position rather of the object of display, perhaps as a way of drawing attention to his own position as entertainer of the court.[124] In both cases Manasses turns a central concern of the twelfth-century writer's situation into a literary theme, just like Prodromos did in several poems,[125] creating a metatextual narrative that concerns his own situation (and that of his peers) rather than his object(s) of praise.

At the same time, it must be underlined that the writer and the object of praise were mutually dependent on each other. As noted by Paul Magdalino, for a rhetorician to perform an encomium at a formal or informal session at the court was an 'initiation rite', an entrance into public life.[126] For more experienced rhetoricians, such as Manasses presumably was in the 1160s and early 1170s, it was an affirmation of one's position in that public life – an opportunity to once again say expected things in an unexpected manner.[127] While occasional texts, as we have seen, most often were concerned with factual events, such as an imperial campaign, an embassy or simply a hunt (real or imagined), and expressed in familiar rhetorical figures and literary topoi, they also had an extraliterary end. To cite Magdalino again, 'Not all encomia were actually honoured with a ceremonial audience. But all, without exception, were offered as gifts in a ritual exchange from which some return was expected.'[128] While Magdalino refers to imperial *encomia* specifically, the same could be said for all occasional texts that were produced in the twelfth century. They

---

[124] Messis and Nilsson 2015: 187.   [125] See Zagklas 2014: 322–5.   [126] Magdalino 1993: 414.
[127] Cf. Magdalino 1993: 418, on the variation of stereotypes and the expectations of the imperial audience.
[128] Magdalino 1993: 425. Cf. Nilsson 2016.

were occasioned by various events, but also by the overarching need for the writer to make a living and defend his position in the system. Written 'by insiders for insiders',[129] the texts were active and referential, not only in relation to the events or objects as such, but perhaps even more in relation to the social circumstances. Hence the need to describe and confirm a space to an audience already in it – not simply as a memory or a representation,[130] but as an interpretation of a reality which could, at least theoretically, be subject to competing interpretations.[131]

---

[129] M. Jeffreys 2003: 92.

[130] In this sense, the ekphrastic topos of the need to describe for the sake of memory says one thing but probably means partly something else; e.g. *Description of a crane hunt* 329–31 (Messis and Nilsson): γέγραπται δή μοι τὰ ὁραθέντα, ἐμοὶ μὲν εἰς ζώπυρον τοῦ πράγματος καὶ ἀνάμνησιν, ἄλλοις δὲ ἴσως ἀνθρώποις εἰς ἐναργὲς προζωγράφημα οὗ μὴ τεθέανται. That is, memory is to be understood as the commemoration of the occasion, somehow fixed in time and space by the art of writing.

[131] See Veikou 2018.

CHAPTER 3

The Occasion of Death
Patronage and the Writer on Command

To write occasional texts is not always a question of writing on command or for a specific patron, but in the twelfth century and in the case of Manasses, they often seem to coincide. In both cases, an essential concern is to find the right voice – the voice that suits the *persona* the writer feels the need to put on display, but that at the same time suits the patron, or at least the occasion for which the particular piece has been composed. Two agents are presumably at work here, the writer and the patron, and discussions of patronage accordingly most often focus on the relationship between the two. Since the influential work of the anthropologist Jeremy Boissevain, that relationship has been defined as reciprocal but asymmetrical, personal and of some duration.[1] Such definitions are still prevalent and sociologists have basically agreed that patronage is a form of power, based on submission and trust, and in that sense often voluntary.[2]

In the case of twelfth-century Byzantium, the sociological perspective has been accepted by several scholars, but employed in rather different ways. Elizabeth Jeffreys has argued for a patron-centred method by looking at the authors who wrote for Sebastokratorissa Eirene, thus defining a more or less stable circle of writers who worked for her.[3] According to such an approach, authors whose works were dedicated to Eirene might have written other pieces for her; in the case of Manasses, who dedicated his *Verse chronicle* and his *Astrological poem* to Eirene, it could be that he also wrote his novel or other works for her.[4] By contrast, Margaret Mullett has

---

[1] Boissevain 1966.
[2] Gellner 1977. See also Saller 1982: 7–39 on definitions (language and ideology). On Byzantium, see Hill 1999: 155–61, along with a useful bibliography on pp. 239–41; more recently, Bernard 2014: 291–333.
[3] E. Jeffreys 1984 and 2014.
[4] On the Komnenian novels and the Sebastokratorissa, see E. Jeffreys 1980 and 2012: 276: 'This reluctance [to write the *Verse chronicle* in political verse] suggests that A&K [*Aristandros and Kallithea*] was also undertaken as a commission from the same sponsor ... although there is little clear evidence for this. It would also be plausible to suggest that Manasses produced A&K as part of

3 The Occasion of Death: Patronage and the Writer

argued for a writer-centred approach, based on the observation that Komnenian writers did not write for only one patron, but rather accepted patronage where they could find it.[5] Such an approach demands a study of networks that radiate from the writer and include various patrons – as in the case of Manasses – rather than patron-centred networks. A third way of looking at patronage, still sociological but aiming at political rather than literary history, may be observed in Paul Magdalino's monograph on Manuel I Komnenos. In the chapter on rhetoric in Komnenian intellectual culture, Magdalino looks at *theatra* in terms of different kinds of relationships at the court of Manuel I, ranging from 'patronage proper' to less firm 'friendships'.[6] His method could perhaps be described as object-centred, since his aim is to understand the role of patronage for the nature of Manuel's rule, not the individual relationships as such.

Although these three methods may be seen as different, they all aim at understanding the function of patronage and should therefore be seen as complementary rather than dissonant.[7] In this chapter I should like to add yet another perspective: persuaded by Mullett's insistence on a writer-centred method, but also influenced by theoretical considerations offered by the musicologist Claudio Annibaldi in his study of musical patronage in the early modern period, my approach could perhaps be described as text-centred, since its aim is to take a point of departure in the individual text itself – its functions and its form – rather than in the writer, the patron or the relationship between the two. While the importance of such aspects cannot be denied, a too strong focus on relationships may lead us to overlook the text and its 'poetics of patronage'.[8] Such a poetics may include not only the writer's own literary *personae*, but also that of the addressee/patron, which must then be properly analysed in its context and not simply taken at face value.[9]

---

the literary rivalry endemic at this period in Constantinople, choosing a form to contrast with the iambics of *R&D* [*Rhodanthe and Dosikles*] and the prose of *H&H* [*Hysmine and Hysminias*].' I find the latter suggestion more plausible, since the alleged reluctance of Manasses to write in political verse is based on rather tenuous evidence; see M. Jeffreys 1974: 158–61 on Manasses, *Verse chronicle* 12–17 (Lampsides).

[5] Mullett 1984. Note esp. Mullett's comment on the place of patronage in relation to audience and readers: 'Patronage comes at an earlier stage in the process than either audience or readership' (Mullett 1984: 180). See also Rhoby 2009: 307–8.
[6] Magdalino 1993: 335–56.
[7] Cf. Mullett's comment on Magdalino 1993 in Mullett 2007: 5 ('Additional notes and comments').
[8] Cf. Annibaldi 1998: 175 (on 'artistic freedom'), with Zetzel 1982 (on 'poetics of patronage'). See also further below.
[9] Noted in Mullett 1984: 180, with reference to Zetzel 1972.

3 The Occasion of Death: Patronage and the Writer

In order to offer a more nuanced definition of what patronage in the twelfth century is and means, I have adapted the anthropological-semiotic model proposed by Annibaldi for the case of musical patronage.[10] Annibaldi's main assumption, that 'music – in its various functions as element of liturgy, ceremony and recreation – was intended to symbolise and represent the social status of the patron commissioning it',[11] fits the twelfth-century situation surprisingly well; we need only to replace 'music' by 'rhetoric'. This assumption, which is based on the workings of hierarchy and convention, has two implications that are just as relevant for the Byzantine situation (and from now on I simply replace the words 'music' and 'musician' in Annibaldi's theory with 'rhetoric/text' and 'rhetorician/writer' in my own adaptation of it). First, the relationship between rhetorician and patron is conceived as the interplay between the rhetorical event (produced by the rhetorician and commissioned by the patron) and the world 'in the presence of which those events took place' – a world 'composed of anyone capable of correlating the events in question to the social rank of the individuals or institutions promoting them'. Second, 'the object of the relationship between [rhetorician] and patron is to be identified not as the composition of the [text] (as customarily thought), but as a performance, even an entirely improvised performance' – an extension of the writer's professional duties 'to any activity required to realise a [rhetorical] performance appropriate to his patron's rank'.[12]

This can be more or less directly transferred to the twelfth-century situation (and probably also to several other Byzantine settings): the relationship between writer and patron is, in practice, an interplay between the occasion at which a text is performed and the surrounding circle of aristocrats and peers (presumably what happens in a *theatron* or at other gatherings); moreover, the object of that interplay is the performative (or occasional) aspects of the text, a perspective that has been increasingly emphasized in studies of Komnenian literature over the last decades.[13] But the question is still what patronage means – in what way music, or indeed rhetoric, 'actually symbolised the rank of the individual or institution commissioning it'. This is an aspect of patronage that has often been overlooked, but Annibaldi's model with its semiotic focus forces us to offer an answer: the performance of the text, along with the text itself

---

[10] See Annibaldi 1998, a summary in English of the theoretical model presented in the introduction to the anthology *La musica e il mondo* = Annibaldi 1993: 9–42.
[11] Annibaldi 1998: 173–4.   [12] Annibaldi 1998: 174.
[13] See esp. Mullett 2003; Marciniak 2007 and 2014; Bourbouhakis 2011 and 2017: 125*–58* (esp. on 'aurality').

3 The Occasion of Death: Patronage and the Writer 61

(its functions and form), demonstrate the 'artistic sensibility and connoisseurship'[14] of the patron; in Byzantine terms it demonstrates his or her *paideia*.

The learnedness and rhetorical skills of the patron or addressee, as described and praised by writers in dedicatory works or *encomia*, have often been taken as *topoi*. This means that such praise remains open to the individual scholar's interpretation of the 'actual' skills of the addressee in question. The advantage of Annibaldi's model is that it forces us to consider the text as an expression of a cultural and semiotic relationship rather than a factual relationship between people. There are two ways, he argues, of using (commissioned) works to represent the social status of the patron, and thus two kinds of patronage, based on 'metaphoric' and 'metonymic' relationships, that is 'similarity' and 'contiguity'.[15] The latter is the means by which 'conventional patronage' achieves its end; the work symbolizes the rank of patron 'through reference to repertoires traditionally associated with the élite class' and thus, in the case of Byzantium, proves to be a sort of rhetorical 'accessory of the élite itself'.[16] In turn, 'humanistic patronage' symbolizes the rank of its patron through the display of his artistic sensibility; it achieves its end by 'similarity', 'by displaying compositional qualities that parallel the sophisticated tastes of the class in question'.[17]

The social status of the patron in twelfth-century Byzantium can certainly be said to reflect these semiotic aspects: contiguity tends to mark more conventional pieces written for the emperor or other members of the imperial court (e.g. *encomia* of the emperor or *epithalamia* brimming with *topoi*) while similarity characterizes pieces written for patrons with whom the writer has a more personal relationship. That said, one should be careful not to make too strict a distinction between the two aspects, since they often overlap and in no way are mutually exclusive: ceremonial texts can display characteristics of rather personal similarity, while encomia and epitaphs of a more personal character can lean towards more formal contiguity. The model proposed here should accordingly not be seen as a strict system according to which rhetoric was produced, but as a tool for

---

[14] Annibaldi 1998: 174.
[15] Annibaldi 1998: 175, drawing on Roman Jakobson's distinction of linguistic communication in those terms.
[16] Annibaldi 1998: 176. Cf. Bernard 2014: 291–332 and his approach to patronage influenced by the 'cultural capital' of Bourdieu.
[17] Annibaldi 1998: 176.

performing a text-based analysis of relationships in a society that depends on patronage.

This cultural-semiotic relationship is to some extent a reflection of the factual relationship, in the sense that the emperor and his close family were more distant from the writer (both ideologically and physically). Moreover, the generosity and philanthropy of the emperor was part of his imperial virtues and in that sense to some extent different from the goodwill of aristocrats.[18] When Eustathios of Thessalonike praises the rhetorical skills of Manuel I Komnenos in his *epitaphios logos*, he borders on similarity in the sense that he displays qualities that he and the emperor shared, but at the same time convention keeps him within the sphere of contiguity rather than expressing some kind of 'kinship'.[19] In the case of Manasses, the distance kept between the writer–observer and the object of praise in the *Description of a crane hunt* and the *Encomium of Emperor Manuel Komnenos*, discussed in the previous chapter, is an expression of contiguity, while cases of similarity are presented and analysed in the present chapter. Since the individual works are the point of departure for my analysis, the aim is not to establish the factual relationships between Manasses and his patrons, but to look at how relationships that appear to be based on patronage are depicted in the texts.

I say 'appear to be based', because the presence of a 'factual' addressee in a text – that is, a historical person that is known also from other documentation – does not necessarily indicate that s/he was a patron, nor does the characterization of the addressee necessarily reflect the 'real' person. While most literary scholars now would accept the idea that the author is not the same as the literary *persona*, which may vary considerably from work to work, there has been less discussion of the *persona* of the addressee. In the case of patronage, it has often been assumed that commissioned texts mirror the wishes and attitudes of the addressees (i.e. patrons) rather than the writers themselves, and that such works should be read as social documents rather than literary works. James Zetzel challenged this idea by arguing for a 'poetics of patronage' that includes the construction of an addressee-patron that is just as carefully wrought as the *persona* of the poet.[20] Based on examples from Roman poets of the first century BCE, Zetzel showed how the choice of addressee is not necessarily a function of

---

[18] Cf. Saller 1982: 41–69 on imperial *beneficia*.
[19] Eustathios of Thessalonike, *The epitaphios for Manuel I Komnenos* 13 (Bourbouhakis), on which see Nilsson 2014: 163–4.
[20] Zetzel 1982.

3 The Occasion of Death: Patronage and the Writer

the relationship between the poet and the person addressed; that is, it does not have to mirror a personal relationship, but 'can be seen as a correlate of both the subject and the style of the poem'.[21] The addressee, which may or may not reflect a real person, is 'an element in a work of art', and the relationship between the writer and the patron, as described in the work, becomes a vehicle for discussing the role of the poet in society.[22] Such an approach seems very useful when we consider twelfth-century texts, in which the writer–patron relationship is often implicitly or explicitly in focus. The combination of this approach with Annibaldi's model of relations marked by contiguity vs similarity can produce a fruitful way of dealing with patronage from a text-centred perspective. This can be illustrated with an example from Manasses.

In the *Description of the Cyclops*, Manasses describes a 'man whose family roots have been registered in old writings and whose love of beauty has been exposed in political affairs' (οὗ καὶ παλαιοῖς λόγοις ἡ ῥίζα τοῦ γένους ἀνάγραπτος κἂν τοῖς πράγμασι δὲ τὸ φιλόκαλον διαφαίνεται), a man who 'both takes pleasure in speeches and is a friend of those who are nourished by speeches' (καὶ χαίρει λόγοις καὶ οἰκειοῦται τοὺς λόγων τροφίμους).[23] The man is not directly addressed, but he is most probably the implied addressee of the ekphrasis, as indicated by the opening paragraph's praise of his intellectual virtues and 'love of beauty'. The text suggests a situation of patronage based on similarity between the addressee and the writer. Yet, though they appreciate the same things, the writer produces them for the addressee, thus indicating an asymmetrical friendship. The word play on παλαιοῖς λόγοις, most probably a pun on the addressee's name Palaiologos, means that the identity of the patron is embedded in the text so that the characterization of him is as much an object as the object of the description (the Cyclops carved in red stone). However, while the indication of the name allows the audience (and modern readers) to identify the patron, the characterization of him does not necessarily reflect the real person at all – from the textual point of view he embodies his function in the socio-cultural system rather than a historical person. As such he is as much part of the literary construction as is the object of the description and the setting in which it has been placed (the house of the patron).[24] While the identification of the patron may help us to see a pattern in the wider network of Manasses' social

---

[21] Zetzel 1982: 88.   [22] Zetzel 1982: 95.
[23] Manasses, *Description of the Cyclops* 17–18 (Sternbach); tr. Nilsson 2011: 127, revised.
[24] Cf. Zetzel 1972 (and Chapter 2 above on the significance of settings).

relations, the primary function of the embedded addressee may be poetic as much as social, since it is probably used for connotation rather than denotation (that is, implicit rather than explicit).²⁵

With a point of departure in this theoretical model, I examine in this chapter Manasses' preserved production of orations related to death, consisting of lamentations and consolatory discourses: the *Monody on the death of Theodora*, the *Consolation for John Kontostephanos*, the *Funerary oration on the death of Nikephoros Komnenos* and the *Monody on the death of his goldfinch*.²⁶ All four texts contain elaborate constructions of *personae* on the part of narrator, addressee and object, while at the same time exploring the relation between writer and patron in more or less explicit terms. A closer analysis of their 'poetics of patronage' allows us to better understand Manasses' careful construction of literary characters – both his own and others'.

Your Sorrow is My Concern

The Byzantines had several literary treatments of death, each related to various parts of the rituals surrounding the deceased. While the *epikedeion*, the *epitaphios logos*, the *monodia* and the *paramythetikos logos* belonged to different rhetorical genres and followed different authoritative models, they were at the same time interrelated – they 'overlapped with each other, and sometimes replaced each other'.²⁷ Since they were all concerned with death, they display many similarities not only thematically, but also as regards the way in which the writer focalizes the sorrow of the addressee or the audience. Such narrative strategies were taken over from the formal genres of oratory and in the twelfth century inserted into narratives such as the novels, where they could function as ways of engaging the audience in the emotional experiences of the protagonists.²⁸ Fictional texts were not

---

²⁵ Cf. Zetzel 1982: 99 (on the use of second-person address for connotation rather than denotation in Catullus).
²⁶ The fragmentarily preserved *Monody on the death of an anonymous man* (Τοῦ λογιωτάτου κυροῦ Μανασσῆ τοῦ ... μονῳδία ἐπὶ τῷ κυρῷ...), possibly Alexios Doukas, is not analysed in any detail here. On this oration, see Sternbach 1901: 193–4 (edition and brief commentary) and Sideras 1994: 191–2. On the four orations addressing members of the imperial family, see Sideras 1994: 190–5 (leaving out the monody on the goldfinch).
²⁷ Littlewood 1999: 23. On the interrelation of the different forms and their use as part of ritual lamentation, see Alexiou 1974. On the rhetorical forms and their generic blending, see Agapitos 1998 and 2003. For a recent discussion of the *epitaphios* and its performative and 'aural' aspects, see Bourbouhakis 2017: 126*–58*.
²⁸ In the case of Manasses' novel, see esp. frg. 3–4 and 73 (Mazal). On lamentation in the Komnenian novels, see Agapitos 2003: 14; see also Nilsson 2017.

the only ones open to such devices; historical writings such as Anna Komnene's *Alexiad* were as well.²⁹ In the case of Manasses, elements of grief were included in his narrative poem the *Itinerary*, as the narrator wished to display his sorrow at losing the intellectual advantages of Constantinople. The different expressions of grief are accordingly to be seen not only as one or several rhetorical genres, but also as a narrative mode that can be used for various occasions and functions. In this sense, lamentation can function in a manner similar to ekphrasis: as a rhetorical discourse that can be used either for individual pieces (orations or letters) or as a means of creating a certain effect in other narrative forms (both in prose and verse).

Manasses' two texts addressed to John Kontostephanos (c.1128–76/82) on the death of his wife Theodora (died c.1175), preserved in the same manuscript,³⁰ offer the possibility of comparing the formal lamentation of the monody and the more personal expression of grief in the consolation. The marriage between Theodora and John had taken place in c.1165 (commemorated in an *epithalamion* by Manganeios Prodromos³¹) and Manasses' texts support the assumption that Theodora died young, leaving behind not only a grieving husband but also small children.³² Since Kontostephanos also played a role in the *Itinerary* (c.1161), being in charge of the search for a new wife for his uncle Manuel I Komnenos, we may assume a long-standing relationship between Manasses as a writer and Kontostephanos as benefactor or patron.

Let us begin by looking at the monody (Μονῳδία ἐπὶ τῇ σεβαστῇ κυρᾷ Θεοδώρᾳ τῇ τοῦ Κοντοστεφάνου Ἰωάννου συζύγῳ), which was most probably written (or at least performed) before the consolation, perhaps at Theodora's funeral.³³ The rhetor opens by drawing attention to his own task:

> Woe is me, tuning again a mournful lyre, striking up again a discordant melody. This solemn meeting is not for beautifully performed dances, not for wedding tunes, not for songs; for the dark night of the garments and the

---

²⁹ Agapitos 2003: 14–15.
³⁰ Marcianus Append. XI, 22, which contains other texts by Manasses: the *Monody on the death of his goldfinch* and the two texts addressing John Kontostephanos are followed by the *Encomium of Michael Hagiotheodorites* and four letters. On these other texts of the same ms, see below, Chapter 4. On the ms, see Mioni 1985: vol. 3, 116–31.
³¹ Castellani 1888, attributing it to Theodore Prodromos, but cf. Magdalino 1993: 496 (*Poem* 33 of Manganeios Prodromos). The *epithalamion* has been preserved in the same ms as the two orations that Manasses wrote for John Kontostephanos, the Marcianus Append. XI, 22.
³² See Sideras 1994: 194. See also below.
³³ See Sideras 1994: 193–5 (on the monody) and 194 (on the dating).

dullness of the clothing is for lamentations, for cries of sadness. This gathering is not for celebrations, nor for revelling, but for tears, for wailing; for the participants' cries are not for a wedding and the melody is sung not for a feast and not for joy. This fire is sad and without joy, not for a bride, not for a wedding. The faces are gloomy, the eyes are downcast, the circles of their eyes are moist with tears.

> Ὤμοι ἐγὼ πάλιν πενθίμην λύραν ἁρμόζομαι, πάλιν μέλος παράμουσον ἀναβάλλομαι. οὐκ ἐπὶ καλλιχόροις χορείαις ὁ θίασος, οὐκ ἐν ὑμεναίοις, οὐκ ἐν ᾠδαῖς· ἡ γὰρ νὺξ τῶν ἀμφίων καὶ τὸ ἀλαμπὲς τῆς ἀναβολῆς ἐν ὀλοφυρμοῖς, ἐν ὀλολυγμοῖς. οὐκ ἐπὶ πανηγύρεσιν οὐδ' ἐπὶ κώμοις ὁ σύλλογος, ἀλλ' ἐπὶ δάκρυσιν, ἀλλ' ἐπ' οἰμωγαῖς· βοᾷ γὰρ ἀνυμέναια καὶ μέλος ἀνέορτον ᾄδει καὶ ἄναυλον. πῦρ σκυθρωπὸν καὶ ἄχαρι τοῦτο τὸ πῦρ, οὐκ ἐπιθαλάμιον, οὐ γαμήλιον. τὰ πρόσωπα συννεφῆ, τὰ βλέφαρα κατηφῆ, τῶν ὀφθαλμῶν οἱ κύκλοι διάβροχοι δάκρυσιν.[34]

He goes on to describe the gloomy occasion in the same kind of negative terms, and then draws even more attention to himself and the function of his voice:

> Woe is me, luckless rhetor pressed by a heavy fate, for standing here as the mourner of such an enormous harm and for drinking in advance of those present here a bowl brimming with grief, trod by Hades and mixed by Death. For the others, who are beginning to walk on the tragic stage, the suffering is so much more moderate, insofar as they have not often known the affairs of those to be mourned; but for me, the more familiar the qualities of the deceased are to me, the more unbearable is the pain.

> Ὦ βαρυδαίμων ῥήτωρ ἐγὼ καὶ βαρύποτμος, ὅτι κακοῦ τοσοῦδε καθίσταμαι πενθητὴρ καὶ τοῖς παροῦσι προπίνω κρατῆρα γόου περιχειλῆ, ὃν ᾅδης ἐληνοβάτησεν, ὃν ἐκέρασε θάνατος. τοῖς μὲν οὖν ἄλλοις, ὅσοι σκηνῆς κατάρχουσι τραγικῆς, τοσούτῳ μετριώτερον τὸ δεινόν, ὅσῳ καὶ τὰ τῶν θρηνουμένων πολλάκις οὐκ ἔγνωσται· ἐμοὶ δὲ ὅσῳ τὰ τῆς κειμένης καλὰ γνωριμώτερα, τοσούτῳ τὸ ἄλγος ἀφορητότερον.[35]

He thus seems to indicate that less experienced rhetoricians might feel and suffer less than he, who has done this many times ('tuning *again* a mournful lyre, striking up *again* a discordant melody') and knew well the deceased. It is not clear whether this is directed at any rhetoricians in particular, those present at the funeral, or just a general expression of his own experience and personal loss. The rhetor then goes on to praise the

---

[34] Manasses, *Monody on the death of Theodora* 1–10 (Kurtz).
[35] Manasses, *Monody on the death of Theodora* 20–5 (Kurtz).

virtues of the dead (she is a garden of self-control, a golden plane tree of virtues, and other common images of female virtue), which make her a decoration for the female sex (later sustained with a series of mythological *exempla*);[36] now she is dying before her time.[37] There are parallels in language and imagery with the *Verse chronicle* and the novel fragments, making it clear that Manasses was still recycling his earlier work in the 1170s, or perhaps simply using his favourite or most successful expressions, drawn from ancient literature, in order to make his narrative voice clear.[38] More important here, the rhetor presents himself as a vicarious mourner, taking on the sorrow of the husband and in this way sharing his love for the deceased wife.[39] Returning to his experience in mourning, the rhetor describes how he is torn between the praise of Theodora's qualities and the lament that is at hand.

> I have mourned many people on many occasions, I have lent my tongue to many and offered my due, but now I wrestle with an ambiguous mind and I am balancing between two divergent pulls of weight; for the stream of qualities and the sweet sea of virtue pulls me to itself, but the sad circumstances draw me in the other direction and force me to strike up the lament – also the law of the craft pushes me that way and as it overtakes me it entirely immerses me in the misfortune.
>
> Πολλοὺς πολλάκις ἐπένθησα, πολλοῖς τὴν γλῶσσαν ἐχαρισάμην καὶ ἀφωσιωσάμην τὴν ὀφειλήν· νῦν δ' ἀλλὰ διπλῇ παλαίῳ γνωσιμαχίᾳ καὶ ταῖς εἰς ἑκατέραν ἀνθολκαῖς ἀντιταλαντεύομαι· ὁ μὲν γὰρ λιμνασμὸς τῶν καλῶν καὶ τῆς ἀρετῆς τὸ γλύκιον πέλαγος ἐφέλκεταί με πρὸς ἑαυτό, τὰ δὲ τῆς συμφορᾶς ἑτέρωθεν ἀντιπεριάγουσι καὶ τὸ πένθιμον ψαλάττειν βιάζονται· ῥέπει δέ μοι πρὸς τοῦτο καὶ τῆς τέχνης ὁ νόμος καὶ ἤδη λαβὼν ὅλον με τοῦ πάθους ποιεῖ.[40]

---

[36] See Manasses, *Monody on the death of Theodora* 32–41 (Kurtz) (on virtue and garden imagery); 42 (on dying before her time); 106–44 (Biblical and Graeco-Roman *exempla*).

[37] As argued by Sideras 1994: 194, this is probably not just the topos of *mors immatura*; the children are mentioned in *Monody on the death of Theodora* 98–101 (Kurtz) (small children present at the funeral) and *Consolation for John Kontostephanos* 191–3 (Kurtz) (an infant).

[38] See e.g. Manasses, *Monody on the death of Theodora* 102 (Kurtz), cf. *Aristandros and Kallithea* frg. 17.3 (Mazal) (a reworking of the popular *Il.* 16.34); *Monody on the death of Theodora* 139 (Kurtz), cf. *Verse chronicle* 814–39 (Lampsides) (the story of Kandaules, drawn from Herodotus); *Monody on the death of Theodora* 164 (Kurtz), cf. *Verse chronicle* 4335 (Lampsides) (Ps. 112:9). On Manasses' recycling of his own work, see below, Chapter 6.

[39] See esp. Manasses, *Monody on the death of Theodora* 63–101 (Kurtz), on the tears needed to mourn and the references to the husband's love, drawing on the *Song of Songs* (employed for erotic effect in, for instance, the contemporary novel by Makrembolites; see Nilsson 2001: 279–80).

[40] Manasses, *Monody on the death of Theodora* 176–82 (Kurtz).

The monody ends where it began, with the focus back on the rhetor himself: 'Woe is me, ill-starred and heavily grieving rhetor – I prepared such a bitter cup, plucked such gloomy strings, played such a mournful song.' (184–7: ὦ ῥήτωρ κακοδαίμων ἐγὼ καὶ βαρυπενθής, οἷον σκύφον πικράζοντα ἤρτυσα, οἵαν κατηφῆ κινύραν ἐψάλαξα, οἷον μέλος γοερὸν ὑπελύρισα.) An audience familiar with the texts by Manasses may recognize in this last line an echo of the rhetor's complaint in the *Itinerary*,[41] and, as noted by Kurtz, the Manassean style – marked by, for instance, a specific vocabulary of neologisms, compounds and gnomic expressions – is recognizable throughout the monody.[42] Moreover, he continuously underlines his position as an experienced rhetor who knows how to channel the sorrow of his addressee.

This resonates also in the consolation (Παραμυθητικὸν εἰς τὸν σεβαστὸν κύρον Ἰωάννην τὸν Κοντοστέφανον),[43] but the tone is different, possibly due to the generic demands. To a modern reader it may even appear as less compassionate, since 'consolation' consists more or less in a demand to stop grieving. But as noted by Antony Littlewood, a well-written consolation is a way of demonstrating one's sincerity,[44] and it is likely that the focus on the addressee here is the rhetor's way of demonstrating, again, his close relationship with his patron Kontostephanos. The consolation begins by recalling the monody and underlining the role of the rhetor:

> I come again to mix you another bowl of rhetoric, you most noble of men; I come to you as a rhetor, not to sing a sad melody, nor to tear open your wounds of grief or to drink in advance for you a cup filled with the bitter herb of lamentation, but I come to subdue the anger of your soul and to tame the rage and gather liquid honey from both branches of sweet grapevine; and soon this drink will seem to you to banish both pain and restlessness, to be superior to the drug of Helen, the one she used to sweeten the bowl of Telemachos.
>
> Ἥκω πάλιν ῥητορικῆς ἕτερον κρατῆρά σοι κερασάμενος, ἀνδρῶν εὐγενέστατε· ἥκω σοι ῥήτωρ, οὐ μέλος ᾄσων ἀνέορτον οὐδ᾽ ἀναξανῶν σοι τὰ ἕλκη τοῦ πένθους οὐδὲ προπιόμενός σοι φιάλην, ἣν ἀψινθία θρήνων

---

[41] Cf. Manasses, *Monody on the death of Theodora* 184 (Kurtz): ὦ ῥήτωρ κακοδαίμων ἐγὼ καὶ βαρυπενθής, with *Itinerary* 2.91–111 (on which see above, Chapter 2). It echoes at the same time Manasses, *Monody on the death of Theodora* 20, cited above (Ὦ βαρυδαίμων ῥήτωρ ἐγὼ καὶ βαρύποτμος). This repetition with variation technique characterizes Manasses' *Itinerary* as a whole.
[42] Kurtz 1900: 623 and 627.
[43] The manuscript contains no attribution of this text to Manasses, but the placement in the ms directly after the monody (ff. 168ʳ–70ᵛ), along with the opening line and the distinct Manassean style, make the attribution certain.
[44] Littlewood 1999.

πληροῖ, ἀλλ' ἥκω σοι τὸ τῆς ψυχῆς ἀγριαῖνον καταστελῶν καὶ τὸ ἀνοιδοῦν
ἡμερώσων καὶ βλίσων πόσιν ἐξ ἑκατέρου γλυκυχύμου τοῦ κλήματος· καὶ
τάχα σοι τοῦτο τὸ πόμα φανήσεται νηπενθές τε καὶ ἄσχολον καὶ ὑπὲρ τὰ
φάρμακα τῆς Ἑλένης, οἷον ἐκείνη τὸν Τηλεμάχου κρατῆρα ἐγλύκανεν.[45]

The drug of Helen (*Od.* 4.219–34) took away all sorrow and pain over a
loved one, but with that it also made the stories told to Telemachos (about
the bravery of his father) even more pleasant, because his pain at the loss of
his father would be subdued. The rhetor continues to say that he has come
to anoint the wound with an antidote at the right time (κατὰ καιρόν),
because the day before yesterday – presumably the day when the monody
was performed – a lack of spirit still reigned due to the festering sore, the
heart and eyes were overwhelmed by tears (12–21). Now, however, the
fierce pain has begun to withdraw and the present discourse will help to
quench the fire and calm the stormy sea (24–5). The soothing power of the
words themselves are thus underlined, and perhaps also (as in the case of
Helen) the soothing power of stories. Because the consolation contains
numerous *exempla*, even more than the monody, drawn from various
Graeco-Roman sources and the Old Testament – the honey drawn from
'both branches of sweet grapevine' (ἐξ ἑκατέρου γλυκυχύμου τοῦ
κλήματος). This suits the noble and learned addressee, underlines the
rhetor, and with this he seems to turn the focus away from himself but
in fact creates a *persona* for his addressee based on similarity with himself:

> I know that your mind, wise in the things of God, is brimming with all that is
> good, like a vessel of good qualities, and that there is nothing that has escaped
> your vast knowledge. If you wish, I will open for you a beautiful garden, whose
> gardeners and caretakers are many, which is irrigated with streams, all deco-
> rated with trees, bearing fruits, bearing flowers, an outright comfort for the
> soul; and you will cull the noble fruit, the fair beauty, the pleasure from our
> Scripture, which the deep river of the spirit has planted, the rays of God's sun
> has matured, and a large number of inspired men have cared for and tended to;
> you will gather a rose from the thorns and grapes from the shrubs (for this is
> what surrounds them),[46] the offsprings of profane and Hellenic wisdom.
>
> Οἶδά σου τὸν θεόσοφον νοῦν, ὡς πλήρης παντὸς ἀγαθοῦ, ὡς δεξαμενὴ τῶν
> καλῶν, καὶ οὐδὲν ὅτι τὴν σὴν γνῶσιν τὴν πολλὴν διαπέφευγεν. εἰ δὲ
> βούλει, κῆπον ἐγώ σοι καλὸν ὑπανοίξω, οὗ φυτουργοὶ πολλοὶ καὶ
> μελεδῶνες,[47] κατάρρυτον ὕδασι, κατάκοσμον δένδρεσιν, ὀπωροφόρον,

---

[45] Manasses, *Consolation for John Kontostephanos* 4–10 (Kurtz). Cf. tr. in Littlewood 1999: 34.
[46] Cf. Luc. 6:44.
[47] The text's μελεδῶνες does not really seem to make sense, so I assume rather the plural of the poetic μελεδωνεύς or the prosaic μελεδωνός, here translated as caretaker.

ἀνθεοφόρον, ἄντικρυς ψυχῆς παραμύθιον· καὶ δρέψῃ μὲν τὴν ὀπώραν τὴν εὐγενῆ, τὴν καλλονὴν τὴν εὐπρόσωπον, τὴν ἐκ τῆς ἡμετέρας Γραφῆς ἡδονήν, ἣν μοσχεύει μὲν τοῦ πνεύματος ὁ βαθὺς ποταμός, ἡλικιοῖ δὲ ὁ θεοῦ καὶ ἀνύστακτος ἥλιος, γεωργοῦσι δὲ καὶ κηπεύουσι πληθὺς πνευματοφορήτων ἀνδρῶν· τρυγήσεις δὲ καὶ ῥόδον ἐξ ἀκανθῶν καὶ σταφυλὴν ἀπὸ βάτου (τοῦτο δὴ τὸ περιφερόμενον), τὰ τῆς νόθου καὶ ἑλληνικῆς σοφίας κυήματα.[48]

This garden of Biblical and Hellenic (pagan) beauties – an anthology in a very literally metaphorical sense[49] – will be provided by the rhetor and will be able to comfort the mourning man, who has unjustly lost his golden ear of corn and bunch of grapes to Hades (66–71).[50] Included among these stories drawn from various sources is the fairly unexpected account of Aristophanes on the origin of man that is told in Plato's *Symposium*. The well-known story of how man was originally whole but then divided into two, which turns life into an eternal search for the other half,[51] is here introduced in the manner of storytelling and used as a way of explaining and soothing the extreme pain of the mourning husband.[52]

After such repeated requests to stop mourning, supported by numerous *exempla*, the rhetor finally returns to the pain of the wound and the need for it to heal, if not for the sake of the husband, then at least for the children (315). The consolation then closes with another reference to the effect of stories and the relation between writer and addressee:

> What do you say? Are you convinced by these stories? Or should I pour out more words and babble on? I think that would suit small-minded and feeble-witted persons, but for an intelligent man even this small selection brings great strength. I shall therefore end the discourse here and will relax now the oar and let the ship rest,[53] but God who creates and transforms

---

[48] Manasses, *Consolation for John Kontostephanos* 57–66 (Kurtz).
[49] Cf. Basil the Great's famous *Address to young men on the right use of Greek literature*, ch. 4, which expresses a related imagery of bees (readers/writers) collecting honey from the flowers (books).
[50] It is interesting to note that the imagery of the passage is very close to that of Theodore Prodromos' poem *To a garden* (Hörandner no. 158), recently suggested to have been written as a book epigram for an anthology; see Zagklas 2014: 395–402. See also Nilsson 2013: 20–4.
[51] Plato, *Symp.* 189e.
[52] Manasses, *Consolation for John Kontostephanos* 145–7 (Kurtz): … διηγήσομαι· ἀλλά με μὴ φιλόμυθον εἶναι νομίσῃς, μηδὲ κατὰ τοὺς ἀγύρτας τῶν γερόντων καὶ λογοπλάστας καὶ μυθολέσχας, … The entire episode with introductory and concluding remarks covers *Consolation for John Kontostephanos* 142–75 (Kurtz).
[53] Cf. Manasses, *Encomium of Michael Hagiotheodorites* 389 (Horna) (cited and translated below, Chapter 4), and Manasses, *Verse chronicle* 6609 (Lampsides): Ἀλλὰ λοιπὸν εἰς σιωπῆς ὅρμον ὁ λόγος στήτω, the first line of the closing passage. Note also the closing verses 6618–20, employing the same ship metaphor: καὶ τοίνυν ἀναψώμεθα κάλων πρυμνήτην ὧδε, | τοῦ πλοῦ τὴν κώπην σχάσαντες καὶ στείλαντες τὰ λαίφη· | οὐ γὰρ περάσιμά φασι τὰ τῶν Γαδείρων πέρα.

everything, the living God, life itself, the indestructible, the everlasting, the consolation, may he, in his comforting, comfort your soul and convince it to carry the burden easier, even if it is heavy and burdensome.

τί φῄς; πείθομέν σε τούτοις τοῖς λόγοις; ἢ δεῖ καὶ πλείονας ἐπαντλεῖν καὶ στομολεσχεῖν; ἀλλ' οἶμαι ταῦτα τοῖς μικροφύεσιν ἀνθρώποις ἁρμόττειν καὶ τοῖς ὀλιγογνώμοσι, παρ' ἀνδρὶ δὲ συνετῷ καὶ τὰ μικρὰ ταῦτα μεγάλην ἐπάγεσθαι τὴν ἰσχύν. ἡμεῖς μὲν οὖν ἐνταῦθα τοῦ λόγου στησόμεθα καὶ χαλάσομεν ἤδη τὴν κώπην καὶ περὶ τὸν πλοῦν μετριάσομεν, ὁ δὲ θεὸς ὁ πάντα ποιῶν καὶ μετασκευάζων, ὁ ζῶν, ἡ ζωή, ὁ ἀνώλεθρος, ὁ ἀείζωος, ἡ παράκλησις, παρακαλῶν παρακαλέσαι σου τὴν ψυχὴν καὶ πεῖσαι ῥᾷον φέρειν τὸ ἄγχος, εἰ καὶ βαρὺ καὶ δυσάγκαλον.[54]

In the consolation, there is accordingly more focus on the creation of an addressee *persona* than in the monody, though always in relation to the *persona* of the narrator. If the monody was performed at the funeral and the second was sent in the form of a letter, the writer being out of town,[55] there may not have been the same need for self-display on the second occasion; the need to shape the *persona* of the patron remained, however, the same. Even if we know little about the relation between Kontostephanos and Manasses and have to rely on the information that can be drawn from these two texts and the *Itinerary*, the composition of two different texts on the occasion of the same event and the way in which the writer in these texts constructs his *persona* and that of the addressee remain important indications of a strong bond between writer and patron. Both texts approach their addressees with a sense of similarity, but this seems to mark the more 'private' consolation to a larger extent than the monody. The more marked traces of contiguity in the latter may be related to its 'public' character (the performance at the funeral).[56]

Yours, As Ever

A writer–patron relationship also seems to be reflected in the *Funerary oration on the death of Nikephoros Komnenos* (Λόγος ἐπικήδειος τοῦ φιλοσόφου κυροῦ Κωνσταντίνου τοῦ Μανασσῆ πρὸς τὸν ἀποιχόμενον ἐπὶ τῶν δεήσεων κυρὸν Νικηφόρον Κομνηνὸν τὸν ἔκγονον τοῦ καίσαρος),

---

[54] Manasses, *Consolation for John Kontostephanos* 317–24 (Kurtz).
[55] Cf. Littlewood 1999: 34 with n. 72. At the end of the *Consolation for John Kontostephanos* (619–22), Manasses refers to it as an *epitymbion* ('lament by the tomb'), having not been present at his death and not having offered any 'monodic libations' (χοὰς μονῳδούς).
[56] Cf. Agapitos 2008 on public and private death in the works of Michael Psellos.

even if such a relation is not known from any other sources.⁵⁷ Nikephoros Komnenos died c.1173, which means that this oration was probably composed a couple of years before the two orations addressed to Kontostephanos. Nikephoros was the grandson of Anna Komnene and Nikephoros Bryennios, son of John Doukas by his second marriage.⁵⁸ As we will see, his relation to these two writing ancestors is significant for the construction of Nikephoros' *persona* in the present oration. Since the object of a funerary lament or oration is dead at the time of the performance, the function of the *persona* is of course different from that of an addressee. However, the characterization can still be based on contiguity and/or similarity and thus follow the same principle of a metonymic relationship between writer and receiver – even if not present, the deceased is still the receiver of the text, addressed in his or her absence to the audience.

The opening passage contains elaborate garden imagery of the kind Manasses employs for various occasions, here used to describe a marvellous tree from Arabia: in its prime providing perfect fruit and gracious beauty, it withers away and dies young.⁵⁹ The gardener is struck by sorrow:

> Now he who has planted the tree and has been toiling for it, not bearing such a sight worthy of tears, takes his fellow farmers and makes them fellow mourners of the misfortune and as though it were a dead man, he grieves over the tree and laments and besprinkles the ground with the brine of tears. This oration is like the one for that tree, even though this is no Arabian fable.
>
> But the high-minded and noble Doukas, having cultivated a well-planted plant, I mean this good Komnenos, and tending him with the dews of education, gardening him with the moistures of wisdom and irrigating him sufficiently with prowess drawn from books ...
>
> ὁ τοίνυν φυτοσκαφήσας τὸ δένδρον καὶ περὶ ἐκεῖνο μογήσας τοιαύτην θέαν οὐ φέρων δακρύων ἀξίαν, τοὺς συγγεωργοὺς παραλαβὼν συνθρηνητάς τε τοῦ πάθους ποιεῖται καὶ ὡς ἐπὶ νεκρῷ τῷ φυτῷ κόπτεται καὶ πενθεῖ καὶ τῶν δακρύων τῇ ἄλμῃ κατάρδει τὸ δάπεδον. ὁ μὲν δὴ κατὰ τὸ δένδρον ἐκεῖνο λόγος τοιοῦτος, εἴ γε τέως μὴ μῦθος τοῦτο ἀρράβιος.

---

⁵⁷ The oration has been preserved in two mss: Vat. Barber. Gr. 240 and Vat. Urb. Gr. 141 (only the beginning); see Kurtz 1910.

⁵⁸ On Nikephoros Komnenos, see Barzos 1984: vol. 2, 87–95. On Nikephoros and his family, see also Sideras 1994: 182–3.

⁵⁹ I have not been able to locate other references to such a story; the only other reference to Arabia in the texts by Manasses is to an Arabic horse in the *Description of a little man* 9 (Messis and Nilsson). Cf. the presence of the 'Indian stone' in the *Address by the way* and the potentially exotic (oriental?) character of Manasses' fragmentarily preserved novel; see below, Chapter 4, n. 116, and Chapter 6.

Ἀλλ' ὅ γε μεγαλόφρων Δούκας καὶ εὐγενὴς καλλιφυὲς γεωργήσας φυτόν,
τὸν καλὸν ἐκεῖνον φημὶ Κομνηνόν, καὶ δρόσοις μὲν παιδείας μοσχεύσας,
σοφίας δὲ νοτίσι κηπεύσας καὶ τὴν ἐκ τῶν βίβλων ἀνδρείαν ἱκανῶς
ἐπαντλήσας αὐτῷ ...[60]

The passage goes on to describe the trouble that Doukas has gone through in educating his son in all possible ways, and the pain of now having to watch him die: death has pierced his heart with an arrow and now only sorrow and lament remain (48–55). The opening section of the oration thus establishes the care that Doukas has taken in educating his son and his position as the primary mourner, but also the *paideia* of the deceased. This becomes a theme in the oration, also permeating the section that is devoted to his glorious ancestry of two heroic families: the Doukai and the Komnenoi (99–110). Considerable space is devoted to Anna and Bryennios (120–69), elaborately praising Anna as a female intellectual and poet equal to her husband in intelligence and learning.[61] She is a Theano and a Sappho, but also a Hypatia and a Cleopatra – combining in her person not just philosophical and poetic capacities, but also a simple yet imperial character. As noted by Leonora Neville, 'Manasses's commemoration of Anna and Nikephoros, in the generation after their death, indicates that they succeeded in leaving a positive legacy as an intellectual couple',[62] but above all the passage supports the characterization of Nikephoros as one in a long line of intellectuals, worthy of the rhetor's praise. Also his father's interest in rhetoric and books is underlined, though it is primarily his success in war that is brought to the fore.[63] His mother is clearly no intellectual, but her basic skills in writing and speaking are still noted by the rhetor, with a special mention of her speed in writing and in taking care of the household – the writer himself has witnessed this and was impressed.[64]

---

[60] Manasses, *Funerary oration on the death of Nikephoros Komnenos* 25–33 (Kurtz).
[61] Two epigrams attributed to Anna Komnene have been preserved; see Sola 1911: 375–6.
[62] Neville 2016: 118. See also Kaldellis 2007: 258 and 284 on the use of ancient and Biblical literature in this part of the oration; *Funerary oration on the death of Nikephoros Komnenos* 90–3 and 124–8 (Kurtz) respectively.
[63] On the father, see Manasses, *Funerary oration on the death of Nikephoros Komnenos* 170–246 (Kurtz).
[64] Manasses, *Funerary oration on the death of Nikephoros Komnenos* 255–64 (Kurtz): ἡ δὲ οὐδὲ γραμμάτων ἔστιν ἀδίδακτος, οὐδ' ὡς οὕτως εἰπεῖν ἀγροικική τις καὶ ἄμουσος, ἀλλ' εὖ μὲν ἐπίσταται γράφειν δακτύλοις πτηνοῖς, εὖ δὲ τὸν λόγον ἐν ὁμιλίαις συνείρειν καὶ ὡς ἄν τις νόμων ἐθὰς διαλεκτικῆς. τοῖς δὲ λόγοις καὶ τὸ ἀστεῖον μὲν ἐπανθεῖ, ἀλλὰ καὶ τὸ στρυφνὸν ἀνακέκραται. καὶ γράφει, καὶ ταῦτα σὺν ταχυτῆτι, καὶ ταῦτα καλῶς τῶν κατ' οἶκον φροντίζει. εἶδον ἐγὼ πρᾶγμα καὶ θάμβους ἐπλήσθην· τὸν μὲν εἰς ἔργον ὀτρύνει, ἄλλου πυνθάνεται, εἰ κατώρθωταί οἱ ἃ ἐπιτέτραπται, τὸν δ' εὐθύνει περὶ τὰ ἐν χερσί, καὶ τοῦτο εὖ μάλα ἠπίως καὶ προσηνῶς, καὶ τὸ ἐπίχαρι σῴζει καὶ τὸ ἡρωικὸν συνεμφαίνει. Compared to other parts of the oration, the language here is surprisingly simple, possibly mirroring the linguistic register of the mother so that she would understand this passage at the performance.

Altogether, the praise of the family prepares for the characterization proper of the deceased, Nikephoros, but it also places the rhetor close to the family, with intimate knowledge of not only famous ancestors – which would be general knowledge – but also the way in which the household is run. The same intimate tone is maintained as the rhetor moves on to the object of the oration: Nikephoros himself. His childhood and early years are described in extreme detail: the way in which he showed a talent for rhetoric and grammar even as a child, how he impressed his teachers and then even the emperor.[65] It is in this context, in the description of Nikephoros as a kind of *Hofliterat*,[66] that the most well-known passage from this oration appears: a description of a grammar competition held at the court, with Nikephoros acting as rhetor or *grammatikos*.

> The moment had come when boys gather to wrestle with each other, those whom the … grammar has bred and made suckle the breast of schedographic foresight and now sends to the palace to fight like brave athletes in speechmaking before the emperor, who is acting as prize giver and game master. And then the command of the emperor to Komnenos – the child soldiers of words were watching his tongue, as though it were the judge of their strength. But what wisdom, what sweetness, what labyrinth of word-traps! How beautiful was there the surface, how cunning was there the depth; the bait was attractive to the eye and the hidden hook strong! The child was gaping, bewitched by what he saw, the trap immediately caught him. So capable was he [Nikephoros] of skilfully arranging a web of words and sneakily hiding a combination of industrious nets, and the praised fallacy … and devising the most efficient hunting implements.

> Ἐνειστήκει καιρός, καθ' ὃν συνίασι παῖδες ἀλλήλοις συμπλακησόμενοι, οὓς ἡ πρ.... γραμματικὴ ὠδινήσασα καὶ σχεδικῆς προνοίας οὖθαρ θηλάσαι ποιήσασα εἰς τὰ βασίλεια πέμπει γενναίους ἀθλευτὰς λογικῶς ἀγωνιουμένους ὑπὸ βραβευτῇ καὶ γυμνασιάρχῃ τῷ αὐτοκράτορι. καὶ τηνικαῦτα τὸ νεῦμα τοῦ βασιλέως ἐπὶ τὸν Κομνηνόν· καὶ οἱ τοῦ λόγου πυγμάχοι παιδίσκοι πρὸς τὴν ἐκείνου γλῶτταν ἑώρων ὡς τῆς αὐτῶν ἰσχύος χρηματίζουσαν βασανίστριαν. ἀλλὰ τῆς σοφίας ἐκείνου, ἀλλὰ τῆς

---

[65] The same representation of Nikephoros appears in the funerary oration written by Eustathios of Thessalonike and edited by Kurtz along with the oration by Manasses, but also and more notably in the letters addressed to him by Eustathios, in which the learned allusions underline the recipient's level of education and invite a playful intellectual and literary relationship; see Eustathios of Thessalonike, *Letters* 1–17, 18(?), 25, 28–29 and 35(?) (Kolovou). It seems likely that Eustathios had been Nikephoros' teacher (see esp. *Letter* 29.4: κατασοφίσῃ σὺ τὸν διδάσκαλον) and thereafter kept in touch and sometimes asked for support (see *Letters* 18 and 35, though the addressee of the latter has been questioned; Kolovou 2006: 151–2*). See also below, nn. 71–2.

[66] Sideras 1994: 183, n. 14. Central to this description of Nikephoros in the *Funerary oration on the death of Nikephoros Komnenos* are lines 453–98.

μελιχρότητος, ἀλλὰ τοῦ λαβυρίνθου τῶν δόλων τῶν λογικῶν. ὡς καλὸν ἐκεῖ καὶ τὸ ἐπιπόλαιον, ὡς εὐφυὲς ἐκεῖ καὶ τὸ κατὰ βάθους, καὶ τὸ κατ' ὄψιν δέλεαρ ἑλκτικὸν καὶ τὸ λανθάνον ἄγκιστρον κραταιόν. ἐπέχαινε μὲν ὁ παιδίσκος τῷ φαινομένῳ θελγόμενος, ἡ δὲ παγὶς εὐθέως συνεῖχεν αὐτόν. οὕτως ἦν ταχὺς λογικὴν πλεκτάνην εὖ διαθέσθαι καὶ τεχνικῶν ἀρκύων ὑπορύξαι πλοκὴν ἐπαινούμενόν τε ψεῦδος ... καὶ θήρατρα μηχανήσασθαι δεξιώτατα.[67]

We may pause here to note the imagery of bird-catching, employed in several texts by Manasses,[68] but the praise of Nikephoros goes on: his rhythm and cadence in all metric varieties was amazing, he was superior to Archilochus as well as to Ion of Achaea and 'the poet of Cilicia' (Aratus, or perhaps Oppian), superior to his contemporaries and receiving the praise of the emperor. It is worth noting that the order in which Nikephoros is praised, first for his schedographic qualities and then for his poetic craft, is common also in other twelfth-century texts.[69] At the end of the long praise, the rhetor-narrator adds again a personal memory: how he recognized a literary borrowing from Polemon of Smyrna in a discourse by Nikephoros and pointed out the 'theft' (κλοπή) by saying 'My dear friend, you have been caught!' (493–4: ὦ κάλλιστε, εἶπον, ἑάλως). Nikephoros was not angry at this, but laughed, as was typical for his nature.[70]

This is the end of the part of the oration that focuses on characterizing Nikephoros as an intellectual, as the rhetor moves on to his other virtues and the consolation for the mourning father, but this characterization of Nikephoros has been carefully created from the very first image of the beautiful tree nurtured by *paideia* and thus covers the major part of the oration (about 500 of the 625 lines of the edition). Nowhere in the oration is it explicitly stated that Nikephoros was Manasses' patron, nor that Manasses had been one of Nikephoros' proud teachers. Eustathios of

---

[67] Manasses, *Funerary oration on the death of Nikephoros Komnenos* 453–66 (Kurtz). The text is damaged and I depend on the partial reconstruction proposed by Kurtz. Cf. tr. in Polemis 1996: 280.
[68] See Manasses, *Description of the catching of siskins and chaffinches*, *Description of a crane hunt* 42–52 (Kurtz), and the description of a grammar competition in the *Encomium of Michael Hagiotheodorites* 264–74 (Horna). All were clearly influenced by the prose paraphrase of Oppian's *Ixeutica*, probably used also for Makrembolites' novel, *Hysmine and Hysminias* 4.12.1. See above, Chapter 2 (on bird-catching), and below, Chapter 5 (on the grammar contests).
[69] See e.g. Nikephoros Basilakes, Prologue to *Oration* 1 (Garzya), on which Pizzone 2014b. See also Zagklas 2017: 239 and n. 71.
[70] Note the use of the verb ἁλίσκομαι, recalling the vocabulary of the bird-catching and thus the grammar contest. On the borrowing of citations and allusions as potential 'thefts', see Marciniak 2013: 107–8, citing and discussing an interesting introduction to an oration by Nikolaos Kataphloron, edited in Loukaki 2001.

Thessalonike too, in his monody to Nikephoros Komnenos, praises his intellectual capacities and mentions the grammar competition.[71] Should we then assume that both authors had witnessed the same or similar events at the court, and that they did so in their capacity as teachers?[72] It is known from other sources that such events took place and that both members of the imperial family and teacher–rhetoricians were present,[73] so even if the description of the event in Manasses' version is strongly coloured by the ancient imagery of bird-catching and thus could be seen as a literary construction (just like the characterization of the deceased), it is likely to reflect a real situation that was closely associated with teaching. It is reasonable to assume that Nikephoros, who was born c.1144 and probably went to school in the 1150s and perhaps early 1160s, had encountered both Eustathios and Manasses during his years of education in Constantinople.[74] Moreover, the way in which Manasses inserts personal experiences of not only Nikephoros himself, but also his mother, seems to indicate a familiarity and 'friendship' that probably should be defined in terms of patronage.

Regardless of exactly what the relation between Manasses and Nikephoros looked like, the text itself offers an image of a writer–patron relationship that is based on a teacher–student relationship in early years. This relation is clearly based on similarity, with the student eventually becoming more or less the teacher's peer.

My Goldfinch is Dead!

While the orations on the deaths of Theodora and Nikephoros were written for members of the Komnenos family and can be dated with some certainty to the later period of Manasses' career, the *Monody on the death of his goldfinch* (Τοῦ κυροῦ Κωνσταντίνου του Μανασσῆ μονῳδία ἐπὶ

---

[71] Eustathios of Thessalonike, *Funerary oration on the death of Nikephoros Komnenos* 229–39 (Kurtz). Eustathios' monody was edited together with the Funerary oration by Manasses, but they are not preserved in the same ms.
[72] On the student–teacher relationship of Eustathios and Nikephoros as read through *Letter* 7 of Eustathios, see Agapitos 2014: 11–12. See also above, n. 65.
[73] Cf. Zagklas 2014: 64 with n. 84, on an unpublished *schedos* in which the emperor himself is named a judge. On *schedos* contests in the eleventh century, see Bernard 2014: 259–66, but cf. Agapitos 2013 and 2014 on the twelfth century.
[74] Cf. Polemis 1996: 280–1, who argues that Manasses was a teacher, perhaps at the Patriarchal School in Constantinople. This question is discussed in further detail below, Chapter 5. On Eustathios as Nikephoros' teacher, see above nn. 65 and 72.

ἀστρογλήνῳ αὐτοῦ τεθνηκότι) is more difficult to place.⁷⁵ It is one of two known monodies on dead pet birds composed in the twelfth century; a *Monody on the death of his partridge* was written by Michael Italikos, probably in the 1130s or 1140s, when he was still teaching in Constantinople.⁷⁶ Texts involving animals are often relegated to the category of 'school texts', expected to have had as their main function the entertainment of bored students. Such cases have been made for the pseudo-Homeric *Batromyomachia* as well as for its Byzantine parody the *Katomyomachia*.⁷⁷ The latter has recently been considered in relation to the *Sketches of the mouse*, a set of two *schede* attributed to Theodore Prodromos but perhaps written by Manasses.⁷⁸ From this perspective, it may seem as if the *Monody on the death of his goldfinch* would belong rather in Manasses' production of educational texts,⁷⁹ but I have chosen to analyse it in this chapter for primarily two reasons. First, the monody is a form of lamentation, regardless of the object and regardless of a serious, playful or pedagogical purpose.⁸⁰ Second, the monody by Manasses is very much concerned with the literary activities of the narrator, which means that it may also shed light on the orations considered above and the way in which they, too, more or less explicitly discuss the situation of the rhetor in twelfth-century Constantinople.

The monody opens in the style of a typical lament, describing the task facing the rhetor:

---

⁷⁵ The text has been preserved in five mss. Three were known to Horna when he prepared his edition: Vindobonensis Phil. Gr. 149, Baroccianus 131 and Laurentianus Conv.soppr. 627; see Horna 1902: 23–6. In addition to these, the text appears also in Vat. Urb. Gr. 134 (which preserves also the *Description of the catching of siskins and chaffinches*) and Istanbul, Grafeia tēs Ekklēsias Panagias (tōn Eisodiōn) of the fourteenth and the eighteenth century respectively. Given that the three mss Kurtz used are of the thirteenth century, the later manuscripts are not that helpful to the text's constitution, but they indicate the enduring interest in this text by Manasses.

⁷⁶ See Horna 1902: 20: 'sie ist jedenfalls während der Lehrtätigkeit des Italikos, also wohl vor 1143 entstanden', and the tentative dating in Agapitos 1989: 60. Note, however, that Agapitos saw the monody not as a classroom text, but as a text for the *theatron*. The text was first edited by Horna together with the monody by Manasses (the Oxford ms contains both texts; see above, n. 75); Horna 1902: 9–10 (text) and 18–21 (commentary).

⁷⁷ For a recent study with references to previous work, see Marciniak and Warcaba 2018.

⁷⁸ See Meunier 2016 and cf. Marciniak 2017 (on the *Schede tou myos*). See further below, Chapter 5.

⁷⁹ Cf. Horna 1902: 17, who associates the monody rather with 'sport literature' such as the hunting ekphraseis and the *Origins of Oppian*; 'Man dürfte kaum fehlgehen, wenn man das Auftreten dieser Sportliteratur mit dem Umstande in Verbindung bringt, daß der Komnenenkaiser Manuel ... ein leidenschaftlicher Liebhaber jeder Art von Jagd war.' On hunting in the Komnenian period, see above, Chapter 2.

⁸⁰ Cf. Agapitos 1989, who shows that the monody by Italikos presents a generic blending of the rhetorical monody with the Hellenistic epigram tradition of dead pets – a merging of a form with a somewhat unexpected content.

> It is now for me to see you dead, my dearest goldfinch, and to pour libations from the bowls of discourse over you, lying there, and to exchange your sweet and siren-like chattering for funerary tunes. It is now for me to view the singing bird voiceless, the song-loving silent, the sweet-voiced speechless, and to tune the mournful lyre of discourse, to grieve over the sweet-speaking in lamenting echoes and to sing a re-echoing dirge for the so delightful music-making birds. Woe this bitter incident! The honey-sweet-voiced lies dead, the golden-winged has been deprived of his ornament, the noblest among birds and happy-voiced is gone.
>
> Ἔκειτό μοι καὶ σὲ νεκρὸν κατιδεῖν, ἀστρόγληνε φίλτατε, κἀκ τῶν τοῦ λόγου κρατήρων σπεῖσαί σοι κειμένῳ χοὰς καὶ τὰ γλυκερά σου στωμύλματα καὶ σειρήνεια μέλεσιν ἐπικηδείοις ἀμείψασθαι· ἔκειτό μοι τὸν λάλον στρουθὸν θεάσασθαι ἄφθογγον καὶ σιωπῶντα τὸν φιλῳδὸν καὶ τὸν μελίγηρυν ἄναυδον καὶ λόγου πενθίμην λύραν ἁρμόσασθαι καὶ γοεροῖς ἀπηχήμασι τὸν καλλίγλωττον κόψασθαι καὶ μέλψαι θρῆνον ἀντίδουπον τοῖς οὕτω τερπνοῖς μουσικεύμασι· φεῦ πικροῦ συναντήματος· κεῖται νέκυς ὁ μελιχρόφωνος, ὁ χρυσεόπτερος ἀπηγλάϊσται, ὁ εὐγενὴς ἐν στρουθοῖς καὶ καλλίστομος ᾤχετο.[81]

No one should resent him for lamenting his dead bird, continues the rhetor, since many brave men of the past have done the same: Alexander the Pheraean, Crassus the Roman and Alexander the Great all mourned their animals, as did Pyrrhus and Caesar (who even took revenge on a man for killing a quail).[82] After these historical and mythological *exempla*, the superior position of this particular goldfinch in relation to other birds is stated, especially as regards its musical skills (signalled already in the opening passage cited above). This is followed by a series of examples drawn from the writer's own life. Not only did the goldfinch sing beautifully, adorned with golden feathers – it was also in possession of generosity (φιλανθρωπία) and 'quick apprehension and capacity to strike up a tune at the right moment' (εὐσυνέτου καὶ τοῦ κατὰ καιρὸν τὴν ᾠδὴν ἀναβάλλεσθαι).[83] The rhetor calls upon the art of words (*logoi*) and the Muses to bewail the deceased, because

> no longer will he fill our ears with his babbling tunes, no longer will he measure himself against the one gaping over books and in the clearest voice

---

[81] Manasses, *Monody on the death of his goldfinch* 3.1–10 (Horna). This passage offers a good example of Manasses' linguistic variety even when he speaks of one and the same bird: the pet bird is surely a goldfinch (ἀστρόγληνος), known for its sweet song, but it is sometimes referred to as sparrow (στρουθός), here most often translated simply as 'bird'.
[82] Manasses, *Monody on the death of his goldfinch* 3.14–4.4 (Horna).
[83] Manasses, *Monody on the death of his goldfinch* 4.27–9 (Horna).

reading what is in them.[84] I was struggling with the Stagirite philosopher and elucidating the darkness of his thoughts; but my dear bird was incited to compete with what was said and exhibited in return his own wisdom. I was leafing through Euclid, intensely studying the mathematical theorem and distinguishing the problem; the goldfinch, as long as he heard my voice, was talkative and babbling and trotting along with the melody and sang most attentively; but when I went silent and allowed my tongue to be still, as I was stooping over the tablet in my hands and poking at the spread-out red pigment with my pencil and drew the figure, he held back the stream of his tongue and was silent and cut off his voice. One would say that he knew: there's a time to be silent and a time to speak.

> οὐκέτι μέλεσι καταλαλήσει τὰς ἀκοάς, οὐκέτι ἀντιφερίσει πρὸς τὸν ἐπιχάσκοντα βίβλοις καὶ τρανεστέρα φωνῇ τὰ ἐν ταύταις ἀναλεγόμενον· ἐγὼ μὲν περὶ τὸν Σταγειρίτην ἐφιλοπόνουν καὶ τῶν παρ' αὐτῷ νοημάτων τὸ σκότιον διελεύκαινον· ὁ δέ μοι φίλος στρουθὸς ἀντεφιλοτιμεῖτο πρὸς τὰ λαλούμενα καὶ τὴν ἐν αὐτῷ σοφίαν ἀντεπεδείκνυτο· ἐγὼ μὲν τὸν Εὐκλείδην ἀνέπτυσσον καὶ τὸ θεώρημα περιειργαζόμην καὶ ἐφιλοκρίνουν τὸ πρόβλημα· ὁ δὲ ἕως μὲν κατήκουε τῆς φωνῆς, λάλος τις ἦν καὶ ἀδόλεσχος καὶ ἐπετρόχαζε τῷ μέλει καὶ ᾖδεν ἐπιμελέστερον· ἐπὰν δὲ αὐτὸς ἐσιώπων καὶ τῇ γλώττῃ ἐπέταττον ἠρεμεῖν, ἐς δὲ τὸ ἐν χερσὶν σανίδιον μετεκύπταζον καὶ τὴν ἐπεστρωμένην μιλτόχροον κόνιν τῷ γραφείῳ σκαλεύων τὸ σχῆμα διέγραφον, ὁ δὲ τῆς γλώττης τὸ ῥεῦμα ἐπεῖχε καὶ ἡσυχίαν ἦγε καὶ ἀνέκοπτε τὴν φωνήν· εἶπέ τις ἄν, ὡς ἠπίστατο· καιρὸς τοῦ σιγᾶν καὶ καιρὸς τοῦ λαλεῖν.[85]

As the paragraph concludes with this Biblical citation (Ecclesiastes 3:6), the writer – demonstrating, once more, the need for blending both traditions[86] – attributes to his pet bird a sort of divine wisdom. Because this, as it turns out, is the true talent of the goldfinch: to support the intellectual in his reading of ancient texts. The example of Aristotle and Euclid is followed by that of Ptolemy, and the bird takes part not only in the private readings of the writer, but also in his encounters with other learned men:

> And once I had Plato's *Phaedrus* in my hands and was learning from it what is good by its nature and what is thought to be good, but then some men who had plentifully benefited from letters and learning came up to me, not to hear about *Phaedrus* and the good, but to tell me the usual things and supposedly to discuss with me, as if I were a friend.

---

[84] Cf. the imagery in Manasses, *Itinerary* 91–102 (Chryssogelos), on which see above, Chapter 2.
[85] Manasses, *Monody on the death of his goldfinch* 4.30–5.10 (Horna).
[86] See Manasses, *Consolation for John Kontostephanos* 58–66 (Kurtz), cited above.

80   3 The Occasion of Death: Patronage and the Writer

καί ποτε Πλάτωνος μὲν ἐγὼ τὸν Φαῖδρον εἶχον ἐν ταῖν χεροῖν καὶ ἐδιδασκόμην ἐκεῖθεν, ὅ τί ποτε τὸ φύσει καλὸν καὶ τὸ νομιζόμενον· ἄνδρες δέ μοι τῶν ἀφθόνως λόγου καὶ παιδείας ἀπηλαυκότων ἐπέστησαν, οὐκ ἀκουσόμενοι Φαίδρου καὶ τοῦ καλοῦ, ἀλλὰ τὰ εἰκότα μοι προσεροῦντες καὶ ὡς συνήθει μοι δῆθεν προσομιλήσοντες.[87]

The goldfinch, as if it were jealous and wanted to manifest its musical skill, began to sing and imitate different kinds of birds.[88] The men could not yet see the goldfinch, but tried to find the different birds that seemed to be singing, until the narrator laughed at them and pointed at the goldfinch. Then they praised it and one even came up with a refashioned (συγκολλῶν καὶ μεταπλάττων) Homeric verse.[89] The bird seemed to be aware of the praise and sang even louder.[90]

If we return to the monody by Italikos for a brief comparison, there are in fact few similarities beyond the title and the presence of a dead bird.[91] Both authors mention the Muses and the Sirens as ways of underlining the musical skills of their birds,[92] both refer to historical-mythological *exempla* (though Italikos only in passing)[93] and both reject potential mockery (though with different arguments).[94] The most apparent difference is the length, which could be seen in relation to Italikos' stated 'improvisation' of his discourse,[95] but the most significant difference is Manasses' focus on the literary activities of the narrator, not even mentioned in the monody by

---

[87] Manasses, *Monody on the death of his goldfinch* 6.14–19 (Horna).
[88] Manasses, *Monody on the death of his goldfinch* 6.19–24 (Horna): ὁ δὲ καλὸς ἐκεῖνος καί – ὅ τι ποτ' ἂν αὐτὸν ὀνομάσω – στρουθός, καθάπερ πρὸς τοὺς ἄνδρας φιλοτιμούμενος καὶ τῶν φωνῶν ἐπιδεικνύμενος τὴν εὐγένειαν καὶ τὸ ἄνθος δημοσιεύων τῆς μουσουργίας, πρῶτα μὲν ἀκανθυλλίδος μέλος ὑπῆρχε, μετὰ μικρὸν δ' ὑπεκελάδησεν ὡς ἀστρόγλησος καὶ μετ' ὀλίγον καθάπερ σπίνος εὐρυφωνότερον ἐλαλάγησε καὶ βοῆς τὸν ἀέρα ἐπλήρωσε.
[89] Manasses, *Monody on the death of his goldfinch* 7.1 (Horna): εἷς οἰωνὸς ἄριστος, ὅσων ἀντάξιος ἄλλων. Cf. *Il.* 12.243 and 11.514.
[90] Manasses, *Monody on the death of his goldfinch* 7.1–3 (Horna).
[91] The only comparison I know of was made by Horna 1902: 20, who notes primarily that Manasses' monody is longer and more carefully composed. Cf. Agapitos 1989: 62, n. 26, arguing that Manasses probably wrote his monody in imitation of Italikos. Horna also adds the *Enkomion of a dog* by Nikephoros Basilakes as somehow related to the two texts (though it seems to belong rather to the hunting ekphraseis; cf. above n. 79).
[92] Manasses, *Monody on the death of his goldfinch* 3.6, 4.20–1 and 4.29 (Horna); Italikos, *Monody on the death of his partridge* 103.6–7 and 104.21 (Gautier).
[93] Manasses, *Monody on the death of his goldfinch* 3.16–4.2 (Horna); Italikos, *Monody on the death of his partridge* 103.14–16 (Gautier).
[94] Manasses, *Monody on the death of his goldfinch* 3.14–16 (Horna); Italikos, *Monody on the death of his partridge* 104.27–32 (Gautier). Manasses finds support in the mythological *exempla*, Italikos in the Biblical tradition.
[95] Italikos, *Monody on the death of his partridge* 104.1–2 (Gautier): σχεδιάζω τὴν μονῳδίαν αὐτοματίσας. Note Agapitos 1989: 64–5, on the 'Improvisationsstil' of Italikos, rather than actual improvisation.

Italikos. While it seems likely that the 'improvised sketch' by Italikos was indeed produced within his activities as a teacher, it is more difficult to argue that Manasses' text is written primarily for students.[96] Instead, it seems to tie in with concerns that are also voiced in the other orations under consideration in this chapter: the tasks of a writer, the relation between the writer–rhetorician and his addressee. So what does the goldfinch signify in this monody? While it is certainly possible that the author had a pet bird whose death he sincerely mourned, we may also ask ourselves what the bird in this particular text represents.

It is clear that the death of the goldfinch becomes an excuse for the writer to expound on his readings of ancient authors, appearing both in the form of allusions/citations and as an enumeration of authors studied under the bird's supervision. From this perspective, the goldfinch functions as a sort of literary muse or even rhetorical alter ego of the writer – singing the most beautiful tunes, much like Manasses does himself in the eulogies of his patrons. The goldfinch also seems to signify the writer himself. However, it is the bird that supports the writer in his study of difficult texts, not the other way around. Moreover, the goldfinch is in possession of generosity (*philanthropia*) – a characteristic that is associated with patrons and especially imperial patronage.[97] Is the bird then to be seen as one of Manasses' patrons, much like the deceased Nikephoros in the oration discussed above?

As noted by Zetzel in the case of Roman poetry, the choice of addressee is not necessarily a function of the relationship between the poet and the person addressed, but it 'can be seen as a correlate of both the subject and the style of the poem'.[98] As an example Zetzel mentioned the substitution of the Muse for the human patron, which then becomes an indication of the poet's attitude to his society and his craft.[99] This mischievous and yet serious way of discussing patronage and society seems to be at play in Manasses' monody, as the writer creates two *personae* based on himself: the *grammatikos*/rhetor stooped over his books, laboriously preparing his classes/orations *and* the Muse/generous patron who supports and inspires his (own) work. The goldfinch, in this case, signifies both *personae*: the

---

[96] The Oxford ms has a title indicating that Italikos' partridge died while playing with students, but the text itself contains no such information; see Italikos, *Monody on the death of his partridge* 104.2–4 (Gautier), on the reason being unknown. The title adds a playful element to the exercise and suggests a school setting, but it cannot with certainty be ascribed to the author himself. The death of Manasses' goldfinch is referred to as the result of winter and perhaps age; Manasses, *Monody on the death of his goldfinch* 5.21 and 8.30–9.1 (Horna).
[97] Cf. above, n. 18.   [98] Zetzel 1982: 88.   [99] Zetzel 1982: 89.

writer and the patron, so that Manasses in this monody addresses himself and thus – within the fiction of the text – functions as his own patron. This literary and somewhat playful representation could be seen as a mirror of the reciprocal relationship between patron and writer: 'I helped you to sing by reading my books for you' – 'I write you a monody because you consoled me during my hard work.'

The monody ends with the dejected question of the writer: 'And who, after you, will ease my pains, who will fill my humble abode with chatter, who will distract me when I am sick?' (9.2–3: καὶ τίς μοι μετὰ σὲ τοὺς πόνους ὑποκουφίσοι, τίς δὲ τῆς ταπεινοκαλύβης μοι καταστωμυλεύσεται, τίς δέ με ψυχαγωγήσοι νοσηλευόμενον;) If one follows the interpretation outlined above, the answer would be: no one but yourself, just as before. The narrative *persona* here seems to be based on an experienced character, knowing that in the end one is left to fend for oneself; at the same time, the activities described in the monody may be associated with an earlier career stage, perhaps that of a teacher. Either *persona* tells us little or nothing about the dating of the text. It is likely that Manasses knew about the monody by Italikos, written one or several decades before, but he turned his own monody into something completely different – an elaborate literary play on the creation of *personae*.

The Good Teacher and the Generous Donor

The aim of this chapter has been to approach patronage from the perspective of texts rather than external evidence, allowing the narrative and literary constructions of characters – writer and addressee as well as object – to be at the centre of analysis. In practice, I have sometimes leaned in the direction of a more patron-centred approach, when the historical context has allowed me to. My theoretical point of departure was that the relationship between writer and patron is to be seen as an interplay between the occasion at which a text is performed and the addressee/audience. At that occasion of performance, the text has the opportunity to demonstrate the rhetorical and literary sensibility of the addressee/patron, who may or may not represent a real person. This anthropological-semiotic model has allowed me to read a series of rhetorical treatments of death as vehicles for discussing the role of the writer in society.[100] The overall question is still, as in the previous chapter, related to self-representation: who is 'Manasses' in these texts? And who are his addressees, beyond being assumed patrons?

[100] Cf. Zetzel 1982: 95.

First of all, one may conclude that the narrative *persona* is very much present in these texts, even when they focalize the sorrow of the addressee (as in the case of the orations at the death of Theodora). He is characterized as an experienced rhetor[101] who has enjoyed a long-term relationship with the families of John Kontostephanos and Nikephoros Komnenos, who were both grandchildren of Anna Komnene.[102] This experienced *persona* of the writer is also employed in the construction of the *personae* of the addressees, as the writer implicitly describes his relationship to them as based on similarity – their *paideia* and rhetorical skills match those of the rhetor himself and their interplay is thus shaped by this similarity.[103] One may note a similar characterization of other characters appearing in the orations, most notably the detailed *personae* of Anna Komnene and Bryennios, who are also – but only to some extent – shaped by means of similarity. Contiguity also comes into play here, probably because of the particularly high status of these two family members.[104] Anna seems to be an exception to an otherwise gendered characterization of family members: Theodora is characterized in a rather conventional manner, based on typically female virtues, as is the mother of Nikephoros Komnenos. However, the 'familiarity' that characterizes the relationship between the writer and his addressees involves also their families, so that the personal details even in the case of female *personae* (Theodora's premature death and young children, the household skills of Nikephoros' mother) offer a slightly different picture than more conventional orations or poems based on contiguity. In the case of Theodora, one may compare her characterization here with the one in the *epithalamion* by Manganeios Prodromos, written for her marriage with John in 1165; the latter is clearly built on contiguity – symbolic praise of the Komnenian power – rather than similarity.[105]

Needless to say, the line between the two is often difficult to draw, as is the line between 'personal' and 'official'. Above we noted a certain difference in the perspective between the (official) monody and the (private) consolation for John Kontostephanos, with more focus on the addressee

---

[101] See esp. *Monody on the death of Theodora* 24–5 and 176–7 (Kurtz).
[102] It is possible that Manasses wrote for yet another grandchild of Anna's: Sideras 1994: 191–2 has suggested that the fragmentarily preserved *Monody on the death of an anonymous man* was written for Alexios Doukas (died 1171); see also Horna 1904: 351. Alexios Doukas has also been suggested as Manasses' benefactor in Cyprus in the *Itinerary*; see above, Chapter 2.
[103] Note esp. the interaction between the rhetor and Nikephoros in Manasses, *Funerary oration on the death of Nikephoros Komnenos* 493–4 (Kurtz).
[104] Cf. Neville 2016: 118, quoted above.   [105] On the *epithalamion*, see above, n. 31.

than on the rhetor in the consolation. It is possible that a more intimate setting could allow the writer to focus less on self-display and more on the addressee and their 'friendship' under such circumstances, but one must also keep in mind that the lamentation as well as the consolatory discourse could be recycled for any number of circumstances and genres. As noted by Kurtz, the two orations on the death of Theodora by Manasses are similar to a monody written by Nikephoros Basilakes on the death of his brother Constantine.[106] Moreover, Basilakes' monody has certain affinities with the novel by Eumathios Makrembolites, *Hysmine and Hysminias*.[107] While such observations are traditionally interpreted as influence in one direction or the other, or even 'plagiarism' on the part of one or the other,[108] it may also be seen as a demonstration of the intense transtextuality of twelfth-century texts, composed by authors familiar with each others' compositions and frequently drawing on each other.[109] This means that the 'personal' or 'official' character of a text can only be understood in light of the occasion at which it was performed; not based only on the text itself. Sometimes the occasion is implied by the generic indication of the title (as in the case of a monody vs a consolation); in other cases, the title seems to be thwarted by the text's content and form.

This is what happens in the case of the *Monody on the death of his goldfinch*, the title of which would normally indicate an official setting, but the content of which points in a different direction. In the interpretation suggested above, Manasses here takes the opportunity to develop his poetics of patronage and take on the role of both writer and patron. While there is no explicit mention of patronage in either oration discussed in this chapter, the emphasis on long-standing relations and the writer's personal insight in family affairs indicate a 'friendship' that can most probably be understood as patronage. This relationship may go back to a teacher–student relation in early years, indicated by the positive memories

---

[106] See Kurtz 1900: 624–5; Horna 1902: 15. For the monody of Basilakes, see the edition by Pignani 1983: 235–52 (text) and 373–82 (tr.).

[107] The parallels were listed by Hilberg in his 1876 edition of *Hysmine and Hysminias*, 228–9 (attributing them to Choricius of Gaza, who was by that time thought to be the author of the monody).

[108] See e.g. Plepelits 1989: 76, n. 158, calling Basilakes' monody 'fast ein aus Teilen vom *Hysmine und Hysminias* zusammengesetzter Cento', while other scholars have taken for granted that Makrembolites imitated Basilakes, e.g. Marcovich 2001: viii.

[109] On the term transtextuality, here employed instead of the more common 'intertextuality', see Genette 1992; the terminology has been employed in Nilsson 2001, 2010 and 2014. The similarities between the two texts by Manasses are, however, more apparent than those to other authors and point in the direction of what Kuttner-Homs has recently termed 'auto-citation' (Kuttner-Homs 2016). See further below, Chapter 6.

presented by the rhetor in his text (such as the grammar competition). Such positive memories suggest that this, the educational situation, is where similarity begins: a good teacher can turn his student not only into an educated member of the elite, but also into a generous donor. From this perspective, the *Monody on the death of his goldfinch* sheds some light on the rhetorical and literary construction of that relationship as a partly pragmatic, partly fictional strategy, as much a part of the storyworld of the narrator as any other authorial techniques.

CHAPTER 4

In Times of Trouble
Networks and Friendships

Closely related to patronage is the concept of friendship, a social force that has been the subject of modest yet increasing scholarly attention since the seminal 1988 article by Margaret Mullett.[1] Mullett introduced to Byzantine Studies the anthropological distinction between emotional, instrumental and 'lop-sided' friendship (i.e. patronage), and suggested that Byzantines in general seem to have had a 'practical' approach to friendship.[2] As an illustration of that approach, one may consider the passage 'About friends' (Περὶ φίλων) from the so-called *Moral poem*, attributed with some uncertainty to Constantine Manasses.[3]

> Either get good friends or avoid friendship;
> those are unsound who are friends because of wealth.
> For the friend is tried by the hardships of a friend,
> whether he pretends friendship or nurtures it deep down;
> and the friend must suffer with his friend in misfortunes.

> Φίλους ἢ κτῆσαι τοὺς χρηστούς, ἢ φεῦγε τὴν φιλίαν·
> σαθροὶ πεφύκασι καὶ γὰρ οἱ πρὸς τὸν πλοῦτον φίλοι.
> Καὶ γὰρ ὁ φίλος ἐν κακοῖς ἐλέγχεται τοῦ φίλου,
> εἰ πλάττεται τὸν φίλιον, εἰ κατὰ βάθος ἔχει·
> καὶ χρὴ τὸν φίλον συμπονεῖν ἐν συμφοραῖς τῷ φίλῳ.[4]

The few lines make the instrumental and practical side of friendship clear: there is certainly an expectation of concrete assistance and the need to help

---

[1] Mullett 1988.
[2] Mullett 1988: 13–14; see also (for Theophylact of Ochrid), Mullett 1990 and 1997: esp. 111–23 and 177–8. For more recent studies on medieval friendship in a cross-cultural perspective, see e.g. the volume edited by Grünbart 2011.
[3] The authorship of the *Moral poem* is discussed below, Chapter 6. It may be noted here that the different parts of the poems are organized not according to a joint theme, but as a collection of gnomic poems on various themes that can be loosely described as 'moral' or simply 'human'. The 'titles' of the individual 'chapters' (as here, 'About friends') were added by the modern editor and not transmitted in the manuscript.
[4] Manasses, *Moral poem* 667–71 (Miller).

4 In Times of Trouble: Networks and Friendships

each other in times of trouble. In modern terms, we would speak of social networking rather than friendship, but in Byzantium friends were 'allies and supporters as much as kindred spirits'.[5]

Such issues have already been touched upon in the previous chapters, since the occasional texts under analysis have been defined as having extratextual aims and accordingly as being by definition instrumental – the text always wants to achieve something, even if it is not explicitly stated in all cases. Most often it is the person behind the text, the writer, who wants something, even if the text is described as a gift to the addressee – whether a commissioner, a patron or just a powerful person in a position to act on behalf of the writer.[6] In this triangulation of text, pretext and authorial voice, a number of questions become urgent and unavoidable: especially those of author, intention and interpretation. To some extent one may perhaps avoid, or rather delay such questions, by speaking of authorial *persona* and authorial voice – as I have indeed done so far in this study. But sooner or later, as in this chapter, the scholarly reader has to make up her mind about how to understand the relation between the historical author and the author in the text, about the intention of the one or the other author and about her own interpretation of that intention. In order to come to grips with such issues, I here rely on a series of literary studies by Umberto Eco, combined with some more recent ideas of Mieke Bal from the field of cultural studies.[7]

The questions of authorship, authorial intention and relation of patron to text are, of course, inextricably intertwined, because the scholarly interpretation of literature is often based on how one understands the intention of the author, even if the term as such has been banished from the humanities in the wake of the 'intentional fallacy' debate.[8] As noted by Bal, intention is problematic primarily for methodological reasons, and that observation seems particularly relevant for the study of historical artefacts. Modern readers simply cannot be sure that they have reconstructed the intentions of the historical author in a correct manner.[9] However, the situation is not that different for modern readers of modern

---

[5] Kazhdan and Constable 1982: 28; cited by Mullett 1988: 19.
[6] On such a process of gift-giving in the eleventh century, see Bernard 2011a, 2011b and 2012.
[7] Eco 1979, 1990, 1992 and 1994 (all dealing from various perspectives with the reader, the author, interpretation and intention); Bal 2002: 253–85 (dealing with art rather than literature).
[8] Bal does not exaggerate when she calls it 'the concept we love to hate'; Bal 2002: 253. It should be noted that Wimsatt and Beardsley's argument in their famous 1946 article on the intentional fallacy did not exclude intentionality as such, but only a certain kind of psychologism; see Staten 2010 for a good survey of the series of misunderstandings that have marked the debate.
[9] See Bal 2002: esp. 254–5 and 262–6 (the example of Caravaggio's *Narcissus*).

authors, simply because the intention of the author sooner or later always meets and often clashes with the intentions of the reader, who may read and interpret something completely different from what the author had in mind.[10] Eco primarily analyses fiction, but the strategies of reading and interpreting are not very different for a reader of non-fictional texts. Moreover, the kind of occasional texts that are under examination in this study have been defined as placing themselves between 'the imaginary' and 'the real', connecting the occasion of the performance to a larger literary, mythological and historical imaginary shared by author and audience.[11] This means that 'reality' is largely a question of literary representation.[12]

But who is the author, then? Are they too but a literary representation, a rhetorical construct or even a whole series of selves? In light of recent studies of eleventh- and twelfth-century authors in Byzantium, it is clear that self-representation was of primary importance for both highborn intellectuals such as Anna Komnene and writers of a more modest origin such as John Tzetzes.[13] At the same time, there is a tendency to read Byzantine authors in light of whatever biographical or historical details are available to us from other sources, though often from the texts of the authors themselves. The use of information offered by the authors themselves to interpret other things they say about themselves has obvious methodological problems, and it even muddles the concept of intentionality – whose intention is being reconstructed here, that of the historical author or that of the author as s/he appears in the text? Most often the latter, I would say, but with a confusion of the two, as if they were, in the end, more or less the same.[14] At the same time, most scholars would probably agree with the seminal statement of Stephen Greenblatt in his study of self-fashioning in the Renaissance: 'After all, there are always

---

[10] In Eco 1994, this is illustrated by examples from Eco's own fictional production and subsequent encounters or communications with readers. Cf. Bal on the intention of modern vs historical artists; Bal 2002: 255–6.
[11] See above, Chapter 1. [12] I return to this issue below, Chapter 6.
[13] Over the past decades, the scholarly focus has moved from genre to author, from author to reader, and to some extent back to the author; see Mullett 1992 and 1997: 223–30, Reinsch 2010, Pizzone 2014a. On self-representation and authorial identities in eleventh- and twelfth-century authors, see Papaioannou 2013: esp. 23–4 and 2014 (Michael Psellos); Cullhed 2014b (John Tzetzes); Bourbouhakis 2014 (Michael Choniates); Pizzone 2014b (Nikephoros Basilakes); Xenophontos 2014 (John Tzetzes), Neville 2013, 2014 and 2016 (Anna Komnene); Lovato 2016 (John Tzetzes), Agapitos 2017 (John Tzetzes); Pizzone 2017 and 2018 (John Tzetzes).
[14] It should be noted that the field is rapidly changing in this regard; in addition to the studies mentioned in the previous note, see also van Opstall 2008: 34–9 for a distinction between the 'je autobiographique', 'je porte-parole' and 'je fictionnel' (John Geometres); Paul and Rhoby 2019: 12–14 for the 'Sprecher-Ich' in the *Verse chronicle* by Manasses; Kubina 2020: 187–99 on the historical author and his literary *persona* (Manuel Philes).

selves – a sense of personal order, a characteristic mode of address to the world, a structure of bounded desires – and always some elements of deliberate shaping in the formation and expression of identity.'[15]

In order to come to grips with this confusion of different selves, one may turn to some of Eco's useful distinctions. The first is that between the 'empirical author' and the 'model author', a division that also transfers to the 'empirical reader' and the 'model reader'. The distinction has certain resemblances with the idea of the implied author,[16] but Eco's definition has an advantage for the study of twelfth-century texts in that he describes the model author as a recognizable 'voice' or even 'style' that appears in one or several works:

> The model author ... is a voice that speaks to us affectionately (or imperiously, or slyly), that wants us beside it. This voice is manifested as a narrative strategy, as a set of instructions which is given to us step by step and which we have to follow when we decide to act as the model reader.[17]

Rather than speaking of the intention of the author or of the reader, Eco places the intention on a textual level – the 'intention of the text'. However, this intention 'is basically to produce a model reader able to make conjectures about it', which means that 'the initiative of the model reader consists in figuring out a model author that is not the empirical one and that, in the end, coincides with the intention of the text'.[18] The author and the reader thus remain closely connected through the intention of the text, which in turn may be defined as a semiotic strategy:

> To recognize the *intentio operis* is to recognize a semiotic strategy. Sometimes the semiotic strategy is detectable on the grounds of established stylistic conventions. If a story starts with "Once upon a time" there is a good probability that it is a fairy tale and that the evoked and postulated model reader is a child (or an adult eager to react in a childish mood).[19]

---

[15] Greenblatt 1980: 1. Greenblatt's study has had some impact on Byzantinists, cited by Papaioannou 2013: 23, n. 63, and more recently Kubina 2020: 190.
[16] The term goes back to Booth 1983 [1961], but has been used in ways that differ quite extensively from the original suggestions made by Booth; see Booth 2005.
[17] Eco 1994: 15. This first essay of the collection offers an excellent, if somewhat simplified, introduction to the concept of the model author, which appears in several of Eco's essays.
[18] Eco 1992: 180.
[19] Eco 1992: 180–1. Cf. Genette 1991: 169–221; this is the essay 'Style et signification', in which Genette tries to develop a semiotic definition of style; note esp. the useful definition on p. 203: 'Le style consiste donc en l'ensemble des propriétés rhématiques exemplifiées par le discours, au niveau « formel » (c'est-à-dire, en fait, physique) du matériau phonique ou graphique, au niveau linguistique du rapport de dénotation directe, et au niveau figural de la dénotation indirecte.'

Again, this is a useful distinction for the study of historical and semiotically charged texts such as the occasional texts under examination here. Stylistic conventions play an important role in communicating meaning to the audience, also when they are used in a subversive or playful manner. And in many cases we have nothing but the texts themselves, so just as in the discussion of patronage in the previous chapter, we are left to perform a text-based analysis.

According to such a model, ascribing meaning to aspects of the 'real' (empirical) author is hardly theoretically legitimate, nor is it a fruitful way of looking for meaning or, indeed, intention. Moreover, it means that the study of patronage, friendship or any other kind of networking most often is the study of texts that represent cultural and semiotic relationships rather than factual relationships between individuals or groups or people.[20] And as was noted in the previous chapter, representation and characterization are not limited to the authorial *persona*, but also to the *personae* of addressees and audiences, who in this case may be defined as the model readers – or in the Byzantine context rather as model receivers of the rhetorical performance. Patrons, objects of description (human or not), peers and friends, but also networks as such can accordingly also be literary constructions, having a tenuous relation to reality.[21] Let us from this perspective return to the poem on friendship cited above, asking ourselves what kind of constructions or strategies it presents, if any.

The poem consists of five fifteen-syllable lines, of which especially the first two offer gnomic advice: either you should get good friends or none – some people are in it only for the money. The use of χρηστούς for 'good' implies also the instrumental or practical idea of friendship in its implication of 'useful'. Then follows a small elaboration on the theme, explaining how to prove and define friendship: friends must support each other at bad times. It is a short poem with few poetic markers beyond the metric form,[22] there is no authorial I and no indication of a specific occasion. For a model recipient, however, it does communicate by its content a shared understanding of friendship (in the Byzantine sense) and its style is reminiscent of the model author Manasses. The latter does not necessarily

---

[20] Cf. Annibaldi 1998 and the discussion of patronage above, Chapter 3.
[21] Cf. Zetzel 1972: 175 on the Scipionic circle of Cicero as a literary construction; note also p. 176, 'historical settings are intended to be vehicles for the dialogues in which they are used, not independent entities'. See also above, Chapter 3.
[22] One may note, however, the resonance of the recurring φ (Φίλους ... φεῦγε ... φιλίαν etc.) and the position of Φίλους and φίλῳ at the beginning and end of the poem. A similar but less pronounced effect in the χρηστούς of the first line and the χρή of the last.

coincide with the empirical author Manasses, because one could be dealing here with a compilation or imitation of the style associated with him.[23] Once the identification of the model author (the style) has been made, the content can be connected with other expressions of the same topic by the same model author: comments on friendship made in the *Verse chronicle*, among the fragments of *Aristandros and Kallithea* or in the texts to be analysed in the present chapter.[24]

This still does not mean that the comments made by the model author always reflect the real-life experiences of the empirical author, but that we can read the text as an expression of a concern that was repeated at different occasions and thus reverberated as a theme associated with that particular style or voice. Such a literary interpretation can then be combined with information drawn from other sources, in order to offer a tentative historical interpretation of the circumstances which are expressed in the texts, but it is important also in this part of the analysis to accept the distinction between the imaginary of the texts and the reality in which the characters lived.[25] With these theoretical and methodological considerations in mind, let us proceed to the analysis.

Rhetorical Skill at Work

The texts to be examined in this chapter have all been preserved in the same manuscript, where they are transmitted without any indication of the author. The manuscript (Marcianus Append. XI, 22) also contains, however, other texts by Manasses: the *Monody on the death of Theodora, wife of John Kontostephanos* and the *Consolation for John Kontostephanos* are followed by an oration addressed to a certain (unnamed) logothete and four letters, of which the fourth is incomplete.[26] Based on the appearance of several texts by Manasses together in the same manuscript, the position of the texts in relation to each other and their – as we will see – distinctly Manassean style, the oration and at least the first three letters can be safely

---

[23] As some scholars indeed argue. See below, Chapter 6.
[24] Some of the novel fragments are similar to the *Moral poem* cited above, which makes sense in light of the importance of good friends in the typical novelistic plot; see Manasses, *Aristandros and Kallithea* frgs. 56, 72, 87 and 151 (Mazal). Friendship does not play a major role in the chronicle, but it does appear: *Verse chronicle* 2529–32, 2745–7, 3079–84 (Lampsides); see also Manasses, *Funerary oration on the death of Nikephoros Komnenos* 621 (Kurtz).
[25] Cf. above Chapter 2 with n. 80, and further below.
[26] On the Marcianus Append. XI, 22 (thirteenth century), see above, Chapter 3 with n. 30. The oration to the unnamed logothete follows directly after the *Consolation for John Kontostephanos* in f. 170^v.

attributed to Manasses.²⁷ Moreover, the oration and the three letters are closely linked by the joint story that they present – a story that is tempting to see as an event in the life of the empirical author. Here it is read primarily as the story of the model author (or perhaps rather model rhetor), addressing a model reader who may appreciate and understand his tale. We will therefore leave the historical circumstances to the side for the moment and proceed directly to the oration.²⁸

It opens with a story from classical antiquity, introduced with a pun on the multiple meaning of the word *logos*:

> This is a Hellenic story; the Hellenes were remarkably clever, so may the story not be unprofitable. May this Hellenic story open my oration.²⁹
>
> Apelles, that man much-famed for painting and so skilful in mixing colours, and great as well at imitating the embellishing nature³⁰ and at rendering animals onto his painting boards as if they were living and moving, now this Apelles, striving to feast his spectators with innovative paintings (for man is a creature that loves novelty; he finds the customary tedious, but desires what is done for the very first time in stories, in songs, in paintings), once artfully devised a new painting to charm the eyes, and the painting was a staircase that filled the entire board. The steps of the staircase indicated great skill: some stood firmly on a solid base and steadfast and safely held up those who stepped on them, but others were painted as cracked, unreliable and slippery, more slippery than the ... of the street, more unreliable than water and treacherous for those who stepped on them. And there was an inscription on the painting: 'The course of fortune'.
>
> Λόγος οὗτος ἑλλήνιος· περιττοὶ τὴν σύνεσιν Ἕλληνες· εἴη ἂν οὖν ὁ λόγος οὐκ ἄχρηστος. ἀρχέτω δή μοι τοῦ λόγου λόγος ἑλλήνιος.
>
> Ἀπελλῆς ἐκεῖνος ὁ τὴν γραφὴν πολυύμνητος καὶ χρώματα μὲν κεράσαι δεινός, πολὺς δὲ τὴν κομμώτριαν φύσιν μιμήσασθαι καὶ ζῷα τυπῶσαι τοῖς πίναξιν ἄντικρυς ἔμπνοα καὶ κινούμενα, ἐκεῖνος τοίνυν ὁ Ἀπελλῆς,

---

²⁷ Horna 1906: 171. The fourth letter may well have been written by Manasses, but does not seem to refer to the same events as the first three and is therefore not included in the present analysis.

²⁸ Horna 1906: 173–84. The missing title has been conjectured by Horna as Λόγος προσφωνητικὸς πρὸς τὸν λογοθέτην τοῦ δρόμου κυρὸν Μιχαὴλ τὸν Ἁγιοθεοδωρίτην· τοῦ Μανασσῆ.

²⁹ Here probably an allusion to the opening of Aelian, *Poikile historia* 13 (Λόγος οὗτος Ἀρκάδιος); Horna 1906: 187. I take 'Hellenic' here to mean 'ancient Greek', with no connotations of 'pagan' or 'Hellenic' (in the ideologic and nationalistic sense); on such problems of terminology, see Page 2008: chs 1–2 (on ethnicity and identity) and 3 (on Niketas Choniates). Cf. Manasses, *Aristandros and Kallithea* frg. 30.11 (Mazal): ἄπαγε, μὴ φιλέλληνες οὕτω μανεῖεν ἄνδρες, taking on a different meaning in the novelistic and pseudo-pagan setting. On the issue of 'Hellenism' in Byzantium, see Kaldellis 2007: esp. 225–316 on the twelfth century as the 'third sophistic'; Manasses' *Encomium of Michael Hagiotheodorites* is not included in Kaldellis' analysis. Cf. also the 'Arabian tale' in the *Funerary oration on the death of Nikephoros Komnenos* 1–29 (Kurtz); see above, Chapter 3.

³⁰ For the same expression, see also Manasses, *Description of a crane hunt* 56 (Messis and Nilsson) and *Monody on the death of his goldfinch* 8.14 (Horna).

καινοτέραις σπεύδων γραφαῖς τοὺς θεατὰς ἑστιᾶν (φιλόκαινον γὰρ ζῷον ὁ ἄνθρωπος καὶ τὸ μὲν σύνηθες ἥγηται προσκορές, λιχνεύεται δὲ περὶ τὰ πρώτως ἄρτι γινόμενα ἐν ἱστορίαις, ἐν ἄσμασιν, ἐν γραφαῖς), τεχνάζεταί τινα γραφὴν νεαρὰν εἰς γοήτευσιν ὀφθαλμῶν, καὶ ἡ γραφὴ κλίμαξ ἦν ὅλον περιλαμβάνουσα πίνακα· αἱ βαθμίδες τῆς κλίμακος πολλὴν τινὰ τὴν σοφίαν ὑπέφαινον· αἱ μὲν ἑστήκεσαν πάγιαι στερεοκρήπιδες ἔμπεδοι καὶ τοὺς ἐπιβαίνοντας ἀκινδύνως ἀνέχουσαι, αἱ δὲ σαθραὶ τινὲς καὶ ἄπιστοι ἐγγεγράφατο καὶ ὀλισθηραί, ὀλισθηραὶ ὑπὲρ τὰς τῶν ὁδῶν..., ὑπὲρ τὸ ὕδωρ ἀβέβαιοι καὶ τῶν ἀναβαινόντων προδότριαι. καὶ ἦν ἐπιγραφὴ τῇ γραφῇ· Τύχης φορά.[31]

The painting of Apelles was then seen by the sculptor Lysippus, who wondered at the workmanship, 'was delighted by the subtlety, praised the precision, rejoiced at the resemblance with reality, but nevertheless he also jeered at the artist and put him to shame and rebuked him' (ἠγάσθη τὴν λεπτουργίαν, ἐπῄνεσε τὴν ἀκρίβειαν, ὑπερηγάσθη τὸ πρὸς τὴν ἀλήθειαν ἐμφερές· ἀλλ' ὅμως καὶ ἔσκωψε τὸν τεχνίτην καὶ κατῄδεσε καὶ ἐπέπληξεν).[32] According to Lysippus, Apelles has wasted his skill on something useless, because he has not represented any of the gods – 'Of eloquent Hermes you have no story nor any image, not of Athena, nor of Apollo' (καὶ Ἑρμοῦ μὲν τοῦ λογίου λόγος οὐδείς σοι οὐδὲ εἰκών, οὐκ Ἀθηνᾶς οὐδ' Ἀπόλλωνος) – and he thus resembles 'the vulgar among athletes, who attack the air and fight shadows in vain' (τοῖς ἀπειροκάλοις τῶν ἀθλητῶν, οἳ καὶ ἀτάκτως τῷ ἀέρι ἐφάλλονται καὶ σκιαμαχοῦσιν ἀνόνητα).[33] Apelles listened to the critique of Lysippus and blushed. He thought for a while and then he mixed his colours again: he now painted Athena – detailed, beautiful and fierce. The spectators could not take their eyes from the painting and Apelles received much praise.[34] The rhetor then immediately explains the function of this Hellenic story.

> So this particular Hellenic story, which became the opening of my discourse, suits me too in many ways, you most clever and renowned of men!

---

[31] Manasses, *Encomium of Michael Hagiotheodorites* 1–15 (Horna). The text cited here follows the edition of Horna, indicating that some words of the manuscript are illegible.
[32] Manasses, *Encomium of Michael Hagiotheodorites* 17–19 (Horna).
[33] Manasses, *Encomium of Michael Hagiotheodorites* 20–1 and 22–4 (Horna).
[34] Manasses, *Encomium of Michael Hagiotheodorites* 24–37 (Horna). This story of Apelles is not known from any other source, though Apelles was known for painting allegorical images; see e.g. the scene described in Lucian's *On calumny*, inspiring Renaissance painting and probably known to someone like Manasses, taking an interest in the representation of slander and envy. Cf. also the interest of Manasses in allegory and ekphrasis, and the remarks on 'art history' in the opening of his *Description of the Earth* 5–22 (Lampsides), not including Apelles.

> For as I was exhausting myself with inappropriate matters and wearing myself out by unprofitable affairs and fighting excessively, struggling in vain, a not ungracious friend turned to me and chastened and instructed me; and he blocked the water-pipe of my discourse to those barren matters and guided instead the channel of my art to you and to your praise and songs. May this then be for my benefit and may a blooming tree be gardened for me by this source, carrying fruit, golden with noble fruits. For before, the care of vines led to no fruit and the tree-tending was useless for me and the toilsome culture of herbs was more unprofitable than collecting weeds.
>
> Ὁ μὲν οὖν ἑλλήνιος λόγος οὗτος ἐκεῖνος, ὅς μοι τοῦ λόγου γέγονε πρόσωπον·³⁵ ἁρμόζει δὲ ἄρα κἀμοὶ ἐν πολλοῖς, ἀνδρῶν ἀγχινούστατε καὶ κλεινότατε· κἀμὲ γὰρ ἐν οὐ καιρίοις ἐκδαπανώμενον καὶ ἀκερδέσιν ἐγγυμναζόμενον πράγμασι καὶ ἀεθλεύοντα μὲν περιττῶς, κάμνοντα δὲ ἀνονήτως ἐπέστρεψέ τε φίλος οὐκ ἄχαρις καὶ ἐσωφρόνισε καὶ ἐφρένωσε· καὶ τὴν ὑδρορρόην τοῦ λόγου τοῖς μὲν ἀκάρποις ἐκείνοις ἀπέφραξεν, εἰς σὲ δὲ καὶ τοὺς σοὺς ἐπαίνους καὶ ὕμνους τὸ τῆς τέχνης ὀχέτιον ἴθυνεν· εἴη δέ μοι τοῦτο γοῦν εἰς καλὸν καὶ κηπευθείη μοι τούτῳ τῷ νάματι δένδρον ἀνθεοφόρον, ὀπωροφόρον, χρυσίζον εὐγένεσι καρποῖς. τὰ γὰρ πρὸ τοῦ φυτηκόματα γεγόνασιν ἄκαρπα καὶ ἡ δενδροκομία μοι ἄχρηστος καὶ ἡ πολύμοχθος λαχανεία βοτάνης χορτολογουμένης ἀχρειοτέρα.³⁶

The story of Apelles is accordingly said to reflect the rhetor's own situation: he has been writing for the wrong people – perhaps also writing the wrong things, composing innovative works, displaying the ways in which fortune works? – but has now been advised by a friend to turn instead to the addressee. The rhetor then turns to the task at hand and indicates, for the first time, the status of his addressee: 'But how and starting where should I praise the magnanimous logothete?' (Ἀλλὰ γὰρ πῶς ἂν ἢ πόθεν ἐγὼ τὸν μεγαλόνουν λογοθέτην ὑμνήσαιμι;).³⁷ His successes are huge, his virtues unrivalled, but the rhetor finds it hard to concentrate – he is much concerned with the ills that have befallen him, all because of dangerous slander:

> False rumour and slander are two related ills; rumour is the daughter of slander. And slander, as if having many years as her lot,³⁸ is more convincing than the Sirens and babbles on and is more efficient than fire, sharper

---

[35] Horna 1906: 188 suggests that Manasses might be referring to Pindar, *Ol.* 5.4: ἀρχομένου δ' ἔργου πρόσωπον χρὴ θέμεν τηλαυγές.
[36] Manasses, *Encomium of Michael Hagiotheodorites* 38–49 (Horna).
[37] Manasses, *Encomium of Michael Hagiotheodorites* 50 (Horna).
[38] That is, being of very old age; cf. Sophocles, *Ajax* 508: μητέρα πολλῶν ἐτῶν κληροῦχον. This Sophoclean play belongs to the so-called Byzantine triad read in school and was thus well-known to

than a knife, hotter than lightning and more effective than a sword, while rumour – the bitter spawn of slander – is quicker than the breezes, more fluid than waters, outflies the winds and is lighter than a feather.[39]

Φήμη ψευδὴς καὶ διαβολὴ δύο κακὰ συγγενῆ· θυγάτηρ ἡ φήμη διαβολῆς· καὶ διαβολὴ μὲν οἷα πολλῶν ἐτῶν κληροῦχος καὶ ἔμπειρος ὑπὲρ τὰς Σειρῆνας πιθανολεσχεῖ καὶ στωμύλλεται καὶ ἔστι δραστικωτέρα πυρός, ὀξυτέρα μαχαίρας, φλεκτικωτέρα πρηστῆρος καὶ ἐνεργεστέρα ξιφῶν, ἡ δὲ φήμη, τὸ πικρὸν τῆς διαβολῆς ἀπομαίευμα, δρομικωτέρα πνευμάτων, ὑγροτέρα ὑδάτων καὶ ὑπὲρ ἀνέμους διίπταται καὶ ὑπὲρ πτερὸν ἐλαφρίζεται.[40]

The rhetor has to slowly drag himself and his discourse away from the gloomy circumstances and tragic mode, regularly recalling the wise Solomon[41] but at one point also citing the comedian Aristophanes, supposedly as a way of cheering things up.[42] The oration then seems to take off in a more proper direction: 'The oration should now concentrate on its aim and turn to the *encomia*' ("Ἤδη δὲ ὁ λόγος τοῦ σκοποῦ καταστοχαζέσθω καὶ ἀπευθυνέσθω πρὸς τὰ ἐγκώμια),[43] followed by a citation from Kallimachos: 'We singers always sacrifice without a fire of our own' (Ἄκαπνα δ' αἰὲν ἀοιδοὶ θύομεν, εἶπεν ἂν ὁ Καλλίμαχος); that is, 'Poets live at others' expense.'[44] With this reminder of his task as a rhetor – to perform in order to get paid – the writer turns to the eulogy proper, starting with the background and childhood of the logothete. He had early

---

teachers and students alike. The Sophoclean expression here lends the passage a tragic tone that goes with the mood of the model author.

[39] On the wording and imagery of this passage, see also below, Chapter 6, on the representation of slander and envy in other texts by Manasses (the *Verse chronicle, Aristandros and Kallithea* and the *Moral poem*).

[40] Manasses, *Encomium of Michael Hagiotheodorites* 71–7 (Horna).

[41] The reference to Solomon is not unique, but represents rather Manasses' consistent way of carefully blending ancient and Biblical allusions. Cf. Kaldellis 2007: 258 on the *Funerary oration on the death of Nikephoros Komnenos* 124–8 (Kurtz).

[42] Manasses, *Encomium of Michael Hagiotheodorites* 93–8 (Horna): Ἀλλ' ἐστάτω μοι μέχρι τούτου τὰ βαρύποτμα ταῦτα καὶ βαρυσύμφορα· κἂν γάρ τις κωμικώτερον ἐπισκώπτων ἐρεῖ. "'Ἐπιφυλλίδες ταῦτ' ἐστὶ καὶ στωμύλματα" (cf. Aristophanes, *Ranae* 92), ἀκούσεται παρ' ἡμῶν ὡς "Καρδίας μὲν οὖν, βέλτιστε, κατωδύνου ταῦτα τὰ ῥήματα, ψυχῆς ταῦτα κυμαινομένης οἰδήματα, πνεύματος χειμαζομένου τὰ ἀπηχήματα, ὅτι μηδὲν ἀδικήσαντες ὡς εὐθυνόμεθα". Note that the verse from the *Frogs* (and in particular the word ἐπιφυλλίδες) is also used by John Tzetzes in the grand epilogue to his *Theogony*; see Agapitos 2017: 47, n. 244. The *Frogs*, like Sophocles' *Ajax*, belongs to the Byzantine triad and would have been widely known.

[43] Manasses, *Encomium of Michael Hagiotheodorites* 99–100 (Horna).

[44] Manasses, *Encomium of Michael Hagiotheodorites* 100–1 (Horna). Cf. Kallimachos, frg. 53P. The line is cited also in Athenaeus (Horna 1906: 188), but without mentioning the name of the poet. Cf. Manasses' use of Athenaeus at the beginning of the *Itinerary* and his status as one of Manasses' 'favourite' authors; see Horna 1904: 347, and above, Chapter 2.

training in and talent for letters, but was also taught how to govern properly by the emperor himself. The deeds of the emperor are praised as 'deeds of a gigantic hero' (ἔργα γίγαντος ἥρωος τούτου τὰ ἔργα), as he runs like a winged sun across the known parts of the world.[45] The connection between the logothete and his emperor is thus made very clear, as is the generosity and wisdom of the addressee.[46] The rhetor then turns to a more personal comment on the skills of the addressee:

> Let others say and write other things about this man; let some tell of the steadfastness of his spirit, let others focus on his great ambition,[47] some on his sound mind, others on his hatred of knavery, let his dignity be applauded by some, let his intelligence be recounted by others; but what I admire more than other things and set him higher for than the rest, those things that I would celebrate to the best of my power, are the charm of his sophistic art, the beautifully worded writings, the beautiful craft in composing iambs, his good memory, his fairness.

> Ἄλλοι μὲν οὖν ἄλλα τῶν τοῦ ἀνδρὸς λεγέτωσαν καὶ γραφέτωσαν· οἱ μὲν τὸ στάσιμον τοῦ φρονήματος διηγείσθωσαν, οἱ δὲ τὸ μεγαλεπήβολον ἀποθειαζέσθωσαν, ἄλλοι τὸ σῶφρον, τὸ μισοπόνηρον ἕτεροι, τοῖς δὲ ἡ σεμνότης κροτείσθω, τοῖς δὲ τὸ ἀγχίνουν περιλαλείσθω· ἐγὼ δὲ ἃ τῶν ἄλλων πλέον τεθαύμακα καὶ οἷς τὸν ἄνδρα τῶν λοιπῶν ὑπερτίθεμαι, ταῦτα δὴ καὶ ὡς ἐφικτὸν ἀνυμνήσαιμι, τὴν ἴυγγα τῆς σοφιστικῆς, τὰς καλλιγλώττους γραφάς, τὴν περὶ τοὺς ἰάμβους καλλιτεχνίαν, τὸ μνῆμον, τὴν ἐπιείκειαν.[48]

The rhetor – now clearly representing his addressee as an equal and a colleague – goes on to praise the rhetorical skills of the logothete:

> There is never a lack of trophies set up by the emperor (for neither does heaven lack stars, nor the sea water or the sun beautiful light); these triumphs, these famous victories must be made known to the city of Byzantion, the sun among towns, the beauty of the Earth, the eye of the Universe.[49] Here the logothete writes beautifully and declaims, he displays the graces of the sophistic art that reared him, attracts with melodious

---

[45] Manasses, *Encomium of Michael Hagiotheodorites* 157–61 (Horna). Cf. the praise of Manuel in the orations discussed above, Chapter 2. This is a common imagery in twelfth-century poetry, e.g. in both Theodore Prodromos and Manganeios Prodromos.
[46] See esp. Manasses, *Encomium of Michael Hagiotheodorites* 162–244 (Horna).
[47] See also *Encomium of Michael Hagiotheodorites* 148 (Horna), *Encomium of Emperor Manuel Komnenos* 55 (Kurtz) and *Verse chronicle* 3146 (Lampsides).
[48] Manasses, *Encomium of Michael Hagiotheodorites* (Horna) 245–52.
[49] Cf. Manasses, *Itinerary* 2.154–5 (Chryssogelos): ὀφθαλμὲ τῆς γῆς, κόσμε τῆς οἰκουμένης, | τηλαυγὲς ἄστρον, τοῦ κάτω κόσμου λύχνε.

writings and delights with beautifully articulated sounds,[50] like the reeds under the lyre.[51]

Οὐκ ἐπιλείπουσί ποτε τρόπαια τῷ αὐτοκράτορι κατορθούμενα (οὐ γὰρ οὐρανῷ ἐλλείπουσιν ἄστρα οὐδὲ ὕδωρ θαλάσσῃ οὐδὲ ἡλίῳ κάλλος φωτός)· ταῦτα δὴ τὰ τροπαιουχήματα, ταύτας τὰς νίκας καὶ περιδόξους χρὴ μαθεῖν καὶ τὴν Βύζαντος, τὸν ἥλιον τῶν χωρῶν, τὸ κάλλος τῆς γῆς, τὸν ὀφθαλμὸν τοῦ παντός. ἐνταῦθα ὁ λογοθέτης εἰς κάλλος γράφει καὶ ῥητορεύει καὶ τὰς τῆς θρεψαμένης σοφιστικῆς ἐπιδείκνυσι χάριτας καὶ εὐκελάδοις ἕλκει γραφαῖς καὶ καλλιστόμοις τέρπει φωναῖς, ὡς οἱ ὑπολύριοι δόνακες.[52]

This can only be admired, states the rhetor, who goes on to describe a grammar contest arranged at the court. The description is strongly reminiscent of the contest described in the *Funerary oration on the death of Nikephoros Komnenos* and the role played by the objects of praise is the same: they both function as some sort of game leaders, 'setting traps' in grammar for the students.[53] Such occasions are filled with charm, comments the rhetor, before moving on to excessively praise the addressee in all other kinds of literary activities, finding him superior even to Herodotus, Xenophon, Sappho and Anacreon.[54] The rhetor's admiration is underlined by the fact that he himself has witnessed this,[55] and all the excellent qualities of the logothete are then expressed by other literary and mythological *exempla*. The oration thus ends with yet another Hellenic story (here referred to as a *diegema*): that of King Pyrrhus – an excellent person – and the Lakonian Hegesandros – a mean-spirited man.[56] This

---

[50] Cf. Manasses, *Monody on the death of his goldfinch*, where similar wording is employed, e.g. καλλίστομος in 3.11 (Horna).
[51] The rather mysterious ὑπολύριοι δόνακες are drawn from Aristophanes, *Ranae* 232–3 (Horna 1906: 190), employed by Manasses also in the *Description of a crane hunt* 20 (Messis and Nilsson). According to Pollux, *Onomasticon* 4.62 (Bethe), these reeds used to be placed on (under?) lyres instead of horns: καὶ δόνακα δὲ τίνα ὑπολύριον οἱ κωμικοὶ ὠνόμαζον, ὡς πάλαι ἀντὶ κεράτων ὑποτιθέμενον ταῖς λύραις. Written in the second century, this explanation is likely to be imaginative rather than technically correct, and it seems likely that Manasses uses the expression as a metonym for pleasant, ancient-sounding music.
[52] Manasses, *Encomium of Michael Hagiotheodorites* 253–60 (Horna).
[53] Manasses, *Encomium of Michael Hagiotheodorites* 264–74 (Horna). The passage is translated and examined below in relation to Manasses' production of schedography and activities as *grammatikos*, Chapter 5. On the *Funerary oration on the death of Nikephoros Komnenos*, see above, Chapter 3.
[54] Manasses, *Encomium of Michael Hagiotheodorites* 279–81 (Horna).
[55] Manasses, *Encomium of Michael Hagiotheodorites* 285 (Horna): εἶδον τὸν ἄνδρα.
[56] Manasses, *Encomium of Michael Hagiotheodorites* 339–79 (Horna). The latter story does not seem to be known from any other source, but that does not necessarily mean that Manasses invented it.

story seems to remind the writer of the virtue and self-control of the addressee, but also of his iambic art.[57]

Framed by these two Hellenic stories, representing the writer–rhetor and his learned addressee respectively, the oration then comes to an end.

> But may the oar of our oration now relax; for the sea of your virtues is endless and cannot be sailed.[58] Accept kindly this refrain and know our gratitude and exchange it for my goodwill. In return: block the ears of the manhunters, I mean those malignant ones and slanderers – who even wall off the emperor from those who have done nothing wrong and try to confuse your soul, imitating in this the cabbage-eating worms,[59] mean root-eaters among animals, who dig mines under the earth and by digging deep pits plunder the plants and strike and kill the heart, but themselves leave without profit. May you watch over us and revive the benumbed and raise those who have fallen and give life to the dead; we shall speak again and sing and sacrifice thank-offerings and we shall make the rhetor even more clearly known to you.

> Ἀλλ' ἡμῖν μὲν τὴν κώπην ἤδη τοῦ λόγου σχαστέον· τὸ γὰρ πέλαγος τῶν σῶν προτερημάτων ἀπέρατόν τι καὶ ἄπλωτον. σὺ δὲ δέξαι προσηνῶς τὸ ἐφύμνιον καὶ τὴν ἡμῶν εὐγνωμοσύνην κατάμαθε καὶ τῆς προαιρέσεως ἄμειψαι. ἡ δὲ ἀμοιβή· τοῖς ἀνθρωπόθηρσι τὰς ἀκοὰς ἀποφράγνυε, τοὺς ἐπιχαιρεκάκους λέγω καὶ διαβόλους, οἳ καὶ βασιλέα τοῖς μηδὲν ἀδικοῦσιν ἀποτειχίζουσι καὶ τὴν σὴν πειρῶνται ψυχὴν συνθολοῦν καὶ μιμοῦνται τοῦτο γε τὸ μέρος τὰς λαχανηφάγους πρασικουρίδας, τὸ φαῦλον ἐν ζῴοις καὶ ῥιζοφάγον, αἵτινες ὑπονομεύουσαι τὴν γῆν καὶ ὑποβοθρεύουσαι ληστεύουσι μὲν τὰ φυτὰ καὶ τὴν καρδίαν κεντοῦσι καὶ θανατοῦσιν, αὐταὶ δὲ μηδὲν ἀπονάμεναι οἴχονται. καὶ εἴης ἡμᾶς ἐποπτεύων καὶ ζωπυρῶν ἀπονεκρουμένους καὶ πίπτοντας ἀνεγείρων καὶ θανατουμένους ζωογονῶν· ἡμεῖς δὲ πάλιν λαλήσομεν καὶ ὑμνήσομεν καὶ χαριστήρια θύσομεν καὶ τρανότερόν σοι γνωριοῦμεν τὸν ῥήτορα.[60]

The aim of the oration is thus stated in surprisingly clear and open terms: help me to get rid of my mean slanderers and I will praise you in return.[61] It is noteworthy that the focus here is on the art of rhetoric: if you help me, says the narrator, you shall know much more deeply my qualities as a

---

[57] On the virtues and iambic art of the logothete, see lines 380–8.
[58] Cf. Manasses, *Consolation for John Kontostephanos* 320–2 (Kurtz): ἡμεῖς μὲν οὖν ἐνταῦθα τοῦ λόγου στησόμεθα καὶ χαλάσομεν ἤδη τὴν κώπην καὶ περὶ τὸν πλοῦν μετριάσομεν. See also Manasses, *Verse chronicle* 6609 and 6618–20 (Lampsides), cited above, Chapter 3, n. 53.
[59] For λαχανηφάγοι, see Manasses, *Aristandros and Kallithea* frg. 76.9 (Mazal); the word occurs only in Manasses and in Photios' *Lexicon*, s.v. ἔμβολος· θηρίδιον λαχανηφάγον.
[60] Manasses, *Encomium of Michael Hagiotheodorites* 389–401 (Horna).
[61] On the motif of slander and envy in texts by Manasses, see below, Chapter 6.

rhetor. The story of the writer–rhetor is clear too: I have been slandered by evil men, but I have done no wrong. Moreover, there is an important message from the model author to the model reader: you and I are the same, we know our sophistic art and use it to serve and praise those in power in order to get favours in return; we understand the Hellenic tradition and can interpret each others' *logoi*.

The Need to Address the Logothete

The first letter follows directly after the oration in the manuscript. It offers a sort of summary of the oration and has the same addressee, the logothete. The message of the letter confirms the interpretation of the oration as a plea for help:

> For the lover of letters (*logos*) is this gift, for the *logo*thete have I composed this speech (*logos*) from a grateful soul. But forgive me, you most blessed of men, that I'm so eager to dress someone as great as you in a poor speech, and this at a time when the defence tower of my soul is being besieged by continuous siege engines of affliction. For as clouds are inimical to the rays of the sun, so hostile grievances are to my heart; if the enemies are many, having no fair reason to make war, which soul would endure, shaken by slander and hit by a battering-ram of false accusations? When an oak falls, it's not as if no one will cut wood from it; when a man is faring ill, it's not, it seems, as if no one will attack him.[62] So intervene in my misfortunes, for I know you can! And don't just intervene in not having my means cut short, but also in keeping away the malign and directing to those who are breathing their last a water-flowing channel, which conducts the stream of imperial benefaction towards us. Perhaps we will become a plant that bears generous fruits, neither useless for our lord nor worth cutting off, and we shall inscribe you as a saviour and raise to you a *stele*[63] among benefactors and proclaim you as giver of good.
>
> Τῷ φιλολόγῳ τὸ δῶρον, τῷ λογοθέτῃ τὸν λόγον ἀπὸ ψυχῆς εὐγνώμονος ἐσχεδίασα. ἀλλά μοι συγγνωμονοίης, ἀνδρῶν ὀλβιώτατε, ὅτι πένητι λόγῳ σὲ τὸν τοιοῦτον περιχλαινίζειν παρώρμημαι, καὶ ταῦτα, ὁπηνίκα μοι τὸ περιπύργιον τῆς ψυχῆς ταῖς συνεχέσιν ἐκπεπολιόρκηται ἑλεπόλεσι θλίψεων. ἡλίου μὲν γὰρ ἀκτῖσι νεφέλαι, καρδίᾳ δὲ λῦπαι πολέμιαι· εἰ δὲ πολλοὶ μὲν οἱ πολεμοῦντες, μηδεμίαν δὲ τοῦ πολεμεῖν αἰτίαν ἔχοντες

---

[62] Cf. Menander, *Sententiae* 123: Δρυὸς πεσούσης πᾶς ἀνὴρ ξυλεύεται. Manasses uses a revised version of the gnomic expression and turns it into a simile: as a fallen tree is cut up for firewood, a man already lying down is easily attacked.

[63] On the image of a text as a *stele*, see also *Hysmine and Hysminias* 11.22.4 (Conca), on which Nilsson 2001: 74–8.

εὔλογον, τίς ἂν ὑποίσοι ψυχή, καὶ διαβολαῖς κατασειομένη καὶ συκοφαντίᾳ κριοκοπουμένη; καὶ δρυὸς μὲν πεσούσης οὐκ ἔστιν ὅστις οὐχὶ ξυλεύεται, ἀνδρὶ δὲ δυσπραγοῦντι οὐκ ἔστιν, ὡς ἔοικεν, ὅστις οὐκ ἐπιτίθεται. ἀλλὰ σύ τι διάφερε τῶν κακῶν· ἔξεστι γάρ· καὶ μὴ μόνον διάφερε τῷ μὴ κολούειν τὰ καθ' ἡμᾶς, ἀλλὰ καὶ τῷ τοὺς βασκαίνοντας εἴργειν καὶ τοῖς ἀπεψυγμένοις ὑδρορρόος χρηματίζειν ἀμάρα, τὸ χεῦμα τῆς βασιλείας ἀγαθοποιΐας εἰς ἡμᾶς ὀχετεύουσα. καὶ γενησόμεθα ἴσως φυτὸν καρποὺς εὐγενεῖς ὀπωροφοροῦν καὶ τῷ δεσπότῃ οὐκ ἄχρηστον οὐδὲ ἄξιον ἐκτομῆς, καὶ σὲ σωτῆρα ἐπιγραψόμεθα καὶ ἐν εὐεργέταις ἀναστηλώσομεν καὶ ὡς ἀγαθοδότην περιλαλήσομεν.[64]

The letter thus functions as both a summary of and a commentary on the oration (the gift), using the same words and imagery to characterize both the author and the addressee. The author is like a garden in need of irrigation, sun and caretaking (money, benefaction, patronage) so that plants may grow and carry fruit (orations and other kinds of rhetorical products).[65] He is the victim of false rumours and slander, and he needs the logothete to intervene on his behalf. The logothete is not only a successful politician with close ties to the emperor, he is also a skilled poet and rhetorician. The latter characteristic means that the relationship between the author and the addressee is based on similarity – the two are of a similar kind, appreciating *paideia* and *logoi*.[66] This similarity is expressed by narrative and stylistic means in both texts, but since the oration is longer it allows for more narrative emphasis: the opening and closing stories signifying a shared Hellenic heritage, but also the stories of how the logothete has displayed his poetic and rhetorical skills. The concentrated form of the letter demands stylistic strategies, starting with the programmatic opening and its play on *logos*, *philologos* and *logothetes*.[67] It connects to the opening of the oration and its play on *logos*, but also to the characterization of both author and addressee as based on a sense of similarity. In Eco's words, one might say that the addressee is the model reader of the two texts whose intention is to make the reader act on the author's behalf.

In order to understand exactly how this is going to happen, we need to turn to the second letter, following directly after the first in the manuscript and still with no indication of the author. In this case, there is, however, an

---

[64] Manasses, *Letter* 1 (Horna); tr. Nilsson 2016, revised.
[65] On this imagery and especially the metaphors of waterworks in Manasses' letters, see Nilsson 2016: esp. 274.
[66] Cf. above, Chapter 3, on patronage based on contiguity vs similarity.
[67] Cf. the emphasis on beauty and the appreciation of it in the opening of the *Description of a crane hunt* (above, Chapter 2) and in the *Description of the Cyclops* (Nilsson 2011: 126–7; also below).

The Need to Address the Logothete

addressee: it is written to a certain *pansebastos kyr* Georgios, son of the *megas domestikos* (Τῷ πανσεβαστῷ κυρῷ Γεωργίῳ, τῷ υἱῷ τοῦ μεγάλου δομεστίκου).[68] The second letter reads as follows.

If somewhere in the world there are human beings who live in the darkness, whom neither a star illuminates nor the bright eye of the sun beholds, let Homer's Muse speak and the tongue of Herodotus boast of them[69] – I myself am presently learning and seeing this in practice, you most noble of men! For I had you as a nobly born star and my sun was the emperor – the emperor, whom God placed like a constellation in heaven, whose successes run across the Earth like rays, and they are shot off like a life-nourishing light and they alight like a tree-rearing fire. As that sun is currently wielding his torch in the wars against the Gepids and in the land by the Istros and you are keeping guard over that sun bringing light to mortals, which the discourse set up as my star, I have in the meantime become gloomy and been placed in the dark like in a world without stars and been bereaved of light like in a world without sun. But may you soon shine out, may you soon bring warmer light and, leaving cold Pannonia and the wintry land of the Gepids, bring light to and beam at the land of Panhellenes. And we shall light up again and be brought back to life and speak eagerly and rhythmically like cicadas[70] and celebrate the right hand of the emperor, the one that is generous to its subjects, murderous to its enemies. The oration for the logothete has been sent, and I really trust that your magnanimity sees to it that the logothete receives this in his hands and reads it. And may you traverse the voyage of life washed by no waves and moor your boat of life in harbours calm and safe from winds and may you live even longer than those immortal founders of your family.

Εἰ μὲν εἰσί που τῆς γῆς ἐν ζόφῳ διάγοντες ἄνθρωποι, οὓς οὔτε ἄστρον αὐγάζει οὔτε ἡλίου βλέφαρον εὐφεγγὲς ἐπιδέρκεται, Ὁμήρου μοῦσα λαλείτω καὶ Ἡροδότου γλῶσσα κομπολεσχείτω· ἐμοὶ δὲ ἄρα ἐπὶ τῶν ἔργων καὶ μανθάνειν τοῦτο πάρεστι καὶ ὁρᾶν, ἀνδρῶν εὐγενέστατε· σὲ μὲν γὰρ εἶχον ἄστρον καλλιφυές, ἥλιος δὲ ἦν μοι ὁ βασιλεύς, βασιλεύς, ὃν καθάπερ ἐν οὐρανῷ θεὸς κατηστέρισεν, οὗ καθάπερ ἀκτῖνες τὰ προτερήματα τὴν ὑπ' οὐρανὸν διατρέχουσι καὶ ὡς φῶς ζωοτρόφον ἀποτοξεύονται καὶ ὡς δενδροτρόφον σέλας πυρσεύουσι. Τοῦ τοίνυν ἡλίου τούτου περὶ τὰ γηπαιδικὰ καὶ τὴν παριστρίαν λαμπτηρουχοῦντος καὶ σοῦ τὸν ἥλιον τοῦτον δορυφοροῦντος τὸν φαεσίμβροτον, ὃν ἐμὸν ἄστρον ὁ λόγος ἐστήσατο, ἐγὼ τέως ἠχλύωμαι καὶ ὡς ἐν ἀνάστροις

---

[68] A *megas domestikos* was a military commander of high rank, having also a courtly function of waiting on the emperor at banquets; see *ODB*, s.v. *megas domestikos*.
[69] On the Cimmerians living in a country forever deprived of sunshine and at the entrance of Hades, see *Od.* 11.14. In addition to this Homeric myth, Herodotus brings up the Cimmerians in several places in his *History*.
[70] Cf. Manasses, *Itinerary* 2.119–21 (Horna): ὃ τέττιγες πάσχουσιν οἱ δροσοφάγοι, | θέρους μὲν ὑπάδοντες ἔμμουσον μέλος, | νεκρούμενοι δὲ τοῦ κρύους πεφθακότος.

ἐσκότωμαι καὶ ὡς ἐν ἀνηλίοις ἐζόφωμαι. ἀλλ' ἐπιφαύσαιτε τάχιον, ἀλλ' ὀξύτερον ἐπιλάμψοιτε καὶ τὴν ψυχρὰν Παννονίαν καὶ τὴν δυσχείμερον ἀπολιπόντες γηπαιδικήν, ἐπὶ τὴν Πανελλήνων καὶ φεραυγήσαιτε καὶ φωτοβολήσαιτε· καὶ ἡμεῖς ἀναζωπυρηθησόμεθα καὶ ζωωθησόμεθα καὶ λαλήσομεν τεττιγῶδες καὶ σύντονον καὶ τὴν βασιλέως ὑμνήσομεν δεξιάν, τὴν τοῖς ὑπηκόοις μεγαλοδότειραν, τὴν τοῖς ἐχθροῖς ἀνδρολέτειραν. Ὁ εἰς τὸν λογοθέτην λόγος ἐστάλη, θαρρῶ δὲ ὅτι πάντως, ὅτι τῇ σῇ μεγαλονοίᾳ μελήσει, ὅπως καὶ εἰς χεῖρας δέξεται τοῦτον ὁ λογοθέτης καὶ ἀναγνώσεται. Καὶ εἴης ἀκυμάντως τὸν πλοῦν τοῦ βίου διαπερῶν καὶ τὸ τῆς ζωῆς σκάφος ὁρμίζων ἐν ἀλεξανέμοις ὅρμοις καὶ εὐγαλήνοις καὶ βιώσαις ὑπὲρ τοὺς ἀρχηγέτας τοῦ γένους ἐκείνους τοὺς δολιχαίωνας.[71]

Here we meet a third agent: another functionary who has a previous relation to the author, supposedly back in Constantinople, and who is now close enough to the logothete to assist the author in making him read the oration and the letter. The practical circumstances of the exchange of the oration and the letters thus becomes clearer: the emperor and the logothete are away from Constantinople, as is this Georgios, in the Hungarian wars 'in the land by the Istros' (the Danube).[72] This is why the oration cannot be performed by the author for the logothete, which explains the need for the letters and the intermediary position of Georgios.

There are certain similarities in the way in which this Georgios and the logothete are characterized and addressed. They are both a means to reach the person who really matters – they are stars around the sun (the emperor).[73] The logothete is ultimately a way of reaching the emperor, and Georgios is a way of making sure that the logothete gets the message; at the same time, Georgios is described as a close attendant of the emperor (δορυφορῶν), so he too must be seen as intimately connected to central power. The level of style is as high in the letter to Georgios as in the letter to the logothete, even though the learnedness of Georgios is not addressed explicitly. The style supposedly reflects the expectations of a person in imperial service, having gone through the educational system of Constantinople, perhaps with someone like the rhetor as one of their teachers. Both the logothete and Georgios will be praised by the rhetor if they help him out.[74] All three texts, the oration as well as the letters, represent from that perspective samples of the skills of the rhetorician.

---

[71] Manasses, *Letter* 2 (Horna).
[72] These wars are mentioned also in the oration, but in a less clear manner in a description of various places to which the emperor travels: Manasses, *Encomium of Michael Hagiotheodorites* 158–61 (Horna).
[73] Cf. above, Chapter 2, on Manuel I Komnenos and the imagery of the sun.
[74] Manasses, *Encomium of Michael Hagiotheodorites* 400–1 (Horna): ἡμεῖς δὲ πάλιν λαλήσομεν καὶ ὑμνήσομεν καὶ χαριστήρια θύσομεν καὶ τρανότερόν σοι γνωριοῦμεν τὸν ῥήτορα; *Letter* 2.15–16

In that capacity, they also allow the reader to catch a glimpse of the character of the rhetor – they not only tell his story, they also reflect his state of mind. The choice of the verb σχεδιάζω for the composition of the oration in the first letter (τὸν λόγον ... ἐσχεδίασα)[75] does not indicate improvisation as such, but rather the alleged haste and urgency with which the oration has been put together. In the oration, this is reflected in the impression given of the author finding himself in emotional turmoil, not being quite able to concentrate on the task at hand because he keeps thinking of his own problems. This impression is, however, the result of a careful rhetorical composition rather than actual haste, especially in the 'published' version that has come down to us in the manuscript.[76] At the same time, the author wishes to underline the urgency of his situation by making a clear distinction between the literary imaginary and the harsh reality in which he finds himself: fiction is for Homer and Herodotus, for me there are only facts (ἐμοὶ δὲ ἄρα ἐπὶ τῶν ἔργων).[77]

Let us then consider, against this textual and transtexual analysis of the three texts, the extratextual circumstances and the identity of the author and addressee. As already mentioned, neither author nor addressee is named in the manuscript, but the author can be safely identified as Manasses based on both manuscript evidence and the clearly Manassean style.[78] From the passages cited above, it should be clear that not only the use of specific words, expressions and citations indicate Manasses as an author, but also the imagery employed for describing the rhetor's situation, the character and activities of the learned addressee and the role of the emperor in Constantinopolitan society. Much of it ties in with types of imagery that have already been observed in the previous chapters, and it is all part of Manasses' self-representation as an occasional writer on command: the struggling rhetor who needs good relations and objects to describe and people to write for, the cicada in need of the nurturing sun of imperial benefaction.[79] It is this imagery – employed to some extent also in the self-representation of other twelfth-century writers[80] – in

---

(Horna): καὶ ἡμεῖς ἀναζωπυρηθησόμεθα καὶ ζωωθησόμεθα καὶ λαλήσομεν τεττιγώδες καὶ σύντονον καὶ τὴν βασιλέως ὑμνήσομεν δεξιάν.

[75] Manasses, *Letter* 1.1–2 (Horna).
[76] Cf. Agapitos 1989: 64–5 on the 'Improvisationsstil' of Italikos, rather than actual improvisation, in his *Monody on the death of his partridge* (discussed above, Chapter 3).
[77] Manasses, *Letter* 2.3–4 (Horna).   [78] Horna 1906.
[79] Cf. the the withering cicada in Manasses, *Itinerary* 2.119–21 (Horna) and the soothing 'dew' dispensed by the benefactor Eirene in the *Verse chronicle* 16–17 (Lampsides): καὶ τὸν τοῦ κόπου καύσωνα καὶ τῆς ταλαιπωρίας | αἱ δωρεαὶ δροσίζουσι κενούμεναι συχνάκις.
[80] See above, n. 13.

combination with a particular style, for instance in the form of Manassean words and images, that creates the specific voice of the model author.

As for the logothete, he too may be identified based on the details offered in the texts combined with external evidence. Horna, the editor of the oration and the letters, identified him as Michael Hagiotheodorites, an influential functionary and logothete of the drome in 1166–70.[81] In 1167, he took part in the war fought by Manuel I Komnenos against the Hungarians,[82] which places him in the kind of situation that is described in the texts.[83] As noted by Paul Magdalino, the administrative positions of logothete and *orphanotrophos* offered both wealth and opportunities for patronage.[84] This is indicated not only by the eulogy of Hagiotheodorites by Manasses, but also by two other orations, written by Eustathios of Thessalonike and Constantine Psaltopoulos respectively.[85] In addition to dispensing charity, directly and through the emperor,[86] Hagiotheodorites was also known as a skilled writer and rhetorician, manifested in his position in imperial administration as well as in his skilfully composed iambic poetry.[87] Manasses is careful to underline this in his eulogy, and it is supported by a preserved example of Hagiotheodorites' art: a verse ekphrasis of a chariot race held in Constantinople on 1 February 1168. This ekphrasis deserves a closer look in regard to the possible relation between Hagiotheodorites and Manasses.

It has as its model a poem by the eleventh-century Christopher of Mytilene, a poem that is incomplete and quite poorly preserved in a Vienna manuscript.[88] According to the first lines of Hagiotheodorites'

---

[81] Horna 1906: 193–4. The *logothetes tou dromou* was a high official whose responsibilities included ceremonial duties, protection of the emperor, collection of political information and supervision of foreign affairs; see *ODB*, s.v. *logothetes tou dromou*.

[82] For the Hungarian campaigns of Manuel and Byzantine–Hungarian relations of the twelfth century, see above, Chapter 2, n. 17.

[83] His presence in the campaign is mentioned also by John Kinnamos, *History* 6.6 (Meineke): Μετ' οὐ πολὺ δὲ βασιλέως κελεύσαντος ἄνδρες τῶν ἐπὶ δόξης παρ' αὐτὸν ἦλθον, Ἰωάννης τε ὁ Δούκας καὶ Μιχαήλ, ὃς λογοθέτης ἐκείνου τοῦ χρόνου ἦν. The full name of this logothete is not mentioned by historians, but appears in Balsamon, *Synod. Cpol. can.* IV (PG 137, 1024 B): μετὰ τοῦ μακαρίτου πρωτονωβελλισιμοϋπερτάτου καὶ λογοθέτου τοῦ δρόμου κυροῦ Μιχαὴλ τοῦ Ἁγιοθεοδωρίτου. His name also appears in protocols; see Horna 1906: 193.

[84] Magdalino 1993: 256–7.

[85] Magdalino 1993: 256 and n. 94. On the oration by Eustathios, see Agapitos 1998.

[86] According to Eustathios, Hagiotheodorites did this not only by dispensing charity directly (for instance in his capacity as *orphanotrophos*), but also by 'wielding the pen with which the emperor granted requests'; see Magdalino 1993: 257. Cf. Manasses, *Encomium of Michael Hagiotheodorites* 255–60 (Horna) on how Hagiotheodorites made imperial news known in the capital.

[87] Horna 1906: 194. See also Magdalino 1993: 314.

[88] The poem was edited in Horna 1906: 194–7 (text) and 197–8 (commentary). For a more recent analysis of Hagiotheodorites' poem and its relation to Manasses, see Marciniak and Warcaba 2014.

poem, the chariot race took place 'during the first indiction and the first winter afternoon of the rainy month February in the twenty-fifth year of the reign of Emperor Manuel', which offers a tentative date for the poem (c.1168).[89] In a recent analysis of the ekphrasis, Przemysław Marciniak and Katarzyna Warcaba have argued that it should be seen not as a poor imitation of Christopher of Mytilene, but rather as a skilful expression of rhetorical, narrative and ekphrastic strategies of the twelfth century, represented by authors such as Manasses. They take that observation further by identifying Manasses as the potential addressee of the poem, the mysterious 'somebody living in the countryside' (τινὰ ἐν ἀγρῷ οἰκοῦντα) that was deciphered by Horna from the faded title of the poem.[90] This somebody, addressed as 'stranger', is in the countryside 'to speak undisturbed with books' (ὡς ἀταράχως προσλαλεῖς τοῖς βιβλίοις), 'where alone like a song-loving sparrow you sing sweet musical melodies, with which you sweeten the hearts of listeners enchanting them with your words' (ὅπου μονάζων ὡς φιλῳδὸν στρουθίον | ᾄδεις λιγυρὰς μουσικὰς μελῳδίας, | δι' ὧν γλυκαίνεις ἀκροατῶν καρδίας, | ἴυγξιν αὐτοὺς ἑλκύων σου τῶν λόγων).[91] As noted by Marciniak and Warcaba, this particular sequence is strongly reminiscent of the imagery used by Manasses in the *Itinerary*, the *Verse chronicle* and the *Monody on the death of his goldfinch*. Based on this, they suggest that Manasses might have been the addressee of the ekphrasis, with lines 10 and 25 drawing on and alluding to his *Itinerary* 2.96.[92] Pointing also to other correspondences with Manasses' work, they tentatively conclude that the ekphrasis may have been sent to Manasses, who was not in Constantinople but either in a monastery or in exile as a result of the problems he had mentioned in his oration to Hagiotheodorites.[93]

While I find that interpretation convincing from a transtextual perspective, now supported by the imagery discussed above in Chapter 2, I would rephrase it in light of the theoretical framework proposed here. The model author of the Hagiotheodorites ekphrasis addresses a model reader, who is characterized in accordance with the model author of several texts attributed to Manasses. It is true that this model author has been characterized

---

[89] Hagiotheodorites, *Ekphrasis* 1–5 (Horna); tr. Marciniak and Warcaba 2014. See also Rhoby 2015: 233.
[90] Horna 1906: 194; tr. Marciniak and Warcaba 2014. As noted by Marciniak and Warcaba, the title, too, is an imitation of the poem by Christopher of Mytilene.
[91] Hagiotheodorites, *Ekphrasis* 10 and 25–8 (Horna); tr. Marciniak and Warcaba 2014: 109, with a brief discussion on the use of 'stranger' rather than 'friend'.
[92] Marciniak and Warcaba 2014: 109–10. They note also the similarities with Manasses, *Itinerary* 1.335–6 (Chryssogelos) and *Verse chronicle* 5764 (Lampsides).
[93] See esp. Marciniak and Warcaba 2014: 110–11.

(in the oration and the letters) not only in relation to his books and activities as a writer, but also in relation to his problems, which makes it possible that the author of the ekphrasis refers to some sort of 'exile' caused by falling out of favour with the emperor, or perhaps simply by losing a lucrative position within the system of patronage. However, within the literary imaginary of the texts one may also find other interpretive options, such as the idyllic countryside across the Bosphoros in the *Description of the catching of siskins and chaffinches*.[94] This text contains both the bird imagery and the ekphrastic discourse that seem to have been part of Manasses' trademark. That imagery is also used to describe the grammar contest in which Hagiotheodorites took part,[95] which opens up a poetic connection between bird-catching as a bucolic idyll and bird-catching as a metaphor for linguistic skills. Interpreted in light of this textual link, the mysterious 'stranger' in the Hagiotheodorites ekphrasis – the addressee within the text, not the empirical author Manasses – may simply be spending some time outside of the capital, finally enjoying his books after last year's upsetting events. Such a literary game, too, would 'make perfect sense', as long as we stay within the world of the texts.[96]

With a Little Help from My Friends

What we have observed so far, then, is a series of texts in which the author presents himself as being in trouble and asks his addressees to help him out. At least one of the addressees can be identified: the mighty Hagiotheodorites, who wrote an ekphrasis which seems to somehow interact on a textual level with these and other works by Manasses. The identification of the other addressee – *pansebastos kyr* Georgios, son of the *megas domestikos* – is more difficult, but his position in the hierarchy is clear: he is of a good family, used to serving the emperor, and is now close to the emperor himself. In light of his noble birth, his position should be higher than that of a secretary.[97] After the texts addressing these important men follows a third letter, written to a certain Michael Angelopoulos

---

[94] See above, Chapter 1.
[95] Manasses, *Encomium of Michael Hagiotheodorites* 264–74 (Horna); see also the *Funerary oration on the death of Nikephoros Komnenos* 453–66.
[96] Cf. Marciniak and Warcaba 2014: 111–12.
[97] As noted by Magdalino 1997: 162, this Georgios is either to be identified with the addressee of the *Description of the Cyclops*, the *megas hetaireiarches* Georgios Palaiologos, or he is yet another of Manasses' instrumental friends. The Georgios of the ekphrasis is praised as *philologos* and *philokalos*, a wordplay similar to the one on *philologos* and *logothetes* in the oration for Hagiotheodorites; see above and Nilsson 2011: esp. 128.

(Τῷ κυρῷ Μιχαὴλ τῷ Ἀγγελοπούλῳ). It is shorter and more informal than the other two letters and takes the form of a note of thanks.

> 'The encouragement of a friend is a good thing',[98] says the epic poet. I therefore deem you to be among my very best friends, you most clever of men, and I took your advice to heart and followed it altogether. May now my troubles come to a good and fruitful end, so that we don't – as the saying goes – play the lyre without food and without gifts[99] or are called greenkeepers and gardeners of infertile plants, whose flower is neither deep red nor fully purple, but ignoble, fading and of an unprofitable and uninteresting kind, and whose fruit is nowhere to be seen. Farewell and remember our friendship and keep its flow clean from salty water and unmixed – indeed the river Alphaeus preserves its stream sweet even in the sea.

> "Ἀγαθὴ δὲ παραίφασίς ἐστιν ἑταίρου" φησὶν ὁ εἰπών. ἐγὼ τοίνυν τοῖς μάλιστα τῶν ἐμοὶ φιλουμένων ἐγκρίνω σε, ἀνδρῶν ἀγχινούστατε, ἐγκάρδιόν τε τὴν σὴν ὑποθημοσύνην ἔσχον καὶ εἰς τέλος ἐξήνεγκα. Εἴη δέ μοι καὶ τὸ τοῦ καμάτου τέλος αἴσιόν τι καὶ ἔγκαρπον, ἵνα μὴ κατὰ τὴν παροιμίαν ἄσιτα φορμίζωμεν καὶ ἀδώρητα ἢ φυτησκάφοι καὶ κηπευταὶ χρηματίζοιμεν ἀγόνων φυτῶν, ὧν καὶ τὸ ἄνθος οὐκ ἐξέρυθρον οὐδὲ περιπόρφυρον, ἀλλ' ἀγενὲς καὶ ἐξίτηλον καὶ τῆς ἀχρειοτέρας μοίρας καὶ ἀσπουδάστου, καὶ ὁ καρπὸς οὐδαμοῦ. ἔρρωσο καὶ τῆς φιλίας μνημόνευε καὶ τήρει τὸ ταύτης ῥεῖθρον καθαρὸν ἁλμυρίας καὶ ἀμιγές· καίτοι καὶ ποταμὸς Ἀλφειὸς κἂν θαλάσσῃ σῴζει τὸ νᾶμα γλυκύ.[100]

The voice is the same, but the tone is different from the more formal letters and gives the impression of a more personal exchange between friends – still of an instrumental kind and based on imagery drawn from ancient literature, but on a more affectionate note than in the poem cited at the beginning of this chapter. At the same time, the story that a reader can extract from the series of texts is more or less an elaboration of the topic expressed in the poem cited at the beginning of this chapter: real friends help each other out when they are in trouble. Both Georgios and Michael could be defined as friends in a Byzantine context, but it may be significant that the concept of friendship (φιλία) is brought up only in the letter to

---

[98] *Il.* 11.793.
[99] Cf. Lycophron, *Alexandra* 137–8 (Mascialino): τοιγὰρ ψαλάξεις εἰς κενὸν νευρᾶς κτύπον, | ἄσιτα κἀδώρητα φορμίζων μέλη, quoted by John Mauropous, *Letter* 57.9–10: κατὰ τὸν εἰπόντα ἄσιτα κἀδώρητα φορμίζω μέλη.
[100] Manasses, *Letter* 3 (Horna). Cf. Manasses, *Encomium of Michael Hagiotheodorites* 200 (Horna). The myth of Alpheius and Arethusa appears in Pausanias 5.7.2, but Manasses may as well have received it from Achilles Tatius, *Leucippe and Clitophon* 1.18.1–2. For the same myth, see also Manasses, *Aristandros and Kallithea* frg. 21.6–12 (Mazal), and Niketas Eugenianos, *Drosilla and Charikles* 4.145–8 (Conca).

Michael.[101] Also the less complex style indicates a more symmetrical relationship than the one with Hagiotheodorites and Georgios, perhaps that of fellow teachers or writers. The letter complements the story told in the preceding texts and refers back to the beginning of the oration and the advice of the good friend that is mentioned there, reflecting Lysippus in the story of Apelles: 'For as I was exhausted at critical times ... , a not ungracious friend turned to me and chastened and instructed me; and he ... guided instead the water-pipe of the art to you and your praise and songs.'[102]

The identity of this friend certainly eludes a modern reader, but that does not mean that the story of the texts has no bearing on a socio-cultural situation. That is to say, even if Manasses invented the whole story as an entertaining fiction, carefully constructing the series of texts as a kind of 'documentary', it would still have value for a modern reader who wishes to understand networking in twelfth-century Byzantium. And even without identifying this particular friend, there are similar stories to be extracted from contemporary authors. One may consider, for instance, Theodore Prodromos and the way in which he addresses his former student Theodore Stypiotes in a *schedos* written in political verse.[103] Stypiotes, addressed as 'best of secretaries, students and friends' (ὦ βέλτιστε γραμματικῶν καὶ μαθητῶν καὶ φίλων), has been successful and now holds a position as imperial secretary.[104] Prodromos begins by reminding his former student of the past, back when the student admired the teacher for his skills,[105] but then he presents his real message: now that you are close to the emperor, you need to share that information with me, so that I have something to write about.[106] The emperor is apparently out of town, which explains the need for an intermediary, because for as long as the emperor is away (ἔκδημος) Prodromos is deprived of means (ἔρημος ὁ Πρόδρομος πραγμάτων).[107] The meaning of πραγμάτων is most likely twofold: as long as the emperor is away, Prodromos has nothing to write about and thus cannot make any money.

---

[101] After all, praise of friendship is a standard topos in epistolography; see Mullett 1981 and 1988: 9–10, as well as Papaioannou 2010.
[102] Manasses, *Encomium of Michael Hagiotheodorites* 40–5 (Horna).
[103] Prodromos, *Poem* 71 (Hörandner). On this poem as a *schedos*, see Agapitos 2015c: 16–17. See also Magdalino 1993: 429–30.
[104] Prodromos, *Poem* 71.1 (Hörandner).   [105] Prodromos, *Poem* 71, esp. 7–10 (Hörandner).
[106] Prodromos, *Poem* 71.33–73 (Hörandner); esp. v. 34: νῦν δὲ παρὼν καὶ συμπαρὼν αὐτῷ τῷ στεφηφόρῳ; v. 62: οὐ μεταδίδως τοῦ καλοῦ τῷ φίλῳ σου Προδρόμῳ.
[107] Prodromos, *Poem* 71.93–5 (Hörandner): λόγισαι, πόσον ἔκδημος ὁ βασιλεὺς ὑπάρχει | καὶ πόσον χρόνον ἔρημος ὁ Πρόδρομος πραγμάτων, | αὐτῆς δὲ μᾶλλον τῆς ζωῆς, αὐτῶν τῶν ἀναγκαίων.

This may be compared to the intermediary function of both the logothete and Georgios, the addressee of the second letter, and one may note also the comment made more or less in passing in Manasses' oration to Hagiotheodorites, speaking of the emperor's successes in war: 'these successes, these famous victories must be made known to the city of Byzantion'.[108] For a rhetor not to have access to such information could apparently be a problem, which meant that a good network that included former students, patrons and friends (sometimes in overlapping functions) was of crucial importance. In the case of Prodromos and Stypiotes, a continuation of the story seems to be offered in another poem by Prodromos, this time addressing the emperor himself. 'As it seems' (Ὡς φαίνεται), opens the poem, the secretary is not doing his job – either he has something against me or he sleeps a lot.[109] While this poem, sometimes referred to as 'the fifth Ptochoprodromic poem', is clearly playful and gradually subverts the lofty opening and turns into a vernacular burlesque,[110] the story about networking and the use of friends is clear. And Prodromos, too, underlines the distinction between the literary imaginary of poets like Homer and the factual situation of poets like himself. In a hexameter poem addressed to Anna Komnene, he opens in an epic style that suits the learned princess, but then inserts himself – or rather his authorial *persona* – into the Homeric song: 'For I shall tell you of the manifold cycles of my suffering' (σοὶ γὰρ ἐμῶν παθέων πολυπληθέα κύκλα μυθεῦμαι).[111] What Prodromos does here is to employ a 'fictional' (Homeric) form for the telling of a 'real' tale, or rather the tale of the model author.[112] More importantly, the intention of the text, here too, is that of a decent donation.

The texts under discussion here are all occasional in the sense that they were composed for specific occasions and had extratextual aims. In that capacity they have an intermediary position between the literary imagi-

---

[108] Manasses, *Encomium of Michael Hagiotheodorites* 256 (Horna).
[109] Prodromos, 'Fifth Ptochoprodromic poem' 1–5 (Maiuri): Ὡς φαίνεται, φιλόχριστε δέσποτα, | δεσποτά μου, | ἀστὴρ τοῦ κόσμου φαεινέ, λαμπτὴρ κοινὲ Ῥωμαίων, | κάλλος τοῦ διαδήματος, ἀγλάϊσμα τοῦ στέφους | καὶ τῆς πορφύρας καύχημα καὶ δόξα βασιλείας, | ὡς φαίνεται, ὁ γραμματικός . . ., and 7: ἢ μάχην εἶχε μετ' ἐμοῦ, ἢ περισσὰ νυστάζη.
[110] See Hörandner 1974: 66. On the usage of 'learned' vs 'colloquial' in the twelfth century, see Agapitos 2015b and Agapitos 2017; on this particular poem, Agapitos 2015c: 34–26. In this series of articles, Agapitos identifies a significant link between schedography and the use of the colloquial or vernacular register.
[111] Theodore Prodromos, *Poem* 38.10 (Hörandner).
[112] Cf. the use of Homer in Manasses, *Description of a little man*; see Messis and Nilsson 2015 and below, Chapter 7.

naries of the Graeco-Roman and Biblical traditions and the real life situation in which the authors found themselves. Stories of this kind – extracted from the texts without arguing (or denying) that the empirical authors are to be identified with the model authors who appear in the texts – may help us to reconstruct the socio-cultural milieu that characterized twelfth-century Constantinople, while still acknowledging our own position as modern interpreters. We can never step into the shoes of someone who was part of the relevant circles at the time, but by recognizing the semiotic structures of the texts, we can do our best to become model readers and interpret the meaning of the text. From this perspective, there is one more text that could be brought into the discussion as a kind of complement to the authorial story that has been traced above.

The so-called *Address by the way* (ἐνόδιον προσφώνημα) was first edited by Konstantin Horna together with Manasses' *Monody on the death of his goldfinch* and Michael Italikos' *Monody on the death of his partridge*, but Horna was reluctant to attribute the text to Manasses.[113] While I agree with his reluctance, due to the lack of a clearly Manassean voice, the *Address by the way* undeniably ties in with the way in which the model author Manasses is characterized in the *encomium* and the letters discussed in this chapter. It is written as a combined *encomium* and note of thanks, most probably addressing Manuel Komnenos. The blazing light and generosity of the emperor, the sun, is contrasted with the suffering of the author, now safe and sound but previously 'sunk in a pit' and 'frozen in the clutch of hunger', just like Daniel in the lions' den.[114] In spite of the lack of a specifically Manassean vocabulary, the imagery is reminiscent of that used in the oration and the letters and it is tempting to read it as an expression of gratitude to the emperor himself, a sort of formal equivalent of the letter of thanks for Angelopoulos. The more conventional tone, marked by contiguity rather than similarity, could in that case explain the

---

[113] See Horna 1902: 21–2 on the rather complicated textual situation. In the Barocc. 131, the *Monody on the death of his goldfinch* is followed by two anonymous texts: a poem consisting of 71 political verses (ibid.: 13–14) and a prose text (ibid.: 12). The poem draws on Biblical material and does not display any significant Manassean characteristics, but the prose text curiously reappears in the same ms, f. 484 and then with an attribution to Manasses (for details, see ibid.: 22). Browning 1966 presented a revised edition and translated the text in his collection of *prooimia* under the name of Manasses, without offering any arguments for the attribution. On the monodies by Manasses and Italikos, see above, Chapter 3.

[114] *Address by the way* 18–20 (Browning): οὕτω καὶ σύ, βασιλεῦ, ἐν λάκκῳ βοθρευομένους ἡμᾶς κατῳκτείρισας, λιμοῦ τε πυράγρᾳ κρυσταλλουμένους καὶ πόρρωθεν ἀνεζώωσας ἀκτῖνας χρυσοῦ ἐπαφείς. The *exemplum* of Daniel is offered in lines 13–18, then referred to again in lines 21–2.

lack of a personal style. But it is also possible that the text was written by another author, perhaps simply as an example of a typical imperial address, as suggested by Horna.[115] In either case, the text's character and its position in the manuscript together with texts more safely attributed to Manasses indicate a certain familiarity with the twelfth-century context in general and perhaps with Manasses in particular.[116]

It was once noted by Paul Magdalino that Manasses 'was remarkably single-minded in attaching himself to his social superiors – an impression reinforced by [his] almost total lack of reference to his social equals'.[117] This impression can be revised based on the analysis proposed here. In the oration and the letters, interaction with both superiors and equals is clearly displayed, ranging from the logothete Michael Hagiotheodorites at the very top (characterized in terms of similarity in regard to his poetic and intellectual skills, but with the social power to help out the author) to the friend Michael Angelopoulos (characterized in terms of 'real' similarity and symmetrical friendship, not just rhetorical similarity in the service of successful patronage).[118] And according to the story that Manasses (the model author) projected here, along with other texts that have come down to us, his choice to follow the advice of his friend turned out to be successful, because he (the empirical author) was still writing for aristocratic patrons in imperial circles in the early 1170s.[119] It is possible that this story is nothing but a literary construct, but it is also possible that

---

[115] Horna 1902: 22.
[116] Of some interest is the reference to the 'Indian stone' in *Address by the way* 6–11 (Browning), employed to describe the character of the emperor (see Horna 1902: 22 on the use of the same image in Theodore Prodromos), but potentially pointing in the direction of magic stones in the novel tradition and the 'Indian' novel by Manasses. The Indian stone is the Heliodoran παντάρβη (*Aethiopica* 8.11.4), as reinterpreted by Eugenianos, *Drosilla and Charikles* 6.399 (Conca) (ἀλλ' Ἰνδικὴν λίθον σε παντάρβην ἔχω), appearing also in other twelfth-century authors, e.g. John Tzetzes, *Chiliades* 6.68 (Leone): Παντάρβη λίθος οὖσα τις τοὺς λίθους ἐπισπᾶται, | ὁμοῦ χρυσόν τε καί τινα βυθοῖς ἐγχαλασθεῖσα, | ὡς ἡ μαγνῆτις σίδηρον εἴωθεν ἐπισπᾶσθαι, | καθάπερ καὶ ἡ ἤλεκτρος, ἥν λέγεις βερενίκην, | καὶ αὕτη ἐπισπᾶται γὰρ τὰς φύσεις τῶν ἀχύρων, | δάκρυον οὖσα δένδρων τι· τὴν ἄλλην γὰρ οὐ λέγω, | ἤλεκτρον τὴν χαλκίζουσαν, τὰς δὲ λοιπὰς δυνάμεις | ἐῶ μετάλλων ἄλλων τε καὶ λίθων διαγράφειν. On Manasses' novel, see below, Chapter 6.
[117] Magdalino 1997: 162. Cf. more recently Foskolou 2018: 79–80 and 95–6 on the 'snobbery' in Manasses' attitude, influenced by Magdalino 1984 and 1997.
[118] Cf. the model proposed above, Chapter 3.
[119] Cf. Chryssogelos 2016: 155–60 on the 'social skills' of Manasses, helping him in his career, and above, Chapter 1. As for John Kontostephanos, it should be noted that he was involved c.1161 in the embassy to Jerusalem and then addressed in the mid 1170s at the death of Theodora, so he seems to have remained a more or less stable presence in the aristocratic circle of Manasses for at least 15 years. For more details, see above, Chapter 3.

it mirrors the kind of life that Manasses the historical person found himself in. In either case it seems fairly certain that a twelfth-century writer on command could save himself from a difficult situation by mobilizing his social network and get a little help from his friends and, importantly, his literary skills.

CHAPTER 5

On an Educational Note
The Writer as Grammatikos

Like many writers of the twelfth century, Constantine Manasses was active not only as rhetor and panegyrist, but also as teacher. In addition to a few texts that may be described as didactic, there is also a series of five *schede* attributed to Manasses, preserved in three different manuscripts.[1] It was Robert Browning, in his study of the Marcianus Gr. XI, 31 and its schedographic content, who first suggested that Manasses had been a teacher at the Patriarchal School of Constantinople.[2] Some ten years later, Odysseas Lampsides agreed with Browning and added that Manasses' short ekphraseis had a 'schulischen Charakter' and accordingly could be connected to his activities as teacher.[3] All five *schede* were then edited and discussed by Ioannis Polemis, who noted that Manasses himself seems to mention his teaching activity (*Lehrtätigkeit*) in other works as well, namely in two passages describing grammar contests held at the imperial court.[4]

One of these passages, included in the *Funerary oration on the death of Nikephoros Komnenos*, represents Nikephoros Komnenos as a kind of game leader, skilfully setting traps for the students in the manner of hunting or bird-catching.[5] The other passage, included in the *Encomium of Michael Hagiotheodorites*, represents the logothete in a similar function and manner.

> At one occasion a contest is arranged for the foster children of grammar in the presence of the emperor; and traps preying on their minds are hidden for them and treacherous nets for their intellects are disguised, like the traps for airborne birds, which bird-catchers contrive with lime and decoy birds and snares. Then indeed the logothete discloses his art and fills all around

---

[1] Marc. Gr. XI, 31, Monac. Gr. 201 and Vat. Pal. Gr. 92, all collections of schedographical texts.
[2] Browning 1976. Browning included two mss containing *schede* by Manasses in his discussion (Marc. Gr. XI, 31 and Mon. Gr. 201); a third ms was added by Gallavotti 1983 (Vat. Pal. Gr. 92).
[3] Lampsides 1988; see also Lampsides 1996: xv.
[4] Polemis 1996, with 'corrected' editions of the *schede* (text of mss in notes) and summaries of their content.
[5] Manasses, *Funerary oration on the death of Nikephoros Komnenos* 453–66 (Kurtz); cited, translated and discussed above, Chapter 3.

the palace with his voice and prepares snares for the young boys. One would then see his skill in the sophistic art and praise his intelligence and admire his skilful contrivance. One of the young boys was caught by the tip of his wing, another was captured by the neck, one had bitter fetters bound around his back, another yet was fluttering his wings as if to fly away but was also caught; no one could get entirely out of the trap.

Ἵσταταί ποτε καὶ παισὶ τροφίμοις γραμματικῆς ἐν ὀφθαλμοῖς βασιλέως ἀγών· καὶ κρύπτονται τούτοις παγίδες νόας θηρεύουσαι καὶ ὑπορύττονται θήρατρα φρενῶν δολωτήρια, καθάπερ ἀεροπόροις ὀρνέοις ἐπιβουλαί, ἃς τεχνάζονται ἰξευταὶ καὶ παλευταὶ καὶ βροχοποιοί. τότε δὴ τότε τὴν ἑαυτοῦ τέχνην ὁ λογοθέτης παραγυμνοῖ καὶ περιλαλεῖ τὰ ἀνάκτορα καὶ ἑτοιμάζει βρόχους τοῖς μείραξιν. Ἴδοι τις ἂν τότε σοφιστικῆς δεξιότητα καὶ ἐπαινέσεται τὸ εὐσύνετον καὶ θαυμάζεται τὸ εὐμήχανον· ὁ μὲν τῶν μειράκων ἄκρας ἑάλω τῆς πτέρυγος, ὁ δ' ἐκ μέσης ἐζωγρήθη δειρῆς, τοῦ δὲ νῶτον δέσμη περιέσχε πικρά, ὁ δὲ πτερύσσεται μὲν ὡς ὑπερπετασθησόμενος, ἡγρεύθη δὲ καὶ αὐτός· καὶ παντελῶς οὐδεὶς τὴν παγίδα ἐξήλυσεν.[6]

In this description, the imagery of bird-catching is even more pronounced than in the other passage, as Michael Hagiotheodorites sets his clever traps and easily catches the children. As in the case of Nikephoros Komnenos, the contest is brought up as a way of underlining the intellectual capacities of the addressee – the focus is not on the contest as such, but on the characterization of the logothete. As has been argued above, such a characterization of the addressee creates a relationship between the author and his addressee that is based on metaphorical similarity, potentially flattering for the addressee and accordingly potentially useful for the author.[7] For Polemis, the interest in the two passages lay rather in the information they may offer on how such grammar contests were staged at the court, supported also by other evidence.[8] He argued that Manasses' interest in these events could only be explained by his own position as a teacher, which allowed him to attend such contests when his pupils were there: 'ein versteckter Beweis des Verfassers selbst für seine Lehrtätigkeit'.[9] This teaching activity took place, according to Polemis (following Browning and Lampsides) at the Patriarchal School, since that would have been a logical part of a career that eventually led Manasses to a position as bishop of first Panion, then Naupaktos.[10]

---

[6] Manasses, *Encomium of Michael Hagiotheodorites* 264–74 (Horna). Cf. tr. Polemis 1996: 281.
[7] See above, Chapters 3 and 4.   [8] See further below.   [9] Polemis 1996: 281.
[10] Polemis 1996: 279, referring to Browning 1976 and Lampsides 1988. Cf. also above, Chapter 1, on the assumed biography of Manasses.

5 On an Educational Note: The Writer as Grammatikos   115

In light of more recent research and within the methodological framework of this study, a number of crucial questions are raised by these important observations and interpretations made by previous scholars. The first concerns the biography of Manasses and his alleged bishop's office in Panion and/or Naupaktos: the evidence supporting such an interpretation has been revised and it is unlikely that the writer Manasses is to be identified with the bishop of Naupaktos, while it is possible, though still uncertain, that he was at some point bishop of Panion.[11] It seems reasonable to assume, however, that he worked at one of the institutions of the Patriarchal School, perhaps at the Orphanotropheion.[12] Second, we cannot be entirely sure that Manasses was present at the grammar contest in his capacity as a teacher, even if it is possible that he was. Since the primary concern of the two passages in question is not the educational system of Constantinople but the characterization of two potential patrons, it is possible that the setting described by Manasses is partly imaginary, even if we know from other sources that such contests did take place. From this perspective, the 'hidden evidence' is rather a part of the characterization strategy mentioned above – to create a relation marked by similarity between author and object/addressee based on similarity in grammatical and rhetorical skills.

This brings us to questions of a more general kind, concerned with the social position(s) of twelfth-century teachers and intellectuals, the environment of teaching and the meaning of so-called school texts. While education in Byzantium has been subject to numerous careful studies for quite some time,[13] and the particular situation of the twelfth century – with its increased and intense use of schedographic material – has received much consideration in the last few years,[14] less attention has been devoted to the way in which writers combined their activities as teachers, rhetors and functionaries at the court or the Church. It has been known for a long time

---

[11] See Rhoby (forthcoming): 'Ob er mit jenem Konstantinos Manasses identisch ist, der auf einem zwischen ca. 1150 und ca. 1170 zu datierenden Siegel als Bischof des ostthrakischen Panion belegt, ist nicht ganz geklärt ... Auszuschließen ist hingegen, dass der Schriftsteller K. identisch ist mit dem gleichnamigen Bischof von Naupaktos, da letzterer erst in das letzte Viertel des 12. Jahrhunderts zu datieren ist.' See also Paul and Rhoby 2019: 4–5.
[12] See e.g. Miller 2003a: 10 and 2003b: 233–7 on the career of teachers at the school of the Orphanotropheion, many of whom became bishops. See also further below.
[13] Markopoulos 2005, 2006 and 2008 with extensive bibliographies.
[14] See e.g. Vassis 1993/94 and 2002; Polemis 1996; Agapitos 2014, 2015a, 2015b and 2017; Nilsson and Zagklas 2017.

that Byzantine writers occupied many positions in society,[15] but methods of 'social localization'[16] have often been discarded in favour of either historical investigations of specific phenomena of Byzantine society (e.g. schools, the court or the Church) or philological close readings of specific authors or specific genres. An interesting exception is the recent study of Theodore Prodromos by Nikolaos Zagklas, which manages to combine a critical edition and philological case study with some interesting sociological observations of what he has termed 'communicating vessels'.[17]

Zagklas' communicating vessels refer to the three different settings in which Prodromos is known to have been active: the court, the rhetorical *theatra* and the classroom. As a teacher and writer of poetry and rhetoric, Prodromos functioned as a 'channel' between the three settings. This model suggests that the contexts for performance of twelfth-century texts could be multi-layered and not necessarily confined to one setting. An important consequence of Zagklas' model is that didactic texts in this manner are allowed to transcend the confined space of the 'classroom' and be acknowledged also as 'literature': 'a didactic purpose does not annul the highly aesthetic value of these texts, nor did it exclude readership outside the class'.[18] Texts could in this manner take on different functions at different stages of a writer's career, being used at some point in an educational setting, at another in a *theatron* or at the court. And one should not take for granted that educational usage always preceded a more prestigious purpose; as noted by Zagklas, the grammar treatise written by Prodromos for the Sebastokratorissa Eirene may well have been used in the classroom, minus the dedications to the imperial patron.[19]

Zagklas' approach has methodological similarities with the recurring argument of Panagiotis Agapitos that the distinction between 'learned' and 'popular' is an artificial and not very useful way of looking at Byzantine texts.[20] Both ways of looking at Byzantine culture as less confined to specific settings, whether performative-functional or linguistic, are useful for the present study of Manasses. Manasses' didactic tendency, his use of political verse and his tendency to mix a generally learned register with occasional 'vernacular' words has probably contributed to the description of him as someone who 'writes only to entertain or to instruct on a very basic level'.[21] In light of the arguments made in previous chapters,

---

[15] See e.g. Mullett 1984: 184–7.   [16] Kazhdan and Franklin 1984: viii; Mullett 1988: 22.
[17] Zagklas 2014: 73–87.   [18] Zagklas 2014: 86.   [19] Zagklas 2014: 83.
[20] Agapitos has for long argued against such artificial boundaries; see most recently Agapitos 2015d and 2017.
[21] Magdalino 1997: 162.

such statements may seem rather exaggerated, so in the following a series of didactic texts by Manasses are analysed in order to see to what extent they corroborate or contradict the idea of didactic, entertaining and 'scholarly' texts as separate categories in the twelfth century.

The selection of texts represents different kinds of didactic texts, likely to have been used in different or overlapping settings, but all displaying a clearly instructive intention:[22] the so-called *Astrological poem*, dedicated to Sebastokratorissa Eirene,[23] the versified *Origins of Oppian*, presumably intended for students, and the five *schede* mentioned above. In addition, the so-called *Sketches of the mouse*, traditionally attributed to Prodromos, is brought into the discussion as a work tentatively attributed to Manasses. Other works by Manasses have been described as didactic, such as the *Verse chronicle*, likewise dedicated to Eirene and presenting itself as 'giving plain teaching in ancient history',[24] and the ekphraseis in their function as rhetorical exercises, progymnasmata.[25] However, since the present analysis is based on thematic rather than generic or chronological concerns, the main focus here is on the model author as teacher, that is, the voice that the writer-narrator projects in his texts and its relation to other texts attributed to him. The real situation of Manasses' teaching activities is of only secondary interest, even though the authorial voice to some extent may be seen to reflect that reality.[26] My main question in this chapter is: does the voice of the *grammatikos* Manasses differ from the voice of the writer Manasses?

Gazing at the Stars

The *Astrological poem* dedicated to the Sebastokratorissa Eirene (Στίχοι συντεθέντες ... τῇ σεβαστοκρατορίσσῃ κυρᾷ Εἰρήνῃ) has been preserved in no fewer than six manuscripts.[27] The poem consists of 593 fifteen-syllable verses and opens with a prologue addressing the Sebastokratorissa:

---

[22] See Hörandner 2019: 461 on the definition of didactic poetry as having an 'instructive intention' rather than being a clearly defined genre.
[23] Previously attributed to Prodromos, also in the edition by Miller, but with Rhoby 2009: 322–9 the attribution to Manasses may be seen as definite. See also Horna 1902: 24–6.
[24] Manasses, *Verse chronicle* 9 (Lampsides): τρανῶς ἀναδιδάσκουσαν τὰς ἀρχαιολογίας. On the *Verse chronicle* as didactic, see Rhoby 2014: 393 and Hörandner 2017: 125. Cf. Reinsch 2002: 84–5 and Nilsson 2019: 523.
[25] Lampsides 1988; see also Lampsides 1996: xv.
[26] For theoretical considerations of these issues, see above, Chapter 4; see also below.
[27] Two of which attribute the poem to Manasses (the others to Prodromos); see Hörandner 1974: 48–9, and Rhoby 2009: 321–2. The edition by Miller was based on only two of these manuscripts, both of which attribute the poem to Prodromos. For recent discussions of this poem, see Hörandner 2017: 98–9 and Chryssogelos 2021. The latter indicates three similar but different

Come now, imperial and most magnificent soul, | brilliant-minded, lover of beauty, lover of history, lover of letters, | thrice-noble, thrice-glorious, sea of graces, | bred by the Muses, breathing the Muses, treasury of wit, | garden filled with beautiful trees of manifold wisdom, | beautifully growing plant, golden vine; | come now, imperial soul, shining by your prudence, | after the many winding stories and digressions | and labyrinths and twists of wisdom-loving books, | which you profit from each day and are enriched with, | turn now towards another height of philosophy, | fly, spread your wings towards astronomy | and learn the configurations and characteristics of the stars, | the movements and paths of the seven planets; | so, listen first to their names and positions.

> Ἄγε ψυχὴ βασίλισσα μεγαλοπρεπεστάτη,
> λαμπρόψυχε, φιλόκαλε, φιλίστορ, φιλολόγε,
> τρισευγενὲς, τρισσοκλεὲς, θάλασσα τῶν χαρίτων,
> μουσόθρεπτε, μουσόπνευστε, συνέσεως ταμεῖον,
> παράδεισε καλλίδενδρε παντοδαπῆς σοφίας,
> φυτὸν ὡραιοβλάστητον, ἀναδενδρὰς χρυσέα·
> ἄγε ψυχὴ βασίλισσα λάμπουσα τῇ φρονήσει,
> μετὰ πολλοὺς τοὺς ἑλιγμοὺς καὶ τὰς ὑπαναπτύξεις,
> καὶ λαβυρίνθους καὶ στροφὰς τῶν φιλενσόφων βίβλων,
> αἷς καθ' ἑκάστην σεαυτὴν ὀλβίζεις καὶ πλουτίζεις,
> μετάβηθι πρὸς ἕτερον ὕψος φιλοσοφίας,
> πετάσθητι, πτερύχθητι πρὸς τὴν ἀστρονομίαν,
> καὶ μάθε τοὺς σχηματισμοὺς καὶ φύσεις τῶν ἀστέρων,
> καὶ τὰς κινήσεις τῶν ἑπτὰ πλανήτων καὶ τοὺς δρόμους,
> καὶ τούτων πρῶτον ἄκουσον τὰς κλήσεις καὶ τὰς θέσεις.[28]

As noted by Andreas Rhoby, this opening not only recalls the way in which Manasses addresses the Sebastokratorissa in the dedicatory hexameter epigram of the *Verse chronicle*, it also employs numerous words that are typical of Manasses' vocabulary,[29] signalling thus the authorship of the text from the start. The prologue may also refer to the long narrative chronicle as a previous commission in verses 8–10: 'the many winding stories and digressions | and labyrinths and twists of wisdom-loving books, | from which you profit each day and are enriched by'.[30] This is then supported by the many similarities with the way in which the stars and planets were

---

versions of the poem, representative of Manasses' tendency to rework and recycle his verses: Chryssogelos is currently preparing a new edition.

[28] Manasses, *Astrological poem* 1–15 (Miller).
[29] See Rhoby 2009: 323–9. On the dedicatory hexameters to Sebastokratorissa Eirene, placed after the *Verse chronicle* in some manuscripts, see below, Chapter 6 and n. 24.
[30] The winding and twisting could also refer metaphorically to the turning of the book's or books' pages, but in either case they are related to the experience of reading on a cognitive and/or physical level.

described in the opening ekphrasis of the *Verse chronicle*,[31] but while the description of the heaven and its stars in the chronicle is ekphrastic and filled with poetic words and garden imagery, the *Astrological poem* initially presents a much drier, scientific and didactic account:

> Saturn holds the first place among the celestial spheres, | Jupiter is after him, Mars is the third star; | the fourth light-bringer is the torch-bearing Sun, | and after him is the light-bringing sphere Venus; | the sixth is Mercury, the seventh is the moon near the Earth. | Such are the names of the seven planets, | this is the order among them and the wisest arrangement | according to astronomers and astrologers; | for according to philosophers their order is different. | But learn now their characteristics and powers.

> Τὴν πρώτην ζώνην ἔλαχεν ὁ Κρόνος ἐν ταῖς σφαίραις
> ὁ Ζεὺς ἐστὶ δὲ μετ' αὐτόν, Ἄρης ἀστὴρ ὁ τρίτος·
> ὁ φεραυγὴς δὲ τέταρτος Ἥλιος ὁ φωσφόρος,
> καὶ μετ' αὐτὸν ἡ φεραυγὴς σφαῖρα τῆς Ἀφροδίτης·
> ἕκτος Ἑρμῆς, ἕβδομος δὲ καὶ πρόσγειος Σελήνη.
> Τὰ μὲν ὀνόματα ταυτὶ τὰ τῶν ἑπτὰ πλανήτων,
> αὕτη τε τάξις ἐν αὐτοῖς καὶ σοφωτάτη θέσις
> κατὰ τοὺς μαθηματικοὺς καὶ τοὺς ἀστερολέσχας·
> κατὰ τοὺς φιλοσόφους γὰρ ἄλλη τούτοις ἡ τάξις.
> Ἤδη δ' αὐτῶν ἐκμάνθανε τὰς φύσεις καὶ δυνάμεις.[32]

As the poem moves on to describe the characteristics of the planets – ranging from the negative effects of dark and cold Saturn (Kronos), causing nothing but envy and malign influence,[33] to the positive workings of a Jupiter–Venus (Zeus–Aphrodite) conjunction, offering love and friendship[34] –, not only words and concepts familiar from the *Verse chronicle* appear but also narratorial interventions such as 'And why should I go on at length and recount everything...' (Καὶ τί με δεῖ μακρηγορεῖν καὶ πάντα καταλέγειν...).[35] At times the didactic tone is abandoned for a

---

[31] Manasses, *Verse chronicle* 104–41 (Lampsides). See Nilsson 2005.
[32] Manasses, *Astrological poem* 16–25 (Miller).
[33] See esp. Manasses, *Astrological poem* 30–5 (Miller): Μέλας μέν ἐστι καὶ ψυχρός, τὴν χρόαν μολιβδώδης, | βαρύς, βραδύς, δυσκίνητος, ἀργὸς περὶ τοὺς δρόμους· | ποιητικὸς δὲ γίνεται φθόνου καὶ βασκανίας, | μερίμνης, ὑποκρίσεως καὶ μονογνωμοσύνης, | πένθους, στυγνότητος, δεσμῶν, χηρείας, ὀρφανίας, | βαθυφροσύνης σκοτεινῆς καὶ σκυθρωπῆς καρδίας. Cf. the motifs of envy and slander in other texts by Manasses, written in various phases of his career; see below, Chapter 6.
[34] Manasses, *Astrological poem* 188–99 (Miller). Cf. the negative conjunction of Ares–Aphrodite, having the negative effects of infidelity and general misery; *Astrological poem* 237–9.
[35] Manasses, *Astrological poem* 36–8 (Miller): Καὶ τί με δεῖ μακρηγορεῖν καὶ πάντα καταλέγειν, | προθέμενον συναγαγεῖν καὶ συνοψίσαι ταῦτα, | καὶ τοῖς μικροῖς περιλαβεῖν πᾶσαν μακρολογίαν; cf. Manasses, *Verse chronicle* 1169 (Lampsides): καὶ τί πολλὰ καὶ περιττὰ μακρηγορεῖν καὶ γράφειν;

more romantic discourse, reminiscent of certain chronicle episodes and even the novel fragments.

> The fifth star is the white-gleaming sphere of Venus. | She causes love, graces and friendship, | she offers both pleasures and desires, | and she takes delight in embellishments and sweet oils, | in bright garments and shimmering robes | of noble women, honoured princesses, | she is the cause of profits, brilliant successes, | and of thrice-famous nuptials, of very brilliant chambers, | she is ruler of affections caused by the Amours, | of adornments, of brightness, of the fairness of a face, | of flutes and musical pipes, of dances and cithara music, | of luxury and a soft life and a rich cuisine, | of hot baths softening, beguiling the bodies.

> Πέμπτος ἀστὴρ λευκοφυὴς σφαῖρα τῆς Ἀφροδίτης.
> Ἔρωτας αὕτη προξενεῖ, χάριτας καὶ φιλίας,
> τὰς ἡδονὰς παρέχει δὲ καὶ τὰς ἐπιθυμίας,
> καὶ χαίρει τοῖς καλλωπισμοῖς καὶ ταῖς μυραλοιφίαις,
> τῶν ἱματίων τοῖς λαμπροῖς καὶ ταῖς φαιδροστολίαις
> ἐξ εὐγενῶν δὲ γυναικῶν ἐντίμων βασιλίδων·
> κερδῶν αἰτία γίνεται, λαμπρῶν εὐτυχημάτων,
> τρισευκλεῶν νυμφείων τε, θαλάμων περιλάμπρων,
> συμπαθειῶν δε πρύτανις τῶν ἀπὸ τῶν ἐρώτων,
> ὡραϊσμῶν, στιλπνότητος, ἰδέας εὐπροσώπου,
> αὐλῶν, συρίγγων μουσικῶν, μολπῶν, κιθαρισμάτων,
> τρυφῆς καὶ βίου μαλακοῦ καὶ λιπαροτραπέζου,
> λουτρῶν θερμῶν, θηλυντικῶν τὰ σώματα θελγόντων.[36]

The model author and teacher thus manifests his presence to his model reader and generous patron by using a voice known from other books written for her (certainly the chronicle, but perhaps also the novel) and by alluding to her privileged position at the court and her happy marriage.[37]

After having explained the workings of the planets and the zodiac, the writer–teacher turns again, in v. 565, to his patron in a rather long epilogue. But when he does, he has already addressed her also in the middle of the poem, inserting a reminder of her generosity: 'Now, imperial and most generous soul, | that the matters of the seven planets have been summarized, | it is time to describe for you the zodiac circle' (Ἤδη, ψυχὴ βασίλισσα μεγαλοδωροτάτη,[38] | ὡς ἐν συνόψει λέλεκτο τὰ τῶν ἑπτὰ πλανήτων, | καιρὸς δὲ διαγράψαι σοι τὸν ζωηφόρον κύκλον).[39] The

---

[36] Manasses, *Astrological poem* 288–300 (Miller). [37] On the novel, see below, Chapter 6.
[38] Cf. Manasses, *Verse chronicle* 15 (Lampsides): αἱ μεγαλοδωρίαι σου καὶ τὸ φιλότιμόν σου.
[39] Manasses, *Astrological poem* 358–60 (Miller). For the formulaic ψυχὴ βασίλισσα, see also vv. 1 and 7 (cited and translated above).

epilogue opens by repeating, for the fourth time, the formulaic ψυχὴ βασίλισσα, now with the same epithet that was used in v. 1: 'Look, imperial and most magnificent soul, I have brought the promised work to completion' (Ἰδοὺ, ψυχὴ βασίλισσα μεγαλοπρεπεστάτη, | τὸ πόνημα τετέληκα τὸ προϋπεσχημένον).[40] This is followed by a justification of the author, in case anyone would blame him for writing about astrology: he does not consider the stars to be gods, but knows that God has created everything, including the sky and its planets.[41] The remaining nine verses address again the Sebastokratorissa directly, underlining the significance of this gift:

> This small gift is from us to you, thrice-fortunate | empress, a modest evidence of gratitude; | for having enjoyed many of your benefactions | I bring you a small gift, I offer you this: | accept it kindly as if it were more valuable than rubies; | for to souls like yours, most loving of letters, | works of words are better than pearls. | And may you now succeed for many more years,[42] | most noble of women, most generous in bestowing riches.

> Τοῦτό σοι δῶρον ἐξ ἡμῶν μικρὸν τῇ τρισολβίᾳ
> τῇ βασιλίδι, πενιχρὸν εὐγνωμοσύνης δεῖγμα·
> πολλῶν γὰρ ἀπολαύσας σου τῶν εὐεργετημάτων
> δῶρον προσάγω σοι βραχύ, τοῦτό σε δεξιοῦμαι,
> ὅπερ καὶ δέξαι προσηνῶς ὑπὲρ λυχνίτας λίθους·
> ταῖς γὰρ ψυχαῖς ταῖς κατὰ σὲ ταῖς φιλολογωτάταις
> τὰ λογικὰ πονήματα κρείττονα καὶ μαργάρων.
> Καὶ τοίνυν εἰς λυκάβαντας ὡς ἀείρεσθαι πλέον,
> εὐγενεστάτη γυναικῶν ὀλβιοδωροτάτη.[43]

Here, too, there are similarities with the way in which the Sebastokratorissa is addressed in the dedicatory epigram of the *Verse*

---

[40] Manasses, *Astrological poem* 565–6 (Miller). Cf. *Verse chronicle* 3 (Lampsides): σὺ δέ, ψυχὴ βασίλισσα καὶ φιλολογωτάτη. Hörandner 2019: 466 refers to the recurring epithet as a 'ring composition', but it seems to be rather a case of repetition with variation. See also Rhoby 2009: 326.

[41] Manasses, *Astrological poem* 567–84 (Miller), ending with a reference to Genesis 1:14. Cf. also the Creation ekphrasis at the beginning of the *Verse chronicle*, making this position of the author very clear.

[42] The Greek printed in Miller's edition does not really make sense. Rhoby 2009: 325 suggested ἀπειρεῖσθαι for ἀείρεσθαι, based on v. 9 of the hexameter dedication to Eirene of the *Verse chronicle*: εἰς τοίνυν λυκάβαντας ἀπειρεσίους ἐλάσειας (Lampsides). This is better, but still not entirely satisfactory. Chryssogelos 2021 suggests a reading based on the ms Kamariotissis 151 (attributing the poem to Manasses, but not known by Miller). Here I have kept Miller's text, translating rather freely with the hexameter dedication in mind.

[43] Manasses, *Astrological poem* 585–93 (Miller).

chronicle, as well as in its opening verses.⁴⁴ More importantly, it seems as if the author is referring – once more – to the chronicle and the generous reward its author had received: this time he brings something small, supposedly in contrast to the 'many winding stories and digressions | and labyrinths and twists' of the previous work.⁴⁵ If this is a correct interpretation, the *Astrological poem* was composed after the chronicle, or at least after the first part and/or version of the chronicle had been presented to the Sebastokratorissa.⁴⁶ The emphasis in the poem on Venus/Aphrodite and the happiness of imperial women could be seen as an indication that Andronikos was still alive when the poem was composed, but it could also be a way of simply reminding Eirene of her lucky marriage, even after the death of her husband (in 1142).

As we have seen, the characterization of Eirene is here based entirely on her position as a generous patron, a lover of letters and learning – this is a clearly asymmetrical relationship, not marked by any attempt at similarity, but by contiguity in the sense of shared intellectual concerns.⁴⁷ Those concerns, however, are shared only to the extent that the author–teacher has the capacity to teach (sell) and the addressee-patron the capacity to learn (buy). The simple style of the poem and its elementary content may be said to speak against the praise of the recipient as φιλολογωτάτη ('most loving of letters'), but the structure of the poem is carefully wrought and the transtextual relations with the *Verse chronicle* create a literary effect that goes beyond that of a simple 'school text'.⁴⁸ At the same time, the

---

⁴⁴ See above, n. 42, but cf. also Manasses, *Verse chronicle* 3 (Lampsides): φιλολογωτάτη; also v. 2 of the hexameter dedication: ὀλβιόδωρε ἄνασσα. Cf. also the address of another Eirene (born Bertha von Sultzbach, first wife of Manuel I Komnenos) in John Tzetzes' *Allegories of the Iliad* as ὁμηρικωτάτη in the title of the work: Ὑπόθεσις τοῦ Ὁμήρου ἀλληγορηθεῖσα παρὰ Ἰωάννου γραμματικοῦ τοῦ Τζέτζου τῇ κραταιοτάτῃ βασιλίσσῃ καὶ ὁμηρικωτάτῃ κυρᾷ Εἰρήνῃ τῇ ἐξ Ἀλαμανῶν (Boissonade). Such superlatives of flattery seem to have been common in the twelfth century.

⁴⁵ Manasses, *Astrological poem* 8–10 (Miller), cited and translated above. On vv. 585–93 as a possible hint at the *Verse chronicle*, see E. Jeffreys 2014: 179–80.

⁴⁶ The large verse chronicle was probably composed in portions, begun for Eirene (perhaps as early as the late 1130s or early 1140s) and then finished or revised under Manuel I Komnenos (at some point after 1143). See Paul and Rhoby 2019: 8, Nilsson 2021a and below, Chapter 6.

⁴⁷ Note esp. the description of Eirene as a 'fosterchild of learning' (Manasses, *Verse chronicle* 7 Lampsides: τροφίμη λόγου) and cf. the 'foster children of grammar' (παισὶ τροφίμοις γραμματικῆς) in the *Encomium of Michael Hagiotheodorites* 264–5 (Horna), indicating that Eirene is still in need of teaching of the Graeco-Roman heritage. This does not necessarily contradict the praise of her as learned and devoted to scholarship; see E. Jeffreys 2014, 182–3. On patronage expressed in terms of contiguity vs similarity, see the model described above, Chapter 3.

⁴⁸ Cf. Katharina Volk's interesting study of the poetics of Latin didactic poetry and her demand for not only 'explicit didactic intent' and a 'teacher-student constellation' in didactic poetry, but also 'poetic self-consciousness' and 'poetic simultaneity' (the latter referring to the creation of a dramatic illusion of a lesson being in progress as the poem progresses); for a discussion of these terms and definitions, see Volk 2002: 6–24.

inscribed intention of the text (to teach astronomy and astrology to the Sebastokratorissa in exchange for a donation) does not exclude other functions beyond that occasional use. As noted by Eric Cullhed in the case of the *Commentaries* on the Homeric epics by Eustathios of Thessalonike, inscribed readers and actual readers are not to be equated or confused.[49] The six manuscripts of the *Astrological poem* indicate a fairly wide reception, which should mean that the text was considered useful by later readers. Accordingly, its instructive (and perhaps also poetic) intention long outlived the occasion for which it was originally composed.

The question remains why the Sebastokratorissa needed or wanted to learn about the stars – was it her idea, that of her writer–teacher Manasses, or did the idea come from somewhere else? The text does not give us any clue, beyond the reference to 'another level of philosophy' in v. 11, which may refer to the expected next stage in the education of the imperial princess.[50] But it is tempting to read the *Astrological poem* in light of the well-documented interest in astrology in the twelfth century, represented by, among others, the emperor Manuel I Komnenos himself.[51] Manuel even wrote a treatise in defence of astrology, refuted by Michael Glykas.[52] We have seen above how Manuel is repeatedly described as the sun, the life-giving centre of the empire, and Paul Magdalino has noted how contemporary poetry described the Komnenian dynasty as 'a constellation of stars sharing in the light of the imperial sun'.[53] With the Sebastokratorissa being one of those stars, an astrological poem for her would certainly not have come as a surprise.

However, one should note the difference in function between the learned and theological debates on astrology, on the one hand, and didactic poetry on the other. While astrology could be seen as potentially harmful to Orthodox society,[54] basic knowledge about the stars was part of classical *paideia* and could thus easily be defended in the manner that Manasses does in his brief apology.[55] Miller, editor of the *Astrological poem* (which he attributed to Prodromos), compared it to a poem by John

---

[49] Cullhed 2014a: 19*–20*. Cf. Cullhed 2016: 9*–11*.
[50] The grammar treatise written for her by Prodromos has already been mentioned above; see Zagklas 2011 and E. Jeffreys 2014: 182.
[51] Magdalino 2015.
[52] For a discussion and translation of both treatises, see George 2001. See also Chryssogelos 2021.
[53] Magdalino 1988: 181, with reference to Manganeios Prodromos, *Poem* 3.75 (Bernardinello). On this kind of imagery of Manuel, see above, Chapter 2.
[54] Magdalino 2006 and 2015.
[55] Note also Magdalino 1997: 163 and n. 122, on the implicit defence of astrology in Manasses' *Verse chronicle*.

Kamateros and stated that the latter was 'plus savant et plus technique, plus développé que celui de Théodore Prodrome'.[56] That is certainly right, because that poem was dedicated to Manuel himself, composed in dodecasyllables and brimming with allusions to ancient astrology – it had nothing to do with basic instruction, because the emperor was already (assumed to be) an expert.[57] From a functional perspective, the two texts have little in common beyond their theme and the fact that they were written for members of the Komnenian court. This is a good example of how 'court poetry' may differ considerably in function and intention, even in cases where generic and thematic similarities seem rather clear.

An Ancient Life in Verse

Another poem by Manasses that has a clear instructive intention is the *Origins of Oppian* (Κωνσταντίνου τοῦ Μανασσῆ γένος Ὀππιανοῦ διὰ στίχων πολιτικῶν ἐμμέτρων), composed in political verse and preserved in three manuscripts.[58] The tradition of writing biographies of authors and poets goes back to antiquity and is accordingly part of a long tradition, with the twelfth century again showing a particularly wide and intense interest in the authorial models of the past.[59] It should be noted, however, that the title of the poem – *genos* and not *bios* – indicates a departure from the biographic tradition.[60] It is possible, perhaps even likely, that the title does not go back to the author but has been drawn from the first verse of the poem; however, as we shall see, the poem does focus more or at least as much on the origin of the ancient author as on his life.

Manasses' poem consists of 52 verses and presents a rather conventional biography, similar to other known tales of Oppian's life. It thus opens with the family and homeland of Oppian:

---

[56] Miller 1872: 50. Cf. Chryssogelos 2021, arguing that Kamateros is likely to have been imitating the poem of Manasses.
[57] It should be noted that Kamateros also wrote a poem in political verse, likewise dedicated to Manuel; see Hunger 1978: 242–3; Kazhdan and Franklin 1984: 172.
[58] First edited by Westerman 1845: 67–8, but based on only two mss (Par. Gr. 2736 and Par. Gr. 2737), both copies of Marc. F. a. 479, edited by Colonna 1964, which transmit Manasses' poem after Oppian's *Cynegetica*.
[59] On authorial biographies in antiquity, see Lefkowitz 2012; this study focuses on the early period and does not include Oppian. On the twelfth-century interest in authorial *personae* of the past, see e.g. Cullhed 2014b and Pizzone 2018.
[60] Cf. the somewhat deceptive title of the modern edition by Colonna (1964): *De Oppiani vita antiquissima*.

The poet Oppian was Cilician by descent | from the most illustrious city called Nazarbos, | born from thrice-happy and esteemed parents, | his father Agesilaos and his mother Zenodote, | the father being filled with wisdom and learning | of the best and very highest kind. | He flourished in the time of Emperor Severus, | Severus who would engender Marcus Antoninus.[61]

> Ὀππιανὸς ὁ ποιητὴς Κίλιξ μὲν ἦν τὸ γένος
> ἐκ λαμπροτάτης πόλεως Ναζάρβου καλουμένης,
> τρισευδαιμόνων γεγονὼς περιφανῶν γονέων,
> Ἀγησιλάου μὲν πατρὸς μητρὸς δὲ Ζηνοδότης,
> σοφίας ὄντος τοῦ πατρὸς ἔμπλεω καὶ παιδείας
> τῆς μείζονος καὶ μάλιστα καὶ τῆς ὑψηλοτέρας.
> Ἤκμαζε δ' οὖν ἐν τοῖς καιροῖς τοῦ κράτορος Σεβήρου,
> Σεβήρου τοῦ γεννήσαντος τὸν Μάρκον Ἀντωνῖνον.[62]

When (Septimius) Severus came to Cilicia to subdue his rivals, continues the narrator, all local Cilician men took part in the campaign – only Oppian's father Agesilaos was missing,

> For he spent his time, night and day, with books, | hunting down the best of all kinds of learning, | at the same time training his son for similar hunts.

> Βίβλοις καὶ γὰρ ἐσχόλαζε νύκτωρ καὶ μεθ' ἡμέραν
> θηρώμενος τὰ κάλλιστα πάντων τῶν μαθημάτων,
> καὶ σκυλακεύων τὸν υἱὸν ἐς τὰς ὁμοίας θήρας.[63]

The emperor was annoyed and angry; he sent for this 'lover of wisdom' (τὸν τῆς σοφίας ἐραστήν)[64] and had him exiled to the island of Melite (probably Malta).[65] Oppian accordingly went away with his father, where he stayed until he was 30, and it was there that he wrote first his treatise on fishing, then the one on hunting and finally the one on bird-catching (τὴν τῶν ἰχθύων ἔγραψεν ἄγραν τὴν ἐναλίαν, | τὴν τῶν θηρίων μετ' αὐτήν, | εἶτα τὴν τῶν ὀρνέων).[66] He also wrote other short books, notes the narrator, but time spared only those on hunting and fishing.[67] Oppian

---

[61] Septimius Severus (193–211) fought his rivalling generals in Cilicia by the beginning of his reign. His son was Marcus Aurelius Severus Antoninus Augustus, formerly known as Antoninus, now as Caracalla (198–217).
[62] Manasses, *Origins of Oppian* 1–8 (Colonna).
[63] Manasses, *Origins of Oppian* 16–18 (Colonna). [64] Manasses, *Origins of Oppian* 20 (Colonna).
[65] Melite could also refer to the island Mljet off the Dalmatian coast, but since we are dealing with a legend here and the geographical location is of little or no importance, I cite the traditional version of Oppian's life and read Melite as Malta.
[66] Manasses, *Origins of Oppian* 25–6 (Colonna).
[67] Manasses, *Origins of Oppian* 27–30 (Colonna): σὺν ἄλλοις πλείοσι, λεπταῖς καὶ βραχυτμήτοις βίβλοις, | ὧνπερ κατεκαυχήσατο χρόνος ὁ πανδαμάτωρ, | τούτων τῶν δύο τέλεον φεισάμενος καὶ μόνων | τῶν εἰς τὰ κυνηγέσια καὶ πρὸς τὴν ἐναλίαν. This description corresponds to the modern situation, though the surviving work on hunting (Κυνηγετικά) now is believed to be the work of a

then went to Rome – 'the older Rome' (τὴν πρεσβυτέραν Ῥώμην)[68] – where he met the new emperor (Antoninus, because Severus had passed away), and 'handed over to him the books at which he had toiled' (καὶ βίβλους ἐνεχείρισεν αὐτῷ τὰς πονηθείσας).[69] His affection for the emperor appeared to be so great that he was awarded a wish, and his father was thus released from his exile. In addition, Oppian received one golden *stater* for each verse of his works.[70] The rest, says the narrator, he will disregard (παρίημι) in order to avoid a long story (μῆκος ἐκφεύγων λόγου), and with this the narrative as such is over.[71] In its place, a list of 'facts' (ὅτι) is presented: that they returned together to Nazarbos, but Oppian died in a plague that afflicted the city; that after his death, the people raised a statue of Oppian, inscribed with elegiac verses;[72] and finally,

> that he [Oppian] suitably succeeds in pronouncing on every subject, | bringing the things he discusses in front of the readers' eyes | and, finally, that smoothness is abundant in his discourses, | enveloping clarity like a flower, | and that he also knows how to handle the density of thoughts, | which is difficult and extremely toilsome for rhetors.

> ὅτι τυγχάνει προσφυῶς πάνυ τοι γνωματεύων,
> τὰ πράγματα δ' ὑπόψια δείκνυσι παραβάλλων,
> καὶ τελευταῖον ὡς πολὺ τὸ λεῖον ἐν τοῖς λόγοις,
> ὃ τοῦ σαφοῦς σκευαστικὸν οἷά περ ἄνθος ἔχει,
> ᾔδ' οἶδε τὴν πυκνότητα τὴν τῶν ἐνθυμημάτων,
> ὃ δυσχερὲς τοῖς ῥήτορσι καὶ παντελῶς ἐργῶδες.[73]

In spite of this apparently simple and typical biography of Oppian, the text accordingly contains quite a few interesting references to the situation of a rhetor-writer, to some extent agreeing with points made by Manasses in

---

different Oppian. It opens (1.1–15) with an invocation of Caracalla and the goddess Artemis; see Spatharakis 2004: 3 and 14. The treatise on fishing (Ἁλιευτικά) consists of *c*.3,500 lines and has a dedication to Marcus Aurelius and his son Commodus, dating it to the time of their joint rule (177–80). The treatise on bird-catching (Ἰξευτικά) has survived only in an anonymous prose paraphrase, perhaps the same that Manasses used for his own descriptions of such hunting methods. See further below.

[68] Manasses, *Origins of Oppian* 31 (Colonna). Cf. Manasses, *Verse chronicle* 2319–21 (Lampsides) on Constantinople as the 'younger' Rome (cited and discussed above, Chapter 2).

[69] Manasses, *Origins of Oppian* 34 (Colonna).

[70] Manasses, *Origins of Oppian* 39–40 (Colonna): ἀπαριθμεῖται καὶ χρυσὸς αὐτῷ πρὸς βασιλέως, | ἑνὸς στατῆρος ὤνιον ἕνα τεθέντος στίχον.

[71] Manasses, *Origins of Oppian* 41–2 (Colonna): καὶ ταῦτα μὲν ἐνταῦθά μοι στήτω τοῦ πρόσω δρόμου· | τὰ γὰρ πολλὰ παρίημι μήκος ἐκφεύγων λόγου.

[72] Manasses, *Origins of Oppian* 45–6 (Colonna): ὅτι θανόντος ἄγαλμα πολυτελὲς ὁ δῆμος | ἔστησαν ἐπιγράψαντες ἔπαινον ἐλεγείοις.

[73] Manasses, *Origins of Oppian* 47–52 (Colonna).

other works. First, the description of Agesilaos studying night and day is reminiscent not only of other didactic poems,[74] but also of passages in Manasses' *Itinerary* depicting the narrator as struggling day and night with books in his youth.[75] Second, the tale of how Oppian went to Rome and handed over his works to the emperor has a clear parallel in contemporary patronage situations, such as the relation between Manasses himself and the Sebastokratorissa Eirene discussed above.[76] Even the choice of verb (πονέω) for his production of books recalls the vocabulary of such toilsome writing on command or for powerful persons.[77] Third, the final paragraph ties in with such activities of the rhetor and offers some technical advice to the reader/listener (presumably a student) as regards the composition of such discourse. Oppian is useful because he offers suitable topics presented in a smooth and clear form, even 'dense' thoughts are handled with skill – something even rhetors struggle with and students therefore need to learn.

Rhetorical instructions have in this manner been inscribed into the poem itself, offering more than just a model of how to write a biography and, at the same time, the story of an ancient author. In contrast to Manasses' poem, the anonymously transmitted *Origins of Oppian* written in prose, most probably belonging in the twelfth century and proposed by Colonna as the model for Manasses' versification,[78] does not contain any of the references to learning or patronage noted above. This brings us to the choice of Oppian for the composition of a biography that had an instructive intention and probably was used in some sort of pedagogical setting: why Oppian? In light of some thematic choices in other works by Manasses – the writing of two ekphraseis on hunting (the *Description of a crane hunt* and the *Description of the catching of siskins and chaffinches*), along with the bird-catching imagery employed in the descriptions of grammar contests at court – it could be suggested that Manasses was interested in hunting, or that the patrons for whom he worked had such interests (such as Emperor Manuel). Such a suggestion, however, would still not explain the function of the texts, at least not beyond the expression of a 'popular' theme. Let us return briefly to the *Description of the catching*

---

[74] As noted by Hörandner 2019, referring to Niketas of Herakleia.
[75] Manasses, *Itinerary* 2.91–7 (Chryssogelos). See above, Chapter 2.
[76] Cf. Hörandner 2019, 'The poem is a typical *vita* completely devoted to detailed information on the life and works of the individual author at hand, without any allusion to the reader or patron.'
[77] See esp. Manasses, *Verse chronicle* 12–13 (Lampsides): ἡμεῖς ἀναδεξόμεθα τὸ βάρος τοῦ καμάτου, | κἂν δυσχερές, κἂν ἐπαχθὲς τὸ πρᾶγμα, κἂν ἐργῶδες; see also the first line of the dedicatory epigram in hexameters: Δέχνυσο τοῖον δῶρον ἀφ' ἡμετέροιο πόνοιο. See also below, Chapter 6.
[78] Colonna 1964: 36–7. Zagklas 2017: 245 suggests that both versions of the *Life* may have been written by Manasses as a demonstration of how to write in prose and verse.

of siskins and chaffinches and see to what extent it ties in with the *Origins of Oppian*, the *Description of the crane hunt* or the passage on Hagiotheodorites' participation in the grammar contest, cited at the beginning of this chapter.

As noted above, the *Description of a crane hunt* contains a short passage that describes the catching of small birds which may refer back to the *Description of the catching of siskins and chaffinches*, possibly written in the early years of the writer's career.[79] In contrast to the description of Emperor Manuel's participation in a brutal and masculine hunt reminiscent of a war, the ekphrasis describing an excursion to the other side of the Bosphoros presents a kind of rustic idyll, with a much longer and more detailed description of the setting of traps for birds. After spending the night in a tent, the narrator and his host wake up at dawn because of the noise caused by the preparations for the bird-catching. In a clearing at some distance from the tent, on high ground but yet protected by the wind, the traps are set up by a group of boys and adolescents, led by a very old man (ἀνὴρ πρεσβυτικὸς καὶ παλαιγενής).[80] They set up the traps: branches are stuck into the earth, covered in sweet bay and thus looking like bushes, but with twigs covered in lime hidden among them.[81] Tame birds of various kinds are brought there in order to fly around the trap and thus attract wild birds.[82] The trap works and a large flock of birds appears, like a cloud in the sky.[83]

Two such flocks of small birds are caught, all while various entertaining (from the perspective of the narrator) things happen: the happy shouting of the boys scares off the birds and angers the old man; the old man gets lime in his beard as he cleans off the caught birds; a falcon hunts a chaffinch; the old man drops his hat and shows off his shiny bald head. A different kind of hunt is then undertaken:

---

[79] Manasses, *Description of a crane hunt* 45–56 (Messis and Nilsson). See above, Chapters 1 and 2.
[80] Manasses, *Description of the catching of siskins and chaffinches* 23 (Horna).
[81] Manasses, *Description of the catching of siskins and chaffinches* (Horna) 40–51. Cf. Manasses, *Funerary oration on the death of Nikephoros Komnenos* 466 (Kurtz): θήρατρα μηχανήσασθαι δεξιώτατα.
[82] Manasses, *Description of the catching of siskins and chaffinches* 51–61. There is also a goldfinch (ἀστρόγληνος), the bird mourned by Manasses in the *Monody on the death of his goldfinch*, in lines 55–61: Παρέφερον δὲ καὶ ἄλλο στρουθίον περικαλλές, ὡραῖον τὴν ὄψιν, καλὸν ἰδέσθαι, λάλον ἀκοῦσαι, ἐπιτερπὲς ὁμοῦ καὶ πολύφωνον· ἡ κεφαλὴ φοινικέῳ περιήνθιστο βάμματι, τὸ δὲ πτερὸν ποικίλως ἐχρώζετο· ἀγλαόπτερον ἦν, περιπόρφυρον ἦν, κατάστρεον, χρυσεόπτερον. Ἀστρόγληνον ὁ γέρων ἐκάλει τὸ στρουθίον ἐκεῖνο τὸ ἐρυθρόκρανον, καὶ ἐνεκαυχᾶτο τῇ τοῦ ζώου καλλιγλωττίᾳ καὶ ὀλβιοδαίμονα ἐκάλει τὸν ἔχοντα ὑπὲρ Κροῖσον, ὑπὲρ Ἀντίοχον.
[83] Manasses, *Description of the catching of siskins and chaffinches* 61–3 (Horna).

An Ancient Life in Verse

Not long after, siskins were seen flying above, and I saw another, stranger kind of hunt. There was a fine and light string; the end of this had been tied to the arrangement of those twigs of sweet bay. Attached to the string was also a live siskin and the siskin was a decoy; the other end of the string had been entrusted to a youngster. As then the siskins approached in large numbers – a countless army, one could say – so the young man slowly touched the string and thus reminded the poor siskin of flying. While it could not, it still fluttered its wings and tried to fly and lured its kin.

Μετ' οὐ πολὺ καὶ σπίνοι ὑπερπετόμενοι ὤφθησαν, καὶ εἶδον ἄγρας τρόπον καινότερον ἕτερον. μήρινθος ἦν τετανὴ καὶ λεπτή· ταύτης τὸ ἄκρον τῇ τῶν καταδάφνων ἐκείνων ῥάβδων φυτείᾳ προδέδετο. Ἐξήρτετο τῆς μηρίνθου καὶ ζῶσα σπίνος καὶ ἦν ἡ σπίνος παλεύτρια· τὸ δὲ ἕτερον ἄκρον τὸ τῆς μηρίνθου παιδαρίσκος πεπίστευτο. Ἅμα τὲ οὖν κατὰ πολλοὺς οἱ σπίνοι προσῄεσαν, στρατός, ἄν εἴποι τις, μυριοπληθής, καὶ ὁ παιδαρίσκος ἠρέμα τὴν μήρινθον ἀνεσόβει καὶ τὴν ταλαίπωρον σπίνον ὑπανεμίμνησκε πετασμοῦ. Ἡ δὲ οὐκ ἔχουσα μέν, ἐπτερύγιζε δ' οὖν καὶ ἐπεχείρει πετάζεσθαι καὶ ἐπάλευε τὸ ὁμόφυλον.[84]

The narrative goes on, but let us stop here and consider the description in relation to the bird-catching imagery employed when Manasses describes the grammar contests. Obviously, the ekphrasis allows for much more detailed description, but what makes the imagery as such so useful for the description of schedography is the setting of traps. They are not described, but referred to in the way in which Hagiotheodorites captures the boys in various manners: one 'by the tip of his wing', another 'by the neck' and so on.[85] The methods are also alluded to in the corresponding passage about Nikephoros Komnenos, where the 'visible bait' is attractive and the 'hidden traps' powerful.[86] An important difference between the ekphrasis of the hunt and the imagery used for grammar contests is the role of the boys: being happy and playful hunters in the description, they are the hunted preys in the contests.

As for the *Origins of Oppian*, probably intended for boys being trained in grammar and rhetoric, it contains no descriptions of hunting at all.

---

[84] Manasses, *Description of the catching of siskins and chaffinches* 157–65 (Horna). This kind of trap is known from the illuminations to Oppian's *Cynegetica* in Marc. Gr. Z 139; see Spatharakis 2004: 24 and fig. 4. The illustrated passage, 1.62–6 (Mair), reflects the overall tone of Manasses' ekphrasis and may have inspired him: Ναὶ μὴν ἰξευτῆρι πόνος γλυκύς· ἢ γὰρ ἐπ' ἄγρην | οὐκ ἄορ, οὐ δρεπάνην, οὐ χάλκεα δοῦρα φέρονται, | ἀλλ' αὐτοῖς ἐπὶ δρυμὰ συνέμποροι ἕσπετο κίρκος | καὶ δολιχαὶ θώμιγγες ὑγρός τε μελίχροος ἰξός | οἵ τε διηερίην δόνακες πατέουσιν ἀταρπόν. Note also fig. 22, likewise illustrating a bird hunt.

[85] Manasses, *Encomium of Michael Hagiotheodorites* 264–74 (Horna), cited and translated above.

[86] Manasses, *Funerary oration on the death of Nikephoros Komnenos* 453–66 (Kurtz), cited and translated above, Chapter 3.

However, two things must be noted. First, the metaphor used for the intellectual ambitions of Oppian's father: 'hunting down the best of all kinds of learning', he trains his son 'for similar hunts'.[87] Hunting imagery is in this manner included in the poem without any direct descriptions of hunting. Second, the fact that such descriptions were made by Oppian himself are indicated by the closing remarks of the poem, pointing out the ekphrastic quality of Oppian's work, 'bringing the things he discusses in front of the [readers'] eyes'.[88] It is of little importance that Manasses did not read Oppian's original *Ixieutika* (*On bird-hunting*) and probably had to rely on the prose paraphrase attributed to Dionysios;[89] within the literary imaginary of the didactic situation, that part of Oppian's work was indeed lost,[90] but his thoughts and style still lived on in his texts and in the characterization of him as an author. The educative intention of the poem accordingly transcends the didactic presentation of anecdotal biography by far – this is a highly self-conscious didactic poem presenting the life of a didactic poet, who also dedicated his work to imperial patrons and wrote in a manner that rivals contemporary rhetor-teachers.

Enigmatic Exercises

Let us in light of these readings turn to the *schede* attributed to Manasses. Do they in any way express the authorial voice – the model author – who, as we have seen, is clear in the *Astrological poem* and certainly

---

[87] Manasses, *Origins of Oppian* 16–18 (Colonna), cited above. The word used for 'training' is even σκυλακεύω, the term used for hunters training puppies. For a similar use of metaphors in a paratext, see John Tzetzes' introductory passage to his scholia on Oppian's *Halieutica* (On fishing): Χρησάμενος, παῖ, τῷ λογισμοῦ δικτύῳ | ἐξ Ὀππιανοῦ τοῦ βυθοῦ τῶν χαρίτων | ἄγραν λόγων πάγκαλον ἀνείλκυσά σοι, | ἐγὼ γὰρ ἵνα μὴ πάθῃς ἀηδίαν, | λαμπρῶς κατεσκεύασα τὴν πανδαισίαν (Colonna 1964: 36). The passage is discussed by Budelmann 2002: 160: 'Tzetzes adapts his metaphors to the subject matter of the *Halieutica*: he pulls up a catch from the depth. The catch is a catch of *logoi*, and ... it is served up for the reader's or audience's pleasure.' Cf. the opening lines of *Sketches of the mouse* 1.2–4 (Papademetriou) on the 'feast of learning' being set for the students. On the popularity of Oppian in the twelfth century, see Rhoby 2010: 169–70.

[88] The ancient handbooks on *progymnasmata* (e.g. Theon and Aphthonios) described the ekphrasis as a way of 'bringing the subject matter vividly before the eyes' of its recipient; see e.g. Webb 2009: 39–59. On the use and function of ekphrasis in Manasses, see Nilsson 2005; in the middle Byzantine period, see Nilsson 2021b.

[89] See Gàrzya 1955/57 and Papathomopoulos 1976. Note also the possible inspiration of *Cynegetica* 1.62–6 cited above, n. 84.

[90] Manasses, *Origins of Oppian* 24–30 (Colonna): ἔνθα συνὼν Ὀππιανὸς αὐτῷ τριακοντούτης | τὴν τῶν ἰχθύων ἔγραψεν ἄγραν τὴν ἐναλίαν, | τὴν τῶν θηρίων μετ' αὐτήν, εἶτα τὴν τῶν ὀρνέων | σὺν ἄλλοις πλείοσι, λεπταῖς καὶ βραχυτμήτοις βίβλοις, | ὧνπερ κατεκαυχήσατο χρόνος ὁ πανδαμάτωρ, | τούτων τῶν δύο τέλεον φεισάμενος καὶ μόνων | τῶν εἰς τὰ κυνηγέσια καὶ πρὸς τὴν ἐναλίαν.

distinguishable in the *Origins of Oppian*? Does the enigmatic form of the *schedos* even allow for such a personalized voice?

The five *schede* that have come down to us under the name of Manasses all have Christian themes: the first narrates the Life of Daniel the Stylite, the second and third address the Theotokos, the fourth describes Mary's entry into the temple and the fifth seems to offer part of a martyrium.[91] The Life of Daniel offers an interesting complement to other *Lives* that are part of Manasses' production – not only the *Origins of Oppian*, but also the biographical sections of orations and the *Verse chronicle* –, so let us begin by taking a closer look at that exercise. In order to give an impression of the kind of challenges the students met, I offer first the 'original' version of the *schedos* as it stands in the manuscript (based on the apparatus offered by Polemis) and then the 'corrected' version as presented in the edition by Polemis, marking the 'traps' in bold. My translation follows the 'corrected' version.[92]

Οὐκ ἔξω παντὸς καιροῦ, ἂν αἱ τῶν ἄθλων ἑτοιμασίαι τὰ κατὰ τὸν μέγαν Δανιὴλ εἰς μέσον ἀγάγωσι καὶ σοὶ **δαῖθ'αἱ λιταὶ ἂν** ποιήσωνται, σύλλογε, **δῖε. τὰ νέων** γὰρ φιλολόγων ἐντεῦθεν παλαίσματα ἐλεγχθήσονται. Ἀλλά μου συναντιλαμβάνου τοῦ πόνου **ὃς** στερρὸν προπύργιον, πάτερ θειότατε, καὶ τῷ τὴν δρόσον ἡμῖν ἐπιχέαι τῶν σῶν προσευχῶν ὑπανάψυχε καὶ **κενῶσαι πάρει γε** τοῖς ὑμνοῦσί σε.

Οὐκ ἔξω παντὸς καιροῦ, ἂν αἱ τῶν ἄθλων ἑτοιμασίαι τὰ κατὰ τὸν μέγαν Δανιὴλ εἰς μέσον ἀγάγωσι καὶ σοὶ **δὲ θελητέαν** ποιήσωνται, σύλλογε, **δίαιταν. Νέων** γὰρ φιλολόγων ἐντεῦθεν παλαίσματα ἐλεγχθήσονται. Ἀλλά μου συναντιλαμβάνου τοῦ πόνου **ὡς** στερρὸν προπύργιον, πάτερ θειότατε, καὶ τῷ τὴν δρόσον ἡμῖν ἐπιχέαι τῶν σῶν προσευχῶν ὑπανάψυχε καὶ **καινῶς ἐπάρηγε** τοῖς ὑμνοῦσί σε.[93]

It is not inappropriate if the preparations of the contests bring the story of the Great Daniel into focus and produce for you, my class, a life to be wished for.[94] For the struggles of young lovers of letters shall thus be brought to the test. But assist me in my labour, most holy father, like a firm bulwark, and pouring over us the dew of your prayers, refresh us and bring new strength to those who sing your praise.

---

[91] See Polemis 1996: 282: 'Die letzte Schede ist ein Bruchteil des Martyriums irgendwelcher Heiliger, die ich nicht bestimmen konnte. Wahrscheinlich handelt es sich um eine Paraphrase zu dem Kapitel von Symeon Metaphrastes, wo er die Antwort niederschreibt, die die Märtyrer auf die Ermutigung des Herrschers, sich für die Götter zu opfern, gaben.'

[92] Cf. the methods of Polemis 1996 and Vassis 1993/94 respectively.

[93] Manasses, *Schedos* 1.1–6 (Polemis).

[94] Cf. Gregory of Nazianzus, *Carmina moralia* 948.7. Here I take θελητέος to be an equivalent of θελητός, which seems to be the case also in Gregory's poem.

Having thus addressed both the presence of the students, greeted as σύλλογε (assembly or meeting), and the contest or struggle that lies ahead of them, and having stated that the day of the class is suitable for Daniel the Stylite (December 11), whom he asks to be gracious, the teacher moves on to the narrative element of the life. Daniel fled from his wealthy parents, not being interested in riches, and went to the large city of Constantinople. He first lived in a church, but then climbed up on a pillar. There he resisted all human pleasures, looking forward only to the delight of the heavenly kingdom. Here the *schedos* turns into dodecasyllable verse, though without breaking off the narrative flow:

> Therefore the grace of the holy spirit | made him produce wondrous omens, | drive away illnesses and banish demons.
>
> Ἐντεῦθεν αὐτῷ πνεύματος θείου χάρις
> αὐτουργὸν εἰργάσατο σημείων ξένων,
> νόσων διώκτην, φυγαδευτὴν δαιμόνων.[95]

There is nothing particular about the story itself as narrated here: it is most likely the version as revised by Symeon Metaphrastes,[96] and the language used is typical for Byzantine hymns and prayers – this is accordingly a useful example for imitation. Moreover, the opening of the *schedos* is interesting in its way of referring to the trial of 'young lovers of letters', that is, students who are trained to become future teachers, functionaries and rhetors.[97] The 'contests' here probably refers to the class itself rather than to the kind of contests arranged at the court and described in other texts by Manasses,[98] but the tests are certainly the same – to find and fix the grammatical problems, while at the same time learning about composition in both prose and verse. Saints' lives are common themes for *schede*, often – as in this case – determined by the day of the class.[99] The Theotokos is also a common theme, useful not only for future writers of poems and sermons, but also for practising panegyrics in general. The closing verses of *Schedos* 2 could certainly be used metaphorically in various situations also beyond a religious setting:

---

[95] Manasses, *Schedos* 1.28–30 (Polemis). The switch from prose to verse is a standard device of the bipartite *schedos*; see Agapitos 2015c.
[96] PG 116, 969–1037.
[97] Cf. Manasses, *Letter* 1 (Horna): Τῷ φιλολόγῳ τὸ δῶρον, τῷ λογοθέτῃ τὸν λόγον, with *Funerary oration on the death of Nikephoros Komnenos* 184 (Kurtz): ὅμως καὶ πῦρ φιλολογίας ἐντρέφεται καὶ ζῆλος χαρίτων ῥητορικῆς, and *Verse chronicle* 3 (Lampsides) (φιλολογωτάτη).
[98] Manasses, *Funerary oration on the death of Nikephoros Komnenos* 453–66 (Kurtz); Manasses, *Encomium of Michael Hagiotheodorites* 264–74 (Horna).
[99] See Vassis 1993/94.

Delivered, then, from wandering in the dark | we walk in a straight path to the unfading light.

Ἀπαλλαγέντες τοιγαροῦν σκότους πλάνης
εὐθυδρομοῦμεν εἰς ἀνέσπερον σέλας.[100]

These two verses are reminiscent of several Biblical passages, referring to the sinful path of man and the light found in Christ.[101] But similar verses could also work, for example, in the context of the imperial light of Emperor Manuel – the eternal sun of the empire – or for the delivery from troubles in the writer's projected life-story.[102] The use of motifs and similes from the Old and New Testaments as well as hymnography is also part of the lesson, as is the variation of epithets and names, particularly notable in *Schedos* 3. It opens with a curse on those who do not praise the virgin: 'May for blasphemers be parched, o gate of God, all words of their filthy mouths, with which they do not proclaim you, the chaste mother of God. For you gave birth, o girl, to a son…' (Ἀποφρυγέσθωσαν, ὦ πύλη Θεοῦ, τοῖς βλασφήμοις, ὅσαι φωναὶ στόματος ῥυπαροῦ, ἐν ᾧ Θεοῦ σε μητέρα μὴ καταγγέλλουσιν ἀδιάφθορον. Σὺ γὰρ ἔτεκες, ὦ κόρη, υἱόν…).[103] After presenting the virgin in a well-known manner as the solution to numerous hardships and pains, the *schedos* culminates in a series of Biblical epithets, so that the closing verses contain no fewer than six words used in the Old Testament but here employed for Mary:

Hail, gold-wrought bed of Solomon, | ladder, ark, jar, bush, lamp.

Ὅ χαῖρε, χρυσότευκτε Σολομῶν κλίνη,
κλῖμαξ, κιβωτέ, στάμνε, βάτε, λυχνία.[104]

Such passages offer practically the entire vocabulary one needs in order to praise the Theotokos and would thus have been highly useful for students.[105] But the question remains: is there any room in this kind of exercise for the model author?

---

[100] Manasses, *Schedos* 2.22–3 (Polemis).
[101] See e.g. Psalms 82:5; Proverbs 4:19; Isaiah 9:2; Jude 1:13; John 8:12 and 12:35.
[102] Cf. esp. Manasses, *Letter* 1.5 (Horna) and *Letter* 2.1–12 (Horna), along with the *Address by the way* 3–5 and 20 (Browning), cited and discussed above, Chapter 4. For the imagery of Emperor Manuel as the sun, see above, Chapter 2.
[103] Manasses, *Schedos* 3.1–4 (Polemis).
[104] Manasses, *Schedos* 3.33–4 (Polemis). κλίνη Song 3:7; κλῖμαξ Gen. 28:12; κιβωτέ Ex. 25:9–10; στάμνε Ex. 16:33; βάτε Ex. 3:2; λυχνία Ex. 25:30–31.
[105] Cf. the two poems on the Theotokos by Theodore Prodromos, edited and commented in Zagklas 2014: 266–75 (Zagklas nos. 8–9 = Hörandner nos. 129–30).

From what has been cited so far, there are few traces in the *schede* of that recognizable authorial voice that has been traced throughout the previous sections of this book. The only thing that stands out at all, and just barely, is the opening of the first *schedos* with its reference to 'lovers of letters' (*philologos*) – a word that Manasses occasionally plays around with[106] – and the request for 'refreshing dew' from the addressed saint, reminiscent of demands for compensation from worldly patrons.[107] But it could, of course, be argued that those words are so common among authors in similar situations that they mean nothing particular here. As noted by Ioannis Vassis, *schede* are known for being difficult to attribute, since not all of them betray an individual author's style,[108] so there is nothing strange about the attribution of these *schede* to Manasses in spite of the lack of his usual voice. However, there is one text that may offer a different perspective of the matter: the so-called *Sketches of the mouse* (*Schede tou myos*), traditionally attributed to Theodore Prodromos but which Horna maintained was written by Manasses.[109]

Horna's attribution of the text to Manasses was based primarily on three arguments: only one manuscript attributes the text to Prodromos,[110] the prose rhythm of the *Sketches of the mouse* adheres to that of Manasses[111] and the close similarities between the *Sketches of the mouse* and a passage in the *Description of the Earth*. Horna's arguments have generally been found inconclusive, but the attribution to Prodromos also remains 'rather weak'.[112] It is not my intention in the present study to try to attribute more texts to Manasses, but to discuss and critically assess such attributions within the frame of Manasses' entire production and the authorial voice that he projects in those works. While neither prose rhythm nor a specific vocabulary may offer conclusive evidence, it is still relevant to

---

[106] Manasses, *Letter* 1 (Horna): Τῷ φιλολόγῳ τὸ δῶρον, τῷ λογοθέτῃ τὸν λόγον; see also above, n. 97.
[107] Manasses, *Verse chronicle* 16–17 (Lampsides): καὶ τὸν τοῦ κόπου καύσωνα καὶ τῆς ταλαιπωρίας | αἱ δωρεαὶ δροσίζουσι κενούμεναι συχνάκις.
[108] Vassis 1993/94: 8, discussing the *schede* by Prodromos on Christian themes (among which a stylite and the Theotokos). This could be the case also for the political verses transmitted in the Barocc. 131 and possibly composed by Manasses; see Horna 1902: 13–14 and 21. For a brief discussion, see above, Chapter 4, n. 113.
[109] Horna 1904; 324, n. 1; Horna 1905: 12–14. See now also Lauxtermann 2021: n. 55.
[110] When Horna made this claim, only two manuscripts were known (Par. Gr. 2652, used by Boissonade, and Vat. Gr. 711, consulted by Horna); since then three more manuscripts have been added for the edition of Papademetriou 1969, but none of them contains any indication of the author.
[111] Based on the analysis made by Maas 1902; see also Hörandner 1981: 144–50 for the same argument.
[112] Marciniak 2017: 510; cf. e.g. Mercati 1927 and, more recently, Meunier 2016: esp. 16, n. 33.

consider the kind of arguments that are proposed or rejected in such discussions, especially in view of Manasses' tendency to recycle his own words and phrases. Let us therefore compare the two passages in question and look at the arguments for and against an attribution to Manasses and Prodromos respectively.

The *Sketches of the mouse* is a kind of schedographic diptych that tells the story of a mouse who cannot resist the temptation of some leftovers and therefore has the misfortune of being caught by a cat. The mouse tries to use rhetoric in order to save himself, posing as a monk and presenting a cento of verses from the Psalms in order to impress the cat. The cat, unmoved, tells him that his mouth will be his grave. The passage that is close to the *Description of the Earth* is placed in the first *schedos* and runs as follows.

> There was also the head of a beautiful mullet, and the mouse hurriedly threw himself at it. Yet, even as he desired [it], he was afraid: he opened his mouth and, shaking, stepped back. While his stomach pushed him towards the food, fear put him to flight. Desire stirred in him, but his cowardly heart held him back. Even as he was running toward it, he was running away from it. He desired food but fled as if from an enemy. He suspected that a cat might be hidden somewhere in the bones. Nevertheless, after a long time he shook off the fear and threw himself at the head of the mullet.
>
> Ἦν ἐκεῖσε καὶ τρίγλης ἀγλαομόρφου κρανίον καὶ τούτῳ φέρων ὁ μῦς ἐπέρριψεν ἑαυτόν. Καὶ ἦν ὁμοῦ λιχνευόμενος καὶ φοβούμενος· ἅμα τὸ στόμα ὑπήνοιγε καὶ ἅμα ὑπότρομος ἀνεπόδιζεν. Ἡ μὲν γαστὴρ ἤπειγεν εἰς τροφήν, τὸ δὲ δέος ἔτρεπεν εἰς φυγήν· τὸ μὲν ὀρεκτικὸν ἀνηρέθιζεν, ἀλλ' ἀντεπεῖχε τὸ δειλοκάρδιον· ἅμα ἐπέτρεχε καὶ ἅμα ἀπέτρεχε· καὶ ὡς ἐδώδιμον ἤθελε καὶ ὡς πολέμιον ἔφευγεν. Ὑπώπτευε γάρ, μή πού τις κατοικίδιος αἴλουρις τοῖς ὀστέοις ἐμπερικρύπτοιτο. Ὅμως δὲ τὸ δέος ὀψέ ποτε ἀποτιναξάμενος τῷ κρανίῳ τῆς τρίγλης ἐνέπιπτε.[113]

The corresponding passage in the *Description of the Earth* is inserted in a long ekphrasis of a mosaic depicting a personification of the Earth as a woman, surrounded by nine tableaux depicting various fruits (fresh and dried), the leftovers of a meal, seafood, fish and a cock. The little mouse is part of the representation of the leftovers.

> A mouse had smelled the heap, for the animal is indeed greedy and quickly grasps the smell of food. It had thus smelled the heap and attacked. In its rush it ignored everything that was there, passed it by without even looking at it, considering it to be useless and tasteless. It had desired the head of the

---

[113] *Sketches of the mouse* 15–23 (Papademitriou), tr. Marciniak 2017: 524.

red mullet and attacked it with frenzy. What clever invention, though! The artist had painted it as both greedy and frightened. It opened its mouth and, at the same time, moved back scared. Its belly pressed it upon the food, but fear put it to flight. Its appetites urged it forward, but cowardice held it back. It advanced and retreated. It wanted the red mullet as a titbit, but avoided it as an enemy, looking at the heap distrustfully, should the cat of the house be hiding inside it. With such an expertise had the painter represented the mouse in its dilemma.

Ἤσθετό ποθεν ἐκείνης τῆς ὀστώσεως μῦς· λίχνον δὲ ἄρα τὸ ζῷον καὶ ταχέως τῆς τῶν γευστῶν ὀσμῆς ἀντιλαμβανόμενον· ᾔσθετο δὴ τῆς ὀστώσεως καὶ αἰσθόμενος ὀξέως ἐπέδραμε καὶ ἐπιδραμὼν τῶν μὲν ἄλλων ὑπερεφρόνησε καὶ παρῆλθεν ὡς ἄχρηστα καὶ ἀφῆκεν ὡς ἄβρωτα καὶ οὐδὲ βλέπειν προσεποιήσατο, ὅλος δὲ τοῦ κρανίου τῆς τρίγλης ἐγένετο καὶ τούτῳ φέρων ἐπέρριψεν ἑαυτόν. Ἀλλ' ὦ τῆς σοφίας! Ἔγραψεν αὐτὸν ὁ τεχνίτης καὶ λιχνευόμενον καὶ φοβούμενον· ἅμα τὸ στόμα ὑπήνοιγε καὶ ἅμα ὑπότρομος ἀνεπόδιζεν· ἡ μὲν γαστὴρ ἤπειγε πρὸς τροφήν, τὸ δὲ δέος ὑπέτρεπεν εἰς φυγήν· τὸ μὲν ὀρεκτικὸν ἀνηρέθιζεν, ἀλλ' ἀντεπεῖχε τὸ δειλοκάρδιον· ἅμα ἐπέτρεχε καὶ ἀπέτρεχε· καὶ ὡς ἐδώδιμον ἤθελε καὶ ὡς πολέμιον ἔφευγε δείλαιος καὶ τὴν σωρείαν αὐτῶν τῶν ὀστέων ὑπώπτευε, μή πού τις ἐν αὐτοῖς κατοικίδιος αἴλουρος παρακρύπτοιτο. Μετὰ τοιαύτης σοφίας ὁ μῦς ἐκεῖνος δυεῖν εἰκόνιστο.[114]

The two passages are close to each other, which to previous scholars suggested a potential influence in one direction or the other. Maas accused Manasses of plagiarizing the work of Prodromos, while Horna argued that the procedure of borrowing from contemporaries would have been unthinkable.[115] As noted by Marciniak in a recent study, it is not unthinkable at all, but rather fairly common in the twelfth century.[116] However, an aspect that complicates the discussion of influence, not noted by any of these scholars, is the probable hypotext of both passages: the opening passage of the so-called Xenia II of Philostratus' *Imagines*, depicting a hare caught in the same moment of hesitation:

> This hare in his cage is the prey of the net, and he sits on his haunches moving his forelegs a little and slowly lifting his ears, but he also keeps looking with all his eyes and tries to see behind him as well, so suspicious is he and always cowering with fear.

---

[114] Manasses, *Description of the Earth* 151–63 (Lampsides), tr. Nilsson 2005: 126, revised.
[115] Maas 1902: 511, n. 1; Horna 1904: 324, n. 1: 'An ein Plagiat zu denken, geht nicht recht an.' See also Lauxtermann 2021: n. 55: 'it is out of the question that Prodromos would plagiarize Manasses in such a manner, or Manasses Prodromos, for that matter: they are both too good for that'.
[116] Marciniak 2017: 511.

Ὁ μὲν ἐν τῷ οἰκίσκῳ λαγωὸς δικτύου θήραμα, κάθηται δὲ ἐπὶ τῶν σκελῶν ὑποκινῶν τοὺς προσθίους καὶ ὑπεγείρων τὸ οὖς, ἀλλὰ καὶ βλέπει παντὶ τῷ βλέμματι, βούλεται δὲ καὶ κατόπιν ὁρᾶν δι' ὑποψίαν καὶ τὸ ἀεὶ πτήσσειν.[117]

The use of Philostratus is rather frequent in the ekphraseis by Manasses, which may speak in favour of his *Description of the Earth* being an 'original' work, not influenced by any other contemporary text, but at the same time the many layers of transtextual relations here complicate the question of influence.[118] At least three explanations for the similarities of the two texts could be proposed, all related to textual and literary rather than moral, philosophical or theological issues.[119]

First scenario: the *Sketches of the mouse* was indeed written by Prodromos, or by any of his fellow teachers, and inspired Manasses to include a mouse in his *Description of the Earth*. In that case, Manasses must have recognized the Philostratean hypertext and decided to underline it by adapting Philostratus also in the introductory part of his ekphrasis.[120] Second scenario: the *Sketches of the mouse* was written by Manasses as an exercise for students and the description of the mouse was recycled in the *Description of the Earth* – or the other way around.[121] The form of the *Sketches of the mouse*, written in prose but ending with dodecasyllable verses, is the same as in the *schede* attributed in the manuscripts to Manasses and analysed above.[122] Third scenario: the *Sketches of the mouse* was written by Prodromos or someone else, imitating the passage of Philostratus, while Manasses composed his *Description of the Earth*

---

[117] Philostratus, *Imagines* 2.26 (Benndorf and Schenkl), tr. Fairbanks.
[118] For the use of Philostratus, see e.g. Manasses, *Description of the Earth* 5–16 (Lampsides) (cf. Philostratus, *Imagines* 1, proem 1–2), *Description of the Earth* 109–14 (cf. *Imagines* 1.6.1), *Description of the Earth* 215–19 (cf. *Imagines* 1.31.1); see also Manasses, *Description of the Cyclops* 46–51 (Sternbach) (cf. Philostratus, *Imagines* 2.18.3). A more thorough search would probably reveal many more examples. For a comparison between the openings of the *Description of the Earth* and the *Description of the Cyclops* in relation to Philostratus, see Nilsson 2011: 127–8. The similarity between the *Description of the Earth*, the *Sketches of the mouse* and Philostratus is noted by Foskolou 2018: 91–2, with texts and translations in the Appendix.
[119] For the moral significance of the mouse as a symbol of greed, see Bazaiou-Barabas 1994: 105–6, 114–15. On philosophical and theological implications, see Meunier 2016 (including also the *Katomyomachia* in her analysis).
[120] See above, n. 118.
[121] One may note that the image of the mouse caught in a trap or net (ἀρκύων at the beginning of the second *schedos*, changed by Papademetriou into σαρκίων, but translated as 'trap' by Marciniak 2017: 525) may be read in relation to both a Philostratean hypertext and the schedographic imagery used by Manasses in the *Encomium of Michael Hagiotheodorites* 264–74 (Horna) and the *Funerary oration on the death of Nikephoros Komnenos* 453–66 (Kurtz).
[122] Cf. Marciniak 2017: 511.

independently of that person's work, but adapting the same Philostratean ekphrasis.

These are not even all the possibilities, but only a few. My point is that we tend to interpret texts and attribute them to certain authors based on preconceived ideas of textual as well as personal relations. From our modern perspective, based on romantic notions of originality, one text has to precede the other. According to the same reasoning, one author has to be more important than the other and therefore more likely to be imitated.[123] But such notions do not seem to characterize writing practices in the twelfth century, and certainly not the production of progymnasmata and schedography. It seems likely that Manasses wrote the *Sketches of the mouse*, but one should still accept the complexity of textual relations in the period in which the text was most probably composed. This does not mean that a search for the model author in the schedographic writing that may or may not be attributed to Manasses is all in vain, but rather that certain kinds of texts may have been produced less for self-display and more for the benefit of the students and future rhetors of Constantinople.

The Model Author and the Teacher

I set out primarily to analyse two poems and five *schede*, but the investigation has taken me beyond the boundaries of those texts, and beyond the boundaries of what is usually defined as didactic or school context. Some of the ekphraseis that I initially tried to exclude have been brought back into the discussion, as has the *Verse chronicle* and, above all, the potentially Manassean *Sketches of the mouse*. So where has this taken us, in terms of understanding the instructive intentions of Manasses the model author and his teaching activities? Let us return once more to Hagiotheodorites and the description of the grammar contest in the presence of the emperor, who must have been Manuel I Komnenos. The textual and social relations between this passage and a number of other texts – the ekphraseis and the *schede*, but also the *Origins of Oppian* – provide a perfect example of the model proposed by Zagklas, that is, the 'classroom' as only one of several 'communicating vessels' between which the teacher–writer would move in twelfth-century Constantinople.

Manasses' praise of the logothete Hagiotheodorites as, among other things, a skilful game leader of grammar contests, offers a transtextual key to understanding the relation between texts and contexts involving

[123] See above, n. 115.

teaching, rhetorical display and patronage. As we have seen above, texts with instructive intentions – whether for patrons or students – may very well be expressed in the regular voice of the model author, but they may also supress that voice in favour of their educational purpose (as in the less personal *schede* discussed above).[124] The use of the same motifs or imagery in texts composed for different occasions and with different functions creates intertextual links that may help the audience to navigate the production of a certain writer, but which also help the writer to make his voice noticed and heard. Even schedography could in this manner 'transcend the classroom',[125] just as didactic poems written for specific addressees could be reused for pedagogical use beyond that primary occasion. Ekphraseis could be used for education, for panegyrics and for rhetorical display – any one function does not exclude the others, and it may be more important to acknowledge the multiple functions than to pin down the 'primary use'.[126]

The different social positions of the writer in society are thus made part of his literary output, since no clear distinction between didactic and other kinds of texts can be made. In fact, Byzantine texts are often didactic, which may be seen in relation to their occasional functions and extratextual messages.[127] Even a text such as the *Encomium of Michael Hagiotheodorites*, with a primary panegyric purpose – praise in exchange for favours – offers teaching in the roles to be assumed by writer and patron, by students and provider of funding (emperor/*orphanotrophos*). It may be relevant from this perspective to consider more carefully the relation between Manasses, Manuel and Hagiotheodorites, and the occasion at which they (allegedly) met to watch the students contend: 'At one occasion a contest is arranged for the foster children of grammar in the presence of the emperor' (ἵσταταί ποτε καὶ παισὶ τροφίμοις γραμματικῆς ἐν ὀφθαλμοῖς βασιλέως ἀγών).[128]

---

[124] Cf. Vassis 1993/94 on similar tendencies in the production of Prodromos.
[125] Zagklas 2014: 75. Cf. Vassis 1993/94 on schedography taking on a new panegyric function, praising patrons. This does not necessarily mean that it became a new 'genre', but rather that it took on a new function according to processes similar to those of the ekphrasis (moving from rhetorical exercise to independent text type). See also the series of articles by Agapitos on schedography and its function beyond the classroom; Agapitos 2015a–c and 2017.
[126] Cf. Zagklas 2014: 81, on the need to distinguish 'between texts designed to be used primarily in a teaching setting and those meant to be inscribed'.
[127] Cf. the discussion of the term *Gebrauchstext*; see Garzya 1981; cf. Lauxtermann 2003: 30. On these functions of Byzantine literature, see also above, Chapter 1.
[128] Manasses, *Encomium of Michael Hagiotheodorites* 264–5 (Horna).

This kind of contest is known from several other sources, the most well-known being a passage in the *Alexiad* of Anna Komnene.[129] Anna describes how the children of the grammar school at the Orphanotropheion, established by her father Alexios I Komnenos, recopy and cite *schede* as a way of learning and practising ancient Greek grammar.[130] As noted by Timothy Miller in his studies of the Orphanotropheion, such contests seem to have been regularly organized by the teachers of the school in the presence of powerful patrons. Miller has paid special attention to two *schede* attributed to a certain Leo of Rhodes, a teacher who feels 'worn out in addressing the tribes of young children' by his hard work at the school of the Orphanotropheion.[131] Both of these *schede* are included in the Vaticanus Palatinus Gr. 92, the manuscript containing numerous schedographic texts, among which two by Manasses.[132] Another teacher associated with the school of the Orphanotropheion, whose *schede* have been preserved in the same manuscript, is Prodromos. His schedographic production was marked by innovation, noted already by his own students, and in particular by the tendency to add dodecasyllable verses at the end of a prose *schedos*.[133]

All this taken together, and especially combined with the fact that Michael Hagiotheodorites held the office of *orphanotrophos* in 1166 and 1170,[134] makes it plausible to associate Manasses with the grammar school at the Orphanotropheion specifically rather than with the Patriarchal School in general. As noted by Miller, many of the teachers of the school eventually became bishops, which would then also support the possibility that Manasses became bishop of Panion at a later stage of his career.[135] If we read the passage carefully, it may even contain an allusion to the teaching situation of Manasses: the 'foster children of grammar' (παισὶ τροφίμοις γραμματικῆς) could be a reference to the Orphanotropheion and its grammar school.[136] Then again, Sebastokratorissa Eirene is addressed in a similar manner at the beginning of the *Verse chronicle* as a 'foster child of learning', presumably without any connotation of the

---

[129] Anna Komnene, *Alexiad* 15.7.9 (Reinsch and Kambylis). The passage is cited and discussed in detail in Agapitos 2014. On other sources for such contests, see Miller 2003a: 17–18; Miller 2003b: 230–2.
[130] On the question of whether Alexios had actually established the school or not, see Miller 2003b: 209–12.
[131] Miller 2003a: 12–13.   [132] On the manuscript, see Gallavotti 1983: 24–30.
[133] See esp. Vassis 1993/94, but also Miller 2003b: 228; Zagklas 2017.
[134] Horna 1906: 193; Magdalino 1993: 256.   [135] Miller 2003a: 10; Miller 2003b: 233–7.
[136] Miller 2003b: 231, n. 88, notes this possible allusion, but without suggesting that Manasses was one of the school's teachers.

Orphanotropheion.[137] And Manasses, due to his association with the logothete and various other imperial and aristocratic patrons, may have taken part in a contest without being one of the school's teachers.

It is possible that more *schede* will eventually be attributed to Manasses or found in yet unexplored manuscripts,[138] perhaps shedding more light on some of the questions raised in this chapter. For the present investigation of Manasses and his self-representation, we can at least conclude that his voice is present also in educational contexts, and that they should not be separated from other social or textual settings in which he displayed his work.

[137] Manasses, *Verse chronicle* 8 (Lampsides): τροφίμη λόγου. See above, n. 47.
[138] As noted by Polemis 1996: 282.

CHAPTER 6

Life, Love and the Past
Self-Quotation and Recycling

All writers repeat themselves. This is to some extent even what characterizes successful authors – the repetition of distinct motifs, turns of phrases and words that make their style recognizable to their readers. They also repeat elements from the tradition on which they rely: this has been part of authorial strategies since antiquity and helps the audience to place a new work in the appropriate setting of already known and accepted conventions, also known as genre systems. While such strategies are well-known and have served as the very basis of philological and literary studies for ages, there is definitely a limit to how much repetition readers – or at least critics – are ready to accept. Carefully constructed circular compositions, poetic works based on repetition with variation, a pronounced intertextuality along with a moderate use of self-reference, are usually appreciated as skilful and artistic, but an excessive use of the same techniques is often condemned as either tedious or problematic – a sign of the writer's lack of imagination, laziness or even plagiarism. This critique may be directed at both ancient and modern authors, but it has been particularly frequent in the case of Byzantine texts.

While questions of imitation, often under the Greek term 'mimesis', and plagiarism have been rather thoroughly studied and discussed,[1] the issue of self-imitation or self-reference in Byzantine literature has received much less attention. That is to say, the self-referential strategy understood as a way of pointing to the author himself has been noted in the cases of, for example, Michael Psellos and John Tzetzes,[2] but self-reference as a textual strategy that points not to the author as a person (nor as a literary

---

[1] From Hunger 1969/70 to Nilsson 2010 and 2014: 94–8, and Marciniak 2013. Note also Nilsson and Nyström 2009.
[2] Papaioannou 2013 and 2014 on Psellos, Pizzone 2018 on Tzetzes. On authorial self-confidence and self-referentiality in the twelfth century, see also several contributions in Pizzone 2014a.

6 Life, Love and the Past: Self-Quotation and Recycling 143

persona) but to the texts themselves is more rarely discussed.³ A recent exception has been provided by Stanislas Kuttner-Homs, who has studied self-referentiality in the case of Niketas Choniates as three different kinds of textual functions: self-representation (of the author), self-quotation (*autocitation*) and textual self-reference (*métapoétique*).⁴ Kuttner-Homs shows that such procedures are a central part of the aesthetic norms to which Choniates adhered, norms – moreover – that had been at play since antiquity and were therefore inherited by Choniates from his literary predecessors. I very much agree with these presumptions and believe that the study of Kuttner-Homs is of great importance when we wish to understand the compositions of twelfth-century writers.

In the present study, the first kind of self-reference defined by Kuttner-Homs, self-representation, is seen primarily as a narrative strategy, 'telling the story' of the author throughout his entire production of texts.⁵ The third kind, metapoetic self-reference that takes place on the level of the text, has been discussed above rather in terms of metaliterary or meta-textual commentary; to offer but one example, drawn from the *Origins of Oppian*, the choice of writing a didactic poem about an author who wrote didactic poems adds a metatextual quality to the text, enhanced by the fact that both authors wrote for imperial patrons.⁶ It is the second kind of self-reference defined by Kuttner-Homs – self-quotation – that is of most interest to me in this chapter, even if we have seen several examples of such procedures also in the preceding chapters. Self-quotation is interesting on linguistic, narratological and stylistic levels, because it helps achieve the recognizable voice of the model author. To accept the fact that such techniques were part of the ancient and Byzantine authors' aesthetic norms and methods of the craft may help modern readers avoid judgemental approaches that condemn repetition in favour of 'originality' and accordingly misunderstand the crucial function of repetition and recycling.

---

³ Nilsson 2001 studied 'auto-mimesis' and 'repetition with variation' (based on Lodge 1976) as a narrative strategy in *Hysmine and Hysminias*, but that study was limited to one work whose author, Eumathios Makrembolites, is not otherwise known (with the exception of a series of riddles, included at the end of Hilberg's edition of the novel; Hilberg 1876: 202–17).

⁴ Kuttner-Homs 2016: vol. 2, 7: 'L'autoréférence subsume trois domaines : la référence à soi, l'autocitation, la métapoétique.' Cf. p. 584: 'L'autoréférence se décline de trois manières : d'abord comme mise en scène de l'auteur par lui-même ; ensuite comme référence interne au sein du corpus nicétéen (autocitation); enfin comme référence des textes à eux-mêmes (métapoétique).' See also the more concise analysis in Kuttner-Homs 2018.

⁵ On the idea of an authorial narrative, see above, Chapter 1. By 'author' I here intend the model author, not the empirical author; see above, Chapter 4.

⁶ See above, Chapter 5.

Repetition and recycling are not failings on the part of the author, but central stylistic, rhetorical and narrative techniques.⁷

In the context of twelfth-century Constantinople, recycling seems to be part of overall authorial strategies, both within individual authors' production and between different authors. Theodore Prodromos recycled much of his material over the years, probably using the same or similar material with different functions in different settings.⁸ His style is later praised and imitated by his students, such as Niketas Eugenianos, whose novel was composed as a response to that of his former teacher.⁹ Imitation was part of both educational and rhetorical practices and thus became an obvious part of literary aesthetics. But contrary to the modern way of understanding imitation as unoriginal and tedious, imaginative and skilful imitation was considered to be innovative. The use of the same story, the same motifs or the same words – equivalent to the manifold colours of a painter – could create novelty. For, as Manasses puts it in his *Encomium of Michael Hagiotheodorites*, 'man is a creature that loves novelty; he finds the customary tedious, but desires what is done for the very first time in stories, in songs, in paintings' (φιλόκαινον γὰρ ζῷον ὁ ἄνθρωπος καὶ τὸ μὲν σύνηθες ἥγηται προσκορές, λιχνεύεται δὲ περὶ τὰ πρώτως ἄρτι γινόμενα ἐν ἱστορίαις, ἐν ᾄσμασιν, ἐν γραφαῖς).¹⁰ Eustathios of Thessalonike makes similar observations when he analyses the Homeric epics, noting the listener's urge for novelty:

> The poet used this method both because it is novel and surprises with its unexpectedness – for to start naturally from the first events has nothing novel and the listener expects it to happen in this way in general – and because it is more forceful, i.e. better arranged.
>
> Ἐμεθώδευσε δὲ ὁ ποιητὴς τοῦτο ἅμα μὲν διὰ τὸ καινοπρεπὲς καὶ τῷ ἀνελπίστῳ ξενίζον, τὸ γὰρ κατὰ φύσιν ἀπὸ τῶν πρώτων ἄρξασθαι οὔτε καινόν τι ἔχει καὶ ὁ ἀκροατὴς δὲ ὡς ἐπὶ πολὺ οὕτως ἐλπίζει γενέσθαι, ἅμα δὲ καὶ διὰ τὸ δεινότερον, τουτέστιν οἰκονομικώτερον.¹¹

---

⁷ Cf. Nilsson 2001: 57 on repetition with variation in *Hysmine and Hysminias*: 'In the light of repetition with variation as a narrative strategy it should, however, be seen as a stylistic and rhetorical effect, and not as a failing on the part of the author.'
⁸ Zagklas 2014: esp. 76.
⁹ This is indicated by a heading preceding the text in one of the mss of Eugenianos' *Drosilla and Charikles*; see Conca 1990: 8–9 and 30.
¹⁰ Manasses, *Encomium of Michael Hagiotheodorites* 6–8 (Horna). See above, Chapter 4.
¹¹ Eust. in *Il*. 1.11.17–20 (van der Valk), tr. van den Berg 2016: 78 (here slightly revised), with discussion p. 79.

This skill in arranging narrative elements is crucial to successful writing – whether epics or oratory – and thus to the successful recycling of both others' and one's own material. In the case of Manasses cited above, it is his placement of the 'Hellenic story' of the ancient painter Apelles at the very beginning of his oration that is both innovative and useful, because the story of Apelles mirrors his own situation.[12] At the very basis of novelty lies thus the craft of letters (*logos* and *grammata* alike), allowing the writer to please his audience with the right combination of what is at the same time customary and new. The same compositional principles apply to the process, whether the writer draws on earlier material, on that of contemporary writers or on his own earlier production. In the latter case, self-quotation becomes a crucial part of creating an individual and recognizable voice.[13]

In this chapter, I turn to three works that employ the same form (political verse) and, moreover, a number of overlapping verses,[14] but which belong to different genres which traditionally are seen as having different functions: the *Verse chronicle* (a chronicle), the fragments of *Aristandros and Kallithea* (a novel) and the so-called *Moral poem* (a didactic poem with a moral aim). The use of political verse is an innovative feature per se when used for historiography and novel, and all three texts are characterized by the individual style or voice of Manasses. They also share some thematic features in their choice of motifs, themes and the use of a large number of gnomes and sayings. Even though the attribution of the *Moral poem* to Manasses has been challenged and should be seen as unsettled, the close relation between the three texts in terms of both content and form makes it relevant to consider them together. My analysis does not focus primarily on relations based on dependence, but I wish to understand the significance of authorial choices in this kind of repeated recycling of one's own (or perhaps someone else's) material – the way in which the same material transgresses genre conventions and contributes to the creation of a Manassean style or voice.

A Pleasant Reading of the Past

The *Verse chronicle* (Σύνοψις Χρονική) is the largest, the most widely known and the most frequently read of Manasses' works. It consists of

---

[12] See above, Chapter 4.
[13] For such procedures as 'theft' or plagiarism, see above, Chapter 3, n. 70. But note Marciniak 2013 on this procedure as an overall accepted part of literary and rhetorical composition in the twelfth century.
[14] Mazal 1967b: 66–9 and 70–3.

more than 6,000 verses and has come down to us in more than a hundred manuscripts.[15] It was continued, imitated and turned into vernacular prose in the Byzantine period,[16] translated into Bulgarian in the fourteenth century,[17] and translated into Latin as early as 1573.[18] Subject to imitation and praise all the way up to the early nineteenth century,[19] it fell into scholarly disgrace rather later due to its poetic form and apparent lack of historical information. In the last few years the *Verse chronicle* has been somewhat rehabilitated, with several studies of both its handling of sources and its literary techniques,[20] along with translations into modern languages.[21] What I should like to offer here is not another study of the literary characteristics of the chronicle, but a reconsideration of the chronicle within the context of Manasses' other preserved texts. I believe that such a perspective may offer a more nuanced picture and help us better understand both the chronicle and its author. Recycling and repetition are indeed central techniques in the chronicle tradition and in this sense Manasses uses the previous tradition pretty much as any other Byzantine chronicler,[22] but the question here is how to understand the recycling of motifs and verses within and across the entire production of Manasses.

As already noted above, the chronicle was written for Sebastokratorissa Eirene and opens with an address to her, referring to the roles of both

---

[15] The large number of mss witness a wide circulation of the text, even if many of them belong to later periods; see Lampsides 1996: lxxvi–cxlix.

[16] For the continuation, see Grégoire 1924. On the vernacular version, see Praechter 1895 and 1898, more recently Genova 1993 and Iadevaia 2000–8. See also further below.

[17] On the Middle Bulgarian translation, see Yuretich 2018: 10–13; Paul and Rhoby 2019: 53–5. The Vatican ms offers the only illuminated version of Manasses' *Verse chronicle*, on which see Boeck 2015.

[18] This was even before the *editio princeps* (Meursius 1616). The translator was Johannes Leunclavius (Löwenklau) (1541–94), a German historian and orientalist who had also translated ancient authors such as Xenophon (1565) and Plutarch (1565). The edition of Meursius included also the translation by Leunclavius; for a list of early editions and translations, see Lampsides 1996: clv–clix; also Paul and Rhoby 2019: 55–7. On another contemporary reader, Martin Crusius (Kraus), renowned Hellenist in Tübingen, see Rhoby 2014 and 2018; Paul and Rhoby 2019: 1–3.

[19] See esp. the Greek enlightenment poet Kaisarios Dapontes, on which Lampsides 1969, along with Romanian polymath and writer Nicolae Iorga (cited above, Chapter 1). On the early modern reception of the *Verse chronicle*, see also Nilsson 2021a.

[20] Reinsch 2002 and 2007; Nilsson 2005, 2006, 2019 and 2020; Kiapidou 2009; Nilsson and Nyström 2009; Rhoby 2014; Taxidis 2017.

[21] English tr. in Yuretich 2018 and German tr. in Paul and Rhoby 2019, the latter with a substantial introduction to various aspects of the chronicle, including its sources, literary form and reception. As noted above, the English translation by Yuretich appeared when I had already made my own translations, which are consistently used in this book. For a recent description of the chronicle from a historiographical perspective taking literary aspects into account, see Neville 2018: 200–4.

[22] Though not quite; see Reinsch 2007 and Nilsson 2005, 2006 and 2021a. For a study of the techniques of 'borrowing' in the Byzantine chronicle tradition, with special focus on the Trojan war episode, see Jouanno 2014.

patron and writer.²³ In addition, a dedicatory poem praising Eirene, but written in hexameters, follows the *Verse chronicle* in some manuscripts. In Lampsides' edition, it was printed before the chronicle, but it was probably composed as a closing book epigram, corresponding to the opening verses of the work.²⁴ Since Manasses' *Verse chronicle* also includes praise of Manuel I Komnenos (vv. 2507–12), his accession to the throne in 1143 has often been seen as a *terminus post quem*, whereas Eirene's death c.1153 provides the latest possible date for the composition of the work. However, it seems plausible to assume that this large work was written in portions, perhaps starting as early as the late 1130s or the early 1140s, and that the references to Manuel were inserted after 1143.²⁵ The episodic structure of the work indicates that it was performed in portions, but in view of its length it seems unlikely that all episodes were ever performed.²⁶ One could easily imagine the performance of certain narrative highlights, such as the programmatic opening offering an elaborate ekphrasis of the Creation,²⁷ or the episodes describing particularly important or intriguing emperors of the past, such as Constantine the Great (306–37), Justinian I (527–65) or Leo the Iconoclast (717–41).²⁸ An indication of such occasional functions is provided by the inclusion of Constantinopolitan details in all of these episodes, placing the historical past in the spatial environment in which the performance took place. Such a combination of past and present is a typical feature of occasional literature, which allows us to see the *Verse chronicle* as occasional in the sense that it was partially performed at specific occasions in the capital, most probably for the Sebastokratorissa and her entourage.²⁹

---

²³ Manasses, *Verse chronicle* 1–26 (Lampsides).
²⁴ See Hörandner 2007: 332–3; Rhoby 2009: 323–5; Paul and Rhoby 2019: 15. The correspondence between the opening verses 1–26 of the *Verse chronicle* and the hexametric epigram is clear in the choice of words (esp. the first line's Δέχνυσο τοῖον δῶρον ἀφ' ἡμετέροιο πόνοιο), in spite of the epigram's focus on Eirene's husband Andronikos (died 1142). This does not necessarily mean that the *Verse chronicle* was composed and handed over in its entirety, but rather that the book epigram belonged to the 'published' version of the work. Cf. Magdalino 1993: 350–1, arguing that the reference to gifts in the opening verses 'is to a series of gifts made before the work was completed'. In my view, the reference might as well be to gifts paid for in portions during the completion of the large commission.
²⁵ On the dating, see Lampsides 1988. Cf. Reinsch 2007: 266–7, dating the chronicle to 1150–53. Cf also Nilsson 2021a; Paul and Rhoby 2019: 7–9.
²⁶ See Paul and Rhoby 2019: 51 with n. 209 on a manuscript marginal note indicating that the *Verse chronicle* was read out loud to the Sebastokratorissa.
²⁷ Manasses, *Verse chronicle* 27–286 (Lampsides), on which Nilsson 2005.
²⁸ On the episodes on Justinian and Leo the Iconoclast, see Nilsson 2021a.
²⁹ See above, Chapter 2. Episodes that lend themselves to romantic or adventurous suspense may also have had performative potential, such as the Trojan war (*Verse chronicle* 1108–1470) or the story of

The opening ekphrasis of the Creation is significant, because it not only sets the tone of the chronicle from the very start – this is not a typical Byzantine chronicle, but rather an ekphrastic and romantic story of the world, that is, the Byzantine empire with Constantinople at its centre –, it also offers a descriptive and narrative model to which the later episodes can allude and refer. The starry sky and the lush garden of Eden are thus the backdrop against which the beauties of Constantinople are set: the shimmering Hagia Sophia, a sun among stars, or the rich library of the adjunct school, a garden of wisdom.[30] The audience can thus follow the history of the city through the poetic imagery of the narrator, creating a significant and in some cases emotional link between the then of historiography (time) and the now of the occasion (space). This spatio-temporal strategy creates a chronicle in which the real protagonist is the City itself – constantly present, in contrast to her interchangeable rulers. Even the passage in which the contemporary ruler Manuel I Komnenos is evoked places the city of Constantinople, the eternally new Rome, at centre stage.[31]

Since much has already been said about the erotic and 'novelistic' qualities of Manasses,[32] here I should like to look instead at some recurring motifs that cause emotional reactions on both intra- and extradiegetic levels: power, wealth and success, leading to anger and envy. While not uncommon motifs in historiography, they are used by Manasses to build up narrative tension and suspense not only in the *Verse chronicle*, but also in other works and thus in the overall story of the model author. An emperor that provides suitable material for such an investigation, while also offering an example of the Constantinopolitan focus described above,

Theodosios II, Pulcheria and Eudokia (*Verse chronicle* 2448–2722); see Nilsson 2006; Nilsson and Nyström 2009.

[30] See e.g. Manasses, *Verse chronicle* 4191–4202 (Lampsides): Τοῦ τεμενίσματος ἐγγὺς τῆς τοῦ Θεοῦ Σοφίας | οἶκος λαμπρὸς δεδόμητο τοῖς πάλαι βασιλεῦσι, | κῆπος, ἄν εἴποι τις, ἁβρὸς βιβλιοφόρων δένδρων, | ἄλσος ἀγλαοφύτευτον παντοδαπῆς σοφίας· | βίβλοι γὰρ ἦσαν ἐν αὐτῷ προτεθησαυρισμέναι | εἰς τρισμυρίας φθάνουσαι πρὸς ἄλλαις τρισχιλίαις· | τὸν τηλικοῦτον κῆπον δὲ καὶ τὸ τοσοῦτον ἄλσος | θεῖος ἀνὴρ πεπίστευτο, προέχων ἐν σοφίᾳ | καὶ πλέον πάντων ταῖς αὐγαῖς τῆς γνώσεως ἐκλάμπων, | ἄλλος, ἄν εἴποι τις, Ἀδὰμ ἔνθεος δενδροκόμος | τοῖς τῆς Ἐδὲμ ἐπεντρυφῶν καλλιβλαστήτοις δένδροις | καὶ φυτευμάτων γεωργὸς τῶν μὴ μαραινομένων. This passage is placed in the reign of Leo the Iconoclast; for a discussion, see Nilsson 2021a. For the description of the Hagia Sophia, placed in the reign of Justinian, see *Verse chronicle* 3223–34 (Lampsides), cited and discussed below.

[31] Manasses, *Verse chronicle* 2506–12 (Lampsides); cf. vv. 2327–9 (brief mention of the capital, but not of Manuel) and 6614–17 (on the Komnenian rulers, whose story is not told but whose deeds here are said to exceed those of Heracles).

[32] On the *Verse chronicle*, see esp. Reinsch 2007; Nilsson 2006, 2014: 98–111 and 2020; Rhoby 2014 and 2018. On the *Itinerary*, see esp. Marcovich 1987; Nilsson 2014: 186–96; Chryssogelos 2017.

is Justinian I, or rather his general Belisarios, whose story takes up most of the almost 200 verses devoted to the reign of Justinian.³³

The episode opens by stating what seems to be the most important characteristic of Justinian: he is 'the builder of that thrice-great church, | more magnificent than previous emperors' (τὸν τοῦ ναοῦ δομήτορα τούτου τοῦ τρισμεγίστου, | τὸν μεγαλοπρεπέστερον ἀνάκτων τῶν προτέρων).³⁴ This is followed by a short note on the 'pure friendship' (φιλίαν καθαράν) that Justinian, before becoming emperor, had enjoyed with Hilderic, king of the Vandals.³⁵ When Justinian found out that Gelimer had taken power and imprisoned Hilderic and his family, Justinian was 'struck in his heart' (πληγείς τε τὴν καρδίαν) and 'affected by great compassion for his unlucky [friend]' (καὶ μέγα παθηνάμενος ὑπὲρ τοῦ δυσπραγοῦντος),³⁶ and this was the reason behind the Vandal wars. This is also where the story of Belisarios takes over in the form of a long digression, leaving Justinian in the background.

Belisarios was sent to Africa as head of the army and justly conquered the Vandals, whereupon the 'hostile Libyans' (δυσμενῶν Λιβύων) joined him.³⁷ This latter fact is explained by a gnomic statement: 'In this manner, righteous dealing is a thing hard to defeat, | it both knows how to turn former haters into friends | and attracts enemies like the magnet attracts iron' (οὕτω τοι πρᾶγμα δύσμαχον ἡ δικαιοπραγία | καὶ φίλους οἶδε καθιστᾶν τοὺς πρώην μισουμένους | ἐφέλκεταί τε τοὺς ἐχθροὺς ὡς σίδηρον μαγνῆτις).³⁸ Then follows an example of Belisarios' goodness and philanthropy, which implicitly turns him into a sort of imperial representative, taking on the character of a just emperor. One of his soldiers had stolen a hen from a private house, and when Belisarios found out he was enraged,

> he found the robber and boiling over with indignation | he exacted a terrible penalty for a small offence: | he orders that the poor man be hanged³⁹ | and suffer this punishment for his unjust attitude.

---

³³ Manasses, *Verse chronicle* 3070–3245 (Lampsides). On the role of envy in Manasses' chronicle, including this episode, see Hinterberger 2013: esp. 396–409. See also Reinsch 2007 and Hinterberger 2011; also further below.
³⁴ Manasses, *Verse chronicle* 3073–4 (Lampsides).
³⁵ On friendship as a motif in Manasses' works, see above, Chapter 4 with n. 24.
³⁶ Manasses, *Verse chronicle* 3085–6 (Lampsides).   ³⁷ Manasses, *Verse chronicle* 3099 (Lampsides).
³⁸ Manasses, *Verse chronicle* 3101–3 (Lampsides). Cf. *Aristandros and Kallithea* frg. 21a (Mazal = Planoudes §4), elaborating on *Aristandros and Kallithea* frg. 21 (Mazal), but probably drawing also from Achilles Tatius, *Leucippe and Clitophon* 1.17.2–3 and/or Longus, *Daphnis and Chloe* 1.137–41. On the Planoudes collection, see further below.
³⁹ For ἀνασκολοπίζω as 'hang' rather than 'impale' (*LSJ*), see Heher 2013. Cf. Yuretich 2018: 132.

ἀνεῦρε τὸν φιλάρπαγα, τῷ ζήλῳ δ' ὑπερζέσας
δεινὴν εἰσπράττεται ποινὴν ὑπὲρ μικροῦ μεγάλην·
κελεύει γὰρ τὸν ἄθλιον ἀνασκολοπισθῆναι
καὶ ταύτην δίκην ὑποσχεῖν τῆς φιλαδίκου γνώμης.[40]

This zeal (ζῆλος) terrified his army, but the local people felt love (ἀγάπη) for him and praised him as equal to God. The praise of Belisarios continues and culminates in an episode in which he saves the emperor from a 'rebellious mob' (τοῦ στασιώδους ὄχλου):[41] 'like a bold-hearted lion he rushed into the crowd | and cut down the swarm of foolish people, | like Moses the Midianites, like Joshua the Hittites' (ὡς λέων θρασυκάρδιος εἰσέπεσεν εἰς μέσον | καὶ τοῦ μωραίνοντος λαοῦ συνέκοψε τὸ σμῆνος, | ὡς ὁ Μωσῆς τὸν Μαδιάμ, ὡς Ἰησοῦς Χετταίους).[42] This was the most brilliant achievement of Belisarios, says the narrator, but it also led to his downfall: 'But the most evil envy did not like this. | Therefore, it looked bitterly upon the general's fame | and charged against his glory with all his powers; | for envy, as they say, does not know what is profitable' (Ἀλλὰ γὰρ ταῦτ' οὐκ ἤρεσε τῷ φθόνῳ τῷ κακίστῳ. | Ἔνθεν πικρὸν ἐνέβλεψε τοῦ στρατηγοῦ τῷ κλέει | καὶ πάσαις ἤλασεν ὁρμαῖς κατὰ τῆς τούτου δόξης· | ὁ φθόνος γάρ, ὡς λέγουσιν, οὐκ οἶδε τὸ συμφέρον).[43] This great warrior accordingly 'was defeated by the savage beast of envy' (φθόνῳ καταστρατηγηθεὶς τῷ χαλεπῷ θηρίῳ).[44] After a description of the miserable fate of Belisarios the narrator addresses envy directly:

O envy, savage beast, bandit, murderer, pursuer, | scorpion of ten thousand goads, man-eating tiger, | poisonous she-snake, deadly plant, | arrow without iron, sharpest spear of all, | what evil you contrive and commit, what harm you concoct!

Φθόνε, θηρίον χαλεπόν, λῃστά, φονεῦ, διῶκτα,
σκορπίε μυριόκεντρε, τίγρις ἀνθρωποβόρε,
δράκαινα φαρμακεύτρια, βοτάνη θανασίμη,
βέλος ἀσίδηρον, αἰχμὴ πασῶν τμητικωτέρα,
οἷα ποιεῖς καὶ κακουργεῖς, οἷα δεινὰ τυρεύεις![45]

---

[40] Manasses, *Verse chronicle* 3108–11 (Lampsides).
[41] Manasses, *Verse chronicle* 3156 (Lampsides).
[42] Manasses, *Verse chronicle* 3170–2 (Lampsides). For the Biblical *exempla*, see Judges 6:8 and Joshua 12:7–8.
[43] Manasses, *Verse chronicle* 3182–5 (Lampsides). The last of these lines is recycled in the *Moral poem*, on which see below.
[44] Manasses, *Verse chronicle* 3191 (Lampsides).
[45] Manasses, *Verse chronicle* 3199–3203 (Lampsides).

Here the narrator has worked up such indignation that he breaks off the narrative – which had already come to a standstill with the lament of Belisarios and the reprimand of envy – and adds an authorial remark.

> Calamity overcomes me, sorrow confuses me | and brings tears from my eyes. | For how long, destroyer, will you then prevail? | Until when, most evil one, will you create turbulence in our lives, | all-scheming tyrant, murderer, weaving your wiles? | For I too, who did not deserve it, fell into your hands | and struck by your arrows I lie down, barely breathing. | These things were said by me as a digression, | for the bitterness of the soul forces people to speak.

> Ὑπερνικᾷ τὸ πάθος με, συγχέει με τὸ πένθος,
> καὶ προκαλεῖται δάκρυον ἐκ τῶν ἐμῶν βλεφάρων.
> ἕως καὶ πότε, λυμεών, οὕτως ὑπερισχύσεις;
> Μέχρι καὶ τίνος, κάκιστε, τὸν βίον συγκυκήσεις,
> τύραννε παντομήχανε, φόνιε, δολοπλόκε;
> Κἀγὼ γάρ, ὡς οὐκ ὤφελον, σαῖς ἐμπεσὼν παλάμαις
> καὶ πειραθείς σου τῶν βελῶν κεῖμαι μικρὸν ἐμπνέων.
> Καὶ ταῦτα μὲν ἐλέχθησαν ἡμῖν ἐν παρεκβάσει·
> ἡ γὰρ πικρία τῆς ψυχῆς λαλεῖν καταναγκάζει.[46]

It is not until after this emotional outburst, taking the audience out of the historical account and into the life of the narrator,[47] that the narrative proper of Justinian's reign is resumed (3213–45). The emotional pathos of the story of Belisarios gives way to an ekphrastic digression on Hagia Sophia and the other churches of Constantinople.

> If someone would compare to the heavenly sphere | the most prosperous city, Constantinople, | and its holy temples to the light-bringing stars, | I do not think he would be far from the appropriate. | For they all shine forth with bounteous beacons | and glitter with graces and illuminate the creation | and are called bright stars by those on Earth, | and the sun sprang up, leaving the beauteous sea[48] | and the lamps of all the stars were dimmed; | for she brightly outshines, as among small stars, | the holy churches as another giant sun, | this church built by God, the beauty of the entire Earth.

> Ἂν οὖν τις παρεικάσειε σφαίρᾳ μὲν οὐρανίᾳ
> πόλιν τὴν ὀλβιόπολιν, τὴν Κωνσταντίνου πόλιν,
> τοὺς δὲ ναοὺς τοὺς ἱεροὺς ἀστέρων φεραυγείαις,

---

[46] Manasses, *Verse chronicle* 3204–12 (Lampsides).
[47] For a discussion of this passage and its function, see Hinterberger 2013: 408. Cf. Yuretich 2018: 135, n. 1436, who reads v. 3212 as a 'rare personal comment from Manasses'. See also further below.
[48] Cf. *Od.* 3.1: Ἠέλιος δ' ἀνόρουσε, λιπὼν περικαλλέα λίμνην.

> οὐκ οἶμαι τοῦ καθήκοντος οὗτος ἀποσφαλεῖται.
> Πάντες μὲν οὖν ἐκλάμπουσιν ἀφθόνοις φρυκτωρίαις
> καὶ στίλβουσι ταῖς χάρισι καὶ κτίσιν δᾳδουχοῦσι
> καὶ χρηματίζουσι φαιδροὶ τοῖς ἐπὶ γῆς ἀστέρες,
> ἥλιος δ' ἀνόρουσε λίμνης περικαλλέος
> καὶ πάντων ἀπεκρύβησαν ἀστέρων αἱ λαμπάδες·
> ὑπερεκλάμπει γὰρ φαιδρῶς, ὡς ἐν μικροῖς ἀστρίοις,
> τοῖς ἱεροῖς τεμένεσιν ἄλλος ἥλιος γίγας,
> ὁ θεοδόμητος ναός, τὸ κάλλος γῆς ἁπάσης.[49]

Here we have an example of the connection between past and present mentioned above, the church itself offered as a 'living' example – a re-presentation – of the eternal beauty of Constantinople.[50] The text itself reflects the same intimate relation between the present verses and the literary heritage of the past, highlighted by the epic grammatical forms in v. 3230, lending the scene a Homeric tone. It is followed by the brief note on how Justinian's wife Theodora also built a church, like a moon to the sun of Hagia Sophia, 'second in beauty to the radiant sun' (v. 3240: εἰς κάλλος δευτερεύοντα τοῦ λαμπραυγοῦς ἡλίου). This church 'for the disciples of the Lord' (v. 3238: τοῖς τοῦ Κυρίου μαθηταῖς) is the Church of the Holy Apostles. We may note here, again, the importance and centrality of Constantinopolitan space in the chronicle, underlining both the setting of history and the setting of the performance of the chronicle in some sort of imperial environment.[51]

Rather than simply arguing that the empirical author Manasses himself had bad experiences of envy and could not stop himself from an emotional outburst,[52] I would suggest that the reasons for the emotional staging of this episode are at least two-fold. First, the emotional staging of the reign of Justinian, or rather the story of Belisarios, made it suitable for rhetorical performance. It should be noted that not only envy is at work here, but also the affection of Justinian for Hilderic, the rage of Belisarios and the love of the Libyan people. These emotions are all at play, causing the sorrow of the narrator, as he thinks of the unfair envy that caused the end of the brave Belisarios. It all makes for an exciting rhetorical performance of pathos, portraying historical characters in a vivid and entertaining

---

[49] Manasses, *Verse chronicle* 3223–34 (Lampsides). Cf. Manasses, *Itinerary* 2.154–5 (Horna): ὀφθαλμὲ τῆς γῆς, κόσμε τῆς οἰκουμένης, | τηλαυγὲς ἄστρον, τοῦ κάτω κόσμου λύχνε.
[50] Cf. Manasses, *Verse chronicle* 4191–4202 and 4204–6 on the library next to Hagia Sophia; see Nilsson 2021a.
[51] See also above, Chapter 2.   [52] For such readings, see further below.

manner.⁵³ Second, the sorrow of the narrator and his 'personal' tale should also be seen in light of the more or less consistent narrative of the model author Manasses, examples of which we have already seen in the chapters above. With this in mind, let us move on to the next text and its representation of similar themes.

Excerpted Love and Envy

The novel by Manasses, *Aristandros and Kallithea*, has come down to us only in excerpts. The last trace of the entire text dates to 1492, when Ianos Laskaris (1445–1535) saw a manuscript containing it in Arta in the collection of a certain Demetrios Trivolis.⁵⁴ Laskaris was employed by Lorenzo de' Medici in Florence as an agent in the purchase of Greek manuscripts from the Ottoman sultan Bayezid II (1447–1512). There is a note on the novel in Laskaris' list of manuscripts preserved in Vat. Gr. 1412, made in relation to an inventory of the library of Lorenzo de' Medici, but noting also titles of manuscripts that he had seen on his journeys and found interesting enough to consider for later copying or acquisition.⁵⁵ In the chapter on Arta he notes: 'An erotic book, the Indian story of Aristandros and Kallithea, by Constantine Manasses' (Κωνσταντίνου τοῦ Μανασσῆ ἐρωτικὸν βιβλίον τὸ κατὰ Ἀρίστανδρον καὶ Καλλιθέαν Ἰνδικὸν διὰ στίχων πολιτικῶν).⁵⁶ Laskaris seems to have been the last to see the novel in its entirety; what we now have at our disposal are two collections of excerpts and one prose paraphrase.

First, the excerpts of Makarios Chrysokephalos (*c.*1300–82), metropolitan of Philadelphia, who included 611 verses in his 'Rose garden' ('Ροδωνιά). This anthology contains excerpts from both pagan and Christian authors, but it has an emphasis on morality (and also includes excerpts from the *Verse chronicle*). It has been preserved in an autograph copy that was later owned by Bessarion, the fourteenth-century Marc. Gr. 452.⁵⁷ Importantly, Chrysokephalos indicates which book of the novel he excerpts and the order of the excerpts in the original book. Second, an anonymous collection containing 765 verses (337 of these are 'new' in

---

⁵³ See Hinterberger 2013: 409 for a similar interpretation. ⁵⁴ Mazal 1967b: 12.
⁵⁵ Edition in Müller 1884, along with a long introduction on Laskaris' travels. On Laskaris and his visits to Greece, see also Speake 1993.
⁵⁶ Müller 1884: 393.
⁵⁷ The presence of the novel in this ms was first noted by Villoison in 1781 and first edited by Boissonade 1819 (as an appendix to the edition of *Drosilla and Charikles*, vol. 2, 322–403). The Marc. Gr. 452 was produced *c.*1328–36; see Turyn 1972: 168–72.

comparison to the excerpts of Chrysokephalos) under the title 'Maxims from the book of the wise Constantine Manasses' (Γνωμικὰ ἐκ τῆς βίβλου τοῦ σοφωτάτου κυροῦ Κωνσταντίνου τοῦ Μανασσῆ). The collection has an emphasis on love and is preserved in two manuscripts.[58] The excerpts are here taken out of sequence and without indication of book number, but as indicated above, about half overlap with those of Chrysokephalos. Third, Maximos Planoudes (c.1260–1305), best known perhaps for his edition of the *Greek Anthology* and his translations from Latin into Greek, wrote prose paraphrases of some excerpts from the novel by Manasses in his 'Very useful compilation of extracts from a variety of books' (Συναγωγὴ ἐκλεγεῖσα ἀπὸ διαφόρων βιβλίων πάνυ ὠφέλιμος).[59]

Together, the excerpts and the prose paraphrases give a fairly good idea of the general content of the novel, but it is obvious that the narrative structure and details of the plot have been lost. The attempt by Mazal to reconstruct the plot, generally accepted by scholars, is based on the idea that all novels followed the same plot pattern.[60] While it is true that the ancient Greek and Komnenian novels share numerous features and motifs, there are also significant differences, and the 'Indian' story of Manasses, the only one of the Komnenian novels to have been written in political verse, may have been rather different from the contemporary novels written by Makrembolites, Prodromos and Eugenianos, not only as regards its metrical form.[61] Laskaris' reference to Manasses' novel as 'Indian' is interesting, because it may indicate a storyworld reminiscent of the ancient novels set in places like Aethiopia and Babylon. Little in the excerpts indicates India as the setting of the story,[62] but they do offer some unusual motifs that are not known from other novels, such as the poisonous eunuch

---

[58] Cod. Phil. Gr. 306, ff. 1–16ᵛ (Vienna, 14th c.) and Cod. Cgm 281, ff. 144ᵛ–63ᵛ (Munich, Bayerische Staatsbibliothek, 16th c.). Mentioned by Krumbacher 1897: 380, but published first in 1967, when the editions of Tsolakes and Mazal both appeared. Mazal's edition and reconstruction (1967b) was preceded by a preliminary version of the anthology text alone (Mazal 1966).

[59] Piccolomini 1874; E. Jeffreys 2012: 278: 'together with excerpts from historians, philosophers and paradoxographical elements, though it should be noted that it was at this time that he was translating Ovid and working on the *Greek Anthology*, and so he might have been interested in *A&K* as a further example of the Greek erotic tradition.' See also Karla 2006.

[60] Mazal 1967b. Cf. E. Jeffreys 2012: 279–80.

[61] While this may have contributed to why it was not preserved in its entirety (see E. Jeffreys 2012: 277), in light of the fragility of any manuscript tradition it may also have been a coincidence. On the diverse form of ancient novels, see Hägg 2006.

[62] India may, in fact, signify any foreign or exotic land; cf. Mazal 1967b: 77–9, suggesting that India is to be identified with Aethiopia. But note also the 'Arabian tale' in the *Funerary oration on the death of Nikephoros Komnenos* 1–29 (Kurtz) and the 'Indian stone' in *Address by the way* 6–7 (Browning); see above, Chapters 3 and 4.

causing the death of a snake,[63] and a large number of gnomic passages on emotions other than erotic desire.[64] Following the non-erotic emotional thread that was considered in the *Verse chronicle*, we will look at two passages that deal with unfair treatment, slander and envy.[65]

The first is one of relatively few long passages that have been excerpted, supposedly drawn from the second book (frg. 31). It opens with an address to a gathering of men, so it must have been originally pronounced by one of the novel's characters, perhaps someone who has been hurt by a slanderer and now is accusing that person.[66] After the opening, stating that a slanderer destroys both countries and families, the image of the serpent – employed also in the *Verse chronicle*, but then for envy – is introduced:

> He is a serpent spewing forth deadly venom, | belching terrible man-slaying poison, | a maritime puffer-toad, a fire-breathing *katobleps* | and a manticore,[67] that man-eating Indian beast | which shoots out darts from its mouth's sinews | and like the far-shooters aims most accurately | bitter heart-biting words that wound worse than arrows.
>
> Ὄφις ἐστὶ θανάσιμον φάρμακον ἀποπτύων,
> ἰὸν ἀπερευγόμενος δεινὸν ἀνθρωποφόντην,
> φύσαλος θαλασσόβιος, πυρίπνοος κατῶβλεψ
> καὶ μαρτιχόρας Ἰνδικὸν ἀνθρωποφάγον ζῷον,
> ὡς ἐκ νευρᾶς τοῦ στόματος ἀποτοξεύων βέλη
> καὶ βάλλων εὐστοχώτατα κατὰ τοὺς ἐκηβόλους
> λόγους πικροὺς θυμοδακεῖς, πλήττοντας ὑπὲρ βέλη.[68]

The exotic animals may indicate an exotic (potentially Indian) setting here, but most of all they enhance the terrifying character and inhumanity of the slanderer. The serpent is most probably an allusion to the devil, who in the disguise of a serpent slandered God and thus convinced Eve to eat from the forbidden tree. The description goes on, comparing the slanderer to different poisonous roots, then again to a serpent, a lion and a vulture.[69] The impossibility of escaping its effects is then illustrated:

---

[63] Manasses, *Aristandros and Kallithea* frg. 80 (Mazal).
[64] For a useful summary, see E. Jeffreys 2012: 280–2.
[65] Hinterberger 2013: 439 argues that envy played a significant role in the novel. I would be a little more careful to assume such a thing based on excerpts that mirror the taste of the excerptors and paraphrases that may not lie very close to the original text. On the role of *phthonos* in Manasses' novel, see also Hinterberger 2013: 403.
[66] For Mazal's reconstruction, see Mazal 1967b: 88–9.
[67] Both are mythical beasts: the *katobleps* has a head so heavy that it hangs down (Aelian, *De natura animalium* 7.6) and the manticore (*martichoras*) has huge fangs reminiscent of those of a tiger (Aelian, *De natura animalium* 4.21).
[68] *Aristandros and Kallithea* frg. 31.5–11 (Mazal), tr. E. Jeffreys 2012.
[69] *Aristandros and Kallithea* frg. 31.12–17 (Mazal).

> If you have a slanderer as a fellow citizen, | you will not escape his venom, you will not evade his goad | even if you become a broad-winged high-soaring eagle, | even if you fly high in the air, even if you flee to the aether. | His tongue spouts venom, his heart rage; | he is an accurate archer, he envenoms his darts; | his missiles reach into the heaven and wound; | his dart is not made of bronze, his missile is not made of iron, | his bow is not made of horn nor its sinew of ox-gut – | but it reaches you and kills, whether you reach for the stars, | whether you soar to the heights of the starless sphere.

> Ἄν συμπολίτην οὖν αὐτὸν τὸν συκοφάντην ἔχῃς,
> οὐ φεύξῃ τούτου τὸν ἰόν, τὸ κέντρον οὐκ ἀλύξεις,
> κἂν ὑψιβάμων αἰετὸς μεγαλοπτέρυξ γένῃ,
> κἂν πετασθῇς μετάρσιος, κἂν εἰς αἰθέρα φύγῃς.
> Ἡ γλῶσσα βλύζει τὸν ἰόν, τὴν λύσσαν ἡ καρδία·
> τοξότης εὔστοχός ἐστι, φαρμάσσει καὶ τὰ βέλη·
> εἰς οὐρανὸν τὸ βέλεμνον φθάνει καὶ τραυματίζει.
> Τούτου τὸ βέλος ἄχαλκον, ἀσίδηρον τὸ βλῆμα,
> τὸ τόξον οὐκ ἐκ κέρατος, οὐδ' ἡ νευρὰ βοεία,
> καὶ φθάνει σε καὶ θανατοῖ, κἂν τῶν ἀστέρων ψαύσῃς,
> κἂν ἕως ὕψους πετασθῇς τῆς σφαίρας τῆς ἀνάστρου.[70]

This seems to imply that not even a person of very high status, such as the emperor himself – described as a broad-winged and high-soaring eagle in other texts by Manasses –, can escape the effects of slander.[71] The passage ends with a gnomic statement, directly connecting slander with envy and repeating the serpent imagery:

> Envy that hates the good is the father of slander, | slander is the conception of deeply jealous envy, | the yet more bitter child and offspring of a bitter father, | an appalling tiger-lion sprung from a wrathful viper.

> ὁ φθόνος ὁ μισόκαλος πατὴρ συκοφαντίας,
> συκοφαντία κύημα φθόνου τοῦ βαρυζήλου,
> πατρὸς πικροῦ πικρότερον καὶ γέννημα καὶ θρέμμα,
> ὡς ἐξ ἐχίδνης θυμικῆς ῥίγιστος τιγρολέων.[72]

The passage ties in with imagery known from the *Verse chronicle*, for example the episode on Belisarios discussed above. But the closing gnomic description of the relation between slander and envy is also close to the *Encomium of Michael Hagiotheodorites*, describing false rumour as the

---

[70] Frg. 31.18–28 (Mazal), tr. E. Jeffreys 2012.
[71] On the imagery of Manuel as an eagle, see above, Chapter 2.
[72] Frg. 31.29–32 (Mazal), tr. E. Jeffreys 2012.

daughter of slander (θυγάτηρ ἡ φήμη διαβολῆς). Slander is 'more efficient than fire, sharper than a sword, swifter than lightning and more effective than a knife' (δραστικωτέρα πυρός, ὀξυτέρα μαχαίρας, φλεκτικωτέρα πρηστῆρος καὶ ἐνεργεστέρα ξιφῶν), while rumour is 'quicker than the breezes, more fluid than waters and outflies the winds and is lighter than wings' (δρομικωτέρα πνευμάτων, ὑγροτέρα ὑδάτων καὶ ὑπὲρ ἀνέμους διίπταται καὶ ὑπὲρ πτερὸν ἐλαφρίζεται).[73]

Let us look at one more passage from the novel that ties in with the same theme, the impossibility of escaping envy, even for high officials and emperors.

> But no one, it seems, has existed who has not experienced envy, | who is unscarred by its bitterly piercing goads, | not an emperor or general or he who relies on words; | indeed the emperor in particular, since he is the most powerful, | is most tormented by envy's thorns.
>
> Ἀλλ' ἦν, ὡς ἔοικεν, οὐδεὶς ἀπείρατος τοῦ φθόνου,
> οὐδ' ἀμωλώπιστος αὐτοῦ τοῖς πικροκέντροις κέντροις,
> οὐ βασιλεύς, οὐ στράταρχος, οὐ λόγοις προσανέχων,
> μᾶλλον μὲν οὖν ὁ βασιλεύς, ὅσῳ καὶ κρείττων πάντων,
> πλείοσι περιπείρεται τοῦ φθόνου ταῖς ἀκάνθαις.[74]

Taken out of context, this passage could even be read as a comment on the episode of Belisarios or an elaboration of that theme, but it is also strongly reminiscent of another passage in the *Verse chronicle*. It is placed as an authorial comment in the episode of Eudokia, wife of Theodosios II (408–50), and runs as follows.

> But there was no success in life, it seems, | unmixed with grief and distress, nor any good fortune | that does not grow together with nettles; | for even the fragrant rose carries many thorns | and clouds obscure the eye of the sun | and envy grows against those who do good | and every virtuous success, every splendid thing in life | comes mixed with misfortune.
>
> Ἀλλ' ἦν οὐδέν, ὡς ἔοικεν, εὐτύχημα τοῦ βίου
> ζάλης καὶ λύπης ἀμιγές, οὐδέ τις εὐποτμία
> μὴ συναναφυόμενον ἔχουσα καὶ τὸ κνίζον·
> καὶ γὰρ καὶ ῥόδον εὔοσμον φρίσσει πυκναῖς ἀκάνθαις
> ἡλίου τε τὸ βλέφαρον σκοτίζουσι νεφέλαι
> καὶ φθόνος ἐπιφύεται τοῖς τὸ καλὸν ἀσκοῦσι

---

[73] Manasses, *Encomium of Michael Hagiotheodorites* 71–7 (Horna), cited and translated above, Chapter 4. Cf. also Manasses, *Letter* 1.7–8 (Horna).
[74] Manasses, *Aristandros and Kallithea* frg. 48 (Mazal), tr. E. Jeffreys 2012. For similar ideas on the mighty as more likely to be envied, see also frg. 171 (Mazal = Planoudes §38).

καὶ πᾶν εὐτύχημα σεμνόν, πᾶν τὸ λαμπρὸν τοῦ βίου
φέρει καὶ τὸ δυστύχημα συνανακεκραμένον.[75]

This passage, too, is reminiscent of the expressed emotion of the narrator in the *Encomium of Michael Hagiotheodorites* and the accompanying letters and then especially the imagery of the sun (fortune/emperor/patronage) being covered by clouds (misfortune/slanderers/envy).[76] The connection made in the novel fragment cited above between the one who holds imperial power and the one who has the power of words (frg. 48, 3: λόγοις προσανέχων) is crucial, because it mirrors the relation based on similarity that is employed in so many of Manasses' representations of author vs addressee – the patron is like the writer, since both are successful and therefore victims of envy.[77] Even the pet bird of the writer, described in the *Monody on the death of his goldfinch* and here interpreted as a characterization of both writer and patron, is subject to potential envy because of its beautiful performance.[78]

It is accordingly clear that Manasses used the same imagery and very similar wording in both the chronicle and the novel, sometimes as authorial interventions and often expressed in gnomic form, and that he used the same material in other works, most notably in the *Encomium of Michael Hagiotheodorites* and the letters, written at a later stage of his career (in the late 1160s).[79] Such recycling does not mean that the audience was supposed to make a connection between the various passages, or between the lives of Belisarios and Manasses himself, but rather that a recurring imagery and its narrative accessories became part of Manasses' recognizable voice. It should be noted that there is a difference between envy between

---

[75] Manasses, *Verse chronicle* (Lampsides) 2600–7. Cf. tr. in Nilsson and Nyström 2009: 48. Cf. also *Aristandros and Kallithea*, frg. 49, 76 and 171 (Mazal).
[76] E.g. *Letter* 1.5–8 (Horna): Ἡλίου μὲν γὰρ ἀκτῖσι νεφέλαι, καρδίᾳ δὲ λῦπαι πολέμιαι· εἰ δὲ πολλοὶ μὲν οἱ πολεμοῦντες, μηδεμίαν δὲ τοῦ πολεμεῖν αἰτίαν ἔχοντες εὔλογον, τίς ἂν ὑποίσοι ψυχή, καὶ διαβολαῖς κατασειομένη καὶ συκοφαντίᾳ κριοκοπουμένη; and *Letter* 2.1–5 (Horna): Εἰ μὲν εἰσί που τῆς γῆς ἐν ζόφῳ διάγοντες ἄνθρωποι, οὓς οὔτε ἄστρον αὐγάζει οὔτε ἡλίου βλέφαρον εὐφεγγὲς ἐπιδέρκεται, Ὁμήρου μοῦσα λαλείτω καὶ Ἡροδότου γλῶσσα κομπολεσχείτω· ἐμοὶ δὲ ἄρα ἐπὶ τῶν ἔργων καὶ μανθάνειν τοῦτο πάρεστι καὶ ὁρᾶν, ἀνδρῶν εὐγενέστατε.
[77] See above, Chapter 3.
[78] *Monody on the death of his goldfinch* 7.14–18 (Horna): καὶ ὁ μὲν παιδίσκος ὁ περὶ τὴν ἐκείνου λατρείαν ταλαιπωρούμενος προβασκανία τοῦ καλάθου ἐξῆρτα, ἔνθα ὁ στρουθὸς ἐκοιτάζετο, καὶ πυκνὰ πυκνὰ περιετίθει περίαπτα, μὴ τηλικούτῳ κάλλει βάσκανον ἐντρανίσῃ τις, μὴ τηλικαύτης φωνῆς ἐν φθόνῳ ἀκούσῃ τις καὶ ἀποβῇ τὸ φθέγμα καὶ τὸ κάλλος οἰχήσεται. See Hinterberger 2013: 140.
[79] For a discussion of the dating of all preserved works, see below, Chapter 7.

individuals (as described in Manasses' authorial story) and envy as a superhuman force – an envious fate – in the chronicle and the novel.[80] At the same time, the emotional theme (how envy affects human conditions both individually and in general) became part of Manasses' authorial repertoire, for those in the audience who followed his production throughout the decades. That is to say, the metanarrative (part of the authorial self-representation) would be relevant only for recurring listeners, while the recycling of words and phrases (voice or style) would be recognizable also for audiences attending or reading only one or a few works.

Parallel with and subsequent to this internal use of the motif, it was also excerpted in its gnomic form and lost its narrative context. It is no coincidence that the two passages on slander and envy were excerpted from the novel, because the theme is also present in the excerpt collections of the *Verse chronicle*; in fact, the last citation above is included in several of the Manassean *gnomologia*.[81] Quite a few collections contain excerpts from both the novel and the chronicle, which makes it even more difficult to determine the relation between the two texts.[82] In fact, Chrysokephalos adjusted the wording of some excerpts in his 'Rose garden' so as to make them more gnomic, which complicates our understanding of the original version of the novel.[83] At the same time, the excerpts point to an important aspect of the reception of Manasses' texts: their usefulness. As noted above, the prose paraphrase of Planoudes was entitled a 'very useful (πάνυ ὠφέλιμος) collection of extracts', and an excerpt collection in the Bodl. Misc. 285 defined the verses from Manasses' chronicle as 'suitable to everyone for the matter at hand' (ἑκάστῳ ἁρμόζων πρὸς τὸ προκείμενον).[84] These excerpts were never supposed to replace the original work, but they were to be used in practice by those who needed to express themselves in speech and writing. It is therefore a more or less impossible task to reconstruct the narrative based on such excerpts, but a comparative analysis may still help us detect their authorial voice.

---

[80] This important distinction is made in Hinterberger 2013.
[81] See Lampsides 1985; Nilsson and Nyström 2009.
[82] See Lampsides 1985. Also Mazal 1967b: 70–3, esp. p. 73: 'Die Verse aus der Chronik des Manasses, die sich in der Romananthologie finden, müßen nicht als Bestand des Romans angesehen werden, etwa in der Funktion von Dubletten.' See also E. Jeffreys 2012: 275: 'A number of lines appear in both *A&K* and the *Synopsis Chronike*, though it is impossible to draw conclusions from these about the texts' compositional priority.'
[83] Lampsides 1985: 127.
[84] Nilsson and Nyström 2009: 50. On the issue of usefulness in the twelfth-century context, see also Cullhed 2014b: 53.

A Moral Poem à la Manasses

The so-called *Moral poem* refers to 916 political verses, divided into 100 'chapters' or short poems on various more or less ethical topics, ranging from faith and friendship to sleep and envy.[85] Most sections have Christian undertones, underlined also in the prologue (vv. 1–76) and the epilogue (vv. 899–916), concluding the poem with an invocation of the trinity. The first editor, Emmanuel Miller, had access to one manuscript (the fourteenth-century Parisinus graecus 2750 A),[86] which indicated no title and no author, but he argued that the poem was written by Manasses, based on stylistic features, vocabulary and the number of verses that correspond with verses in the anthologies of Manasses' novel. The presence of these verses was explained as self-imitation: 'il est naturel de supposer que notre poète a usé du droit qu'ont toujours eu les écrivains de se copier eux-mêmes'.[87] It should be noted that Miller assumed that the poem provided verses for the novel, not the other way around: 'le poème moral devait fournir des citations qui étaient de nature à s'adapter aux différentes situations des personnages, situations amenées par les péripéties du roman'.[88] Miller added the headings that appear in his edition (e.g. α'. Περὶ πίστεως), drawing on the headings of the anonymously transmitted treatise that precedes the Manassean verses in the Paris manuscript, now attributed to Andronikos Palaiologos (1259–1332).[89]

About a century after Miller's edition, Otto Mazal argued that the *Moral poem* was not written by Manasses himself, but by a plagiarist or imitator with no restraints: 'einen Nachahmer des Manasses, der sein Vorbild ungehemmt ausgeschöpft hat'.[90] This had, in fact, already been suggested by Karl Krumbacher just a few years after Miller's edition, so Mazal was leaning on Krumbacher's opinion.[91] Mazal identified 228 verses drawn from the novel among the 916 verses of the *Moral poem*, arguing that this was evidence of someone else having composed the poem. He did not accept Miller's idea of self-imitation, but argued that such a procedure would be unthinkable: 'Auch bei Berücksichtigung aller Unselbständigkeit der Byzantiner in literarischer Hinsicht wäre es für Manasses ein zu großem Armutszeugnis, sich selbst in derart grossem Umfang

---

[85] First edited by Miller 1875.
[86] The manuscript is originally from Athos, re-bound; text on ff. 89ʳ–107ᵛ. [87] Miller 1875: 29.
[88] Ibid.
[89] The so-called *Kephalaia*; see Konstantinidis 1989 and Simelidis 2015. See also below, n. 96.
[90] Mazal 1967a: 249. See also Mazal 1967b: 62–9. Cf. Hunger 1978: 126, agreeing with Mazal.
[91] Krumbacher 1897: 379.

abgeschrieben zu haben.'[92] For Mazal, the poem was thus primarily an indirect witness to Manasses' novel, strictly belonging to the Nachleben of his work.[93] In the same year that Mazal's edition of the novel fragments appeared, the Greek scholar Eudoxos Tsolakis published his edition of the same material.[94] Contrary to Mazal, he found it probable that the poem was written by Manasses. He refuted Krumbacher's ideas and added further arguments for Manasses as the author, composing the *Moral poem* with verses drawn from his novel.[95]

The question of authorship has not been resolved, since no irrefutable evidence to prove one or the other interpretation has been published.[96] The present analysis aims at a discussion of previous arguments and likely scenarios, rather than a solution of the problem. Let us begin by taking a closer look at 'chapter' 8, the section on envy, and compare it with the expression of the same topic in the *Verse chronicle* and the novel fragments. The passage runs as follows.

> I shall speak of terrible envy, I shall accuse and blame it, | even if I'm completely attached to it, even if I nurture it within. | For envy, as they say, does not know what is profitable. | It is a deadly serpent, terrible, man-slaying, | belching poison, spewing forth venom, | a maritime puffer-toad, a man-eating beast, | a truly fire-breathing manticore, a *katobleps*, | a wildly fighting unicorn, a poisonous dragon, | a bear, a savage cobra, a liver-eating lion, | a vulture not invading the nest, nor digging out the eyes, | but rather invading the powers of the soul, the mind, the emotions. | For envy is tenfold worse than murder, | as the letters say, when one sound is missing.

> Εἴπω τοῦ φθόνου τὸ δεινόν, ἐλέγξω, στηλιτεύσω,
> κἂν ὁλικῶς ἐξέχωμαι τοῦτον ἐντὸς κἂν τρέφω.
> Ὁ φθόνος γάρ, ὡς λέγουσιν, οὐκ οἶδε τὸ συμφέρον.[97]
> Ὄφις ἐστὶ θανάσιμος, δεινός, ἀνθρωποφόντης,
> ἰὸν ἀπερευγόμενος, φάρμακον ἀποπτύων,
> φύσαλος θαλασσόβιος, ἀνθρωποφάγον ζῷον,

---

[92] Mazal 1967a: 267.   [93] Mazal 1967b: 69. See also E. Jeffreys 2012: 278.
[94] Tsolakis 1967. The novel was subject to much attention in the 1960s. See also Anastasi 1965 and 1969, along with the comment on Tsolakis' work by Mazal 1967b: 15.
[95] Tsolakis 1967: 22–31. See also Tsolakis 2003, maintaining the same opinion.
[96] However, Giulia Paoletti is currently finishing her doctoral dissertation 'Two chapter collections in different metre' at Oxford, offering a new edition of the *Moral poem* and arguing that Andronikos Palaiologos is the author; perhaps her work will change the picture altogether, but since it is not finished I will not take it into account in the following discussion.
[97] Cf. Manasses, *Verse chronicle* 3185 (Lampsides): ὁ φθόνος γάρ, ὡς λέγουσιν, οὐκ οἶδε τὸ συμφέρον. On this expression, see Hinterberger 2013: 116 with n. 88; see also Hinterberger (forthcoming).

καὶ μαρτιχώρας ἀληθῶς πυριπνόος, κατώβλεψ,⁹⁸
θυμομαχὴς μονόκερως, δράκων φαρμακορύκτης,
ἄρκος, ἀσπὶς ἀνήμερος, ἡπατοφάγος λέων,
γὺψ οὐκ εἰσδύνων καλιάν, οὐδ' ὀφθαλμοὺς ὀρύττων,
ἀλλ' εἰς δυνάμεις τῆς ψυχῆς, εἰς νοῦν, εἰς τὰς αἰσθήσεις.
Καὶ γὰρ δεκάκις πέφυκε χείρων ὁ φθόνος φθόνου (leg. φόνου),
ὡς λέγουσι τὰ γράμματα, μόνης (leg. φωνῆς) μιᾶς λειπούσης.⁹⁹

Out of these 13 verses, one is known from the *Verse chronicle* and four from the fragments of *Aristandros and Kallithea*. After the first two verses, expressing the narrator's aim, the gnomic statement cited above (originally belonging in the story of Belisarios) is placed: 'For envy, as they say, does not know what is profitable.' This is immediately followed by an elaboration in the form of four verses that are very close to four novelistic verses, though with the words slightly rearranged, and followed by more examples of envy's beastly nature. The 'chapter' closes with two verses that are quite incomprehensible as they stand in Miller's edition, but with the corrections suggested above offer a word play on the relation between the word *phthonos* (envy) and the word *phonos* (murder), differing by only one 'sound', i.e. the letter theta. The pun may be inspired by a passage in Paul's *Letter to the Romans* and appears also in authors such as George of Pisidia and Michael Attaleiates.¹⁰⁰

It is fair to say that the chapter is a cento, with at least one-third of its verses drawn from works by Manasses.¹⁰¹ It is, however, based on the text itself, impossible to say whether it was composed by him or by someone else. That said, Mazal's arguments that no author would copy himself in the form of a cento, and that the use of the novel characterizes a working method 'nur zu deutlich als plagiatorisch',¹⁰² are simply not valid. As we

---

[98] Cf. Manasses, *Aristandros and Kallithea* frg. 31.5–8 (Mazal): ὄφις ἐστὶ θανάσιμον φάρμακον ἀποπτύων, | ἰὸν ἀπερευγόμενος δεινὸν ἀνθρωποφόντην, | φύσαλος θαλασσόβιος, πυρίπνοος κατώβλεψ | καὶ μαρτιχόρας Ἰνδικὸν ἀνθρωποφάγον ζῷον.

[99] *Moral poem* 147–59 (Miller) = 8. *On envy* (η'. Περὶ φθόνου). For φθόνος φόνου, cf. Romans 1:29: μεστοὺς φθόνου, φόνου, ἔριδος, δόλου, κακοηθείας (full of envy, murder, strife, deceit and malice), on which see Basil of Caesarea, *On envy* 3 (cited in Hinterberger 2013: 137, n. 196). For φωνή as 'sound' in the sense of 'letter', see e.g. Dionysius of Halicarnassus, *Hist et Rhet, de Demosthenis dictione*, 52.14: ἐκμάθωμεν, πρῶτον μὲν τὰ ὀνόματα τῶν στοιχείων | τῆς φωνῆς ἀναλαμβάνομεν, ἃ καλεῖται γράμματα. Cf. the conspicuous combination of φωνή and φθόνος (φωνῆς ἐν φθόνῳ) in *Monody on the death of his goldfinch* 7.14–18 (Horna), cited above, n. 78.

[100] See Hinterberger 2013: 137 with n. 197.

[101] Since the poem contains both the novel and the chronicle, it seems reasonable to assume that the poem was composed later than both of those works, but the opposite cannot be excluded on any philological grounds.

[102] Mazal 1967a: 268. See also Mazal 1967b: 62: 'Wir können nich annehmen, daß Manasses selbst sich in der Form eines Cento kopiert hätte.'

have seen throughout this study, Manasses recycled his own work to a large extent, both verbatim and in revised form. On a larger scale, the different versions of the *Itinerary* suggest that the first part of the poem was used both separately (perhaps for a performance in the capital while the poet was still out of town) and as part of a larger edition (perhaps revised and 'published' after the original plans of the embassy had been thwarted).[103] And as noted above, it seems likely that the *Verse chronicle* was written and performed in portions and subsequently edited over a few years. Accordingly, it does not seem unlikely that Manasses would put together a cento using his own verses, presenting it to a new addressee or for a new occasion – especially if his particular style, as demonstrated in the novel and the chronicle, had turned out to be successful throughout his career.[104] The pious tone of the poem, especially in the prologue and the epilogue, may seem to differ from Manasses' regular interests, but one should keep in mind that the preserved texts may not be representative of his entire production and that, even among those texts that have come down to us, the Graeco-Roman and the Christian heritage play an equally important role. In the *schede*, the Biblical and patristic heritage even dominate, probably for the benefit of the students.[105]

Moreover, the addressee of the poem is unnamed but male, evoked in v. 1 as 'the best of all living in accordance with the (divine) spirit' (πάντων, βέλτιστε, τῶν κατὰ πνεῦμα ζώντων) and in v. 899 as 'divine person' or 'leader' (θεία κεφαλή). The latter indicates, according to Miller, a male member of the imperial family,[106] while Mazal added the possibility of a church dignitary and Tsolakis argued for a monastic superior.[107] In light of the pious tone of the poem and its emphasis on Christian virtues, a church dignitary seems most probable. If one assumes that Manasses did indeed compose the cento, drawing on his earlier work at a later stage of his career, the poem could be seen as a gift to a spiritual advisor attached to a church or a monastery, perhaps presented as the writer was awarded a position as bishop or took on the monastic garb.[108] The recycling of secular works in such a spiritual context, including the exchange of pagan references for

---

[103] On the different versions of the poem, see above, Chapter 2, n. 86. On the manuscripts and the versions, see Chryssogelos 2017: 87–95.
[104] Cf. Mazal 1967b: 62: 'Es is nicht vor der Hand zu weisen, daß sich ein Schriftsteller gelegentlich selbst zitiert; wohl aber erscheint es unwahrscheinlich, daß er sein eigenes Werk in umgearbeiteter Form in anderem Gewand wiederholt.'
[105] See above, Chapter 5.   [106] Miller 1875: 30.
[107] Mazal 1967a: 250; Tsolakis 1967: 24–5; Tsolakis 2003: 17–18.
[108] On Manasses' assumed career, see above, Chapters 1 and 5.

Christian, would offer an interesting example of the flexibility of a twelfth-century writer.[109] Such an interpretation is, however, based on a series of assumptions that remain hypothetical until supported by further evidence.

The idea of an imitator is, of course, just as likely. Mazal suggested that an admirer composed the *Moral poem* as a cento around 1200 or later in the thirteenth century, when Manasses' novel 'noch in frischer Erinnerung war'.[110] Planoudes used the novel in the second half of the thirteenth century and the two anthologies of novel excerpts – the one anonymous, the other by Chrysokephalos – were put together in the fourteenth century, so such a use of Manasses' novel over a rather long period would not be surprising.[111] To the thirteenth century belongs also a continuation of the *Verse chronicle*, of which only 79 political verses have survived. The content, narrating events that took place during the Fourth Crusade, seems to be drawn from the *History* of Niketas Choniates, but the form is that of Manasses.[112] In the same period, or somewhat later, the *Verse chronicle* was also turned into prose, changing the linguistic register into vernacular Greek. This paraphrase has survived in not fewer than 24 known manuscripts, some containing continuations of the chronicle all the way up to the Ottoman sultans.[113] Such undertakings have important consequences for our understanding of the status of Manasses' texts in the later Byzantine period and support the attribution of the *Moral poem* to an imitator rather than to Manasses himself.[114]

There is, however, an important difference between the anthologies and the poem, since a cento recycles in a different manner, taking on the voice of the original author by adding new verses in the same style.[115] By doing so, the imitator not only impersonates the voice of his model author, creating the kind of confusion modern scholars now find themselves in, but in this case he also creates a didactic poem in the style of an author

---

[109] Cf. Zagklas 2014: 79 on the case of Theodore Prodromos.   [110] Mazal 1967b: 63.
[111] Mazal 1967b: 63, and note the comparison between Planoudes' excerpts and the *Moral poem* on pp. 63–5; see also Mazal 1967a.
[112] On this continuation, see Grégoire 1924, arguing for an early date (1204/5). Briefly on this matter from the perspective of Choniates, see Simpson 2013: 109–10.
[113] First discussed in Praechter 1895 and 1898, but note the more recent Genova 1993, adding new manuscripts and defining two redactions of the original paraphrase of Manasses' text. See also the recent edition in Iadevaia 2000–8, not taking into account the manuscripts added by Genova. The oldest manuscript dates to the fifteenth century, but it is possible that the first paraphrase of the *Verse chronicle* was written earlier than that, perhaps not very long after its composition.
[114] Cf. above, n. 96.
[115] Even if we assume that the poem contains more verses drawn from the novel (as suggested by Mazal), it is still likely that new verses have been added. Cf. the *Christos Paschon*, which has more verses added by the author than drawn from Euripides; see Marciniak 2004: 89.

who himself composed didactic poems in the very same metre (the *Astrological poem* for Sebastokratorissa Eirene).[116] The model author thus becomes also a model teacher, something that is also indicated in an epigram added at the end of one of the anthologies of the novel fragments and, partially, in one manuscript of the *Verse chronicle*.[117] It is written in dodecasyllables and thus resembles some of the book epigrams associated with the ancient and Komnenian novels,[118] but it does not refer to the novel but addresses the author himself:

> But O Manasses, heart-entrancing mouth,
> young Orpheus better than the old,
> tune your sweet kithara once more
> and reveal your countenance to your friends
> and address your pupils as in the past;
> for if sweet speech could soften
> the deaf hair-stuffed ears of dreaded Hades,
> you would have accomplished this after going to Hades,
> being yourself a self-charming self-sweetness.

> Ἀλλ' ὦ Μανασσῆ θελξικάρδιον στόμα,
> Ὀρφεῦ νεαρὲ τοῦ παλαιοῦ βελτίων,
> τὴν γλυκερὰν ἅρμοσον αὖθις κιθάραν
> καὶ σὴν πρόσοψιν ὑπόδειξον τοῖς φίλοις
> καὶ προσλαλήσαις τοῖς μαθηταῖς ὡς πάλιν·
> εἰ γὰρ μαλάσσειν εἶχε γλυκερὸς λόγος
> ὦτα λασιόκωφα δυσμενοῦς Ἅιδου,
> τοῦτ' αὐτὸς ἂν ἔδρασας ἐλθὼν εἰς Ἅιδην
> ὡς αὐτοθελκτήριος αὐτογλυκύτης.[119]

The epigram has been read by Elizabeth Jeffreys as evidence for an early dating of the novel (and the chronicle), arguing that the evocation of Manasses as a 'young Orpheus' refers to his young age at the time of the epigram's and thus the novel's composition.[120] While I agree with the early dating of the novel, I find it problematic to use the epigram as

---

[116] Cf. the strategy used by Manasses himself when composing the didactic poem on the origins of Oppian (though not writing in hexameter); see above, Chapter 5.
[117] Mazal 1967b: 152. See also below, n. 120.
[118] A parallel noted by Mazal 1967b: 152; see now Nilsson and Zagklas 2017 for more material and a wider perspective.
[119] Manasses, *Aristandros and Kallithea*, frg. 181 (Mazal); tr. E. Jeffreys 2012, slightly revised. See also Paul and Rhoby 2019: 58–9; the first five verses are preserved in Par. Gr. 2087, following immediately after the hexameter verses to Sebastokratorissa Eirene; the extended version in Vind. Phil. Gr. 306 and Monac. gr. 281.
[120] E. Jeffreys 2012: 275–6: 'The most striking evidence comes from the epilogue to the novel … it refers to Manasses with a word that suggests he is under, say, twenty-five'.

evidence of Manasses' age at the composition of the novel. First, the reference to Manasses as a new Orpheus more likely refers to his poetic skills than to his actual age,[121] and second, the call to 'address pupils as in the past' does not necessarily mean that the author of the epigram was a former student of Manasses.[122] Any reader familiar with the work of Manasses, or at least with the chronicle, would most probably acknowledge his didactic qualities and could have addressed him as a 'teacher of the past' without having any personal experience of his teaching.[123] The dating of the epigram might accordingly belong to a later period, perhaps the thirteenth or even the fourteenth century when Manasses' work was read, appreciated and appropriated and the *Moral poem* may have been composed. If that is the case, the author of the epigram chose a strategy that is different from that of the potential imitator of the *Moral poem*: rather than imitating the voice of Manasses and impersonating his model author, he addressed him directly and thus created an addressee that reflected the model author found in the text – a successful teacher and poet, similar to the image offered by Manasses himself.[124]

Whose Emotions, Whose Life?

The emotional motifs that have been considered in some detail in this chapter, the unstable fortune of life and the dangers of envy, appear in rather different kinds of works: they have been both recycled by the author himself and then excerpted by his readers in order to be used in new contexts. The usefulness of such passages is obvious, especially in the case of short gnomic statements, such as the first lines of frg. 49 of *Aristandros and Kallithea*:

> Nothing is certain for mortal men, but the wheel of Fortune
> frequently rotates and turns intentions
> and plans and human fate upside down.

---

[121] On Orpheus as a common encomiastic topos, see Paul and Rhoby 2019: 59 with n. 243.
[122] Cf. E. Jeffreys 2012: 337, n. 283 on Manasses' involvement in teaching. Also n. 284 offers a biographical reading of the poem that presumes that the author was familiar with details of Manasses' life and thus belonged in twelfth-century Constantinople: 'The summons to re-tune, to appear to his friends and pupils again suggest that Manasses had spent a period out of the public eye, perhaps caught up ca. 1143–45 with the troubles surrounding the sevastokratorissa Irene.'
[123] Cf. Mazal 1967b: 72, who refers to the poem as 'ein Opus eines seiner Schüler oder Kopisten einer Handschrift'.
[124] Cf. below, Chapter 7, on the possible imitation of a Manassean voice in this epigram. On other book epigrams on the *Verse chronicle*, see Paul and Rhoby 2019: 59–61 and below, Chapter 7.

> Οὐ γάρ τι βέβαιον θνητοῖς, ὁ δὲ τροχὸς τῆς Τύχης
> συχνάκις κυλινδούμενος ἄνω καὶ κάτω ῥέπει
> σκέμματα καὶ βουλεύματα καὶ τύχας ἀνθρωπίνας.[125]

We have already seen examples of very similar elaborations of the same theme, and the explicit mention of the wheel of Fortune (ὁ τροχὸς τῆς Τύχης) in this passage also brings to mind 'The force of Fortune' (Τύχης φορά) painted by Apelles, described by Manasses in the opening of his *Encomium of Michael Hagiotheodorites*, which later develops the theme of envy and adversity.[126] In light of other writings of the Byzantine period, the emotional themes of envy and personal misfortune are not unique, and it is clear that these issues were felt to be relevant to Manasses and his fellow writers.[127] However, this does not mean that the expression of the motifs and themes reflect the personal lives of the empirical authors.

In the case of Manasses, this kind of reading has been recurring in research on the *Verse chronicle* and the novel fragments, even though neither text is explicitly autobiographical or even very 'personal' in character. Thus Tsolakis interpreted the address of envy and the authorial comment on its power in *Verse chronicle* 3199–3210, cited above, as a personal comment of the empirical author: 'Τὸ νόημα τοῦ στίχου αὐτοῦ [3210] εἶναι βέβαια, ὅτι ἕως τῇ στιγμῇ ποὺ ὁ ποιητὴς ἀσχολεῖται μὲ τὴ συγγραφὴ τοῦ ἱστορικοῦ του ἔργου δὲν ἔχει περάσει πολὺς καιρὸς ἀπὸ τὴν ἡμέρα ποὺ γλίτωσε ἀπὸ τὰ βέλη τοῦ φθόνου καὶ γιὰ τὸ λόγο αὐτὸ κεῖται μικρὸν ἐμπνέων.'[128] For Tsolakis, this experience was indicated also in the *Encomium of Michael Hagiotheodorites* and in the *Itinerary*, but it should be noted that these works are dated to the early 1160s, perhaps as much as twenty years after the first compositional phase of the chronicle. Also Odysseas Lampsides took the authorial comments of Manasses at face value, arguing that his problems were related to Sebastokratorissa Eirene's falling out of favour with Emperor Manuel.[129]

Paul Magdalino took a different but related approach in his analysis of Manasses as a 'typical courtier', reading his 'preoccupation with the power of envy and the Wheel of Fortune' as 'courtly not only in the sense that it reveals a secular, semi-pagan outlook on life, but also, and primarily, because he almost always expresses it in connection with court situations.'[130] Such

---

[125] Manasses, *Aristandros and Kallithea*, frg. 49.1–3 (Mazal), tr. E. Jeffreys 2012, slightly revised.
[126] Manasses, *Encomium of Michael Hagiotheodorites* 1–15 (Horna). Cited and translated above, Chapter 4. On the wheel of fortune, Cupane 1993.
[127] See esp. Hinterberger 2013: 168–71, on envy among Byzantine intellectuals.
[128] Tsolakis 1967: 20.   [129] Lampsides 1996: xix.   [130] Magdalino 1997: 162.

an approach places the thematic interest of Manasses partly in a sociocultural context, but Magdalino then goes on to connect the expression of the themes in both the chronicle and the novel to personal experiences: 'He was certainly influenced by his own personal experience of Envy at the court of Manuel I, and that experience surely lies behind his bitter comments on eunuchs, both in his history and in his romance...'[131] While there is always a connection between the personal experience of the world and the way in which that world is represented in different kinds of writing, including fiction,[132] it seems hard to prove these kinds of certain correlations between the empirical author's emotions and his works.[133] In the case of envy, Martin Hinterberger has argued against such interpretations, based on the difference between envy as a human emotion and envy as a force of fate: 'Dagegen spricht allerdings auch, daß Phthonos bei Manasses größere Bedeutung als Schicksalsmacht denn als menschliche Emotion hat.'[134]

It thus seems reasonable to read Manasses' frequent use of motifs based on envy and misfortune more as an expression of an overall interest in human life, of relevance in the court environment and shared by both aristocrats and peers. This explains the presence of such elaborations in works of different kinds and with different functions: from the chronicle and the novel to the *Monody on the death of his goldfinch*, the *Encomium of Michael Hagiotheodorites* and the letters. Their emotional character is more likely to be related to rhetoric than to personal feelings, which explains the appearance of 'startlingly personal reminiscences in highly depersonalised literary contexts', as Magdalino aptly puts it in the case of the *Itinerary*.[135] The recycling of the same themes and motifs in different texts probably indicates not in the first place their personal importance for the authors, but their relevance in the court context, for aristocrats and patrons. For Manasses, they seem to have been part of a stock of verses, half-verses or expressions that could be recycled for different occasions,[136] something that later became an advantage also for excerptors and perhaps imitators.

---

[131] Magdalino 1997: 162. On the image of eunuchs in the novels, including that of Manasses, see Messis 2014: 229–34.
[132] For a discussion of this relation, see above, Chapter 1.
[133] For the case of Manasses, see Reinsch 2007: 269, n. 11 (arguing against Lampsides), and Nilsson and Nyström 2009: 45, n. 15.
[134] Hinterberger 2013: 409. Cf. also Cairns 2014 on the 'principle of alternation' and its function in Greek narrative.
[135] Magdalino 1993: 402. Cf. other readings of the *Itinerary* referred to above, Chapter 2.
[136] Cf. Zagklas 2014: 79 on similar recycling in the case of Prodromos.

Regardless of whether the *Moral poem* was written by an aged Manasses, recycling previous material in a spiritual setting, or composed by 'another' Manasses, they were both projecting the voice of the model author and thus expressing his 'emotions', not necessarily their own at that specific moment in time.

CHAPTER 7

Occasional Writing as a Creative Craft

This study set out to investigate the 'personal' and consistent voice of Constantine Manasses, based on the assumption that a clear and individual, yet flexible style was necessary in order to have a successful career as a writer in twelfth-century Constantinople. Part of such a winning voice was authorial self-representation – the tale of the person behind the text, inscribed in both fictional and factual writings and representing the model author rather than the empirical writer. In modern terms one would speak of 'author branding', considered crucial for the development of one's 'writer platform'. To cite a popular online manual on the topic: 'The author who can tap into what their readers yearn for – and construct an entire experience around what they crave – is the author that earns the devoted fan base.'[1] Numerous guides for aspiring authors advocate author branding as a key to success, most often emphasizing the need for proper understanding of one's intended audience and consumer. As underlined by Donna Zuckerberg, applying the concept of author branding to ancient Greek literature, 'brand construction is far from a unilateral undertaking; it often involves input and influence from multiple sources, including the creator, the consumer, and the critic'.[2] Accordingly, the strategy was well known also to ancient and medieval authors, working under the constraints of performativity and patronage; creating a 'public *persona*' (as Zuckerberg argues in the case of Aristophanes) or an 'authorial *persona*' (as I argue in the case of Manasses) was a process that had to be undertaken in careful consideration of the consumers' explicit and implicit wishes.

Such strategies presuppose a diachronic perspective, since a 'brand' is created over periods of various lengths. This is particularly relevant in the case of Manasses, who was active for at least 30 years and who, as we have seen, kept recycling his own work as a procedure that would underline

---

[1] Grabas 2015. For the significance of branding in a wider, cultural perspective, see Holt 2004.
[2] Zuckerberg 2016: 162.

both his position in the socio-cultural system and his firm handling of *logoi* (in the senses of writing, learning and literature). He could thus create a coherent body of work while, at the same time, 'crafting a narrative of development and reinvention over time'.[3] This narrative has sometimes been read as a personal narrative of the empirical author Manasses,[4] but the aim here has been to show that it belongs rather to the author as projected in his texts – an authorial narrative that is based on, but does not necessarily coincide with, the 'real' Manasses. In this final chapter I return to some of these theoretical concerns, and then especially to the relationship between author, text and pretext in occasional literature, reconsidered in light of the textual analysis undertaken above.

Recycling the Past, Recycling the Present (1)

The way in which Manasses' work has traditionally been described in scholarship is very much marked by his alleged imitation of ancient literature, his so-called 'novelistic' characteristics and his innovative use of political verse. In the words of Otto Mazal,

> Das literarische Werk des Manasses ist weitgehend vom Romanhaften und von der Nachahmung der Antike bestimmt. Das zeigt sich schon in seinem Hauptwerk, der Chronik, die ebenfalls in politischen Versen verfasst ist und auf ihrem Gebiet etwas neues darstellte.[5]

This is true at least for the most well-known works by Manasses: the novel *Aristandros and Kallithea* and the *Verse chronicle*. Political verse was a form used by several other authors writing for the court circles, but as far as we know it had never been used for a novel or a chronicle. While the step from twelve- to fifteen-syllable verses in the novel is rather small, writing history in verse was probably a greater challenge and led to the impression of a literary, poetic or indeed novelistic chronicle.[6] The *Itinerary*, written in dodecasyllables, is also often read as a 'novelistic' poem, describing the experiences of the narrator with an emphasis on emotion and personal feelings.[7] However, this generally accepted description of Manasses' work

---

[3] Zuckerberg 2016: 152, with reference to Holt 2004.
[4] For the distinction between empirical and model author, see above, Chapter 4.
[5] Mazal 1967b: 11. For a similar evaluation of the novelties of Manasses' *Verse chronicle*, see Lampsides 1996: xl–xlv.
[6] For recent discussion, see Nilsson 2019 and 2021a; see also above, Chapter 6.
[7] See above, Chapter 2.

needs to be modified in light both of his other works that have come down to us and the tendencies of twelfth-century literature at large.

While it is true that most of Manasses' works rely on the ancient tradition, the same could be said for practically all Byzantine literature. His way of using ancient authors is not different from that of his peers, and includes a wide range of works from the Homeric epics and Pindar to numerous imperial authors such as Philostratus, Oppian and Athenaeus. In the same manner, he relies on the rhetorical handbooks of Menander and Hermogenes to the same extent as all of his contemporaries. Importantly, and often neglected in discussions of Byzantine imitation of antiquity, his linguistic imitation of Greek authors, sustained by citations and allusions, is combined with references to Roman literature and an intense use of Biblical and patristic texts. The result is a dense fabric of literary and cultural references, spanning a semiotic and hermeneutic field that is much wider and more complex than the concept of 'antiquity' denotes: woven into this fabric are also Byzantine texts and artefacts going all the way up to Manasses' own time. The novel, for instance, was most probably written in dialogue with the other Komnenian novels, in turn relying on the ancient novel tradition – it is inevitably 'novelistic' because of its generic constraints. The chronicle, although presenting history in a new, poetic form, retells ancient and Byzantine (pagan and Christian) history and thus necessarily follows similar generic conventions; its narrative form is 'novelistic' in the sense that it reminds modern readers of techniques that are traditionally associated with the novel (e.g. episodic structure, descriptions and suspense). It is, however, important to note that such associations are subjective and depend on the reader's own expectations – as noted above, Nicolae Iorga associated the *Verse chronicle* rather with the epic and Milton.[8] Moreover, such 'novelistic' strategies were used by numerous twelfth-century authors, so even if the *Itinerary* also seems to present the same 'typically Manassean' character, narrating a potentially romantic event in an entertaining manner, it may be seen as part of an overall trend of the period.[9]

So while Manasses, as most of his peers, constantly mixed ancient Greek imagery, rhetoric, citations and allusions with references to Roman and Biblical literature, modern scholars have been more keen to discuss literary expressions of 'Hellenism'.[10] This probably depends on the higher status of classical literature and the long philological tradition of trying to identify

---

[8] See above, Chapter 1.   [9] See Nilsson 2014.
[10] In the vein of Kaldellis 2007; cf. above, Chapter 4, n. 29.

'new' ancient Greek texts in the form of citations in Byzantine authors. The use of Biblical, patristic and hagiographical texts has often been seen as less interesting, or perhaps simply taken for granted, even though the techniques involved are very similar and should be investigated together. The references to Roman literature have been more or less ignored, since the great majority of Byzantine authors did not read Latin texts in the original, did not cite them in Latin and accordingly offer little more than anecdotal notes.[11] While such notes bring nothing 'new' to the knowledge of Roman literature, they do show how Byzantine authors understood and related to the Roman heritage beyond linguistic differences and therefore deserve our attention.[12]

The proportions of Greek, Roman and Biblical material in a text depend on the occasion for which it was written. In a somewhat simplified manner one could perhaps say that the occasion determines the generic model (e.g. a *schedos* for teaching or a monody for a death), while the choice of references depends on the specific triangulation of text, pretext and authorial voice. For the chronicle, the generic model (history) was indicated by the pretext / the wish of the dedicatee, while the specific form (political verse) may have depended partly on the specifications of the dedicatee ('a clear treatise'),[13] partly on the authorial voice (political verse as a 'trademark' of Manasses). For a text like this, the proportions of Graeco-Roman and Biblical material depend to some degree on the Byzantine understanding of what a history should contain, but on a strictly textual level (words, imagery, citations, allusions) it is up to the author to craft his own version of history. Manasses thus casts the Creation as an ekphrasis composed in a poetic, partly Homeric vein, while the origin of the Trojan War is presented as a miniature novel.[14] Such genre-bending was probably a way of making certain narrative highlights suitable for performance in front of an audience that was used to ekphrastic and novelistic forms and identified with the Greek, the Roman and the Christian heritage of Byzantium.

---

[11] For exceptions, see e.g. Xenophontos 2014 and Lovato 2016.
[12] Manasses offers a case in point in his *Origins of Oppian*, referring to Oppian as an author making money off his writings for the Roman emperor; see above, Chapter 5. Note also Manasses' use of Athenaeus and his relation to the wealthy patron Publius Livius Larensis; see above, Chapter 2. In both cases, Manasses interacts with Roman socio-cultural settings through texts written in the imperial period.
[13] Manasses, *Verse chronicle* 8 (Lampsides): εὐσύνοπτόν σοι καὶ σαφῆ γραφὴν ἐκπονηθῆναι.
[14] Nilsson 2006 and 2021a.

By contrast, the preserved *schede* by Manasses all rely on Christian stories, drawn from Biblical and hagiographical contexts, while the novel depends primarily on the discourses of the ancient Greek novel and its Komnenian predecessors. However, this does not mean that the *schede* are entirely free from profane references or that the novel fragments are devoid of Christian references – hypertextuality is more complex than that. The motif of envy, for instance, is an originally ancient concept that was absorbed and developed by Christian writers, and Manasses uses it in various texts and contexts, including the novel.[15] And the *schede*, although intended for training in Christian discourses, contain material that could be used in various contexts, sometimes referring openly to the Olympic gods and accordingly offering examples of how to both critically appraise and integrate the pagan heritage in one's own writings.[16]

Most often, Manasses offers examples of how such blending may be achieved by mixing the Greek, the Roman and the Christian, turning the three into one. This is perhaps most obvious in his representation of Manuel I Komnenos as Alexander, David and Augustus in the *Encomium of Emperor Manuel Komnenos*.[17] The representation is combined with citations and allusions to all three areas, thus connecting them to the *persona* of the emperor and the empire that he represents. The technique makes the ancient past and the Christian imaginary merge in a text that, due to its occasional status, is both 'real' and 'factual'. At the same time, it creates an effect that is mostly associated with fiction – a sort of fairy-tale quality that envelops the *persona* of Manuel.[18] A similar case appears in the representation of Nikephoros Komnenos through the *personae* of his grandparents Anna Komnene and Nikephoros Bryennios, who are represented as ancient poets of the past.[19] The ancient Greek past (of Sappho and Archilochus) here merges with recent Byzantine history (of Anna and Bryennios) in order to shape the character of the addressee Nikephoros. The pretext (to praise the deceased Nikephoros) compels the authorial voice to recycle not only the cultural memory of Byzantium, but

---

[15] On envy, see above, Chapter 6.
[16] Manasses, *Schedos* 4 (Polemis). Note also Manasses' explicit awareness of the need for such a mixture of profane and Christian in his *Consolation for John Kontostephanos* 4–10 and 57–66 (Kurtz), discussed above, Chapter 3.
[17] Manasses, *Encomium of Emperor Manuel Komnenos* 280–6 (Kurtz). See above, Chapter 2.
[18] Cf. Kaldellis 2007: 284. See also Magdalino 1992: 201–3 on Manuel's need, at the beginning of his reign, to create a winning *persona* at the court despite his young age.
[19] Manasses, *Funerary oration on the death of Nikephoros Komnenos* (Kurtz) 120–69. See above, Chapter 3.

also more recent memories that in themselves represent the Roman identity of the Byzantines.[20]

While thus recycling both the distant and the recent past, Manasses draws on the cultural and literary arsenal at hand and shapes his texts in accordance with the occasion for which they are produced. His authorial voice remains more or less stable throughout various texts and across genres, thanks to the ways in which he recycles the same motifs, images, settings, figures of speech, words and so on. He even seems to have a literary mascot in the songbird, occurring in various texts in the guise of a goldfinch or a sparrow, sometimes simply in the form of fluttering wings.[21] In the case of poetry, the technique sometimes recalls formulaic poetry, especially in the texts written in political verse (*Origins of Oppian, Aristandros and Kallithea, Verse chronicle, Astrological poem, Moral poem*), between which words, verses and half-verses are frequently recycled. This lends an 'oral' quality to the works, since such techniques have traditionally been associated with oral poetry rather than written, and most notably with the Homeric epics. As stated in one of the standard works on narrative from a diachronic perspective, Robert Scholes and Robert Kellogg's *The Nature of Narrative*:

> In the writings of no known literary poet is the percentage of verbatim repeats even in this vicinity. Quite the contrary: literary poets strive to make each line unique, reserving repeated phrases for very special rhetorical effect.[22]

This statement, still largely representative of prevalent ideas in comparative literature, offers a point of departure for two important observations on the character of Manasses' narrative and literary techniques. First, the kind of intense repetition that is characteristic of the writings of Manasses (and numerous other Byzantine authors) has generally been understood as an 'oral' quality if not as a sign of poor talent or even laziness.[23] Second, 'oral' has been seen as the opposite of 'literary', which means that any techniques seen as 'oral' automatically exclude 'literariness'. Both assumptions have contributed to pejorative ideas about the exaggerated 'rhetoric' and repetitiveness of Byzantine literature in general. Such ideas are now being

---

[20] The *Alexiad* of Anna Komnene is certainly a case in point; see Neville 2012 and 2016; cf. Stouraitis 2014 and now also Kaldellis 2019.
[21] See above, esp. Chapter 3. [22] Scholes, Phelan and Kellogg 2006: 21 (first published in 1966).
[23] This attitude is apparent in e.g. Otto Mazal's insistence that no author would 'plagiarize' themselves to the extent that Manasses did, had he been the author of the *Moral poem*; see above, Chapter 6. See now also Yuretich 2018: 9, 'It is perhaps only slightly more surprising to discover that Manasses quotes extensively from his own writings, particularly his novel, *Aristandros and Kallithea*.'

reappraised and important studies of rhetorical performance have led scholars to focus on the 'aural' characteristics of rhetoric rather than its 'orality'.[24]

In the case of Manasses, the 'oral' effect is related to the use of political verse, the occasional use of vernacular or simple language,[25] the performative purpose of at least certain passages and, most importantly, his creation of a consistent authorial voice. The 'verbatim repeats' here accordingly have a function that goes well beyond rhetorical effect. The consistent recycling is rather a kind of self-imitation or hypertextual repetition with variation, making his texts recognizable for his audience. This is not unique, since a similar case could be made for several other authors of his time, not only in Byzantium but also in the West. Moreover, similar patterns may be observed in ancient literature, both Greek and Roman, since the same educational system based on imitation and rewriting was the basis of ancient authorship. Wordsworth's romantic definition of poetry as 'spontaneous' and 'original' has come to dominate also modern thinking about poetics.[26] However, not only the medieval, but also the ancient model stands in sharp contrast to such notions. Pindar too wrote occasional poetry, and such texts – written as a response to certain needs or demands – are clearly not less creative or less valuable than others. They have only been viewed that way because post-romantic readers have failed to recognize ancient and medieval notions of authorship and creativity. Sometimes Byzantinists themselves have fallen into the trap of apologetic introductions to critical editions of texts they seem to dislike, and even if such attitudes are less and less common, one should be aware of these critical double-standards that disadvantage Byzantine literature.

Recycling the Past, Recycling the Present (2)

In spite of my argument for a coherent and recognizable Manassean voice stretching over decades of production of occasional texts, it must be acknowledged that absolute stylistic coherence can never be expected, since all authors (and artists and musicians) sometimes depart from their usual manners. This has already been discussed above in the case of *schede*, whose use as didactic instruments most often affects the voice of their

---

[24] See Bourbouhakis 2011 and 2017: 125*–58*. For Manasses, see Paul and Rhoby 2019: 51 on dramatic elements of the *Verse chronicle* and their significance for its performance.
[25] On this aspect of language in Manasses' *Verse chronicle*, see Lampsides 1996: xliv–v; Trapp 1993: 119; Paul and Rhoby 2019: 48–9.
[26] See above, Chapter 1.

authors in a way that makes them less recognizable.²⁷ Such works tend to be less attractive to scholars or sometimes even called into question because of their divergence from what is seen as 'normal', especially in the case of ancient literature where canonical authors are often supplied with various so-called Pseudo-texts. As noted above, style then becomes a kind of paternity test, not really allowing for variation or experimentation on the part of the author.²⁸ In the case of Manasses, such discussions have marked in particular the *Moral poem* (as a text probably not composed by Manasses) and the *Sketches of the mouse* (as a text probably composed by Manasses), but another text that merits consideration is the neglected *Verses on how Darius came to power* (Στίχοι τοῦ Μανασσῆ εἰς τὴν τοῦ Δαρείου ὑπόθεσιν ὅπως ἐβασίλευσεν ὁ Δαρεῖος).

These verses have almost completely escaped the notice of scholars, with the exception of the two editors, both avid readers of Manasses. The text has been preserved in a single manuscript, the Vaticanus Gr. 915, and consists of 16 verses, of which Leo Sternbach presented an edition in 1902.²⁹ Some 85 years later (1987), Odysseas Lampsides edited the same text, seemingly unaware of Sternbach's edition.³⁰ As indicated by the title, the verses narrate the well-known story of how Darius became king (emperor) of Persia. The text runs as follows.

> Since they had no one to be king according to the law, | the mightiest of the Persians, as by divine agreement, | appointed to be emperor | whoever's horse indicated him as such by neighing. | Now the resourceful and shrewd groom | of Darius, knowing of the madness for a certain mare of that horse | that used to carry the future king of Persians, | took the urine of its partner mare on a sponge | and, pretending to clean its bit and bridle, | provoked the horse to search for his mate | with plentiful neighing, noises sounding from the nostrils. | Seeing this, the others descended from their horses | and prostrated themselves before Darius, bending their knees to the ground. | Because of this, until now, the habit has dominated | that most men get off their horses when they meet | the most powerful and radiant and famous men.

---

²⁷ See above, Chapter 5.   ²⁸ See above, Chapter 1.
²⁹ The poem is to be found on f. 45r of the ms, which dates to the end of the thirteenth or beginning of the fourteenth century and contains secular poetry of a great variety; on this ms, see Schreiner 1988: 125–37.
³⁰ The most significant difference between the two editions is that Lampsides reads the first verse as part of the title; his version of the poem accordingly has only 15 verses. Here I rely on the edition by Sternbach, who may have studied the manuscript in situ (though it is not entirely clear whether he refers to the manuscript or a copy), whereas Lampsides had a photocopy of possibly low quality (Lampsides 1987: 335, n. 6).

> Ἐπιλειπόντων τελέως τῶν νόμῳ βασιλέων
> Περσῶν οἱ κρατιστεύοντες ὡς ἐκ θείας συνθήκης
> ἐκεῖνον ἐπεκλήρωσαν ἔσεσθαι βασιλέα,
> ὃν χρεμετίσας σημανεῖ τοῦτον ὁ φέρων ἵππος.
> Ὁ τοίνυν ποικιλότροπος, ἀγχίνους ἱπποκόμος,
> ὁ τοῦ Δαρείου, συνιδὼν θηλυμανῆ τὸν ἵππον,
> ὃς εἶχε φέρων ἔποχον τὸν ὕστερον Περσάρχην,
> οὖρον λαβὼν ἐν σπογγιᾷ φορβάδος τῆς συννόμου
> καὶ προσχηματισάμενος τὸν χαλινὸν καθαίρειν,
> πυκνοῖς πυκνοῖς χρεμετισμοῖς, μυκτηροκόμποις ψόφοις
> ἀναζητεῖν ἠρέθιζε τὴν σύντροφον ἱππάδα.
> Ὅπερ ἰδόντες οἱ λοιποὶ τῶν ἵππων ἀποβάντες
> Δαρείῳ προσηκύνησαν, κλίναντες γῇ τὸ γόνυ·
> ἐξ οὗπερ ἐπεκράτησεν ἕως τοῦ δεῦρο χρόνου
> τοὺς πλείους ἀφιππάζεσθαι, πηνίκα συναντῷεν
> τοῖς μεγιστᾶσι καὶ λαμπροῖς καὶ περιφανεστέροις.[31]

The anecdote of how Darius came to rule over Persians is here used as an explanation of a habit that dominates 'until now', turning the historical event into an explanation of a supposedly contemporary custom. In this way, the short version of a longer narrative told by Herodotus becomes an independent story in the form of a self-contained poem, pointing in the Herodotean direction for a learned audience and offering an entertaining and edifying tale.[32] It is easy to imagine a school setting and an exercise for students, either for making history memorable or as an example of how to rewrite stories of the past.

Both Sternbach and Lampsides compared the *Verses on how Darius came to power* with a passage of Manasses' *Verse chronicle*, in which the same story of Darius and his horse is narrated in verses 883–906. Here the anecdote is part of a longer account of the Persian empire, spanning over some 35 verses. After an opening passage on the internal power struggles and intrigues of the Magi, the seven most prominent Persians kill the Magi and then decide the future of Persian rule.

> After long deliberations about the empire | they finally decided that he whose horse | was observed to neigh first of all horses, | just as the light-bringing sun would light up the Earth, | he would rule over Persians, he would be their commander. | This was agreed, but the groom of Darius | was capable of conceiving the following plan: | investigating and finding out which mare | Darius' horse liked more than all others, | he took, after the

---

[31] Manasses, *Verses on how Darius came to power* (Sternbach).
[32] For the original story, see Herodotus, *Hist.* 85–6. See also below, n. 34.

two horses had mated, her urine | and smeared it around the nostrils of the stallion. | They rode off all at once, and Darius' horse, | excited by the smell of the urine of the mare, | was snorting and was observed to neigh. | And the novel and wondrous thing was that thunder | and lightning appeared, terrifying those present, | who, when they saw this, got off their horses | and prostrated themselves for Darius, as was the Persian custom.

> πολλὰ δὲ βουλευσάμενοι καὶ περὶ βασιλείας
> τὸ τελευταῖον ἔκριναν, οὗ τινος τούτων ἵππος
> χρεμετισμῷ χρησάμενος πρὸ πάντων φωραθείη,
> ἄρτι πυρσεύοντος τὴν γῆν τοῦ φεραυγοῦς ἡλίου,
> οὗτος κατάρξειε Περσῶν, οὗτος ἀρχηγετήσει.
> ἦν ταῦτα τὰ συνθήματα, Δαρείῳ δ' ἱπποκόμος
> ἦν ἱκανὸς τεχνάζεσθαι τοιαύτας ἐπινοίας·
> οὗτος μαθὼν καὶ διαγνοὺς ὁποίαν ἵππον στέργει
> τῶν ἄλλων πλέον ἁπασῶν ἵππος ὁ τοῦ Δαρείου,
> μετὰ τὴν μῖξιν τοῖν ἀμφοῖν οὖρον λαβὼν ἐκείνης
> ἐκ τούτου περιέχρισε μυκτῆρας τοὺς ἱππείους.
> ἅμα δὲ καθιππάσαντο, καὶ πρῶτος ὁ Δαρείου,
> ἐκ τῆς ὀσμῆς συγκινηθεὶς τῶν οὔρων τῆς θηλείας,
> καὶ φριμαγμοῖς ἐχρήσατο καὶ χρεμετίζων ὤφθη·
> καὶ τὸ καινὸν καὶ θαυμαστὸν ὅτι βροντώδεις ἦχοι
> καὶ στεροπαὶ γεγόνασι θαμβοῦσαι τοὺς παρόντας,
> οἳ ταῦθ' ὡς ἐθεάσαντο, τῶν ἵππων ἀποβάντες
> Δαρείῳ προσεκύνησαν, ὡς ἔθος παρὰ Πέρσαις.[33]

To readers who are used to Manasses' tendency to recycle verses or parts of verses, words and expressions, these two versions of the same story appear as curiously different. Here, we are not dealing with different events told in similar words, as in many of the cases we have seen above, but with the same event told in different words and, to some extent, a different voice. The two versions have a few unavoidable keywords in common (e.g. ἱπποκόμος, οὖρον λαβών, χρεμετίσας/χρεμετίζων, προσεκύνησαν), all of which go back to the ancient story by Herodotus.[34] Considering the fact that the poem is preserved in a single manuscript, one might even be

---

[33] Manasses, *Verse chronicle* 889–906 (Lampsides).
[34] While there are similarities in vocabulary, there are also two significant differences between Manasses' version(s) and the original story: (a) in Herodotus, Darius talks to the groom (Oebares) beforehand and asks him to come up with a plan (3.85.1–2); (b) the night before the race, Oebares brings both horses to a place outside the city (where he knows the horses will pass the next morning) and allows them to mate (3.85.3), but Herodotus then adds an alternative version: some people say that Oebares rubbed his hand on the mare's vulva and then, in the morning, smeared the nostrils of the stallion (3.86). On Herodotus as a general model for Manasses, see E. Jeffreys 1979: 213–14; Paul and Rhoby 2019: 22 and 51.

tempted to argue for a Pseudo-Manasses, offering his own take on the story told in the *Verse chronicle*. But in that case, the imitator has studied carefully both his model and other works by Manasses, because upon a closer examination there is a verbatim correspondence beyond single words[35] and the *Verses on how Darius came to power* contain rare words employed in other texts by Manasses.[36] Also the rhythm is the same in the poem as in the political verses of the *Verse chronicle*: the caesura is always after the eighth syllable, which in most cases is either oxytonic or proparoxytonic. And certain verses, like v. 10 (πυκνοῖς πυκνοῖς χρεμετισμοῖς, μυκτηροκόμποις ψόφοις), have an unmistakable Manassean ring, not least through the opening repetition of πυκνοῖς, recalling the πυκνὰ πυκνὰ of the *Description of a crane hunt*, the *Monody on the death of his goldfinch* and the *Sketches of the mouse*.[37]

This is not clear evidence that the poem was written by Manasses, because style can be deceptive and book epigrams with similar adaptations of the Manassean voice have been preserved. One was discussed above, preserved in manuscripts of both the *Verse chronicle* and the novel fragments. While the poem speaks to Manasses the teacher and the poet, it does so by using the rare word θελξικάρδιος, used by Manasses in both the *Verse chronicle* and other texts. This means that at least part of the authorial voice of the addressee is inscribed in the epigram.[38] Two more book epigrams, preserved in manuscripts of the *Verse chronicle*, are cited, translated and discussed in the introduction to the German translation by Anneliese Paul and Andreas Rhoby, making these important witnesses to the reception of Manasses known to a wider audience. While the first epigram speaks in the voice of a reader, the second speaks in the voice of the book itself ('I am the book…') and the third brings in the voice of the scribe, a certain Alexios.[39] Such versatility is typical of book epigrams and indicates the intimate relation between text, reader and scribe in

---

[35] The two half-verses τῶν ἵππων ἀποβάντες | Δαρείῳ προσηκύνησαν appear in *Verse chronicle* 905–6 (Lampsides) and in *Verses on how Darius came to power* (Sternbach) 12–13, in the same metrical position.

[36] See e.g. μυκτηρόκομπος in *Verse chronicle* 3629 and 5801 (Lampsides), originating in Aeschylus, *Seven against Thebes* 464, but used only by Manasses in the twelfth century. One may also note the rare ἀφιππάζεσθαι, which appears only in this poem according to *LBG*.

[37] Manasses, *Description of a crane hunt* 52–3 (Messis and Nilsson); *Monody on the death of his goldfinch* 6.27 and 7.16 (Horna); *Sketches of the mouse* 1.28 (Papademetriou). Cf. Lampsides' reading of v. 10 (his v. 9): πυκνοῖς χρεμετισμοῖς, μυκτηρόκομποις ψόφοις; Lampsides 1987: 335.

[38] Noted by Paul and Rhoby 2019: 59. In addition to the *Verse chronicle* 311 (Lampsides), see also *Description of a crane hunt* 254 (Kurtz) and *Monody on the death of his goldfinch* 4.26 (Horna).

[39] Paul and Rhoby 2019: 59–61. The first and third epigram are included in DBBE; the second in Bekker's 1837 edition of the *Verse chronicle*, p. 287.

manuscript transmission.⁴⁰ But more interesting for us here, the second and third epigrams also employ words used in the chronicle itself – thus recalling not only the story and the physical book, but also the voice of the author-narrator.⁴¹

To conclude, I see no compelling reason to question Manasses as author of the *Verses on how Darius came to power*. It seems likely that we are dealing with two independent adaptations of Herodotus, written by the same author for different occasions and accordingly with different functions: one for the chronicle and one for a separate, probably educational setting. For both occasions, Herodotus is a suitable model and the anecdote itself entertaining. What I wish to underline with this discussion – along with similar discussions above in this study – is that imitation and recycling can take many forms. Both procedures have a tendency to turn readers' expectations upside down, which complicates the reliance on style as a proof of authorship, context or dating. The use, function and pretext of each text all affect the voice of the model author, sometimes making it less recognizable in terms of vocabulary, rhythm or thematic focus. Inductive reasoning does not always work for artistic production, not even in times and places that we see as controlled by generic and metric constraints. Sometimes authors do things differently, and that novelty is what makes their craft interesting.⁴²

Occasional Literature Between History and Fiction

The in-between status of occasional literature, placing itself between 'the real' and the 'imaginary', has already been touched upon in the discussion of recycling: citations of or allusions to ancient or Christian characters or events may function as fictional markers that confuse any clear boundaries between the past and the present, the factual and the fictional.⁴³ This does not make the text's content less 'real', but rather underlines the interplay between author, text and audience in any occasional setting. In the case of Manuel I Komnenos, the characterization of the contemporary person of

---

⁴⁰ DBBE has made this important material more widely available and led to innovative studies of the relation between ancient and Byzantine literature; see e.g. Bértola 2019 and 2021.
⁴¹ Paul and Rhoby 2019: 60–1. The words in question are τριπέμπελος as an epithet for Rome (second epigram, v. 6; *Verse chronicle* 3778 and 4452 [Lampsides]) and θεὸς πανεργάτης (third epigram, v. 1; *Verse chronicle* 63 [Lampsides]).
⁴² Manasses voices this concern in his *Encomium of Michael Hagiotheodorites* 6–8 (Horna), cited and discussed above, Chapters 4 and 6.
⁴³ For a more detailed discussion, see above, Chapter 1.

the emperor was made by reference to leading characters of the past, turning the addressee (Manuel himself) into a re-presentation imbued with historical and mythical, *qua* fictional significance. The result is a very powerful characterization that not only merges the three cultural traditions on which Byzantium is founded, but also acknowledges the interplay of fiction and reality. In the words of Paul de Man,

> The stress falls not so much on the fictional status of literature – a property now perhaps somewhat too easily taken for granted – but on the interplay between these fictions and categories that are said to partake of reality, such as the self, man, society, . . . Hence the emphasis on hybrid texts considered to be partly literary and partly referential.[44]

Occasional texts are referential in the sense that they want to achieve something for someone (the author, the addressee or the commissioner), but by looking at them from this perspective they are also fictional in the sense that they freely employ fictional imagery and thus often 'fictionalize' both historical and contemporary characters. The occasional settings of Constantinople offered ample opportunities for such merging of the real and the imaginary, not least in ekphrastic discourses which in themselves contain an inherent rivalry between truth and fiction, art and nature.[45]

As we have seen above, Manasses' *Description of a little man* offers an example of how an 'unrealistic', yet 'true' or even 'natural' sight (*theama*) is brought before the eyes of the beholders, who are the listeners of the performance (*drama*). The little man may be understood as both a realistic representation (of an actual event at the Constantinopolitan court) and a metaphor (signifying the author himself).[46] The fictional markers (referring to Homer and Achilles Tatius) blur the boundaries between the real world and the imaginary, but they do not cancel the message of the text: a potential comment on the author's own situation. A similar situation may be detected in the *Description of the catching of siskins and chaffinches*, which takes the beholder/listener from the reality of Constantinople (a hot place in late summer, suffering from draught) to the other side of the Bosphoros (a *locus amoenus* with plenty of water and lush gardens). The simple and rustic life that reigns over there may be seen as a charming contrast to the hustle and bustle of the big city and thus 'realistic' (as Iorga seems to have read it), but the narrator takes his audience straight into a

---

[44] de Man 1979: 3.   [45] See above, Chapters 2 and 6.
[46] See above, Chapter 1; in more detail, see Messis and Nilsson 2015 and 2021.

storyworld of the Second Sophistic – the deceptively plain countryside which (in the case of both Philostratus and Manasses) turns out to be a carefully wrought literary and rhetorical construction, or perhaps even a painting.[47]

Ekphrastic strategies were also an important part of the historical narrative that Manasses composed for the *Verse chronicle*, not merely as decorative elements, but as significant ways of linking the past and the present. The great church of Hagia Sophia, its adjunct library and the Church of the Holy Apostles built by Theodora all offer 'living' examples of Constantinople's eternal beauty, connections between its long and glorious past and the everyday reality of the writer and his audience.[48] Such strategies are part of all historiographical writing and it is therefore important to acknowledge this technique of blending facts and fiction, while keeping in mind the distinction between the two kinds of referentiality at work here: the text's connection to the occasion (pretext/performance) and its (literary/potentially fictive) representation of a 'reality' that is relevant to that occasion.[49] There is no way to 'de-narrativize' an event or a character of a historical text in order to reveal the 'true' historical event; as noted by Hayden White, 'since these conceptions have their origins in ethical considerations, the assumption of a given epistemological position by which to judge their cognitive adequacy would itself represent only another ethical choice'.[50] Accordingly, one has to accept the narrative conceptions of authors as they have come down to us, even if they seem to contradict one's modern understanding of 'truth' vs 'fiction'.

Gérard Genette made an attempt to come to terms with such problems in his *Fiction et diction*, which consisted of four theoretical essays that ultimately aimed at defining what makes some texts literary and others not.[51] In the essay 'Récit fictionnel, récit factuel', Genette considered the differences between fictional and factual narrative, arguing that the only narratological categories that make any difference between the two are 'mode' (mood) and 'voix' (voice).[52] According to Genette's model, various types of focalized narrative may constitute fictional markers, and especially embedded narrative: 'La présence du récit métadiégétique est donc un

---

[47] Cf. Manasses, *Description of the catching of siskins and chaffinches*, with the illuminations of Oppian's *Cynegetica*, esp. fig. 4 and 22 in Spatharakis 2004. Likewise, the *Description of the Earth* should be compared with mosaic representations of various kinds, including the *asarotos oikos* floor mosaic, the 'unswept room' that was described by, for instance, Pliny the Elder as early as the second century BCE (*Natural History* 36.184). See now Foskolou 2018: 89–90 and 92.
[48] See above, Chapters 2 and 6.   [49] See above, Chapter 1.   [50] White 1973: 26.
[51] Genette 1991.   [52] Genette 1991: 141–68, esp. 151–63.

indice assez plausible de fictionnalité – même si son absence n'indique rien.'⁵³ In practice, this means that a factual text can be formally constructed exactly like any fictional narrative as regards order, duration and frequency, and that its fictional aspects are indicated only (and not even necessarily) by means of focalization and metadiegetic insertions.

Such strategies are at the core of Manasses' way of inserting himself and his own story into 'factual' texts occasioned by specific events. By inserting a secondary narrative that has bearing on the writer's situation, but casting it as a fictional strategy, he produces a metanarrative that is subtle enough to avoid criticism but at the same time clear enough to be noted by attentive readers/listeners. This is particularly clear in the *Monody on the death of his goldfinch*, where the bird is cast as both the writer and his patron, creating a situation in which Manasses addresses himself and thus – within the fiction of the text – functions as his own patron.⁵⁴ The way in which Manasses accordingly characterizes himself, his addressees and his objects of praise, sometimes also his enemies,⁵⁵ by means of fictional strategies offers yet another connection between the real world that occasions his works and the literary imaginary to which he has access through his knowledge of the Graeco-Roman and Biblical heritage. His voice and his story are 'individual' in the sense that they are a unique combination of the many pieces offered by those traditions, but they are firmly rooted in a joint discourse.

This is how the 'empty formalism' and 'full concretism' of twelfth-century literature were brought together by an individual performer. As noted by Paul Magdalino, these aspects of Komnenian literature were merely 'two sides of the same coin, coined by performers showing off their way with words in a theatre of talent, ambition and patronage'.⁵⁶ The adaptability and skills in 'social relations' that were demanded by such a 'theatre' called for a creative and firm handling of factual and fictional strategies, both relying on rhetorical learning. The very notion of 'empty formalism' thus needs finally to be reappraised, since form clearly is filled with both semiotic and concrete meaning. When Manasses praises Oppian's rhetorical skills, he is ultimately praising himself and his navigation of the society in which he works: he expresses suitable opinions and knows how to handle dense ideas, he brings the things he discusses before the audience's eyes and he does all this in a smooth manner.⁵⁷

---

⁵³ Genette 1991: 154.   ⁵⁴ See above, Chapter 3.   ⁵⁵ See Manasses, *Letter* 1.6–13 (Horna).
⁵⁶ Magdalino 1993: 356.   ⁵⁷ Manasses, *Vita Oppiani* 47–52 (Colonna). See above, Chapter 5.

The Voice, Story and Career of Constantine Manasses

Manasses' authorial voice and narrative cannot be immediately equated with the empirical author who lived in Constantinople in the twelfth century. This does not mean that they are unrelated to him and to his socio-cultural environment – on the contrary, they offer important information on the way in which a writer understood himself as a professional within the Komnenian system. Scholars have often read twelfth-century voices as personal voices, expressing the emotions or feelings of the empirical authors, driven by the need for self-promotion and an ultimately profitable projection of a confident self.[58] The problem with such an approach is that it neglects the complex processes of self-representation, self-projection and self-imitation that have been observed in this study of Manasses. A prerequisite for such observations is an inclusive and comparative perspective, taking into account not only individual works – which may indeed seem egocentric and emotionally charged when studied in isolation – but the entire preserved production of one author. When Magdalino noted the function of individual self-projection by twelfth-century authors, including Manasses, as 'inherent in their professional self-confidence' he was certainly right,[59] and it was his careful reading of numerous authors that allowed him to draw such a conclusion. The present analysis of all preserved texts by one author complements and corroborates Magdalino's pioneering study of Komnenian culture by showing how self-projection was a consistent strategy on linguistic, narratological and metadiegetic levels.

While the linguistic and narratological techniques are fairly easy to detect, the metadiegetic level is methodologically more challenging. In the case of authorial comments, inserted extradiegetically in the text, the message may seem rather clear, but other stories are more ambiguously conveyed and demand a more detailed analysis. For instance, my reading of the *Monody on the death of his goldfinch* as a representation of the complex relationship between writer and patron offers one more piece of the Manassean authorial story, but at the same time it can be read as a demonstration of rhetorical techniques for students, in which case it adds to our understanding of Manasses' teaching activities. The one does not exclude the other; the multiple readings rather show how a twelfth-century writer and teacher would produce texts that could be useful in different settings and for different purposes. More importantly, the adaptability and

---

[58] See above, Chapters 2 and 4.   [59] Magdalino 1993: 402.

recycling of motifs and sayings create difficulties for scholars who wish to extract a chronologically coherent and teleological narrative of the author. The temptation to read the chronological development of the life and career of the author into the metanarrative comments and interpretations may, in fact, thwart the function of the authorial *persona* projected by Manasses. An author brand does not build on change, but on consistency, and the thematic recurrence of, for instance, envy and misfortune in Manasses' work should not be read as part of an overall authorial tale in which these themes are sometimes more prevalent than others. The very distribution of such motifs across Manasses' production speaks against such an approach; that kind of reconstructed authorial tale should therefore not be used to date individual works.

That said, the works were to some extent written in a certain order, but – importantly – some of them were most probably composed over periods of time and recycled in or adapted for different settings. We should therefore consider not only chronological, but also simultaneous models of composition. The *Verses on how Darius came to power* may have been written while Manasses was working on the corresponding passage of the *Verse chronicle*, just as the novel and the chronicle may have been composed more or less simultaneously, though it seems likely that the *Verse chronicle* took much longer to produce. However, since my analysis of Manasses' works has been undertaken thematically, I should like to add a few words on how I tentatively understand their sequence. Such a sequence remains hypothetical, especially since we most probably possess only a small part of Manasses' entire production and we cannot assume that what we have can be distributed evenly over his career. However, the stylistic and thematic coherence of the works that have come down to us makes it likely that they are representative of the particularly Manassean voice that has been traced in this study. Moreover, the kinds of texts that have been preserved point at two kinds of core activities in Manasses' career: teaching and performative rhetoric. Based on that, and on the identifiable persons to which individual texts are addressed, I would divide Manasses' production into two periods: the first stretching from the late 1130s or early 1140s to the end of the 1150s, the second from *c.*1160 to the 1170s.

The first period is characterized by teaching and commissions for Sebastokratorissa Eirene. If one accepts Odysseas Lampsides' dating of Manasses' birth to *c.*1115,[60] he would have been in his mid-twenties by

---
[60] Lampsides 1988. See also above, Chapter 1.

the end of the 1130s and could have already been active as a teacher and writer on commission. This is the most difficult period in terms of dating, since the only texts by Manasses that can be firmly dated to before 1161 are the *Astrological poem* and the *Verse chronicle*, both written for Eirene, who died in 1153.[61] The dating of the chronicle has varied from the 1140s to the 1150s, but it seems likely that it was written and performed in portions over a few years.[62] In order to get such a commission of writing a history for Eirene, an important and prestigious assignment, Manasses would have already had to prove himself an appreciated teacher–rhetorician, perhaps as a teacher associated with the school of the Orphanotropheion.[63] Both the *Origins of Oppian* and the *schede*, perhaps also the *Verses on how Darius came to power*, belong to an educational setting and may thus be placed in the late 1130s or early 1140s, but they do not possess the rhetorical or literary force that would have granted future commissions.

It is therefore possible that the novel *Aristandros and Kallithea* and perhaps some of the ekphraseis (*Description of the Earth* and *Description of the catching of siskins and chaffinches*) were written before the chronicle, and that the success of ekphrastic discourse and political verse caused the commission of the chronicle.[64] The reference to a 'larger work' in the *Astrological poem*, composed in political verse for the same Eirene, seems to indicate such a sequence, but it is also possible that Manasses here refers to the novel (or to some other work that has not been preserved).[65] In either case, it seems likely that all works written in political verse belong to this early stage of Manasses' career. In light of the potentially educational use of three other texts, the *Monody on the death of his goldfinch*, the *Description of the Cyclops* and the *Description of a little man*, I would place them too in this early phase but slightly later, perhaps in the 1150s. Such an interpretation is based on the way in which they comment upon the system of patronage and the situation of a writer, which is done in a different manner in the texts I see as earlier.[66]

---

[61] For the most recent study of Eirene, see E. Jeffreys 2014.
[62] Nilsson 2021a; Paul and Rhoby 2019: 7–9. For a dating to the 1140s, see also E. Jeffreys 2012: 274. Cf. Lampsides 1988: esp. 110–11.
[63] See above, Chapter 5.
[64] If one accepts the *Schede tou myos* as a work by Manasses, it should perhaps be placed in proximity to the *Description of the Earth* and other ekphraseis drawing heavily on Philostratus. See above, Chapter 5.
[65] Cf. E. Jeffreys 2012: 275–6, on the dating of *Aristandros and Kallithea*.
[66] Cf. e.g. the story of the *Origins of Oppian* and its implicit reflection of a writer on commission, offering a playful model to students (above, Chapter 5), with the almost sarcastic tone of the *Description of a little man* (Messis and Nilsson 2015 and 2021).

My understanding of this early period remains an educated guess, based on the presumed settings of the individual texts, their transtextual relations and the voice of the model author. In contrast, the texts of the second period, spanning the 1160s and 1170s, can all be dated with some certainty to the period in question and their internal sequence is more or less clear. The *Itinerary* was written around 1161, but most probably edited in one or two different versions.[67] The *Encomium of Michael Hagiotheodorites* and the three letters that relate to the composition and delivery of the oration may be placed in the late 1160s, when the logothete accompanied Manuel on his military campaign in Hungary.[68] The *Encomium of Emperor Manuel Komnenos* is probably to be dated somewhat later, *c.*1170 or in the early 1170s, and as I have argued above I believe the *Description of a crane hunt* to have been delivered in relative proximity to the oration.[69] In the early 1170s belong also the fragmentarily preserved oration to an anonymous Komnenos, which has not been included in my analysis,[70] and the *Funerary oration on the death of Nikephoros Komnenos*, dated to *c.*1173. Finally the two texts written for John Kontostephanos on the death of his wife Theodora, a monody and a consolation, belong to *c.*1175.[71]

The texts of this later period are marked by the writer's relation to not only one patron, as in the case of Eirene's position in his early career, but several patrons and 'friends'. They all belong to the inner circles of Komnenian society, ranging from relatives of the emperor and high functionaries to the emperor himself. Some of the connections that Manasses had with these persons may have been related to his earlier (or present) position at the school of the Orphanotropheion or at some other teaching institution of Constantinople. The texts are characterized by the kind of authorial comments and metadiegetic allusions that imbue also some texts of the early (or middle) period (the *Monody on the death of his goldfinch*, the *Description of the Cyclops* and the *Description of a little man*). An important difference is that the direct address of the patrons/friends in question allows for a more 'personal' expression that includes the characterization of not only the writer himself, but also his addressees.[72] It should be noted that the characterization of the addressee in terms of similarity, as in the case of Michael Hagiotheodorites and Nikephoros

---

[67] See above, Chapter 2.   [68] See above, Chapters 2 and 4.   [69] See above, Chapter 2.
[70] Manasses, *Monody on the death of an anonymous man*, identified as Alexios Doukas in Sideras 1994: 190–2.
[71] On the orations to Nikephoros Komnenos and John Kontostephanos, see above, Chapter 3.
[72] See above, Chapter 3.

Komnenos, is different from the teacher–pupil relationship that marks Manasses' characterization of Sebastokratorissa Eirene in the early period.[73]

Based on this description of the two phases of Manasses' career it may be tempting to see a development or change in his authorial voice, from the teaching voice of the early years to the experienced rhetorician of the later period. There is, however, a certain risk of falling again into a biographical trap by assuming such a change. From the theoretical perspective that has been applied here, the change lies not in Manasses' style or self-projection, but in the different relations he now upholds and the different occasions of the texts he produces. When a writer of occasional literature underlines his own experience and skills in relation to others, he does it as a way of showing that he remains the same: Manasses remains a songbird in the service of his friends. There is no sign of a 'late style' in Edward Said's sense in twelfth-century Constantinople, only functions that come with experience and relationships, such as becoming a bishop.[74] If Manasses did indeed write the *Moral poem* it would probably belong in the later period,[75] but not because it represents a 'late style'. Said's idea of development or evolution in literary careers – that an author's work grows and changes as they themselves get older and more mature, becoming more experimental, more ambitious – does not apply to the twelfth-century situation. Towards the end of his career, Manasses was still flexible and adaptable, constrained by commission and convention, but experimental in a manner that was consistent.

This is another reason for not reading a teleological narrative into the authorial story, since the consistency of style and the complex recycling of material easily leads the reader in the wrong direction. My tentative sequence of the works attributed to Manasses is based on my analysis of the texts in question, but that sequence should not in turn be used as a basis for conclusions about the empirical author and his texts. It is possible, as has been suggested, that Manasses fell out of favour in the late 1140s and 1150s, after he had been working for Sebastokratorissa Eirene, who was in disgrace with her nephew Manuel,[76] but the authorial comments and motifs on which such interpretations are based recur more or less consistently throughout his entire production. As discussed above, this

---

[73] See above, Chapter 6.
[74] The concept of 'late style' was developed in the posthumously published Said 2006.
[75] On the question of authorship, see above, Chapter 6.
[76] For details, see E. Jeffreys 2014: 178 with n. 7. On the *Verse chronicle* and the Sebastokratorissa, see above, Chapter 6.

does not mean that his references to envy and misfortune were not relevant or 'factual', but that they had a significance that went beyond his personal life at that moment in time and involved a number of writers working in Komnenian Constantinople.

The storyworld sketched in Manasses' texts is accordingly useful not only for understanding the way in which he worked and looked at his own role in society, but also for considering twelfth-century writing in general. Manasses was probably not unique, even if he – like several other writers – managed to create an authorial brand that was. The kind of analysis that has been undertaken here, reading the texts by a Komnenian author through the lens of occasional literature, may be methodologically useful also for the study of other authors. Stepping back from the biographically centred focus on empirical authors, one may thus recognize the model author as a kind of textual geography in which the reader learns to navigate.

Bibliography

1. TEXTS BY CONSTANTINE MANASSES

Address by the way (Τοῦ Μανασσῆ κυροῦ Κωνσταντίνου ἐνόδιον προσφώνημα) – authorship contested
Ed. K. Horna, 'Einige unedierte Stücke des Manasses und Italikos', *Progr. Sophiengymnasium* (Vienna 1902) 3–26: 12; ed. and English tr. by R. Browning, 'Notes on Byzantine Prooimia', in H. Hunger, *Prooimion: Elemente der byzantinischen Kaiseridee in den Arengen der Urkunden*. Wiener Byzantinistische Studien 1: Supplement (Vienna 1966) 26–7.

Aristandros and Kallithea (Τὰ κατ' Ἀρίστανδρον καὶ Καλλιθέαν; preserved only as excerpts)
Ed. O. Mazal, *Der Roman des Konstantinos Manasses. Überlieferung, Rekonstruktion, Textausgabe der Fragmente*. Wiener Byzantinistische Studien 4 (Vienna 1967); ed. E. Th. Tsolakis, *Συμβολὴ στὴ μελέτη τοῦ ποιητικοῦ ἔργου τοῦ Κωνσταντίνου Μανασσῆ καὶ κριτικὴ ἔκδοση τοῦ μυθιστορήματός του "Τὰ κατ' Ἀρίστανδρον καὶ Καλλιθέαν"* (Thessaloniki 1967).
Italian tr. by F. Conca, *Il romanzo bizantino del XII secolo* (Turin 1994) 684–777; English tr. by E. Jeffreys, *Four Byzantine Novels: Theodore Prodromos, Rhodanthe and Dosikles; Eumathios Makrembolites, Hysmine and Hysminias; Constantine Manasses, Aristandros and Kallithea; Niketas Eugenianos, Drosilla and Charikles* (Liverpool 2012) 284–337.

Astrological poem (Στίχοι συντεθέντες . . . τῇ σεβαστοκρατορίσσῃ κυρᾷ Εἰρήνῃ)
Ed. E. Miller, 'Poèmes astronomiques de Théodore Prodromos et de Jean Camatère', *Notices et extraits des manuscrits de la Bibliothèque nationale et autres bibliothèques* 23.2 (Paris 1872) 1–39; cf. S. Lampros, 'Κωνσταντίνου Μανασσῆ στίχοι συνοψίζοντες τὰ προχειρότερα περὶ τῶν ἀστέρων', *Neos Hellenomnemon* 16 (1922) 60–6.

Consolation for John Kontostephanos (Παραμυθητικὸν εἰς τὸν σεβαστὸν κύρον Ἰωάννην τὸν Κοντοστέφανον)
Ed. E. Kurtz, 'Dva proizvedenija Konstantina Manassi, otnosjashchiesja k smerti Theodori Kontostefanini', *VizVrem* 7 (1900) 621–45 (636–45).

Description of a crane hunt (Τοῦ Μανασσῆ κυροῦ Κωνσταντίνου ἔκφρασις κυνηγεσίου γεράνων)

Ed. E. Kurtz, 'Eshje dva neizdannyh proizvedenija Konstantina Manassii', *VizVrem* 12 (1906) 69–98 (79–88); ed. Ch. Messis and I. Nilsson, '*The Description of a Crane Hunt* by Constantine Manasses: Introduction, text and translation', *Scandinavian Journal for Byzantine and Modern Greek Studies* 5 (2019) 9–89 (45–65).

Modern Greek tr. by Th. A. Nimas, *Η « Ἔκφρασις κυνηγεσίου γεράνων » του Κωνσταντίνου Μανασσή. Εισαγωγή, Κείμενο, Μετάφραση, Σχόλια, Γλωσσάριο* (Thessaloniki 1984); English tr. in Messis and Nilsson (as above) 66–79.

Description of a little man (Τοῦ Μανασσῆ κυροῦ Κωνσταντίνου ἔκφρασις ἀνθρώπου μικροῦ)

Ed. L. Sternbach, 'Constantini Manassae ecphrasis inedita', *Symbolae in honorem L. Cwiklinskii* (*Symbolae philologorum Polonorum, quibus amici et discipuli Ludovico Cwiklinski quinque lustra felicissime peracta congratulantur*) (Lemberg 1902) 11–20; ed. Ch. Messis and I. Nilsson, 'Constantin Manassès, *La Description d'un petit homme* : introduction, texte, traduction et commentaires', *JÖB* 65 (2015) 169–94 (188–90).

French tr. in Messis and Nilsson (as above), 192–4; English tr. in Ch. Messis and I. Nilsson, 'Constantine Manasses, *Description of a little man* (translation with brief introduction and comments)', in *Texts on Byzantine Art and Aesthetics: The Visual Culture of Later Byzantium (1081–c.1350)*, ed. C. Barber and F. Spingou (Cambridge 2021).

Description of the catching of siskins and chaffinches (Ἔκφρασις ἁλώσεως σπίνων καὶ ἀκανθίδων τοῦ σοφωτάτου κυροῦ Μανασσῆ)

Ed. L. Sternbach, 'Analecta Manassea', *Eos* 7 (1902) 181–94; ed. K. Horna, *Analekten zur byzantinischen Literatur* (Vienna 1905) 6–12.

German tr. (partial) by H.-G. Beck, *Das Byzantinische Jahrtausend* (Munich 1978) 325–8.

Description of the Cyclops (Τοῦ ἔκφρασις εἰκονισμάτων ἐν μαρμάρῳ κυκλοτερεῖ κατὰ μέσον ἐχόντων τὸν Κύκλωπα τοὺς Ὀδυσσέως ἑταίρους διασπαράσσοντα καὶ ἐσθίοντ‹α› καὶ Ὀδυσσέα οἴνου ἀσκὸν προφέροντα καὶ δεξιούμενον πόσει τὸν Κύκλωπα)

Ed. L. Sternbach, 'Beiträge zur Kunstgeschichte', *Jahreshefte des Österr. Arch. Institut* 5 (1902) Sp. 65–94 (83–5).

Description of the Earth (Τοῦ φιλοσόφου καὶ ῥήτορος κυροῦ Κωνσταντίνου τοῦ Μανασσῆ ἔκφρασις εἰκονισμάτων ἐν μαρμάρῳ κυκλωτερεῖ, κατὰ μέσον μὲν τυπούντων τὴν γῆν ἐν μορφῇ γυναικός, κύκλῳ δὲ παρόντων ὀπωρῶν καί τινων ζῴων θαλασσίων καὶ ἄλλων διαφόρων)

Ed. R. Hercher, 'Constantini Manassis ecphrasis imaginum nunc primum edita', *Nuove memorie dell'istituto di corrispondenza archeologica* II (1865) 491–500; ed. L. Sternbach, 'Beiträge zur Kunstgeschichte', *Jahreshefte des Österr. Arch. Institut* 5 (1902) Sp. 65–94 (74–83); ed. O. Lampsides, 'Der vollständige Text der Ἔκφρασις γῆς des Konstantinos Manasses', *JÖB* 41 (1991) 189–205.

Modern Greek tr. by P. A. Agapitos and M. Hinterberger in *Εικών και λόγος· έξι βυζαντινές περιγραφές έργων τέχνης*, ed. P. A. Agapitos (Athens 2006) 41–73 (tr.) and 175–99 (notes).
Encomium of Emperor Manuel Komnenos (Τοῦ αὐτοῦ. Πρὸς τὸν βασιλέα κυρὸν Μανουὴλ τὸν Κομνηνόν)
Ed. E. Kurtz, 'Eshje dva neizdannyh proizvedenija Konstantina Manassii', *VizVrem* 12 (1906) 69–98 (88–98).
Encomium of Michael Hagiotheodorites (no title in ms)
Ed. K. Horna, 'Eine unedierte Rede des Konstantin Manasses', *Wiener Studien* 28 (1906) 171–204 (173–84).
Funerary oration on the death of Nikephoros Komnenos (Λόγος ἐπικήδειος τοῦ φιλοσόφου κυροῦ Κωνσταντίνου τοῦ Μανασσῆ πρὸς τὸν ἀποιχόμενον ἐπὶ τῶν δεήσεων κυρὸν Νικηφόρον Κομνηνὸν τὸν ἔκγονον τοῦ καίσαρος)
Ed. E. Kurtz, 'Evstafija Fessalonikijskago i Konstantina Manassii monodii na konchiny Nikifora Komnina', *VizVrem* 17 (1910) 283–322 (302–22).
Itinerary – *Hodoiporikon* (Τοῦ Μανασσῆ κυροῦ Κωνσταντίνου εἰς τὴν κατὰ τὰ Ἱεροσόλυμα ἀποδημίαν αὐτοῦ)
Ed. K. Horna, 'Das Hodoiporikon des Konstantin Manasses', *BZ* 13 (1904) 313–55; ed. and modern Greek tr. K. Chryssogelos, *Κωνσταντίνου Μανασσῆ Ὁδοιπορικόν* (Athens 2017).
Partial German tr. by A. Külzer, in *Peregrinatio graeca in Terram Sanctam: Studien zu Pilgerführern und Reisebeschreibungen über Syrien, Palästina und den Sinai aus byzantinischer und metabyzantinischer Zeit* (Frankfurt 1994) 281–7; Dutch tr. by W. J. Aerts, 'Het Hodoiporikon ('Reisverlag') van Konstantinos Manasses', *Tetradio* 11 (2002) 9–53; English tr. (with reprint of Horna's ed.) by W. J. Aerts, 'A Byzantine Traveller to one of the Crusader States', in *East and West in the Crusader States: Contexts – Contacts – Confrontations III*, ed. K. Ciggaar and H. Teule (Leuven and Dudley, Mass., 2003) 165–221; Italian tr. by E. Gori, 'Lo Hodoiporikon di Constantino Manasse', *Porphyra* 12 (suppl. 2011).
Letters: *To Michael Hagiotheodorites* (no title in ms); *To pansebastos George, son of the* megalos domestikos (Τῷ πανσεβάστῳ κυρῷ Γεωργίῳ, τῷ υἱῷ τοῦ μεγάλου δομεστίκου); *To Michael Angelopoulos* (Τῷ κυρῷ Μιχαὴλ τῷ Ἀγγελοπούλῳ); *To Gerasimos the younger* (Εἰς Γεράσιμον τὸν νέον; incomplete)
Ed. K. Horna, 'Eine unedierte Rede des Konstantin Manasses', *Wiener Studien* 28 (1906) 171–204 (185–7).
Monody on the death of an anonymous man (Τοῦ λογιωτάτου κυροῦ Μανασσῆ τοῦ ... μονῳδία ἐπὶ τῷ κυρῷ...; incomplete)
Ed. L. Sternbach, 'Analecta Manassea', *Eos* 7 (1901) 180–94 (193–4).
Monody on the death of his goldfinch (Τοῦ κυροῦ Κωνσταντίνου τοῦ Μανασσῆ μονῳδία ἐπὶ ἀστρογλήνῳ αὐτοῦ τεθνηκότι)
Ed. K. Horna, 'Einige unedierte Stücke des Manasses und Italikos', *Progr. Sophiengymnasium* (Vienna 1902) 3–26 (3–9 [text] and 15–17 [commentary]).

Monody on the death of Theodora, wife of John Kontostephanos (Μονῳδία ἐπὶ τῇ σεβαστῇ κυρᾷ Θεοδώρᾳ τῇ τοῦ Κοντοστεφάνου Ἰωάννου συζύγῳ)

Ed. A. Papadopoulos-Kerameus, 'Ῥητορικὸν γύμνασμα τοῦ Μανασσῆ', *VizVrem* 5 (1898) 671–7; ed. E. Kurtz, 'Dva proizvedenija Konstantina Manassi, otnosjashchiesja k smerti Theodori Kontostefanini', *VizVrem* 7 (1900) 621–45 (630–5).

Moral poem (no title in ms) – authorship contested

Ed. E. Miller, 'Poème moral de Constantin Manassès', *Annuaire de l'Association pour l'encouragement des études grecques en France* 9 (1875) 23–75.

Origins of Oppian (Κωνσταντίνου τοῦ Μανασσῆ γένος Ὀππιανοῦ διὰ στίχων πολιτικῶν ἐμμέτρων)

Ed. A. Colonna, 'De Oppiani vita antiquissima', *Bollettino del Comitato per la preparazione della edizione nazionale dei classici greci e latini* 12 (1964) 33–40 (38–9).

Schede: *On the Life of Daniel the Stylite* (no title in ms); *On the Theotokos* (no title in ms); *On the Theotokos* (no title in ms); *On Mary's entry into the temple* (no title in ms); *On a martyrium* (no title in ms)

Ed. I. D. Polemis, 'Fünf unedierte Texte des Konstantinos Manasses', *RSBN* 33 (1996) 279–92.

Sketches of the mouse – *Schede tou myos* (Τὰ Σχέδη τοῦ Μυός) – authorship contested

Ed. J. T. Papademetriou, 'Τὰ Σχέδη τοῦ Μυός: new sources and text', in B. A. Milligan (ed.), *Classical Studies Presented to Ben Edwin Perry by his Students and Colleagues at the University of Illinois, 1924–60* (Urbana 1969) 219–22. English tr. by P. Marciniak, 'A pious mouse and a deadly cat: The *Schede tou Myos*, attributed to Theodore Prodromos', *GRBS* 57 (2017) 507–27 (523–7).

Verse chronicle – *Synopsis chronike* (Σύνοψις Χρονική)

Ed. I. Bekker, *Breviarium historiae metricum*. CSHB 5 (Bonn 1837); ed. O. Lampsides, *Constantini Manassis Breviarium Chronicum*. CFHB 36/1–2 (Athens 1996).

Modern Greek tr. by O. Lampsides, Κωνσταντίνου Μανασσῆ Σύνοψις Χρονική. Κείμενα Βυζαντινῆς Ιστοριογραφίας 11 (Athens 2003); English tr. by L. Yuretich, *The Chronicle of Constantine Manasses* (Liverpool 2018); German tr. by A. Paul and A. Rhoby, *Konstantinos Manasses, Verschronik (Synopsis Chronike)* (Stuttgart 2019).

Verses on how Darius came to power (Στίχοι τοῦ Μανασσῆ εἰς τὴν τοῦ Δαρείου ὑπόθεσιν ὅπως ἐβασίλευσεν ὁ Δαρεῖος)

Ed. L. Sternbach, 'Constantini Manassae versus inediti', *WSt* 24 (1902) 473–7; O. Lampsides, 'Verse des Konstantinos Manasses über Darius I.', *BZ* 80 (1987) 334–5.

2. PRIMARY SOURCES BY OTHER AUTHORS

Achilles Tatius, *Leucippe and Clitophon*, ed. J.-P. Garnaud, *Achille Tatius d'Alexandrie, le roman de Leucippé et Clitophon*, Paris 2002.

Anna Komnene, *Alexiad*, ed. A. Kambylis and D. R. Reinsch, *Annae Comnenae Alexias* (CFHB 40/1), Berlin and New York 2001. English tr. by E. R. A. Sewter, *Anna Comnene: The Alexiad*, Revised with Introduction and Notes by Peter Frankopan, London 2009 (first published 1969).
Eumathios Makrembolites, *Hysmine and Hysminias*, ed. F. Conca, *Il romanzo bizantino del XII secolo. Teodoro Prodromo – Niceta Eugeniano – Eustazio Macrembolita – Costantino Manasse*, Turin 1994, 499–687.
Eustathios of Thessalonike, *Commentary on the Iliad*, ed. van der Valk, *Eustathii archiepiscopi Thessalonicensis commentarii ad Homeri Iliadem pertinentes*, 4 vols., Leiden 1971–87.
Eustathios of Thessalonike, *Epitaphios for Manuel I Komnenos*, ed. E. C. Bourbouhakis, *Not Composed in a Chance Manner: The epitaphios for Manuel I Komnenos by Eustathios of Thessalonike*, Uppsala 2017.
Eustathios of Thessalonike, *Funerary oration on the death of Nikephoros Komnenos*, ed. E. Kurtz, 'Evstafija Fessalonikijskago i Konstantina Manassii monodii na konchiny Nikifora Komnina', *VizVrem* 17 (1910) 283–322 (290–302).
Eustathios of Thessalonike, *Letters*, ed. F. Kolovou, *Die Briefe des Eustathios von Thessalonike: Einleitung, Regesten, Text, Indizes*, Munich and Leipzig 2006.
Eustathios of Thessalonike, *Orations*, ed. P. Wirth, *Eustathii Thessalonicensis Opera Minora* (CFHB 32), Berlin 2000.
John Kinnamos, *History*, ed. A. Meineke, *Rerum ab Ioannes et Alexio [sic] Comnenis Gestarum* (CSHB), Bonn 1836.
John Mauropous, *Letters*, ed. A. Karpozilos, *The Letters of Ioannes Mauropous Metropolitan of Euchaita* (CFHB 34), Thessaloniki 1990.
John Tzetzes, *Allegories of the Iliad*, ed. J. F. Boissonade, *Tzetzae Allegoriae Iliadis: accedunt Pselli Allegoriae quarum una inedita*. Paris 1851 (repr. 1967).
John Tzetzes, *Chiliades*, ed. P. L. M. Leone, *Ioannis Tzetzae Historiae*, Naples 1968.
Lycophron, *Alexandra*, ed. L. Mascialino, *Lycophronis Alexandra*, Leipzig 1964.
Manganeios Prodromos, *Poems*, ed. S. Bernardinello, *Theodori Prodromi de Manganis* (Studi Bizantini e Neogreci 4), Padua 1972.
Manganeios Prodromos, *Epithalamion for the wedding of Theodora Komnene*, ed. C. Castellani, *Epitalamio di Teodoro Prodromo per le nozze di Teodora Comnena e Giovanni Contostefano*, Venice 1888.
Michael Hagiotheodorites, *Description of a chariot race*, ed. K. Horna, 'Eine unedierte Rede des Konstantin Manasses', *Wiener Studien* 28 (1906) 171–204, 194–7.
Michael Italikos, *Monody on the death of his partridge*, ed. P. Gautier, *Michel Italikos: Lettres et discours* (Archives de l'Orient Chrétien 14), Paris 1972, 103–4.
Michael the Rhetorician, *Encomium of Manuel I Komnenos*, ed. V. Regel and N. Novosadskij, *Fontes Rerum Byzantinarum rhetorum saeculi XII orationes politicae*, vol. 1, Leipzig 1982, 165–82.
Michael Psellos, *Chronographia*, ed. D. R. Reinsch, *Michaelis Pselli Chronographia*, Berlin and Boston 2014.

Michael Psellos, *Letters*, ed. S. Papaioannou, *Michael Psellus: Epistulae*, Berlin and Boston 2019.
Nikephoros Basilakes, *Progymnasmata and monodies*, ed. A. Pignani, *Progimnasmi e monodie* (Byzantina e Neo-Hellenica, Collana di studi e testi 10), Naples 1983.
Nikephoros Basilakes, *Orations*, ed. A. Garzya, *Nicephori Basilacae orationes et epistolae*, Leipzig 1984.
Niketas Eugenianos, *Drosilla and Charikles*, ed. F. Conca, *De Drosillae et Chariclis amoribus* (London studies in classical philology 24), Amsterdam 1990.
Oppian, *Cynegetica*, ed. and tr. A. W. Mair, *Oppian, Colluthus, Tryphiodorus* (Loeb Classical Library), London 1928.
Philostratus, *Imagines*, ed. O. Benndorf and K. Schenkl, *Philostrati maioris imagines* (Leipzig 1893). English tr. A. Fairbanks, *Philostratus Imagines – Callistratus, Descriptions* (Loeb Classical Library), London 1931.
Pollux, *Onomasticon*, ed. E. Bethe, *Pollucis onomasticon*, 2 vols. Leipzig 1931.
Strategikon of Maurice, ed. G. T. Dennis and E. Gamillscheg, *Das Strategikon des Maurikios* (CFHB 17), Vienna 1981. English tr. by G. T. Dennis, *Maurice's Strategikon*, Philadelphia 1984.
Theodore Prodromos, *Poems*, ed. W. Hörandner, *Theodoros Prodromos, Historische Gedichte*, Vienna 1974.
Theodore Prodromos, 'Fifth Ptochoprodromic poem', ed. A. Maiuri, 'Una nuova poesia di Teodoro Prodromo in greco volgare', *BZ* 23 (1920) 397–407.
Theodore Prodromos, 'Fifth Ptochoprodromic poem', ed. A. Maiuri, *Poem and epigrams*, ed. N. Zagklas, *Theodore Prodromos: The Neglected Poems and Epigrams (Edition, Translation, and Commentary)*, diss. Vienna 2014.
Theophylaktos of Ochrid, *Orations*, ed. P. Gautier, *Théophylacte d'Achrida: Discours, Traités, Poésies* (CFHB 16/1), Thessaloniki 1980.

3. SECONDARY LITERATURE

Aerts, W. J. (2003) 'A Byzantine traveller to one of the Crusader states', in *East and West in the Crusader States: Contexts – Contacts – Confrontations III*, ed. K. Ciggaar and H. Teule. Leuven and Dudley, Mass., 165–221.
Agapitos, P. A. (1989) 'Michael Italikos: Klage auf den Tod seines Rebhuhns', *BZ* 82: 59–68.
  (1998) 'Mischung der Gattungen und Überschreitung der Gesetze: Die Grabrede des Eustathios von Thessalonike auf Nikolaos Hagiotheodorites', *JÖB* 48: 119–46.
  (2003) 'Ancient models and novel mixtures: the concept of genre in Byzantine funerary literature', in *Modern Greek Literature: Critical Essays*, ed. G. Nagy and A. Stavrakopoulou. New York and London, 5–23.
  (2007) 'Blemmydes, Laskaris and Philes', in *Byzantinische Sprachkunst: Studien zur byzantinischen Literatur gewidmet Wolfram Hörandner zum 65. Geburtstag*, ed. M. Hinterberger and E. Schiffer. Berlin and New York, 1–19.

(2008) 'Public and private death in Psellos: Maria Skleraina and Styliane Psellaina', *BZ* 101: 555–607.
(2013) 'Anna Komnene and the politics of schedographic training and colloquial discourse', *Nea Rhome* 10: 89–107.
(2014) 'Grammar, genre and politics in Komnenian Constantinople: redefining a scientific paradigm in the history of Byzantine literature', *JÖB* 64: 1–22.
(2015a) 'Learning to read and write a schedos: the verse dictionary of Par. gr. 400', in *Pour une poétique de Byzance : Hommage à Vassilios Katsaros*, ed. P. Odorico, S. Efthymiadis and I. D. Polemis. Paris, 11–24.
(2015b) 'Literary *haute cuisine* and its dangers: Eustathios of Thessalonike on schedography and everyday language', *DOP* 69: 225–41.
(2015c) 'New genres in the twelfth century: the *schedourgia* of Theodore Prodromos', *MEG* 15: 1–41.
(2015d) 'Contesting conceptual boundaries: Byzantine literature and its history', *Interfaces: A Journal of Medieval European Literatures* 1: 62–91.
(2017) 'John Tzetzes and the blemish examiners: a Byzantine teacher on schedography, everyday language and writerly disposition', *MEG* 17: 1–57.
Alexiou, M. (1974) *The Ritual Lament in Greek Tradition*. Cambridge.
(1986) 'The poverty of écriture and the craft of writing: towards a reappraisal of the Prodromic poems', *BMGS* 10: 1–40.
(1999) 'Ploys of performance: games and play in the Ptochoprodromic poems', *DOP* 53: 91–109.
Anastasi, R. (1965) 'Per una nuova edizione del romanzo di Costantino Manasse', *Helikon* 5: 1–20.
(1969) 'Sul romanzo di Costantino Manasse', *Rivista di cultura classica e medioevale* 11: 214–36.
Anderson, J. C. and M. J. Jeffreys (1994) 'The decoration of the Sebastokratorissa's tent', *Byz* 64: 8–18.
Angelidi, Ch. and G. Calofonos (2014) *Dreaming in Byzantium and Beyond*. Farnham, Surrey.
Annibaldi, C. (ed.) (1993) *La musica e il mondo: mecenatismo e committenza musicale in Italia tra Quattro e Settecento*. Bologna.
(1998) 'Towards a theory of musical patronage in the Renaissance and Baroque: the perspective from anthropology and semiotics', *Recercare* 10: 173–82.
Augerinou-Tzioga, M. (2003) *Η Σύνοψις Χρονική του Κωνσταντίνου Μανασσή: συμβολή στην υφολογική μελέτη μιας έμμετρης χρονογραφίας*. Diss. Thessaloniki.
Bakhtin, M. M. (1981) *The Dialogic Imitation: Four Essays*. Ed. M. Holquist, tr. C. Emerson and M. Holquist. Austin, Texas.
Bal, M. (2002) *Travelling Concepts in the Humanities: A Rough Guide*. Toronto.
Barber, C. and S. Papaioannou (eds) (2017) *Michael Psellos on Literature and Art: A Byzantine Perspective on Aesthetics*. Notre Dame, Ind.
Barzos, K. (1984) *Ἡ γενεαλογία τῶν Κομνηνῶν*. Thessaloniki.

Bawarshi, A. S. (2003) *Genre and the Invention of the Writer: Reconsidering the Place of Invention in Composition*. Logan, Utah.

Bazaiou-Barabas, Th. (1994) 'Τo εντοίχιο ψηφιδωτό της Γης στο Ιερό Παλάτιο και οι Εκφράσεις του Κωνσταντίνου Μανασσή και Μανουήλ Φιλή· ρεαλισμός και ρητορεία', *Byzantina Symmeikta* 9/2: 95–115.

Beaton, R. (1987) 'The rhetoric of poverty: the lives and opinions of Theodore Prodromos', *BMGS* 11/1: 1–28.

Bees, N. (1930) 'Manassis der Metropolit von Naupaktos ist identisch mit dem Schriftsteller Konstantinos Manasses', *Byzantinisch-neugriechische Jahrbücher* 7: 119–30.

Berensmeyer, I. et al. (2012) 'Authorship as cultural performance: new perspectives in authorship studies', *Zeitschrift für Anglistik und Amerikanistik* 60.1: 5–29.

Bernard, F. (2011a) 'Greet me with words: gifts and intellectual friendships in eleventh-century Byzantium', in *Geschenke erhalten die Freundschaft: Gabentausch und Netzwerkpflege im europäischen Mittelalter*, ed. M. Grünbart. Münster, 1–11.

(2011b) 'Exchanging *logoi* for *aloga*: cultural capital and material capital in a letter of Michael Psellos', *BMGS* 35/2: 134–48.

(2012) 'Gifts of words: the discourse of gift-giving in eleventh-century Byzantine poetry', in *Poetry and its Contexts in Eleventh-Century Byzantium*, ed. F. Bernard and K. Demoen. Aldershot, 37–51.

(2014) *Writing and Reading Byzantine Secular Poetry, 1025–1081*. Oxford.

Bértola, J. (2019) 'Book epigrams bizantinos sobre novelas griegas antiguas', *Anales de Filología Clásica* 31.1: 25–36.

(2021) 'An unedited cycle of Byzantine verse scholia on Herodotus in the light of twelfth-century verse scholia on ancient historians', in *Byzantine Poetry in the 'Long' Twelfth Century (1091–1204)*, ed. B. van den Berg and N. Zagklas. Cambridge, forthcoming.

Boeck, E. N. (2015) *Imagining the Byzantine Past: The Perception of History in the Illustrated Manuscripts of Skylitzes and Manasses*. Cambridge.

Boissevain, J. (1966) 'Patronage in Sicily', *Man* 1: 18–33.

Booth, W. C. (1983 [1961]). *The Rhetoric of Fiction*. 2nd edition with added final chapter. Chicago.

(2005) 'Resurrection of the implied author: why bother?', in *A Companion to Narrative Theory*, ed. J. Phelan and P. J. Rabinowitz. Malden, Mass., 75–88.

Bourbouhakis, E. C. (2007) '"Political" personae: the poem from prison of Michael Glykas: Byzantine literature between fact and fiction', *BMGS* 31/1: 53–75.

(2011) 'Rhetoric and performance', in *The Byzantine World*, ed. P. Stephenson. London and New York, 175–87.

(2014) 'The end of ἐπίδειξις: authorial identity and authorial intention in Michael Chōniatēs' Πρὸς τοὺς αἰτιωμένους τὸ ἀφιλένδεικτον', in *The Author in Middle Byzantine Literature: Modes, Functions, and Identities*, ed. A. Pizzone. Berlin, 201–24.

(2017) *Not Composed in a Chance Manner: The Epitaphios for Manuel I Komnenos by Eustathios of Thessalonike.* Uppsala.
Browning, R. (1961) 'The death of John II Comnenus', *Byz* 31: 229–35.
  (1962) 'The Patriarchal School at Constantinople in the twelfth century', *Byz* 32: 167–202.
  (1966) 'Notes on Byzantine *prooimia*', in *Prooimion: Elemente der byzantinischen Kaiseridee in den Arengen der Urkunden. Wiener Byzantinistische Studien I: Supplement*, ed. H. Hunger. Vienna, 26–7.
  (1976) 'Il codice Marciano gr. XI, 31 e la schedografia bizantina', in *Miscellania Marciana di Studi Bessarionei*. Padua, 26–7 (= idem, *Studies on Byzantine History, Literature and Education*, London 1977, no. XVI).
Budelmann, F. (2002) 'Classical commentary in Byzantium: John Tzetzes on ancient Greek literature', in *The Classical Commentary: Histories, Practices, Theory*, eds. R. K. Gibson and C. Shuttleworth Kraus. Leiden, 142–69.
Butler, J. A. (2003) 'Poetry 1798–1807: *Lyrical Ballads* and *Poems, in Two Volumes*', in *The Cambridge Companion to Wordsworth*, ed. S. Gill. Cambridge, 38–54.
Cairns, D. (2014) 'Exemplarity and narrative in the Greek tradition', in *Defining Greek Narrative*, ed. D. L. Cairns and R. Scodel. Edinburgh, 103–36.
Chryssogelos, K. (2013a) 'The prophetic dream in the *Itinerary* of Constantine Manasses', *Parekbolai* 3: 65–76.
  (2013b) 'Παρατηρήσεις στο Ὁδοιπορικὸν του Κωνσταντίνου Μανασσῆ. Το μοτίβο της Τρικυμίας και της Ξηρασίας', *Byzantina Symmeikta* 23: 33–43.
  (2016) 'Κωμική λογοτεχνία και γέλιο τον 12ο αιώνα. Η περίπτωση του Κωνσταντίνου Μανασσῆ', *Byzantina Symmeikta* 26: 141–61.
  (2017) *Κωνσταντίνου Μανασσῆ Ὁδοιπορικόν.* Athens.
  (2021) 'Milieu, editorial problems and Quellenforschung of Constantine Manasses' astrological poem', in *Byzantine Poetry in the 'Long' Twelfth Century (1081–1204)*, ed. B. van den Berg and N. Zagklas. Cambridge, forthcoming.
Conca, F. (ed.) (1990) *Niketas Eugenianos, De Drosillae et Chariclis Amoribus.* Amsterdam.
Cullhed, E. (2014a) *Eustathios of Thessalonike, Parekbolai on Homer's Odyssey 1–2.* Uppsala.
  (2014b) 'The blind bard and "I": Homeric biography and authorial personas in the twelfth century', *BMGS* 38/1: 49–67.
  (2016) *Eustathios of Thessalonike: Commentary on Homer's Odyssey, vol. 1: On Rhapsodies α–β.* Uppsala.
Cupane, C. (1993) 'La figura di Fortuna nella letteratura greca medievale', in *Origini della letteratura neograeca*, ed. N. Panagiotakis. Venice, 413–37.
Dauterman Maguire, E. and H. Maguire (2007) *Other Icons: Art and Power in Byzantine Secular Culture.* Princeton.
Delobette, L. (2005) 'L'empereur et la chasse à Byzance du XIe au XIIe siècle', in *La forêt dans tous ses états : de la Préhistoire à nos jours*, ed. J.-P. Chabin. Besançon, 283–96.

de Man, P. (1979) *Allegories of Reading: Figural Language in Rousseau, Nietzsche, Rilke, and Proust*. New Haven.
Dennis, G. T. (2009) 'Some notes on hunting in Byzantium', in *Anathemata Erotika: Studies in honor of Thomas F. Mathews*, ed. J. D. Alchermes, H. C. Evans and T. K. Thomas. Mainz, 131–4.
Drpić, I. (2016) *Epigram, Art, and Devotion in Later Byzantium*. Cambridge.
Eco, U. (1979) *The Role of the Reader*. Bloomington.
  (1990) *The Limits of Interpretation*. Bloomington.
  (1992) *Interpretation and Overinterpretation*. Cambridge, Mass.
  (1994) *Six Walks in the Fictional Woods*. Cambridge, Mass.
Eliot, T. S. (1950) 'Tradition and the individual talent', in *Selected Essays*. New York, 3–11. First published in *The Egoist* (1919), then in *The Sacred Wood* (1920).
Ferguson, F. (2003) 'Wordsworth and the meaning of taste', in *The Cambridge Companion to Wordsworth*, ed. S. Gill. Cambridge, 90–107.
Foskolou, V. (2018) 'Decoding Byzantine ekphraseis on works of art: Constantine Manasses's description of earth and its audience', *BZ* 111/1: 71–102.
Galatariotou, K. (1993) 'Travel and perception in Byzantium', *DOP* 47: 221–41.
Gallavotti, C. (1983) 'Nota sulla schedografia di Moscopulo e suoi precedenti fino a Teodoro Prodromo', *Bollettino dei Classici*, ser. III, 4: 3–35.
Garzya, A. (1955/57) 'Paraphrasis Dionysii poematis de aucupio', *Byz* 25/27: 195–240.
  (1981) 'Testi letterari d'uso strumentale', *JÖB* 31/3: 263–87.
Geertz, C. (1973) 'Thick description: toward an interpretive theory of culture', in *The Interpretation of Cultures: Selected Essays*. New York, 3–30.
Gellner, E. (1977) 'Patrons and clients', in *Patrons and Clients in Mediterranean Societies*, ed. E. Gellner and J. Waterbury. London, 1–6.
Genette, G. (1991) *Fiction et diction*. Paris.
  (1992) *Palimpsestes : la littérature au second degré*. Paris.
Genova, N. (1993) 'Vorläufige Bemerkungen über eine anonyme spätgriechische Prosaparaphrase des Konstantinos Manasses', in *Origini della letteratura Neogreca: Atti del Secondo Congresso Internazionale 'Neograeca Medii Aevi' (Venezia, 7–10 novembre 1991)*, vol. 2, ed. N. M. Panagiotakis. Venice, 545–50.
George, D. (2001) 'Manuel I Komnenos and Michael Glycas: a twelfth-century defence and refutation of astrology', *Culture and Cosmos* 5/1: 3–47.
Goldwyn, A. (2014) '"I come from a cursed land and from the depths of darkness": life after death in Greek laments about the fall of Constantinople', in *Wanted: Byzantium – The Desire for a Lost Empire*, ed. I. Nilsson and P. Stephenson. Uppsala, 93–108.
  (2017) *Byzantine Ecocriticism: Humans, Nature, and Power in the Medieval Greek Romance*. New York.
Grabas, K. (2015) 'How to build your author brand from scratch (and why you need to)', www.thebookdesigner.com/2015/12/how-to-build-your-author-brand-from-scratch-and-why-you-need-to/ (last accessed 20 January 2020).

Greenblatt, S. (1980) *Renaissance Self-fashioning: From More to Shakespeare*. Chicago.
Grégoire, H. (1924) 'Un continuateur de Constantin Manassès et sa source', in *Mélanges offerts à M. Gustave Schlumberger*, vol. 2. Paris, 272–81.
Grünbart, M. (ed.) (2011) *Geschenke erhalten die Freundschaft: Gabentausch und Netzwerkpflege im europäischen Mittelalter*. Münster.
Hägg, T. (2006) 'The ancient Greek novel: a single model or a plurality of forms?', in *The Novel*, vol. 1, ed. F. Moretti. Princeton, 122–55.
Hegel, G. W. F. (1970) *Vorlesungen über die Ästhetik*, vol. 3. Frankfurt am Main.
Heher, D. (2013) 'Der Tod am Pfahl', *JÖB* 63: 127–51.
Herman, D. (2002) *Story Logic: Problems and Possibilities of Narrative*. Lincoln, Nebr. and London.
 (2014) 'Cognitive narratology', in *Handbook of Narratology*, vol. 1, ed. P. Hühn et al. Göttingen, 46–64.
Hilberg, I. (1876) *Eustathii Macrembolitae Protonobilissimi de Hysmines et Hysminiae Amoribus Libri xi*. Vienna.
Hill, B. (1999) *Imperial Women in Byzantium 1025–1204: Power, Patronage and Ideology*. Harlow.
Hinterberger, M. (2011) 'Phthonos als treibende Kraft in Prodromos, Manasses und Bryennios', *MEG* 11: 83–106.
 (2013) *Phthonos: Mißgunst, Neid und Eifersucht in der byzantinischen Literatur*. Wiesbaden.
 (forthcoming) 'The neighbour's unbearable wellbeing: phthonos/envy in Byzantine literature and beyond', in *Managing Emotion: Passions, Emotions, Affects, and Imaginings in Byzantium*, ed. M. Mullett and S. Ashbrook Harvey. Abingdon.
Holt, D. B. (2004) *How Brands Become Icons: The Principles of Cultural Branding*. Boston.
Hörandner, W. (1974) *Theodoros Prodromos: Historische Gedichte*. Vienna.
 (1981) *Der Prosarhythmus in der rhetorischen Literatur der Byzantiner*. Vienna.
 (1987) 'Customs and beliefs as reflected in occasional poetry: some considerations', *ByzF* 12: 235–47.
 (1993) 'Das Bild des Anderen: Lateiner und Barbaren in der Sicht der byzantinischen Hofpoesie', *BSl* 54: 162–8.
 (2003) 'Court poetry: questions of motifs, structures and functions', in *Rhetoric in Byzantium: Papers from the Thirty-fifth Spring Symposium of Byzantine Studies, Exeter College, University of Oxford, March 2001*, ed. E. Jeffreys. Aldershot, 75–85.
 (2007) 'Zur Topik byzantinischer Widmungs- und Einleitungsgedichte', in *Dulce melos: La poesia tardoantica e medievale*, ed. V. Panagal. Alessandria, 319–36.
 (2017) *Forme et fonction : remarques sur la poésie dans la société byzantine*. Paris.
 (2019) 'Teaching with verse in Byzantium', in *The Brill Companion to Byzantine Poetry*, ed. W. Hörandner, A. Rhoby and N. Zagklas. Leiden, 459–86.

Horna, K. (1902) 'Einige unedierte Stücke des Manasses und Italikos', *Progr. Sophiengymnasium*. Vienna, 3–26.
  (1904) 'Das Hodoiporikon des Konstantin Manasses', *BZ* 13: 313–55.
  (1905) *Analekten zur byzantinischen Literatur*. Vienna.
  (1906) 'Eine unedierte Rede des Konstantin Manasses', *Wiener Studien* 28: 171–204.
Hunger, H. (1969/70) 'On the imitation (MIMHSIS) of antiquity in Byzantine literature', *DOP* 23–4: 17–38.
  (1978) *Die hochsprachliche profane Literatur der Byzantiner* (Handbuch der Altertumswissenschaft 12.5.1–2). Munich.
Iadevaia, F. (2000–8) *Anonymi Historia Imperatorum: Introduzione, testo critico, versione italiana, note e indici*, vol. 1 and 2a–c. Messina.
Iorga, N. (1934) *Histoire de la vie byzantine: empire et civilisation; d'après les sources*, vol. 3: *L'Empire de pénétration latine (1081–1453)*. Bucharest.
Jannidis, F. (2000) 'Autor und Interpretation. Einleitung', in *Texte zur Theorie der Autorschaft*, ed. F. Jannidis et al. Stuttgart, 7–29.
Jeffreys, E. (1979) 'The attitudes of Byzantine chroniclers towards ancient history', *Byz* 49: 199–238.
  (1980) 'The Comnenian background to the *romans d'antiquité*', *Byz* 50: 455–86.
  (1984) 'Western infiltration of the Byzantine aristocracy: some suggestions', in *The Byzantine Aristocracy: IX to XIII Centuries*, ed. M. Angold. Oxford, 202–10.
  (2010) 'Rhetoric in Byzantium', in *A Companion to Greek Rhetoric*, ed. I. Worthington. Malden, Mass., 166–84.
  (2012) *Four Byzantine Novels: Theodore Prodromos, Rhodanthe and Dosikles; Eumathios Makrembolites, Hysmine and Hysminias; Constantine Manasses, Aristandros and Kallithea; Niketas Eugenianos, Drosilla and Charikles*. Liverpool.
  (2014) 'The *sebastokratorissa* Irene as Patron', in *Female Founders in Byzantium and Beyond*, ed. L. Theis, M. Mullett and M. Grünbart = *Wiener Jahrbuch für Kunstgeschichte* 60/61 (2011/2012): 175–92.
Jeffreys, E. and M. Jeffreys (2001) 'The "wild beast from the west": immediate literary reactions in Byzantium to the second crusade', in *The Crusades from the Perspective of Byzantium and the Muslim World*, ed. A. E. Laiou and R. P. Mottahedeh. Washington, D.C., 101–16.
Jeffreys, M. (1974) 'The nature and origin of political verse', *DOP* 28: 141–95.
  (2003) '"Rhetorical" texts', in *Rhetoric in Byzantium: Papers from the Thirty-fifth Spring Symposium of Byzantine Studies, Exeter College, University of Oxford, March 2001*, ed. E. Jeffreys. Aldershot, 87–100.
Jouanno, C. (2014) 'Pratique de l'emprunt dans les chroniques universelles byzantines: l'exemple de la matière troyenne', *Kentron* 30: 83–108.
Jusdanis, G. 2010. *Fiction Agonistes: In Defence of Literature*. Stanford.
Kaldellis, A. (2007) *Hellenism in Byzantium: The Transformations of Greek Identity and the Reception of the Classical Tradition*. Cambridge.

(2009a) *The Christian Parthenon: Classicism and Pilgrimage in Byzantine Athens.* Cambridge.
(2009b) 'Classical scholarship in twelfth-century Byzantium', in *Medieval Greek Commentaries on the Nicomachean Ethics*, ed. C. Barber and D. Jenkins. Leiden, 1–43.
(2019) *Romanland: Ethnicity and Empire in Byzantium.* Cambridge, Mass.
Karla, G. (2006) 'Maximos Planudes: Dr. Bowdler in Byzanz? Zensur und Innovation im späten Byzanz', *Classica et Mediaevalia* 57: 213–38.
(2008) 'Das literarische Porträt Kaiser Manuels I. Komnenos in den Kaiserreden des 12. Jh.', *BZ* 101: 669–79.
Karpozilos, A. (2009) Βυζαντινοί ιστορικοί καί χρονογράφοι. Τόμ. Γ (*1105–1205 αί.*). Athens.
Kazhdan, A. and G. Constable (1982) *People and Power in Byzantium.* Washington, D.C.
Kazhdan, A. P. and A. W. Epstein (1985) *Change in Byzantine Culture in the Eleventh and Twelfth Centuries.* Berkeley.
Kazhdan, A. P. and S. Franklin (1984) *Studies on Byzantine Literature of the Eleventh and Twelfth Centuries.* Cambridge and Paris.
Keller, A., E. Lösel, U. Wels and V. Wels (eds.) (2010) *Theorie und Praxis der Kasualdichtung in der frühen Neuzeit.* Amsterdam and New York.
Kiapidou, E.-S. (2009) 'Ὁ λογοτέχνης Κωνσταντίνος Μανασσής συγγράφει Σύνοψη Χρονική. Οι πηγές του για την εξιστόρηση της πρωτοβυζαντινής περιόδου', in *Realia Byzantina*, ed. S. Kotzabassi and G. Mavromatis. Berlin and New York, 57–66.
Kislinger, E. (2008) 'Von Drachen und anderem wilden Getier. Fremdenfeindlichkeit in Byzanz?', in *Laetae segetes iterum*, ed. I. Radová. Brno, 389–404.
Kolovou, F. (2006) *Die Briefe des Eustathios von Thessalonike: Einleitung, Regesten, Text, Indizes.* Munich and Leipzig.
Konstantinidis, D. C. (1989) 'Ἀνδρονίκου Παλαιολόγου Κεφάλαια περὶ ἀρετῆς καὶ κακίας. Κριτική ἔκδοση', *Byzantina* 15 (1989) 179–236.
Koukoules, F. (1932) 'Κυνηγετικὰ ἐκ τῆς ἐποχῆς τῶν Κομνηνῶν καὶ τῶν Παλαιολόγων', *Epistimoniki Etaireia Byzantinon Spoudon* 9: 3–33.
(1952) Βυζαντινῶν Βίος καὶ Πολιτισμός, vol. 5. Athens.
Krumbacher, K. (1897 [1891]). *Geschichte der byzantinischen Litteratur von Justinian bis zum Ende des oströmischen Reiches (527–1453)* (Handbuch der klassischen Altertumswissenschaft 9.1). Munich.
Kubina, K. (2018) 'Manuel Philes – a begging poet? Requests, letters and problems of genre definition', in *Middle and Late Byzantine Poetry: Texts and Contexts*, ed. A. Rhoby and N. Zagklas. Turnhout, 147–81.
(2020) *Die enkomiastische Dichtung des Manuel Philes: Form und Funktion des literarischen Lobes in der Gesellschaft der frühen Palaiologenzeit.* Berlin.
Kulhánková, M. (2008) 'Parallelen zur antiken Literatur in der byzantinischen Betteldichtung', *Sborník prací* 13/1: 81–95.

(2010) 'Die byzantinische Betteldichtung: Verbindung des Klassischen mit dem Volkstümlichen', in *Imitatio – variatio – aemulatio: Internationales wissenschaftliches Symposion zur byzantinischen Sprache und Literatur, Wien 22–25 Oktober 2008*, ed. A. Rhoby and E. Schiffer. Vienna, 57–79.

Külzer, A. (1994) *Peregrinatio graeca in Terram Sanctam. Studien zu Pilgerführern und Reisebeschreibungen über Syrien, Palästina und den Sinai aus byzantinischer und metabyzantinischer Zeit*. Frankfurt am Main.

(2002) 'Byzantine and early post-Byzantine pilgrimage to the Holy Land and to Mount Sinai', in *Travel in the Byzantine World*, ed. R. Macrides. Aldershot, 149–61.

(2003) 'Konstantinos Manasses und Johannes Phokas – zwei byzantinische Orientreisende des 12. Jahrhunderts', in *Erkundung und Beschreibung der Welt*, ed. X. von Ertzdorff. Amsterdam, 185–209.

(2018) 'Some notes on falconry in Byzantium', in *Raptor and Human – Falconry and Bird Symbolism throughout the Millennia on a Global Scale*, ed. K.-H. Gersmann and O. Grimm. Kiel and Hamburg, 699–706.

Küpper, J., P. Oster and C. Rivoletti (eds.) (2018) *Gelegenheit macht Dichter. L'Occasione fa il poeta. Bausteine zu einer Theorie des Gelegenheitsgedichts*. Heidelberg.

Kurtz, E. (1900) 'Dva proizvedenija Konstantina Manassi, otnosjashchiesja k smerti Theodori Kontostefanini', *VizVrem* 7: 621–45.

(1906) 'Eshje dva neizdannyh proizvedenija Konstantina Manassii', *VizVrem* 12: 69–98.

(1910) 'Evstafija Fessalonikijskago i Konstantina Manassii monodii na konchiny Nikifora Komnina', *VizVrem* 17: 283–322.

Kuttner-Homs, S. (2016) *L'héritage de la littérature antique autoréférentielle dans l'œuvre de Nicétas Chôniatès*, 2 vols. Diss. Caen.

(2018) 'Le roman de Thèbes : l'autocitation comme stratégie narrative dans l'*Histoire* de Nicétas Chôniatès', in *Storytelling in Byzantium: Narratological Approaches to Byzantine Texts and Images*, ed. Ch. Messis, M. Mullett and I. Nilsson. Uppsala, 235–62.

Lampsides, O. (1969) 'Κωνσταντίνος Μανασσῆς καὶ Καισάριος Δαπόντες', *Parnassos* 11: 84–8.

(1980) *Δημοσιεύματα περὶ τὴν Χρονικὴν Σύνοψιν Κωνσταντίνου τοῦ Μανασσῆ*. Athens.

(1984) 'Zur Sebastokratorissa Eirene', *JÖB* 34: 91–105.

(1985) 'Les « gnomologia » tirés de la Chronique de K. Manassès', *Byz* 55: 118–45.

(1987) 'Verse des Konstantinos Manasses über Darius I.', *BZ* 80: 334–5.

(1988) 'Zur Biographie von K. Manasses und zu seiner *Chronike Synopsis* (CS)', *Byz* 58: 97–111.

(1991) 'Der vollständige Text der Ἔκφρασις γῆς des Konstantinos Manasses', *JÖB* 41: 189–205.

(1996) *Constantini Manassi Breviarium Chronicum*. Athens.

Lardinois, A. (1989) 'Lesbian Sappho and Sappho of Lesbos', in *From Sappho to de Sade: Moments in the History of Sexuality*, ed. J. Bremmer. London and New York, 15–35.
  (2010) 'Lesbian Sappho revisited', in *Myths, Martyrs, and Modernity: Studies in the History of Religions in Honour of Jan N. Bremmer*, ed. J. Dijkstra, J. Kroesen and Y. Kuiper. Leiden and Boston, 13–30.
  (2014) 'Introduction', in D. J. Rayor, *Sappho: A New Translation of the Complete Works*. Cambridge, 1–17.
Laurent, V. (1946) 'Nicolas Iorga, historien de la vie byzantine', *REB* 4/1: 5–23.
Lauxtermann, M. D. (2003) *Byzantine Poetry from Pisides to Geometres: Texts and Contexts*, vol. 1. Vienna.
  (2009) 'Byzantine didactic poetry and the question of poeticality', in *« Doux remède... » Poésie et poétique à Byzance*, ed. P. Odorico, P. A. Agapitos and M. Hinterberger. Paris, 37–46.
  (2014) 'Tomi, Mljet, Malta: critical notes on a twelfth-century Southern Italian poem of exile', *JÖB* 64: 155–76.
  (2021) 'Of cats and mice: the *Katomyomachia* as drama, parody, school text, and animal tale', in *Byzantine Poetry in the 'Long' Twelfth Century (1081–1204)*, ed. B. van den Berg and N. Zagklas. Cambridge, forthcoming.
Lefkowitz, M. R. (2012 [1981]). *The Lives of the Greek Poets*. Baltimore.
Littlewood, A. R. (ed.) (1995) *Originality in Byzantine Literature, Art and Music: A Collection of Essays*. Oxford.
Littlewood, A. R. (1999) 'The Byzantine letter of consolation in the Macedonian and Komnenian periods', *DOP* 53: 19–41.
Livanos, C. (2006) 'Michael Choniates, poet of love and knowledge', *BMGS* 30/2: 103–14.
Ljubarskij, J. (2003) 'How should a Byzantine text be read?', in *Rhetoric in Byzantium: Papers from the Thirty-fifth Spring Symposium of Byzantine Studies, Exeter College, University of Oxford, March 2001*, ed. E. Jeffreys. Aldershot, 117–25.
Lodge, D. (1976) 'The language of modernist fiction: metaphor and metonymy', in *Modernism: A Guide to European Literature 1890–1930*, ed. M. Bradbury and J. McFarlane. London, 481–96.
Lord, L. E. (1935) 'Horace as an occasional poet', *The Classical Journal* 31/3: 152–66.
Loukaki, M. (2001) 'Τυμβωρῦχοι καὶ σκυλευτὲς νεκρῶν: Οι απόψεις του Νικολάου Καταφλώρον για τη ρητορική και τους ρήτορες στην Κωνσταντινούπολη του 12ου αιώνα', *Symmeikta* 14: 143–66.
Lovato, V. F. (2016) 'Hellenizing Cato? A short survey of the concepts of Greekness, romanity and barbarity in John Tzetzes', in *Cross-Cultural Exchange in the Byzantine World, c. 300–1500 A.D.*, ed. K. Stewart and J. M. Wakely. Oxford and New York, 143–57.
Lytle, G. F. and S. Orgel (1981) *Patronage in the Renaissance*. Princeton.
Maas, P. (1902) 'Rhythmisches zu der Kunstprosa des Konstantinos Manasses', *BZ* 11: 505–12.

MacAlister, S. (1996) *Dreams and Suicides: The Greek Novel from Antiquity to the Byzantine Empire*. London and New York.
Macrides, R. and P. Magdalino (1988) 'The architecture of ekphrasis: construction and context of Paul the Silentiary's poem on Hagia Sophia', *BMGS* 12: 47–82.
Magdalino, P. (1984) 'Byzantine snobbery', in *The Byzantine Aristocracy: IX to XIII Centuries*, ed. M. Angold. Oxford, 58–78.
   (1988) 'The phenomenon of Manuel I Komnenos', in *Byzantium and the West c. 850–c. 1200*, ed. J. D. Howard-Johnston. Amsterdam, 171–200.
   (1992) 'Eros the king and the king of amours: some observations on *Hysmine and Hysminias*', *DOP* 46: 197–204.
   (1993) *The Empire of Manuel I Komnenos, 1143–1180*. Cambridge.
   (1997) 'In search of the Byzantine courtier: Leo Choirosphaktes and Constantine Manasses', in *Byzantine Court Culture from 829 to 1204*, ed. H. Maguire. Washington, D.C., 141–65.
   (2000) 'Constantinople and the outside world', in *Strangers to Themselves: The Byzantine Outsider*, ed. D. C. Smythe. Aldershot, 149–62.
   (2006) *L'orthodoxie des astrologues: La science entre le dogme et la divination à Byzance (VIIe–XIVe siècle)*. Paris.
   (2015) 'Debunking astrology in twelfth-century Constantinople', in *'Pour une poétique de Byzance': Hommage à Vassilis Katsaros*, ed. Ch. Messis and P. Odorico. Paris, 165–75.
Maguire, H. (1992) 'Byzantine art history in the second half of the twentieth century', in *Byzantium: A World Civilization*, ed. A. E. Laiou and H. Maguire. Washington, D.C., 119–55.
   (2011) '"Signs and symbols of your always victorious reign": the political ideology and meaning of falconry in Byzantium', in *Images of the Byzantine World: Visions, Messages and Meanings. Studies Presented to Leslie Brubaker*, ed. A. Lymberopoulou. Farnham, 135–46.
Makk, F. (1989) *The Arpads and the Comneni: Political Relations between Hungary and Byzantium in the 12th Century*. Budapest.
Mango, C. (1963) 'Antique statuary and the Byzantine beholder', *DOP* 17: 55–75.
   (1972) *The Art of the Byzantine Empire, 312–1453: Sources and Documents*. Englewood Cliffs, N.J.
   (1975) 'Byzantine literature as a distorting mirror'. An inaugural lecture delivered before the University of Oxford on 21 May 1974. Oxford.
Marciniak, P. (2004). *Greek Drama in Byzantine Times*. Katowice.
   (2007) 'Byzantine theatron: a place of performance?', in *Theatron: Rhetorische Kultur in Spätantike und Mittelalter*, ed. M. Grünbart. Berlin and New York, 277–86.
   (2013) 'The undead in Byzantium: some notes on the reception of ancient literature in twelfth-century Byzantium', *Troianalexandrina* 13: 95–111.
   (2014) 'The Byzantine performative turn', in *Within the Circle of Ancient Ideas and Virtues: Studies in Honour of Professor Maria Dzielska*, ed. K. Twardowska et al. Krakow, 423–30.

(2017) 'A pious mouse and a deadly cat: the *Schede tou Myos*, attributed to Theodore Prodromos', *GRBS* 57: 507–27.

Marciniak, P. and K. Warcaba (2014) 'Racing with rhetoric: a Byzantine ekphrasis of a chariot race', *BZ* 107/1: 97–112.

(2018) 'Theodore Prodromos' *Katomyomachia* as a Byzantine version of mock-epic', in *Middle and Late Byzantine Poetry: Texts and Contexts*, ed. A. Rhoby and N. Zagklas. Turnhout, 97–110.

Marcovich, I. (1987) 'The *Itinerary* of Constantine Manasses', *Illinois Classical Studies* 12/2: 277–91.

(2001) *Eustathius Macrembolites, De Hysmines et Hysminiae amoribus libri XI*. Munich and Leipzig.

Markopoulos, A. (2005) 'Βυζαντινή εκπαίδευση και οικουμενικότητα', in *Byzantium as Oecumene*, ed. E. Chrysos. Athens, 183–200.

(2006) 'De la structure de l'école byzantine. Le maître, les livres et le processus éducatif', in *Lire et écrire à Byzance*, ed. B. Mondrain. Paris, 85–96.

(2008) 'Education', in *The Oxford Handbook of Byzantine Studies*, ed. E. Jeffreys et al. Oxford, 785–95.

Mazal, O. (1966) 'Neue Excerpte aus dem Roman des Konstantinos Manasses', *JÖB* 15: 231–59.

(1967a) 'Das moralische Lehrgedicht in Cod. Par. gr. 2750A – ein Werk eines Nachahmers und Plagiators des Konstantinos Manasses', *BZ* 60: 249–68.

(1967b) *Der Roman des Konstantinos Manasses: Überlieferung, Rekonstruktion, Textausgabe der Fragmente*. Vienna.

Mercati, S. G. (1927) 'Intorno agli Σχέδη μυός', *Studi Byzantini* 2: 13–17.

Messis, Ch. (2014) *Les eunuques à Byzance, entre réalité et imaginaire*. Paris.

Messis, Ch., M. Mullett and I. Nilsson (eds) (2018) *Storytelling in Byzantium: Narratological Approaches to Byzantine Texts and Images*. Uppsala.

Messis, Ch., and I. Nilsson (2015) 'Constantin Manassès, *La Description d'un petit homme*: introduction, texte, traduction et commentaires', *JÖB* 65: 169–94.

(2019) 'The *Description of a Crane Hunt* by Constantine Manasses: introduction, text and translation', *Scandinavian Journal for Byzantine and Modern Greek Studies* 5: 9–89.

(2021) 'Constantine Manasses, *Description of a little man* (translation with brief introduction and comments)', in *Texts on Byzantine Art and Aesthetics: The Visual Culture of Later Byzantium (1081–c.1350)*, ed. C. Barber and F. Spingou. Cambridge, in press.

Meunier, F. (2016) *Théodore Prodrome: Crime et châtiment chez les souris*. Paris.

Miller, C. R. (1984) 'Genre as social action', *Quarterly Journal of Speech* 70: 151–67.

Miller, E. (1872) 'Description d'une chasse à l'once par un écrivain byzantin au XIIe siècle de notre ère', *Annuaire de l'Association pour l'encouragement des études grecques en France* 6: 28–52.

(1875) 'Poème moral de Constantin Manassès', *Annuaire de l'Association pour l'encouragement des études grecques en France* 9: 23–75.

Miller, T. S. (2003a) 'Two teaching texts from the twelfth-century Orphanotropheion', in *Byzantine Authors: Literary Activities and Preoccupations*, ed. J. W. Nesbitt. Leiden, 9–20.
  (2003b) *The Orphans of Byzantium: Child Welfare in the Christian Empire*. Washington, D.C.
Mioni, E. (1985) *Bibliothecae divi Marci Venetiarum codices graeci manuscripti: Thesaurus antiquus*, 3 vols. Rome.
Müller, K. K. (1884) 'Neue Mitteilungen über Janos Laskaris und die Mediceische Bibliothek', *Centralblatt für Bibliothekswesen* 1, 9/10: 333–411.
Mullett, M. (1981) 'The classical tradition in the Byzantine letter', in *Byzantium and the Classical Tradition*, ed. M. Mullett and R. Scott. Birmingham, 75–93.
  (1984) 'Aristocracy and patronage in the literary circles of Comnenian Constantinople', in *The Byzantine Aristocracy: IX to XIII Centuries*, ed. M. Angold. Oxford, 173–97.
  (1988) 'Byzantium: a friendly society?', *Past & Present* 118: 3–24.
  (1990) 'Patronage in action: the problems of an eleventh-century bishop', in *Church and People in Byzantium*, ed. R. Morris. Birmingham, 125–47.
  (1992) 'The madness of genre', *DOP* 46: 235–43.
  (1995) 'Originality in the Byzantine letter: the case of exile', in *Originality in Byzantine Literature, Art and Music*, ed. A. R. Littlewood. Oxford, 39–58 (reprinted in Mullett 2007 as no. IV).
  (1997) *Theophylact of Ochrid: Reading the Letters of a Byzantine Archbishop*. Aldershot.
  (2002) 'In peril on the sea; travel genres and the unexpected', in *Travel in the Byzantine World*, ed. R. Macrides. Aldershot, 259–84.
  (2003) 'Rhetoric, theory and the imperative of performance: Byzantium and now', in *Rhetoric in Byzantium*, ed. E. Jeffreys. Oxford, 151–71.
  (2007) *Letters, Literacy and Literature in Byzantium*. Aldershot.
  (2010) 'No drama, no poetry, no fiction, no readership, no literature', in *A Companion to Byzantium*, ed. L. James. Oxford, 227–38.
  (2013a) 'Tented ceremony: ephemeral performances under the Komnenoi', in *Court Ceremonies and Rituals of Power in Byzantium and the Medieval Mediterranean: Comparative Perspectives*, ed. A. Beihammer, S. Constantinou and M. G. Parani. Leiden, 487–513.
  (2013b) 'Experiencing the Byzantine text, experiencing the Byzantine tent', in *Experiencing Byzantium*, ed. C. Nesbitt and M. Jackson. Farnham, 269–91.
  (2017) 'Performing court literature in Byzantium: tales told in tents', in *In the Presence of Power: Courts and Performance in the Premodern Middle East, 700–1600*, ed. M. Pomerantz and E. Birge Witz. New York, 121–41.
  (2018) 'Object, text and performance in four Komnenian tent poems', in *Reading Byzantium*, ed. T. Shawcross and I. Toth. Cambridge, 414–29.
Nesseres, E. Ch. (2014) *Η Παιδεία στην Κωνσταντινούπολη κατά τον 12ο αιώνα*. Diss. Ioannina.

Neville, L. (2012) *Heroes and Romans in Twelfth-Century Byzantium: The Material for History of Nikephoros Bryennios*. Cambridge.
  (2013) 'Lamentation, history, and female authorship in Anna Komnene's *Alexiad*', *GRBS* 53/1: 192–218.
  (2014) 'The authorial voice of Anna Komnēnē', in *The Author in Middle Byzantine Literature: Modes, Functions, and Identities*, ed. A. Pizzone. Berlin, 263–74.
  (2016) *Anna Komnene: The Life and Work of a Medieval Historian*. Oxford.
  (2018) *Guide to Byzantine Historical Writing*. Cambridge.
Nilsson, I. (2001) *Erotic Pathos, Rhetorical Pleasure: Narrative Technique and Mimesis in Eumathios Makrembolites' Hysmine & Hysminias*. Uppsala.
  (2005) 'Narrating images in Byzantine literature: the ekphraseis of Konstantinos Manasses', *JÖB* 55: 121–46.
  (2006) 'Discovering literariness in the past: literature vs. history in the *Synopsis Chronike* of Konstantinos Manasses', in *L'écriture de la mémoire: la littérarité de l'historiographie*, ed. P. Odorico, P. A. Agapitos and M. Hinterberger. Paris, 15–31.
  (2010) 'The same story but another: a reappraisal of literary imitation in Byzantium', in *Imitatio – variatio – aemulatio: Internationales wissenschaftliches Symposion zur byzantinischen Sprache und Literatur, Wien 22–25 Oktober 2008*, ed. A. Rhoby and E. Schiffer. Vienna, 195–208.
  (2011) 'Constantine Manasses, Odysseus and the Cyclops: on Byzantine appreciation of pagan art in the twelfth century', in *Ekphrasis: la représentation des monuments dans les littératures byzantine et byzantino-slaves – Réalités et imaginaires* = *BSl* 69: 123–36.
  (2012) 'La douceur des dons abondants: patronage et littérarité dans la Constantinople des Comnènes', in *La face cachée de la littérature byzantine: le texte en tant que message immédiat*, ed. P. Odorico. Paris, 179–93.
  (2013) 'Nature controlled by artistry: the poetics of the literary garden in Byzantium', in *Byzantine Gardens and Beyond*, ed. H. Bodin and R. Hedlund. Uppsala, 15–29.
  (2014) *Raconter Byzance: la littérature au XIIe siècle*. Paris.
  (2016) 'Words, water, and power: literary fountains and metaphors of patronage in 11th- and 12th-century Byzantium', in *Fountains and Water Culture in Byzantium*, ed. P. Stephenson and B. Shields. Cambridge, 265–80.
  (2017) 'Comforting tears and suggestive smiles: to laugh and cry in the Komnenian novel', in *Greek Laughter and Tears: Late Antiquity, Byzantium and Beyond*, ed. M. Alexiou and D. Cairns. Edinburgh, 291–311.
  (2019) 'The past as poetry: two Byzantine world chronicles in verse', in *The Brill Companion to Byzantine Poetry*, ed. A. Rhoby, W. Hörandner and N. Zagklas. Leiden and Boston, 517–38.
  (2021a) 'The literary voice of a chronicler – the *Synopsis Chronike* of Konstantinos Manasses', in *The Brill Companion to Byzantine Chronicles*, ed. R. Tocci. Leiden, in press.

(2021b) 'Describing, experiencing, narrating: the use of ekphrasis in the eleventh to thirteenth centuries', in *Texts on Byzantine Art and Aesthetics: The Visual Culture of Later Byzantium (1081–c.1350)*, ed. C. Barber and F. Spingou. Cambridge, in press.

Nilsson, I. and E. Nyström (2009) 'To compose, read, and use a Byzantine text: aspects of the chronicle of Constantine Manasses', *BMGS* 33/1: 42–60.

Nilsson, I. and N. Zagklas (2017) '"Hurry up, reap every flower of the *logoi*!" The use of Greek novels in Byzantium', *GRBS* 57: 1120–48.

Nimas, Th. A. (1984) Η « Ἔκφρασις κυνηγεσίου γεράνων » τοῦ Κωνσταντίνου Μανασσῆ. Εἰσαγωγή, Κείμενο, Μετάφραση, Σχόλια, Γλωσσάριο. Thessaloniki.

Ödekan, A., E. Akyürek and N. Necipoğlu (eds) (2010) *First International Sevgi Gonul Byzantine Studies Symposium: Change in the Byzantine World in the Twelfth and Thirteenth Centuries*. Istanbul.

Page, G. (2008) *Being Byzantine: Greek Identity before the Ottomans*. Cambridge.

Papaioannou, S. (2010) 'Letter-writing', in *The Byzantine World*, ed. P. Stephenson. London and New York, 188–99.

  (2012) 'Fragile literature: Byzantine letter-collections and the case of Michael Psellos', in *La face cachée de la littérature byzantine: le texte en tant que message immédiat*, ed. P. Odorico. Paris, 289–328.

  (2013) *Michael Psellos: Rhetoric and Authorship in Byzantium*. Cambridge.

  (2014) 'Voice, signature, mask: the Byzantine author', in *The Author in Middle Byzantine Literature: Modes, Functions, and Identities*, ed. A. Pizzone. Berlin, 21–40.

Papathomopoulos, M. (1976) Ἀνωνύμου παράφρασις τὰ Διονυσίου Ἰξευτικά. Ioannina.

Patlagean, E. (1992) 'De la chasse et du souverain', *DOP* 46: 257–63.

Paul, A. and A. Rhoby (2019) 'Einleitung', in *Konstantinos Manasses, Verschronik (Synopsis Chronike). Übersetzt und erläutert von Anneliese Paul und Andreas Rhoby*. Stuttgart, 1–61.

Peers, G. (2017) 'Sense lives of Byzantine things', in *Knowing Bodies, Passionate Souls: Sense Perceptions in Byzantium*, ed. S. Ashbrook Harvey and M. Mullett. Washington, D.C., 11–30.

Piccolomini, E. (1874) 'Intorno ai Collectanea di Massimo Planude', *Rivista di filologia e d'istruzione classica* 2: 101–17 and 149–63.

Pizzone, A. (2011) 'Sulle nere ali dei sogni. Constantino Manasse e l'ambiguità onirica', *BZ* 103/2: 679–98.

Pizzone, A. (ed.) (2014a) *The Author in Middle Byzantine Literature: Modes, Functions, and Identities*. Berlin.

  (2014b) 'Anonymity, dispossession and reappropriation in the Prolog of Nikephōros Basilakēs', in *The Author in Middle Byzantine Literature: Modes, Functions, and Identities*, ed. A. Pizzone. Berlin, 225–43.

  (2017) 'Tzetzes' *Historiai*: a Byzantine "Book of Memory"?', *BMGS* 41/2: 182–207.

(2018) 'The autobiographical subject in Tzetzes' *Chiliades*: an analysis of its components', in *Storytelling in Byzantium: Narratological Approaches to Byzantine Texts and Images*, ed. Ch. Messis, M. Mullett and I. Nilsson. Uppsala, 287–304.

Plepelits, K. (1989) *Eustathios Makrembolites, Hysmine und Hysminias. Eingeleitet, übersetzt und erläutert von Karl Plepelits*. Stuttgart.

Polemis, I. D. (1996) 'Fünf unedierte Texte des Konstantinos Manasses', *RSBN* 33: 279–92.

Praechter, K. (1895) 'Eine vulgärgriechische Paraphrase der Chronik des Konstantinos Manasses', *BZ* 4: 272–313.

(1898) 'Zur vulgären Paraphrase des Konstantinos Manasses', *BZ* 7: 588–93.

Reinsch, D. R. (2002) '*Historia ancilla litterarum*? Zum literarischen Geschmack in der Komnenenzeit: das Beispiel der *Synopsis Chronike* des Konstantinos Manasses', in *Pour une «nouvelle» histoire de la littérature byzantine*, ed. P. Odorico and P. A. Agapitos. Paris, 81–94.

(2007) 'Die Palamedes-Episode in der Synopsis Chronike des Konstantinos Manasses und ihre Inspirationsquelle', in *Byzantinische Sprachkunst: Studien zur byzantinischen Literatur gewidmet Wolfram Hörandner zum 65. Geburtstag*, ed. M. Hinterberger and E. Schiffer. Berlin and New York, 266–76.

(2010) 'Der Autor ist tot – es lebe der Leser. Zur Neubewertung der imitatio in der byzantinischen Geschichtsschreibung', in *Imitatio – variatio – aemulatio, Internationales wissenschaftliches Symposion zur byzantinischen Sprache und Literatur, Wien 22–25 Oktober 2008*, ed. A. Rhoby and E. Schiffer. Vienna, 23–32.

Rhoby, A. (2009) 'Verschiedene Bemerkungen zur Sebastokratorissa Eirene und zu Autoren in ihrem Umfeld', *Nea Rhome* 6: 305–36.

(2010) 'Zur Identifizierung von bekannten Autoren im Codex Marcianus graecus 524', *MEG* 10: 167–204.

(2014) 'Quellenforschung am Beispiel der Chronik des Konstantinos Manasses', in *The Transmission of Byzantine Texts: Between Textual Criticism and Quellenforschung*, ed. I. Pérez Martín and J. Signes Codoñer. Turnhout, 391–417.

(2015) '"When the year ran through six times of thousands …": the date in (inscriptional) Byzantine epigrams', in *'Pour une poétique de Byzance': hommage à Vassilis Katsaros*, ed. S. Efthymiadis, P. Odorico and I. Polemis. Paris, 223–42.

Rhoby, A. (ed.) (2018) *Byzantinische Epigramme in inschriftlicher Überlieferung*, vol. 4. Vienna.

(forthcoming) 'Konstantinos Manasses', in *Lexikon byzantinischer Autoren*, ed. M. Grünbart and A. Riehle.

Rhoby, A. and N. Zagklas (2011) 'Zu einer möglichen Deutung von Πανιώτης', *JÖB* 61: 171–7.

Ryan, M.-L. (2003) 'Cognitive maps and the construction of narrative space', in *Narrative Theory and the Cognitive Sciences*, ed. D. Herman. Stanford, 214–42.

Said, E. W. (1983) *The World, the Text and the Critic*. Cambridge, Mass.
  (2006) *On Late Style: Music and Literature Against the Grain*. New York.
Saller, R. (1982) *Personal Patronage under the Early Empire*. Cambridge.
Schmidt, T. (2016) 'Protective and fierce: the emperor as a lion in contact with foreigners and his subjects in twelfth- and early thirteenth-century court literature', in *Cross-Cultural Exchange in the Byzantine World, c. 300–1500 A.D.*, ed. K. Stewart and J. M. Wakely. Oxford and New York, 159–73.
Scholes, R., J. Phelan and R. Kellogg (2006) *The Nature of Narrative*, 40th anniversary edition, revised and expanded. Oxford.
Schreiner, P. (1988) *Codices vaticani graeci: Codices 867–932*. Vatican City.
Shapiro, G. (1975) 'Hegel on the meanings of poetry', *Philosophy and Rhetoric* 8/2: 88–107.
Sideras, A. (1994) *Die byzantinischen Grabreden: Prosopographie, Datierung, Überlieferung; 142 Epitaphien und Monodien aus dem Byzantinischen Jahrtausend*. Vienna.
Signes Codoñer, J. (2005) 'Poesía clasicista bizantina en los siglos X–XII, entre tradición e innovación', in *Poesía medieval*, ed. V. Valcárcel Martínez and C. Pérez González. Madrid, 19–66.
Simelidis, Ch. (2015) 'Lustrous verse or expansive prose? The anonymous chapters in Parisinus gr. 2750A and Vaticanus gr. 1898', in '*Pour une poétique de Byzance': hommage à Vassilis Katsaros*, ed. S. Efthymiadis, P. Odorico and I. Polemis. Paris, 273–94.
Simpson, A. (2013) *Niketas Choniates: A Historiographical Study*. Oxford.
Sola, J. N. (1911) 'De Codice Laurentiano X plutei V', *BZ* 20: 373–83.
Spanos, A. (2014) 'Was innovation unwanted in Byzantium?', in *Wanted: Byzantium – The Desire for a Lost Empire*, ed. I. Nilsson and P. Stephenson. Uppsala, 43–56.
Spatharakis, I. (2004) *The Illustrations of the Cynegetica in Venice: Codex Marcianus Graecus Z 139*. Leiden.
Speake, G. (1993) 'Janus Lascaris' visit to Mount Athos in 1491', *GRBS* 34: 325–30.
Spiegel, G. (1990) 'History, historicism, and the social logic of the text in the Middle Ages', *Speculum* 65.1: 59–86.
Staten, H. (2010) 'Art as *techne*, or, The intentional fallacy and the unfinished project of formalism', in *A Companion to the Philosophy of Literature*, ed. G. L. Hagberg and W. Jost. Chichester, 420–35.
Stephenson, P. (1996) 'Manuel I Comnenus, the Hungarian crown and the "feudal subjection" of Hungary, 1162–1167', *BSl* 57: 33–59.
  (2000) *Byzantium's Balkan Recovery: A Political Study of the Northern Balkans, 900–1204*. Cambridge.
Sternbach, L. (1901) 'Analecta Manassea', *Eos* 7: 180–94.
  (1902) 'Beiträge zur Kunstgeschichte', *Jahreshefte des Österr. Arch. Institut* 5: Sp. 65–94.
Stouraitis, I. (2014) 'Roman identity in Byzantium: a critical approach', *BZ* 107/1: 175–220.

Taxidis, I. (2017) 'Ekphraseis of persons with deviational behaviour in Constantine Manasses' *Synopsis Chronike*', *Byzantina* 35: 145–59.
Theis, L., M. Mullett and M. Grünbart (eds) (2014) *Female Founders in Byzantium and Beyond* = *Wiener Jahrbuch für Kunstgeschichte* 60/61 (2011/2012). Vienna.
Tompkins, J. T. (1980) 'The reader in history: the changing shape of literary response', in *Reader-Response Criticism: From Formalism to Post-Structuralism*, ed. J. T. Tompkins. Baltimore and London, 201–32.
Trapp, E. (1993) 'Learned and vernacular literature in Byzantium: dichotomy or symbiosis?', *DOP* 47: 115–29.
Treadgold, W. (2013) *The Middle Byzantine Historians*. New York.
Tsolakis, E. Th. (1967) Συμβολὴ στὴ μελέτη τοῦ ποιητικοῦ ἔργου τοῦ Κωνσταντίνου Μανασσῆ καὶ κριτικὴ ἔκδοση τοῦ μυθιστορήματός του "Τὰ κατ' Ἀρίστανδρον καὶ Καλλιθέαν". Thessaloniki.
(2003) 'Το λεγόμενο «ηθικό ποίημα» του Κωνσταντίνου Μανασσή', *Hellenika* 53: 7–18.
Turyn, A. (1972) *Dated Greek Manuscripts of the Thirteenth and Fourteenth Centuries in the Libraries of Italy, I.* Urbana.
van den Berg, B. (2016) *Homer and Rhetoric in Byzantium: Eustathios of Thessalonike on the Composition of the Iliad*. Diss. Amsterdam.
van Opstall, E. (2008) *Jean Géomètre: Poèmes en hexamètres et en distiques élégiaques*. Leiden and Boston.
Vassis, I. (1993/94) '*Graeca sunt, non leguntur*. Zu den schedographischen Spielereien des Theodoros Prodromos', *BZ* 86/87: 1–19.
(2002) 'Τῶν νέων Φιλολόγων Παλαίσματα. Η συλλογή σχεδῶν του κώδικα Vaticanus Palatinus gr. 92', *Hellenika* 52: 37–68.
Veikou, M. (2018) '"Telling spaces" in Byzantium: ekphraseis, place-making and "thick description"', in *Storytelling in Byzantium: Narratological Approaches to Byzantine Texts and Images*, ed. Ch. Messis, M. Mullett and I. Nilsson. Uppsala, 15–32.
Volk, K. (2002) *The Poetics of Latin Didactic: Lucretius, Vergil, Ovid, Manilius*. Oxford.
Wassiliou-Seibt, A.-K. (2016) *Corpus der byzantinischen Siegel mit metrischen Legenden*, vol. 2: *Siegellegenden von Ny bis inklusive Sphragis*. Vienna.
Webb, R. (2003) 'Praise and persuasion: argumentation and audience response in epideictic oratory', in *Rhetoric in Byzantium: Papers from the Thirty-fifth Spring Symposium of Byzantine Studies, Exeter College, University of Oxford, March 2001*, ed. E. Jeffreys. Aldershot, 127–35.
(2009) *Ekphrasis, Imagination and Persuasion in Ancient Rhetorical Theory and Practice*. Farnham.
(2017) 'Spatiality, embodiment, and agency in ekphraseis of church buildings', in *Aural Architecture in Byzantium: Music, Acoustics, and Ritual*, ed. B. Pentcheva. London and New York, 163–75.
Wels, V. (2010) 'Einleitung: "Gelegenheitsdichtung" – Probleme und Perspektiven ihrer Erforschung', in *Theorie und Praxis der Kasualdichtung in der frühen Neuzeit*, ed. A. Keller et al. Amsterdam and New York, 9–31.

Wetzel, M. (2000) 'Autor/Künstler', in *Ästhetische Grundbegriffe*, vol. 1, ed. K. Barck et al. Stuttgart, 480–544.

White, H. V. (1973) *Metahistory: The Historical Imagination in Nineteenth-Century Europe*. Baltimore.

Wilson, N. (1978) 'A Byzantine miscellany: ms. Barocci 131 described', *JÖB* 27: 157–79.

Xenophontos, S. (2014) '"A living portrait of Cato": self-fashioning and the classical past in John Tzetzes' *Chiliads*', *Estudios bizantinos* 2: 187–204.

Yuretich, L. (2018) *The Chronicle of Constantine Manasses*. Liverpool.

Zagklas, N. (2011) 'A Byzantine grammar treatise attributed to Theodoros Prodromos', *Graeco-Latina Brunensia* 16: 77–86.

(2014) *Theodore Prodromos: The Neglected Poems and Epigrams (Edition, Translation, and Commentary)*. Diss. Vienna.

(2017) 'Experimenting with prose and verse in twelfth-century Byzantium: a preliminary study', *DOP* 71: 229–48.

(2018) 'Metrical *polyeideia* and generic innovation in the twelfth century: the multimetric poetic cycles of occasional poetry', in *Middle and Late Byzantine Poetry: Texts and Contexts*, ed. A. Rhoby and N. Zagklas. Turnhout, 43–70.

Zetzel, J. E. G. (1972) 'Cicero and the Scipionic circle', *Harvard Studies in Classical Philology* 76: 173–9.

(1982) 'The poetics of patronage in the late first century B.C.', in *Literary and Artistic Patronage in Ancient Rome*, ed. B. K. Gold. Austin, Texas, 87–102.

Zuckerberg, D. (2016) 'Branding irony: comedy and crafting the public persona', in *Brill's Companion to the Reception of Aristophanes*, ed. P. Walsh. Leiden, 148–71.

Index locorum

This *index locorum* contains only references to works of Constantine Manasses; for other authors, please consult the general index.

Aristandros and Kallithea

31.5-11, 155
31.18-28, 156
31.29-32, 156
48, 157
49.1-3, 166–7
60.1, 54
181, 165

Astrological poem

1-15, 118
16-25, 119
36, 119
288-300, 120
358-60, 120
565-6, 121
585-93, 121

Consolation for John Kontostephanos

4-10, 68–9
57-66, 69–70
317-24, 70–1

Description of a crane hunt

1-19, 36
25-9, 37
30-6, 37
63-5, 38
66-82, 38–9
83-4, 39
125-6, 39
250-4, 40
315-16, 41

45-56, 44–5
57-60, 45

Description of the catching of siskins and chaffinches

1-8, 5
157-65, 129
206-7, 5

Description of the Cyclops

17-18, 63

Description of the Earth

151-63, 135–6

Encomium of Emperor Manuel Komnenos

1-22, 29–30
23-41, 31–2
58-62, 32–3
276-9, 33
280-6, 33–4
329-30, 34

Encomium of Michael Hagiotheodorites

1-15, 92–3, 167
6-8, 144
17-19, 93
21-2, 93
22-4, 93
38-49, 93–4
40-5, 108

50, 94
71-7, 94–5, 157
99-100, 95
100-1, 95
245-52, 96
253-60, 96–7
259, 16
389-401, 98
264-74, 113–14

Funerary oration on the death of Nikephoros Komnenos

25-33, 72–3
453-66, 74–5
493-4, 75

Itinerary

1.1-12, 47–8
1.331-6, 52–3
1.335-6, 54
2.87-90, 50
2.91-111, 50–1
2.119-28, 51
2.130, 52
2.132, 52
2.141-7, 52

Letters

1, 99–100
2, 101–2
3, 107

Monody on the death of his goldfinch

3.1-10, 78
3.10, 16
4.27-9, 78
4.30-5.10, 78–9
6.14-19, 79–80
7.1-3, 80
8.14, 45
9.2-3, 82

Monody on the death of Theodora, wife of John Kontostephanos

1-10, 65–6
20-5, 66

176-82, 67
184-7, 68

Moral poem

1, 163
147-59, 161–2
667-71, 86
899, 163

Origins of Oppian

1-8, 125
16-18, 125
25-6, 125
34, 126
47-52, 126

Schede

1.1-6, 131
1.28-30, 132
2.22-3, 133
3.1-4, 133
3.33-4, 133

Sketches of the mouse

15-23, 135

Verse chronicle

565, 16
889-906, 178–9
2320-26, 26
2600-7, 157–8
3073-4, 149
3085-6, 149
3101-3, 149
3108-11, 149–50
3170-2, 150
3182-5, 150
3191, 150
3199-3203, 150
3204-12, 151
3223-34, 151–2
3240, 152

Verses on how Darius came to power

1-16, 177–8

General Index

Achilles Tatius, 22–3, 182
addressee, 12, 24, 46, 54, 59, 64, 68–72, 81–4, 87, 90, 94, 96–8, 100, 103, 105–6, 109, 114–15, 122, 158, 163, 166, 174, 180, 182, 184, 188
Agesilaos, father of Oppian, 125, 127
Alexander the Great, 33, 78, 174
Alexios Doukas, 52, 55
Alexios I Komnenos, 140
Anna Komnene, 41, 65, 72–3, 83, 88, 109, 140, 174
Antoninus (Caracalla), 125–6
Apelles, 92–4, 108, 145, 167
Arabia, 72–3
Archilochus, 75, 174
Ares, 36–7, 40
aristocracy, 10, 13, 15, 19, 21, 41, 43, 45, 111, 141
Aristophanes, 70, 95, 170
Aristotle, 79
astrology, 25, 117–24
Athenaeus, 47–9, 55, 172
attribution, 14, 16, 77, 86, 92, 110–11, 117, 123, 134–8, 141, 145, 160–6, 181
audience, 1, 5, 7, 9, 12, 16–17, 22–3, 26–8, 41, 45, 49, 52, 56–7, 63–4, 68, 72, 82, 88, 90, 139, 142, 145, 148, 151, 158–9, 170, 173, 176, 178, 180–4
Augustus, 33, 174
author, 1, 4, 6, 9, 11–23, 47, 62, 91, 100, 114–15, 130, 142–4, 158, 176–7, 181–2, 185–90
 author branding, 170–1, 186, 190
 authorial comments, 13, 21, 157–8, 167, 185, 188–9
 authorial I, 37, 90
 authorial narrative, 4, 21, 49, 53, 55, 109–10, 148, 159, 171, 185, 189
 empirical author, 89–90, 92, 106, 110–11, 152, 167–8, 189

 model author, 49, 89–90, 92, 99, 104–5, 109–11, 117, 120, 130, 133, 138–9, 143, 148, 153, 164–6, 169, 181, 188, 190
Bal, Mieke, 87
beauty, 2–3, 29, 35, 41, 44, 50, 54, 63, 69, 72, 96, 118, 151–2, 183
Belisarios, 149–52, 156–8, 162
benefaction, 52, 99–100, 103, 121
biography, 20, 115, 124, 126–7, 130
bird(s), 32, 52–4, 82, 106, 158, 184
 bird hunting, 5, 46, 75–6, 106, 113–14, 125, 127, 129–30
 songbird, 52, 175, 189
bitterness, 68, 78, 95, 114, 150–1, 155–7, 168
Bosphoros, 106, 128, 182
Byzantion (Constantinople), 96, 109

ceremony, 6–7, 56, 60–1
chaffinch, 44, 128
characterization, 4, 43, 83, 90, 100, 114–15, 122, 130, 158, 182, 188
Christ, 52, 133
Christopher of Mytilene, 104–5
Church of the Holy Apostles, 152, 183
cloud(s), 37, 99, 128, 157
commission, 3, 7–10, 12, 14, 17, 19, 24, 60, 62, 87, 118, 182, 186–7, 189
communicating vessels, 116, 138
Constantine Manasses
 Address by the way, 110–11
 Aristandros and Kallithea, 14, 44, 67, 91, 145, 153–62, 166–7, 171–2, 174–5, 187
 Astrological poem, 58, 117–24, 130, 165, 175, 187
 Consolation for John Kontostephanos, 64–5, 68–71, 83–4, 91
 Description of a crane hunt, 2, 27, 35–46, 56, 62, 127, 180, 188

Constantine Manasses (cont.)
Description of a little man, 22–3, 27, 43, 56, 182, 187–8
Description of the catching of siskins and chaffinches, 2, 4–5, 9–11, 27, 44–5, 106, 127–9, 182, 187
Description of the Cyclops, 27, 43, 63–4, 187–8
Description of the Earth, 27, 43, 134–8, 187
Encomium of Emperor Manuel Komnenos, 2, 27–35, 40–1, 53, 56, 62, 174, 188
Encomium of Michael Hagiotheodorites, 15, 91–9, 104, 113–14, 138–41, 144–5, 156, 158, 167–8, 188
Funerary oration on the death of Nikephoros Komnenos, 14, 64, 71–6, 97, 113, 129, 174–5, 188
Itinerary, 2, 16, 27, 46–56, 65, 71, 105, 127, 163, 167–8, 171–2, 188
Letters, 14, 21, 91, 99–110, 168, 188
Monody on the death of his goldfinch, 45, 64, 76–82, 84–5, 105, 110, 158, 168, 180, 184–5, 187–8
Monody on the death of Theodora, wife of John Kontostephanos, 64–8, 71, 83–4, 91
Moral poem, 86–7, 90–1, 145, 160–6, 168, 175, 177, 189
Origins of Oppian, 117, 124–30, 138, 143, 175, 187
Schede, 14–15, 131–4, 138–41, 174, 187
Sketches of the mouse, 77, 117, 134–8, 177, 180
Verse chronicle, 2–3, 14–16, 20–1, 24, 26–7, 58, 67, 91, 105, 117, 119, 122, 131, 138, 140, 145–53, 157, 159, 161, 163–5, 167, 171–2, 175, 178–80, 183, 186–7
Verses on how Darius came to power, 177–80, 186–7
Constantine Psaltopoulos, 104
Constantine the Great, 25–6, 147
Constantinople, 4, 9, 22, 24–8, 34, 44, 46–54, 56, 65, 76–7, 102, 104–5, 110, 113, 115, 132, 138, 144, 148, 151–2, 170, 182–3, 185, 188–90
contiguity, 61–3, 71–2, 83, 110, 122
convention, 1, 4, 17–18, 60–2, 83, 89–90, 110, 142, 145, 172, 189
court, 7, 10, 13, 18, 20, 22–3, 25–7, 35, 43, 46, 56, 59, 61, 74, 76, 97, 113–16, 120, 124, 127, 132, 167–8, 171, 182
crane, 37–8, 40–2, 45
Creation, 147–8, 173
cricket, 51–3
Crusius, Martin, 2
Cyclops, 43, 63
Cyprus, 50, 52

Daniel the Stylite, 131–2
Danube (Istros), 31, 101–2
Dapontes, Kaisarios, 2
Darius, 177–9
darkness, 50, 65, 79, 101, 119, 133
de Man, Paul, 182
death, 36, 64–82, 155, 173
Demetrios Trivolis, 153
desire, 89, 92, 120, 135, 144, 155
didactic function, 14, 24, 113–41, 143, 145, 164, 176
dreaming, 47–8
dwarf, 22, 43, 56

eagle, 29, 32–3, 35, 38, 40, 42, 54, 156
Earth, 50, 96, 101, 119, 135, 151, 178
Eco, Umberto, 87–90
education, 14, 18–19, 50, 72, 76–7, 84, 102, 113–41, 144, 176, 181, 187
ekphrasis, 2–5, 35–47, 63, 65, 104–6, 119, 128–9, 135–8, 147, 173
emotion, 20, 37, 40, 64, 86, 103, 148, 151–3, 155, 158–9, 161, 166–8, 171, 185
envy, 20, 119, 148–68, 174, 186, 190
epic, 3, 40, 107, 109, 152, 172
eroticism, 37–8, 45, 148, 155
Euclid, 79
Eudokia, wife of Theodosios II, 157
Eumathios Makrembolites, 44, 84
Eustathios of Thessalonike, 62, 76, 104, 123, 144
excerpts, 14, 153–5, 159, 164, 166, 168
exile, 49, 105, 125–6

falcon, 35, 37, 40, 42, 128
falconry, 35
fear, 40, 49, 135–6
fiction, 2, 5, 22–4, 46, 48, 64, 82, 85, 88, 103, 108–9, 168, 170, 174, 181–4
fire, 33, 36, 66, 69, 94–5, 101, 155, 157, 161
flower(s), 32, 54, 69, 107, 126
focalization, 4, 54, 56, 184
fortune, 92, 94, 157–8, 166–7
friendship, 5, 12, 14, 59, 63, 76, 84, 86–7, 90–1, 94, 106–11, 119–20, 149, 160, 188
fruit, 69, 72, 94, 99–100, 107, 135

garden(s), 5, 25, 31, 50, 53–4, 67, 69–70, 72–3, 94, 100, 118–19, 148, 182
gardener, 69, 72, 107
Genette, Gérard, 183–4
genre, 17–18, 20–1, 24, 28, 64, 84, 116, 142, 145, 173, 175
George of Pisidia, 162

Georgios Palaiologos, 43
gift(s), 31, 56, 87, 99–100, 107, 121, 163
gnomic form, 16, 68, 90, 145, 149, 155–6, 158–9, 162, 166
goldfinch, 44, 76–82, 175
grammar competition, 15, 75–6, 85, 97, 106, 113–14, 127, 129, 132, 138–41
Greek Anthology, 154

Hades, 66, 70, 165
Hagia Sophia, 148, 151–2, 183
hare, 37, 136
Hegel, Friedrich, 8–10
Herodotus, 97, 101, 103, 178–9, 181
Homer, 16, 22–3, 38, 40, 69, 77, 80, 101, 103, 109, 123, 144, 152, 172–3, 175, 182
honey, 55, 68–9, 78
Hörandner, Wolfram, 7, 41
horse, 36, 177–9
Hungarian wars, 29, 32, 102, 104, 188
hunting, 2, 5, 35–46, 56, 74, 98, 113, 125, 127–30
  fishing, 125

Ianos Laskaris, 153–4
imaginary, 10–13, 22–3, 88, 91, 103, 106, 109, 115, 130, 174, 181–2, 184
imitation, 22–3, 91, 105, 132, 142, 144, 146, 171–2, 176, 181
  imitator, 160, 164, 166, 168, 180
India, 153–5
intention, 21, 24, 87–90, 100, 109, 117, 123–4, 127, 130, 134, 138–9, 166
Iorga, Nicolae, 1–4, 172, 182

Jeffreys, Elizabeth, 58, 165
John Doukas, son of Andronikos Doukas, 42
John Doukas, son of Anna Komnene, 72
John Kinnamos, 42
John Kontostephanos, 47–8, 55, 65–76, 83, 188
John Tzetzes, 88, 142
Justinian, 147–9, 151–2

katobleps, 155, 161
Katomyomachia, 77
King David, 33, 174

lament, 50, 64–8, 72–3, 77–8, 84, 151
Leo the Iconoclast, 26, 147
light, 52, 96, 101, 110, 119, 133, 151, 178
lightning, 95, 157, 179
lion, 33, 38, 110, 150, 155–6, 161
logos, 30, 53, 92, 99–100, 171
Lorenzo de' Medici, 153

love, 29, 36, 63, 67, 69, 92, 99, 118–20, 122, 125, 131–2, 134, 144, 150, 152, 154
lyre, 65–6, 78, 97, 107
Lysippus, 93, 108

Magdalino, Paul, 13, 56, 59, 104, 111, 123, 167–8, 184–5
Makarios Chrysokephalos, 153
Manganeios Prodromos, 18, 23, 65, 83
manticore, 155, 161
Manuel I Komnenos, 2, 13, 18, 26, 28–35, 42–3, 45–6, 50, 54, 59, 62, 65, 104–5, 110, 123, 127, 133, 138–9, 147–8, 167, 174, 181, 188–9
Maximos Planoudes, 154
Menander, 27, 172
metaphor, 23, 25, 43, 48, 61, 70, 106, 114, 130, 132, 182
Michael Angelopoulos, 106, 110–11
Michael Attaleiates, 162
Michael Glykas, 123
Michael Hagiotheodorites, 99–109, 111, 114, 128–9, 138–40, 188
Michael Italikos, 77, 80–2, 110
Michael Psellos, 42, 142
Milton, John, 2, 172
misfortune, 49, 67, 72, 86, 99, 135, 157, 167–8, 186, 190
mouse, 135–7
Mullett, Margaret, 6, 58–9, 86
Muses, 29, 78, 80, 118
music, 18, 36, 51, 59–60, 78, 80, 105, 120, 176

nature, 22, 29, 37, 44–5, 92, 182
Nikephoros Basilakes, 84
Nikephoros Bryennios, 72–3, 83, 174
Nikephoros Komnenos, 71–6, 83, 113–14, 129, 174, 189
Niketas Choniates, 143, 164
Niketas Eugenianos, 44, 144, 154
novelty, 92, 144, 181

occasional literature, 3–13, 21–4, 147, 174, 176, 181–4, 189–90
Oppian, 34, 75, 124–30, 172, 184
originality, 1, 4, 17, 138, 143, 176
Orphanotropheion, 115, 140–1, 187–8
Orpheus, 24, 165–6

paideia, 61, 73, 75, 83, 100, 123
painting, 42, 46, 92–3, 144, 183
Patriarchal School, 15, 26, 113–14, 115, 140

patronage, 6, 8, 13–14, 58–64, 76, 81–4, 86, 90, 100, 104, 106, 111, 127, 139, 158, 170, 184, 187
  poetics of patronage, 59, 62, 64, 84
performance, 4, 6–7, 11, 13–14, 17, 22, 41, 60, 71–2, 82, 88, 90, 116, 147, 152, 158, 163, 173, 176, 182–3
Persia, 31, 33, 177–9
persona, 12, 20–1, 23, 34, 52, 54, 58, 62, 69, 71–2, 82–3, 87, 109, 174, 186
Philostratus, 172
Pindar, 9, 172, 176
plagiarism, 84, 136, 142
  plagiarist, 160
planets, 118–21
Plato, 70, 79
pleasure, 4–5, 20, 36–9, 41–2, 45, 47, 55, 63, 69, 120, 132
poison, 150, 154–5, 161
Polemon of Smyrna, 75
politics, 6, 8, 10, 12, 17, 20, 28, 59, 63, 100
Ptochoprodromos, 51, 109
Publius Livius Larensis, 55
Pyrrhus, 78, 97

reader, 1, 3, 7, 11–12, 21–2, 24, 45, 63, 68, 87–8, 100, 103, 107–8, 116, 123, 126–7, 130, 142–3, 166, 170, 172, 176–7, 179–80, 184, 189–90
  model reader, 89–90, 92, 99–100, 105, 110, 120
  reader-response criticism, 1, 13
reality, 2, 8, 10–11, 21, 23, 28, 30, 32, 46, 48, 57, 88, 90–1, 93, 103, 117, 182–3
recycling, 12, 21, 24, 49, 67, 142–68, 170–81, 186, 189
referentiality, 10, 12–13, 22–3, 26, 56, 182–3
repetition, 142–3, 146, 175–6, 180
  repetition with variation, 12, 16, 142
rhythm, 75, 101, 134, 180–1
Rome, 127
  New Rome (Constantinople), 26
  Rhomaian, 31, 33, 38, 50
  Roman (ancient), 33–4, 55, 62, 81, 172–3, 175
rose, 69, 157

Said, Edward, 11, 189
Sappho, 1, 73, 97, 174
schedography, 14–15, 74–5, 77, 108, 113, 115, 117, 129–41, 163, 173–4, 176, 187
sea, 5, 26, 31, 46, 48, 67, 69, 96, 98, 118, 151

Sebastokratorissa Eirene, 14–15, 26, 58, 116–18, 121–3, 127, 140, 146–7, 165, 167, 186, 189
self-imitation, 142, 160, 176, 185
self-quotation, 143, 145
self-reference, 142–3
self-representation, 4, 16, 21, 23, 49, 55, 82, 88, 103, 141, 143, 159, 170, 185
Septimius Severus, 125–6
serpent, 155–6, 161
Sirens, 80, 94
siskin, 44, 129
slander, 94–5, 98–100, 155–9
snake, 32, 150, 155
Solomon, 95, 133
sorrow, 36, 64, 67–9, 72–3, 83, 151–2
space, 4, 23, 25–8, 41, 43, 54–7, 148, 152
sparrow, 45, 50, 54, 105, 175
stars, 50, 53, 96, 101–2, 118, 120–1, 123, 148, 151, 156
storm, 47–8, 69
storyworld, 23, 85, 154, 183, 190
struggle, 32, 34, 56, 127, 131–2, 178
style, 4, 15–16, 19–20, 24, 63, 68, 81, 89–91, 102–4, 108–9, 111, 122, 130, 134, 142, 144–5, 159, 163–4, 170, 177, 180–1, 189
sun, 29–31, 33, 50–1, 53, 69, 96, 99–103, 110, 119, 123, 133, 148, 151–2, 157, 178
Symeon Metaphrastes, 132

tears, 50, 66, 69, 72, 151
Theodora, wife of John Kontostephanos, 64–71, 83
Theodora, wife of Justinian, 152, 183
Theodore Prodromos, 44, 77, 108, 116, 134, 144
Theodore Stypiotes, 108
Theotokos, 131–3
thorns, 69, 157
toad, 155, 161
toil, 47, 50–1, 72, 94, 126–7
tradition, 1, 22, 142, 146
  Biblical, 21, 34–5, 69–70, 79, 95, 110, 133, 163, 172–5, 184
  Graeco-Roman, 12, 21, 43, 69, 79, 110, 163, 172–3, 184
  Hellenic, 34, 69–70, 92–4, 97, 99–100, 145
trap(s), 5, 44–5, 74, 97, 113–14, 128–9, 131
tree(s), 5, 50, 67, 69, 72, 75, 94, 99, 101, 118, 155
Turgenev, Ivan, 1–2

voice, 1, 3–4, 8–9, 11–14, 17, 20–1, 32, 45, 50–1, 58, 66–7, 78–9, 87, 89, 91, 104, 107, 110, 114, 117, 120, 130, 134, 139, 141, 143, 145, 158–9, 164, 166, 169–70, 173–4, 176, 179–81, 183, 185–9
vulture, 155, 161

war, 27, 29–30, 32, 36, 38, 40–2, 73, 99, 101–2, 104, 109, 128, 149, 173, 188
water, 4–5, 31, 50, 54, 92, 94–6, 99, 107–8, 157, 182
wings, 29, 31–2, 37–8, 40, 44, 52–3, 114, 118, 129, 157, 175
Wordsworth, William, 3, 176